Studies in Human Ecology and Adaptation

Series editors

Daniel G. Bates, Hunter College, City University of New York,
New York, NY, USA
Ludomir R. Lozny, Hunter College, City University of New York,
New York, NY, USA

More information about this series at http://www.springer.com/series/6877

Ludomir R. Lozny • Thomas H. McGovern
Editors

Global Perspectives on Long Term Community Resource Management

With a Foreword by Carole L. Crumley

 Springer

Editors
Ludomir R. Lozny
Hunter College, CUNY
New York, NY, USA

Thomas H. McGovern
Hunter College, CUNY
New York, NY, USA

ISSN 1574-0501
Studies in Human Ecology and Adaptation
ISBN 978-3-030-15799-9   ISBN 978-3-030-15800-2 (eBook)
https://doi.org/10.1007/978-3-030-15800-2

© Springer Nature Switzerland AG 2019
This work is subject to copyright. All rights are reserved by the Publisher, whether the whole or part of the material is concerned, specifically the rights of translation, reprinting, reuse of illustrations, recitation, broadcasting, reproduction on microfilms or in any other physical way, and transmission or information storage and retrieval, electronic adaptation, computer software, or by similar or dissimilar methodology now known or hereafter developed.
The use of general descriptive names, registered names, trademarks, service marks, etc. in this publication does not imply, even in the absence of a specific statement, that such names are exempt from the relevant protective laws and regulations and therefore free for general use.
The publisher, the authors, and the editors are safe to assume that the advice and information in this book are believed to be true and accurate at the date of publication. Neither the publisher nor the authors or the editors give a warranty, express or implied, with respect to the material contained herein or for any errors or omissions that may have been made. The publisher remains neutral with regard to jurisdictional claims in published maps and institutional affiliations.

This Springer imprint is published by the registered company Springer Nature Switzerland AG
The registered company address is: Gewerbestrasse 11, 6330 Cham, Switzerland

Foreword

This book examines the aspects of the contemporary and historic management of resources held in common. The very existence of such management strategies runs counter to the long-held assertion that they are obsolete and must be removed from local management and subjected to state, corporate, or other external controls. A brief look at the not-so-distant history of this view can provide context for this important volume.

It may surprise some readers that the main point of Garrett Hardin's 1968 *Science* article 'The Tragedy of the Commons' is that *overpopulation* is the chief source of environmental degradation, not that communities are incapable of sustained management of the commons. At the time of its publication, the article was the focus of an enormous controversy about what was soon referred to as the 'population bomb' (Ehrlich and Ehrlich 1968). In the same period, but with a broader perspective more characteristic of contemporary opinion, the Club of Rome's *The Limits to Growth* (Meadows et al. 1972) argues that the number of humans is only part of the larger problem: the Earth's resources are finite.

Concerns of the tumultuous late 1960s to early 1970s reflect a long struggle to define the role of humanity in the degradation and depletion of resources. Which elements of society are at fault? For some, the 'overpopulation question' was key to a solution. It was also an opportunity to revisit the early twentieth-century ideas of progress and social engineering, the fundamental assumptions guiding the policies of Western nation-states (Scott 1999).

In the early twentieth century, the tenets of nationalism and of scientific racism proved particularly compatible, offering a solid justification for colonialism, class privilege, and persecution of minorities. Equally attractive was the argument that Europe and North America were doubly blest with the world's most intellectually invigorating climate and its most enlightened population.

In shifting blame away from the colonists and onto the colonized, Hardin's argument echoed the earlier concern about overpopulation. But it also cemented the idea that aside from the progressive, competitive West, the human impact on resources was the result of an outdated strategy of collaboration.

The rise of eugenics (the application of the principles of selective animal breeding to humans) between the two World Wars coincided with the apogee of Western domination of subject peoples and countries all over the globe in the name of progress, with a potent subtext of racism. In Germany, National Socialism adopted a suite of ideas that combined geographical determinism (drawing on Tacitus' *Germania*), cultural determinism (promoting the work of the linguist and archaeologist Gustaf Kossinna), and genetic determinism (the idea that human social and behavioural qualities are manifest in the form of 'racial character'). By 1933, the Nazis had embraced the work of several prominent American scholars, among them, physical anthropologists Aleš Hrdlička and Charles Davenport and geographers Walter Christaller and Ellsworth Huntington, a founder and early president of the Ecological Society of America.

Following statist economic perspectives and genetic theories that still bore the mark of this history, Hardin, who was an anti-immigrant and an advocate of forced sterilization and held white nationalist sentiments, asserts that individual's self-interest inevitably undermines communal action. Hardin's education by the interwar generation of scholars (BS zoology 1936, PhD ecology 1941) and his own predilections follow these earlier trends in ecology, economics, and state planning.

Today, there is abundant evidence that, throughout human history and to the present day, communities have found precise and equitable ways to organize their collective and individual tasks without central authority. Ethnographic, archaeological, and documentary evidence points to a wide range of strategies that can benefit individuals, groups, and communities. Such equitable forms of governance go by many names: communitarian, collective, anarchist, and many others. Of particular current interest are communities that successfully manage common property (jointly held) as well as common-pool (open access) resources.

In 2009, anthropologists and archaeologists found Lin Ostrom and her colleagues' work especially welcome: Ostrom's Nobel Prize in Economics shone a light on Hardin's adherence to unsupported claims with carefully documented fieldwork, much of it drawn from anthropology. They identified 'design principles' of common-pool resource management that include local knowledge, effective communication, clear rules, monitoring, sanctions, paths for conflict resolution, internal trust, and recognition of self-determination by higher-level authorities (Ostrom 1990). These are principles that apply equally to agricultural collectives, anarchist squats, fishing communities, community-owned gardens, and employee-owned corporations.

This volume is a broad and sophisticated update on the commons, employing ethnographic accounts as well as archaeological and historical records. The authors examine how a diverse group of communities integrate communal enterprises and organizations into frameworks that necessarily include ranked, nested, and networked structures (e.g., governance at all levels, associations, individual rights, community norms). The authors of this volume emphasize the specificity of the enterprise, which is always necessary due to the diversity of historical, cultural, legal, and environmental parameters. They argue that risk management is a local, social enterprise, not amenable to imposition from above. Most importantly, their careful work gives back to our human future a skill that is as old as the human experiment itself and as useful as ever: that of self-organization.

Carole L. Crumley
University of North Carolina
Chapel Hill, NC, USA

References

Ehrlich, P., & Ehrlich, A. (1968). *The Population Bomb*. New York: Ballantine Books.
Hardin, G. (1968). The tragedy of the commons. *Science 162*(3859), 1243–1248.
Meadows, D. H., Meadows, D. L., Randers, J., & Behrens, W. W., III. (1972). *The limits to growth: A report for the Club of Rome's project on the predicament of mankind*. New York: Universe Books.
Ostrom, E. (1990). *Governing the commons: The evolution of institutions for collective action*. Cambridge: Cambridge University Press.
Scott, J. C. (1999). *Seeing like a state: How certain schemes to improve the human condition have failed*. New Haven: Yale University Press.

Contents

Foreword v
Carole L. Crumley

Introduction. 1
Ludomir R. Lozny and Thomas H. McGovern

The Tragedy of the Commons: A Theoretical Update. 9
James M. Acheson

**Who Is in the Commons: Defining Community, Commons,
and Time in Long-Term Natural Resource Management** 23
Michael R. Dove, Amy Johnson, Manon Lefebvre, Paul Burow,
Wen Zhou, and Lav Kanoi

**Managing Risk Through Cooperation: Need-Based
Transfers and Risk Pooling Among the Societies
of the Human Generosity Project** 41
Lee Cronk, Colette Berbesque, Thomas Conte, Matthew Gervais,
Padmini Iyer, Brighid McCarthy, Dennis Sonkoi,
Cathryn Townsend, and Athena Aktipis

**Trolls, Water, Time, and Community: Resource
Management in the Mývatn District of Northeast Iceland** 77
Ragnhildur Sigurðardóttir, Anthony J. Newton, Megan T. Hicks,
Andrew J. Dugmore, Viðar Hreinsson, A. E. J. Ogilvie, Árni Daníel
Júlíusson, Árni Einarsson, Steven Hartman, I. A. Simpson,
Orri Vésteinsson, and Thomas H. McGovern

The Organizational Scheme of High-Altitude Summer Pastures: The Dialectics of Conflict and Cooperation 103
Ludomir R. Lozny

Large-Scale Land Acquisition as Commons Grabbing: A Comparative Analysis of Six African Case Studies 125
Tobias Haller, Timothy Adams, Desirée Gmür, Fabian Käser, Kristina Lanz, Franziska Marfurt, Sarah Ryser, Elisabeth Schubiger, Anna von Sury, and Jean-David Gerber

Open Access, Open Systems: Pastoral Resource Management in the Chad Basin 165
Mark Moritz, Paul Scholte, Ian M. Hamilton, and Saïdou Kari

Mollusc Harvesting in the Pre-European Contact Pacific Islands: Investigating Resilience and Sustainability 189
Frank R. Thomas

Environment and Landscapes of Latin America's Past. 213
Vernon L. Scarborough, Christian Isendahl, and Samantha Fladd

The Scale, Governance, and Sustainability of Central Places in Pre-Hispanic Mesoamerica 235
Gary M. Feinman and David M. Carballo

The Native California Commons: Ethnographic and Archaeological Perspectives on Land Control, Resource Use, and Management 255
Terry L. Jones and Brian F. Codding

Identifying Common Pool Resources in the Archaeological Record: A Case Study of Water Commons from the North American Southwest 281
Michael J. Aiuvalasit

Index. 307

Introduction

Ludomir R. Lozny and Thomas H. McGovern

Sustainability concerns the maintenance of societies through a combination of cultural continuation and change and is best understood through examination of long-term perspectives on the complexity of interactions between people and their environments. Such longitudinal studies reveal alternative views on how community-managed strategies mitigate a variety of ecological problems through time. They expose that adaptation to environmental pressures, shifting relationships between local and regional authorities, and external political challenges resonate in policies towards common-pool resources such as water, land, pastures, forest, and entire ecosystems. On the other hand, they also show that optimal adaptation, for instance locally resilient systems of production and exchange, can generate destabilizing positive feedback relations, as often seen in times of major perturbation such as drought, climatic shifts, market upheavals, or political conflict.

Our book presents 12 empirical studies of recurring patterns and trajectories of successes and failures in communal resource management. The participants address the dilemma of competition versus cooperation and examine cases of inter-scalar interactions with direct relevance to current efforts to manage global commons. They conclude that sustainability concerns an admixture of cultural continuation and change. In discussing the pressing issues of governance, sustainability and well-being, cooperation, and management of the commons, they link archaeology and anthropology with human and historical ecology and environmental sciences in a unique interdisciplinary approach to systematically study the commons in synchronic and diachronic scales. Such improved understanding of successful past and present strategies to solve managerial issues offers insightful framework for foster-

L. R. Lozny (✉) · T. H. McGovern
Hunter College, CUNY, New York, NY, USA
e-mail: llozny@hunter.cuny.edu

ing locally contingent approaches to the commons. Here are examples of what the contributors offer:

- They demonstrate that management of the commons and communal use of resources have been often successful on the millennial scale, for instance, in the North Atlantic, and such strategies were key to long-term communal survival and mitigation of systemic vulnerabilities.
- They demonstrate how forms of communal governance provide economic buffering, mitigate subsistence risk, foster cooperation, and serve as foundations for social organization.
- They argue that the use of certain commons, such as pastures, is best organized as an open system, in which a combination of individual decision-making and coordination of movements leads to an ideal type of distribution of mobile pastoralists.
- They show compelling evidence that the development of property rights is associated with scarcity of resources, rising populations, and increasing competition and suggest that such rights should be based on the ability to solve collective-action problems, which depend on several interactive variables, including competition, illegal activity, discount rate, government action, characteristics of communities, and changes in stocks of resources.
- They offer provocative hypothesis that because centralization of decision-making weakens communal cooperatives and contributes to local economic and social crises, participatory polycentric governance seems a viable alternative.
- They discuss recent successes and failures in communal resource management as articulated by the transdisciplinary theory of cooperation and collective-action and offer wider theoretical outlooks on varied strategies to link local segments into larger administrative systems to manage public goods and to solve cooperator problems.
- They offer conclusions that collective polities, by necessity, extensively reorganize the base of society, whether in rural communities or urban neighbourhoods, in such a way as to augment the degree of community-level paragovernmental management capability. Such new systems of local organization combine administrative policies with the new moral codes that emphasize the importance of individual obligation to society beyond the local community.

This book joins a range of studies that address sustainable development and governance of the commons. Authors of those studies also submitted their work to our volume. It thus expands the view regarding long-term communal resource managerial tactics and strategies.

Among the recently published works, Cooper and Sheets (2012) offered a selection of discussions regarding human-environment relations analysed in a diachronic scale. On the other hand, Purvis and Grainger (2004), Rogers et al. (2007), and Blewitt (2008) presented a general overview of sustainable development in a synchronic approach.

Our book offers insights from evolutionary biology, political science, economics, anthropology, and other fields to explain how interactions between our evolved selves and the institutional structures we have created make cooperation possible.

Cooperation is about equalizing chances; it does not contradict economic rules, but allows those who are less-fitted to survive and even prosper. Several authors discuss the dillema of cooperation vs. competition. Their studies expand the research presented in academic papers and books, by, for instance, Kohn (1992) and van der Dennen and Fogler (2012), who offered substantial critique of competition, or Sennett (2012), who discussed psychological fundamentals of cooperation. The contributors also address the theoretical aspect of cooperation presented recently by Cronk and Leech (2012). The key point being that, contrary to the commonly accepted wisdom, competition does not seem basic to human nature.

E. Ostrom et al. (2002) covered extensively the issue of governance of the commons in the fundamental volume *The Drama of the Commons*. The contributors examined the state of knowledge on the "drama of the commons" in the beginning of the twenty-first century. They offered empirical and theoretical approach in a synchronic scale of observation.

Dove and Kammen (2015) produced a volume in which they presented their insights on an interdisciplinary perspective for the natural and social science of sustainability. The authors argued that failures of conservation and development must be viewed systemically. Their book addresses a blind spot within the academic research community to focus attention on the seemingly common and mundane beliefs and practices that ultimately play the central role in the human interaction with the environment.

All contributors to our book, either directly or indirectly, point out to the significance of indigenous knowledge in designing policies and arranging access to commons. Indigenous knowledge has been recognized as a source of ideas that should be included in all programs dealing with resource management (see the contributions in Sillitoe 2017) and environmental stewardship. It has been regarded as significant by the recipient of a Nobel Prize in Physiology in 2015, the Chinese physiologist Tu Youyou, who combined traditional Chinese medical texts with modern research to discover antimalaria drug. Her efforts did not help to advocate indigenous knowledge as much as the Nobel Prize awarded to Elinor Ostrom in Economics in 2009, which significantly influenced the research on cooperation and governance of local resources globally.

Local or indigenous knowledge is not well-defined. Sillitoe (2002, pp. 8–13) proposed to view it as an understanding rooted in local culture that includes all knowledge held collectively by a community that informs interpretation of the world. It contributes, among other things, to promoting sustainable practices in resource use and to outline agendas for future work. Local ecological knowledge corresponds to and changes according to modifications in the environment and social context. It offers clues in understanding of such pressing issues as food security in small scale, sustainable use and conservation of critical resources, and prevention of environmental degradation.

The book presented here consists of 12 chapters and their authors discuss 23 case studies from Europe (Iceland, France), Africa (Kenya, Tanzania, Uganda, Madagascar, Gabon, Cameroon, Morocco, Ghana, Sierra Leone, Kenya, and Malawi), Asia (India, Mongolia), Southeast Asia, South America, Mesoamerica, North America (American West, American Southwest, and California), and the

Pacific Islands (Fiji, Kiribati). Below is a brief overview what the reader might expect in each chapter.

Jim Acheson opposes Hardin's proposition that access to commons should be based on coercive regulations and claims that Hardin's theory is based on culture-bound assumptions that do not hold true cross-culturally. The author offers a theoretical update and new directions to study the commons. Firstly, Acheson points out to the crucial distinction between open access and communally owned and managed resources. Secondly, he argues that all societies that use common resources regulate access to such resources through a variety of means. Thirdly, he points out to the misunderstanding of such terms as "open access", "state property", and "communally owned property". They, in fact, indicate a variety of managerial strategies. The new theory of the commons incorporates multiple claims such as private goods, public goods, toll goods, and common goods in a coherent concept of management and use. Acheson's case studies support the idea that development of common property or private property depends on their economic defendability. That is, when the costs of protecting an area are high relative to the value of the goods in that area, a commons will develop.

Michael Dove and his coauthors discuss practical aspects of cooperation and resource management strategies at community level. They define cooperating community and analyse interactions between such communities and outsiders, especially international organisations and states. Employing five case studies, the authors discuss the gendered politics of reforestation in Madagascar, different mode of care located in indigenous efforts to protect the bison in American West, while the cases from Gabon and India illustrate how the state and private partners actively engage in delineating commons and structuring their use by local communities. Both sections contribute to better understanding of inclusion/exclusion dialectics in community's coherence. The fifth case relates to the significance of swidden agriculture for indigenous wellbeing in general. Dove et al. conclude that changes in attitudes reflect the confrontation between local and metropolitan visions of proper relations between society and its environment. The authors declare that if the aim of community resource management is to determine these relationships through the promotion of specific practices, we must be mindful about who participates in decision-making.

Ragnhildur Sigurðardóttir and coauthors tackle the historical ecology of the Mývatn area in Northeast Iceland that has been occupied by farming communities since the arrival of Viking settlers in the late ninth century. Despite its inland location, and relatively high elevation, this lake basin was affected by continuous human occupation through periods of harsh climate, volcanic eruptions, epidemics, and also the world's economic system. The Mývatn's residents practiced farming, fishing, egg collecting, and hunting for over one millennium. They managed the landscape and its resources with the use of traditional knowledge, which included the story of the troll woman, Kráka. The story, the authors claim, provides a striking metaphor for the landscape history including water resources and environmental changes that the local agricultural community sustained overtime.

Ludomir Lozny discusses the organizational scheme of summer high-altitude pastures associated with transhumance in the Hautes-Pyrénées, France. His objective is to identify and analyse cultural codes used to regulate access to scarce resources managed as commons. Lozny employs linguistic, ethnographic, and historic data on the communal-level collective action and rules that regulate access to vital but limited resources and hypothesizes that high likelihood of conflict forces their users to engage in cooperative interactions. He further theorizes on socioeconomic rationale of such arrangements and concludes that access to sparse resources must be regulated and communal rational cooperation becomes a viable strategy to mitigate conflict (risk) and ensures sustainable group wellbeing.

Lee Cronk and coauthors examine risk management frameworks and describe how societies manage risk socially. The authors use terms such as "need-based transfers" and "debt-based transfers" because these underlie the logic of formal, contractual risk management arrangements found in the eight societies they discuss in their chapter. They focus especially on "need-based transfers", an approach to buffer the effects of disasters and ecological uncertainty. Cronk et al. conclude that given the risk's inevitability, managing it is an important component of both individual and community strategies to adapt to local conditions. The authors provide abundant evidence that need-based transfers are a common strategy for the social management of risk. The Human Generosity Project, a transdisciplinary effort to examine both biological and cultural influences on human cooperation, has documented and analysed these and many other examples of social risk management.

Tobias Haller and coauthors discuss the results of two research projects carried out to examine large-scale land acquisitions in Africa. They examine case studies form Morocco, Ghana, Sierra Leone, Kenya, Tanzania, and Malawi. The authors analyse the drama of grabbed commons and economic consequences that affect marginalized groups. Their research revealed that foreign investors made new land deals with the local state officials and elites. The new rules made the land traditionally held as commons available for market-oriented productions. They further allowed transfer of the assets into state-, local elite-, or international company-owned properties. These changes adversely affected the traditional land rights scheme. New institutional changes eliminated communal ownership and access to land-related commons such as water, pasture, fisheries, forestry, non-timber forest products, and wildlife, all vital for local sustainable livelihoods. The authors analyse how local groups reacted to these dramas and what strategies they used to reinstall access to the commons. They conclude that only bottom-up institutional buildup provides essential basis for securing resilient livelihoods. These studies allow for better understanding how to use the commons in the future on local, national, and international level.

Mark Moritz and coauthors offer provocative discussion that counters Hardin's tragedy of the commons argument that pastoralists are responsible for overgrazing the range. The authors have shown that grazing ecosystems are much more complex and dynamic than was previously assumed and that they can be managed adaptively as commons. A longitudinal study that the authors conducted of pastoral mobility and primary production in the Logone floodplain in the Far North Region of Cameroon suggests that open access does not have to lead to a tragedy of the commons. They argue that pastoral system they study is best conceptualized as an open system, in which a combination of individual decision-making and coordination of movements leads to an ideal-free type of distribution of mobile pastoralists. The authors conclude that self-organizing system of open access works and its implications are critical for theories of management of common-pool resources and our understanding of pastoral systems.

Frank Thomas analyses distributions of mollusc shells in archaeological sites in the Pacific Islands. The author draws primarily from direct observations and semi-structured interviews among mollusc gatherers in Kiribati, Eastern Micronesia, and examines selected case studies of archaeological shell deposits that could shed new light on marine resource management to complement the more widespread research conclusions that depict human impact in largely negative terms. Documented changes in species size, richness, and abundance have often been used as proxies for assessing environmental change as well as human impact and interpreted as evidence of resource abuse by shellfish gatherers. Thomas argues that while such assumption may be valid in some cases, archaeologists need to consider other variables to explain change (or stability) in shell distribution. The author concludes that a better understanding of ecological and biological characteristics of shell midden deposits may result in a reinterpretation of past human behaviour.

Vernon Scarborough and coauthors discuss the landscapes and natural environments of the tropics, which they consider as the setting for a particular understanding of modern ecological principles. Quoting Alexander von Humboldt and Charles Darwin, they argue that contemporary views of coupled human-nature dynamics were first "discovered" in the New World. The authors point out that unlike the prominent worldview identifiable in the Near East and subsequently in early colonizing Europe, Central and South American settings show the inextricable affinity between humanity and the slowly modified biogeography. They conclude that "technological thresholds and breakthroughs seldom accelerated through time; and the role of labour in an environment without widespread domesticated animals and zoonotic diseases made for a different ecological emphasis and a worldview that cultivated the role of plants, animals and their interplay".

Gary Feinman and David Carballo examine frameworks that have traditionally been employed in studies of the rise, diversity, and fall of preindustrial urban aggregations. They suggest that a comparative theoretical perspective, which foregrounds collective-action problems, unaligned individual and group interests, and the social mechanisms that promote or hamper cooperation, advances our understanding of variability in these early cooperative arrangements. They apply such a perspective to examine pre-Columbian Mesoamerican urban centres and to demonstrate tendencies for more collective systems to be larger and longer lasting than less collective ones, likely reflecting greater sustainability in the face of the ecological and cultural perturbations specific to the region and era. The authors conclude that although historical particulars are critical to understanding individual cases, there are scholarly and policy rationales for drawing broader implications regarding the growing corpus of cross-cultural data germane to understanding variability in the constitution of human societies, past and present.

Terry Jones and Brian Codding examine the effects of prehistoric hunting on indigenous fauna through the California archaeological records. The authors briefly discuss the overkill hypothesis and optimal foraging concepts. They further point out that countering such over-exploitation, theories of native conservation typically argue for masterful management of the western North American resource landscape via such methods as controlled burning and ritually mediated resource sharing. The authors argue that the archaeological evidence does not corroborate either overkill or native stewardship. They discuss evidence for prehistoric extinction of the flightless duck (*Chendytes lawi*) along the California coast over a period of 8000 years, while shellfish on the southern California Islands show definite diminution over time due to increasingly frequent human harvest. The authors conclude that human population in most of California was below the carrying capacity, and fisheries were so rich that native peoples had no effect on them—negative or positive. Sociopolitical organization in most of western North America was defined by innumerable small autonomous polities with owned/tightly controlled resource patches within them. The degree to which such structures were intended to accomplish "stewardship" is at best debatable as they mostly promoted the exclusive use of localized resources for groups and individuals. Anadromous fisheries in Northwestern California were effectively shared and remained highly productive, but at the same time there is no evidence for large-scale cooperative agreements to manage other resources whose distributions transcended the limits of small political units such as migrating waterfowl or sea mammals. Nonetheless, most resources remained abundant owing to an epiphenomenal demographic situation that included an almost unthinkably rich and diverse resource base.

Michael Aiuvalasit discusses the case of indigenous water management in American Southwest. The author focuses on the question how the management of water as a common-pool resource affected sustainability of Ancestral Puebloan communities in the Jemez Mountains of New Mexico and presents the results of chronological analyses of 15 water reservoir features at nine Ancestral Puebloan village sites. Independent chronologies of water-related infrastructures serve as proxies for the emergence of social institutions to govern public access and distribution of water for household use. By testing reservoirs across the Jemez and Pajarito Plateaus, two adjoining regions settled by dryland maize agriculturalists between AD 1100 and 1700, Aiuvalasit shows how long-term archaeological records can be used to examine concepts central to the study of the commons and sustainability, such as institutional governance and inherent trade-offs at the nexus of mitigating food-water insecurities.

Communal-level resource management successes and failures comprise complex interactions that involve local, regional, and (increasingly) global-scale political, economic, and environmental changes, shown here to have recurring patterns and trajectories. The human past provides examples of long-term millennial and century scale successes followed by undesired transitions ("collapse") and rapid failure of collaborative management cooperation on the decadal scale. Thus, the book connects the past, present, and future by presenting geographically and chronologically spaced out case studies and overviews of the current cutting-edge research regarding managerial strategies of common-pool resources. The lesson learnt from studying past responses to various ecological stresses is that we must not wait for a disaster to happen to react, but must react, to mitigate conditions for emerging disasters.

This realization suggests that risk management underlined by strategies to minimize risk rather than to maximize gains would be the focal point behind sustainable development in the Twenty-first century.

Thus in opposition to the "tragedy of the commons" we foster the "joy of the commons," an approach to argue that cognitive (generosity) and practical (cooperation) attributes govern collective action to mitigate risk and sustain communal wellbeing.

We suppose that our book will attract readers among college students and participants of graduate level classes and seminars on culture change, indigenous and modern strategies for the management of resources, anthropology and archaeology classes on culture change and the rise of social complexity, historical and human ecology, human-environment dynamics, governmentality, sustainable development and management of critical resources, etc.

The book will also be of interest to professionals including college professors, governmental planners, and decision-makers of different levels of the political structure. It will serve as a guiding tool and reference for regional or global advisory boards and commissions, such as the EU, UN, etc.

The book sprung from a very successful session presented during the 112th AAA Annual Meeting in Chicago, November 2013, organized by Ludomir Lozny and Tom McGovern. We thank all the participants who agreed to present their papers and submitted chapters to this volume. Additionally, we have invited scholars who study sustainable development, governance schemes, and management of common-pool resources (commons), and they offered new insights from the perspective of their filed of specialty.

References

Blewitt, J. (2008). *Understanding sustainable development*. Abingdon: Routledge.
Cooper, J., & Sheets, P. (Eds.). (2012). *Surviving sudden environmental change. Answers from Archaeology*. Boulder: University Press of Colorado.
Cronk, L., & Leech, B. L. (2012). *Meeting at grand central: Understanding the social and evolutionary roots of cooperation*. Princeton, NJ: Princeton University Press.
Dove, M. R., & Kammen, D. M. (2015). *Science, society and the environment. Applying anthropology and physics to sustainability*. Abingdon: Routledge.
Kohn, A. (1992). *No contest: The case against competition* (2nd ed.). Boston: Houghton Mifflin.
Ostrom, E., Dietz, T., Dolšak, N., Stern, P. C., Stovich, S., & Weber, E. U. (Eds.). (2002). *The drama of the commons*. Washington, DC: National Academy Press.
Purvis, M., & Grainger, A. (Eds.). (2004). *Exploring sustainable development: Geographical perspectives*. London: Routledge.
Rogers, P. P., Jalal, K. F., & Boyd, J. A. (2007). *An introduction to sustainable development*. London: Routledge.
Sennett, R. (2012). *Together: The rituals, pleasures, and politics of cooperation* (p. 2012). New Haven, CT: Yale University Press.
Sillitoe, P. (2002). Participant observation to participatory development. Making anthropology work. In P. Sillitoe, A. Bicker, & J. Pottier (Eds.), *Participating in development. Approaches to indigenous knowledge* (pp. 8–13). London/New York: Routledge.
Sillitoe, P. (Ed.). (2017). *Indigenous knowledge. Enhancing its contribution to natural resources management*. Wallingford/Boston: Centre for Agriculture and Biosciences International.
van der Dennen, J., & Fogler, V. (2012). *Sociobiology and conflict: Evolutionary perspectives on competition, cooperation, violence and warfare*. New York: Springer Science.

The Tragedy of the Commons: A Theoretical Update

James M. Acheson

Tragedy of the Commons

In the past decades, the world has become increasingly concerned with environmental destruction. Every year there are thousands of articles on fisheries failure, soil erosion, deforestation, loss of wildlife habitat, depletion of soil, acid rain, etc. The most popular explanation for all of these phenomena is the theory of common property resources. According to this theory, all properties held in common (such as oceans, communal forests and grazing lands, rivers, and the atmosphere) are bound to be overexploited. The reason is that in the absence of ownership rights, the users of these resources are caught in a situation in which it is only logical that they place no limits on exploitation rates. Why should a fisherman limit the amount of herring he takes when other boat owners will take the remaining fish in the school within a matter of hours? As a result, resources without owners can be stripped bare quickly. By way of contrast, privately owned resources will not be overexploited since they gave a private owner an incentive to protect them. Private ownership results in conservation; a commons yields resource destruction. From this modest beginning, the theory was expanded to include several bodies of theory and far more than a concern with natural resources.

The idea that the commons are a problem has a long history in Western thought, but the work of Garrett Hardin in the 1960s gave it substantial popularity at the height of the ecology movement at that time.

Basically, Hardin argued that freedom to produce children inevitably produces disaster in a world with limited resources. The example he used was a pasture owned in common. The first few sheep added to the pasture cause no problem. But as more sheep are added, overgrazing occurs, and yields fall. But even then, herdsmen

J. M. Acheson (✉)
University of Maine, Orono, ME, USA
e-mail: acheson@umaine.edu

continue to add sheep; each herder gains the full output of the sheep he adds, while the costs in terms of overgrazing are shared by all herdsmen jointly. Thus, each herd owner increases herd size without limit, resulting in complete destruction of the pasture. The result is what Hardin called "the tragedy of the commons." Each herdsman has acted rationally, but the result is tragedy for a larger group. For Hardin, "therein lies the tragedy. Each man is locked into a system that compels his share—in a world that is limited. Ruin is the destination toward which all men rush, each pursuing his own best interest in a society that believes in the freedom of the commons." Freedom in a commons brings ruin to all (Hardin 1968).

He concludes the problem cannot be solved by voluntary action. Coercion is necessary to get people to restrain their use of the commons. We cannot expect them to voluntarily restrain their resource. "The coercion may be mutually agreed upon, but it need not be just" (Hardin and Baden 1977, p. 275). The alternative to the commons is too horrifying to contemplate. "Injustice is preferable to total ruin." Hardin saw nothing but disaster looming for societies in the Third World, because he did not believe their governments could limit their populations. The publication "The Tragedy of the Commons" in 1968 and the follow-up book in 1977 (Hardin and Baden 1977) created a firestorm because they openly suggested that the solution to ecological problems such as population pressure, overfishing, and over-harvesting of trees could only be solved by action of governments, imposed by autocratic means, and that victims of such actions deserved their fate.

Hardin's analysis and solutions have been criticized on a number of grounds, but none articulated what I see as the key problems: it rests on questionable assumptions that are highly culture bound. The theory's assumptions do not hold true cross-culturally and do not even hold for all situations in the United States. As we shall see, some societies have been able to solve commons problems at a local level by democratic means.

Economic Theory and the Commons

At root, the classic theory of the commons links resource problems with the absence of property rights. It was economists who first suggested that absence of ownership rights leads to serious problems. Property rights lower transaction costs (the costs of negotiating agreements with others).

If property rights are complete and clear, there is little difficulty in deciding who can claim benefits from the resource and who must be compensated if that property is destroyed. Common property makes such negotiation very costly. How can people whose trees have been destroyed by acid rain be compensated easily? They do not own the air, and only an expensive lawsuit can force owners of the coal-fired plant putting effluents into the atmosphere to pay for the damage they are doing to the land owner's trees (Acheson 1989).

Private property is also said to be more efficient because it leaves an owner able to use the land in ways that are most beneficial to him. He can farm the land, develop housing tracts on it, rent it out, or sell it, whichever confers the most advantage to him. He has no incentive to make poor use of the land. Users of a commons have an incentive to use resources before someone does; only rarely does this lead to efficient use.

Overcapitalization is usually the fate of common property. In industries using common property, abnormally high profits are to be made since all of the costs of production are not being paid (e.g., costs of growing fish). As a result, far more firms using more capital are attracted to such industries than are needed to harvest the resource (Acheson 1989).

All of these problems inherent in using commons stem from the fact that incomplete ownership results in externalities. Externalities exist when one person's actions affect the payoffs of others.

Externalities may be positive or negative, and they always result in non-optimal solutions. If a landowner is allowed to pollute a stream, then he is being permitted to foist negative externalities on land owners downstream. He is also being permitted to act in a way that is not optimal for the society as a whole. Private property does away with such externalities and with them the temptation to act in ways that are not in the best interests of the society. Incomplete property rights lead to waste, inefficiency, and high transaction costs. With common property, there is always a divergence between what is in the best for the individual and what is in the best interest of the society. It is said to always result in escalating abuse of resources (Acheson 1989).

According to economists interested in the commons, the solution is fairly simple. Since the problem is traceable to a lack of property rights, the solution is to generate property rights. As a result, large numbers of resource economists have proposed solving commons problems by the invention of institutions such as quotas or licensing schemes of various sorts. Others, following Hardin, have argued that the solution is actions by the government.

Three of the earliest critiques of the theory of the commons are among the most important. First, early on social scientists pointed out that communally owned property was not always subject to overexploitation. Only property that can be overexploited by everyone without charge is subject to problems. Ciriacy-Wantrup and Bishop (1975) point out that the forests of Germany have been well managed even though they have been communally owned for centuries. Access to the forests is strictly controlled, however. It is "open access" resources that are subject to overexploitation, not communally owned resources. This is a crucial distinction.

Second, despite the work of Hardin, who assumes that people cannot and will not generate institutions to control resource exploitation rates, anthropologists have discovered case after case where people have done exactly that. Some involve the imposition of property rights of some kind or another; others involve restrictions on the way hunting or fishing may be done or the size of animals that can be taken. Other societies use secrecy as a means of controlling access to a select group of *cognoscenti*. Most important is the near universality of such rules. When commenting on fisheries, Fikret Berkes noted "These assets are almost never truly open access"

(Berkes 1985, p. 204). The same point can be made for other community-owned assets (e.g., forests, pasture). Open access always results in escalating abuse of resources, etc. None of this is to suggest that natural resources are always well-managed. In peasant and tribal societies, real tragedies of the commons exist. The well-advertised demise of the American bison is a case in point.

Third, at the time of Hardin's writing, "common property" was a cover term (Berkes and Farver 1989) used to describe open access, state property, and communally owned property. The problem is that they are quite different and all three can be managed well in many instances (Feeny et al. 1990).

A New Conception of Property Rights

In the 1970s, the commons was defined in terms of joint ownership, meaning that it was free for any member of the society to use. In the 1990s, a new conception of the commons came into general use—one that defines common goods as one of four kinds of goods based on difficulty of exclusion and subtractability. Exclusion refers to how easy it is to exclude others from using the good; subtractability refers to one person's use that is not available to others. For example, fish caught by one skipper are not available for use by others, but the weather report he used in deciding to go to sea can be used by others. Arraying these attributes provides a general classification of goods: private, public, toll good, and common-pool resources. Each one of these is a huge continent by itself (Ostrom et al. 1994, pp. 6–8). Private goods are characterized by ease of exclusion and subtractability. Public goods are the opposite of private goods in both attributes. Toll goods share with private goods the ease of exclusion, and with public goods the high cost of exclusion.

Common property has high exclusion costs and subtractability problems. It is difficult to exclude others from using it and disastrous if one cannot do so (Ostrom et al. 1994, p. 16). This means that good management of a commons is subject to some complicated types of dilemmas. It also means that dealing with good management of a commons means dealing with one of four types of goods. None of these four can be analyzed alone.

In the expanding literature on property rights, some interesting work has been done on relations between property rights and types of goods produced. There is increased appreciation of the fact that property is very complicated. Within the same society, rights can be configured to create what von Benda-Beckmann and von Benda-Beckmann (2006) call master categories (private properties, state properties). Moreover, within the same society, different rights to a single object may be allocated to different combinations of people to create a complex matrix of claims (Schlager and Ostrom 1992).

Multiple Claims to Property: The Case of Maine Forest Land

Rights to property may be contested. Legal pluralism may exist so that two or more normative orders may apply to the same situation (Edwards and Steins 1996). The Maine forest land situation allows a chance to explore relations between types of goods and types of property in some detail. The relations are very complicated, and illustrate how one type of property can produce several types of goods. Maine forests produce all four types of goods described by Ostrom et al. (1994)—private goods, public good, toll goods, and common goods—at the same time.

Distinguishing between bundles of rights and the kinds of goods produced is essential to understanding the Maine forest scene, which is undergoing considerable change. In Maine, most forest land is said to be privately owned because 88% is deeded to individuals or private entities (Hagen et al. 2005, p. 9). However, land owners do not hold the entire bundle of rights over the land. There are restrictions on activities of land owners. First, the State of Maine has regulations about wildlife and fish. Second, private Maine forests have long been used by the public as a kind of recreational commons. The right to use the recreational commons is currently being heavily contested by land owners. Both sides have an ideology and legal arguments to support their positions. As a result, new kinds of property are coming into being.

Maine is the most heavily forested state in the nation with over 90% of land in forest. The northern part of the state is virtually uninhabited and was formerly held in huge blocks by pulp and paper companies. Land in this area is now for the most part in the hands of large investment companies who bought out the paper companies. The central part of the state has been cleared of forests. Communities here are small, population is sparse, there is little industry, and the forest land is divided into small parcels. The three southern counties are heavily populated and urbanized.

Land owners have full legal title to their property. They can pass it on to their heirs and can get all income from sale of goods from their land. At the same time, the public uses large amounts of Maine forest land for hunting, trapping, camping, snowmobiling, bird-watching, and cross-country skiing. Groups of campers and canoeists take trips on this land lasting for weeks.

Members of the public generally feel they have a right to use this land. Some ask permission, others do not. When land is posted against trespassing, it is very common for members of the public to destroy the sign with no hesitation or guilt.

The general use of private land by the public goes by several names. Some speak of Maine's "hunting tradition"; and the phrase "open land" tradition is widely used. Ideas and feelings about the rights of the public to use northern forests as a virtual commons were on full display in the case of Roxanne Quimby. In the recent past, Quimby, a large land owner and founder of the highly successful Burt's Bees company, proposed to give thousands of acres of her land to the federal government for a national park. Her request immediately created a firestorm of protests. Those who opposed said she was wrecking the local economy, closing off large amounts of logging roads to trucks, and reducing hunting. The complainants were largely people who said they supported private property ownership (Austin 2003).[1]

The legal system hardly helps to clarify rights of Maine land owners. The open land tradition is very old in New England. The public's right to use private land is encoded in the 1641 "Great Pond" Law of Massachusetts, which became part of Maine law when Maine became a state in 1820. In essence, this law allows all ponds over 10 acres to be utilized by the public for fishing, fowling, and cutting ice. Since virtually all large land owners have a great pond on their property, they do not have a clear-cut right to keep the public off their land, if this means cutting off access to a great pond. People in Maine have become used to using land of large land owners and think they have been deprived if someone tries to keep them off private land. On the other hand, there is a well-developed body of common law concerning trespass. This conflict of laws makes it difficult for land owners to know what their rights are.

Public policy hardly helps. Maine has a long tradition of encouraging private land owners to allow the public to use private property by limiting the liability of land owners if someone is hurt on their land while engaged in a recreational activity. The objective is to boost tourism—Maine's largest industry.

Maine forest land presents forest users with a cultural bind. There is little consistency in expected behavior. Many studies show cultural support for two different types of behavior. One study indicated that 69% of the public said that the public does not have a right to use private land, while in another study 57% said they did not (Acheson and Acheson 2010, p. 558).

Hunters and land owners accommodate to each other in a variety of ways. First, they avoid each other. When one is using part of a forest, the other is not. Hunting clubs stress the importance of getting owners' permission to ease tensions. And both emphasize a policy of exchange, i.e., we both use each other's land. Most of the time conflict is controlled by avoidance.

More important, forest land produces every type of property right, and right of withdrawal is owned by still different groups. Private land produces timber, pulpwood, and agricultural goods. When used by hunters, it produces common property in the form of game and hunting benefits. It can also produce public goods in the form of snowmobiling, bird-watching, and cross-country skiing.

Some private land is sold for conservation easements in which long-term development rights are held by one group and rights to timber, pulp, and hunting are used by someone else. Rental rights can be held by still other groups to create toll goods (e.g., hunting right to land owned by hunting clubs). Cases where several types of goods have been produced by a single property regime have been noted by other authors. Short (2008) points out that common land in England and Wales has evolved to produce three classes of goods. A similar situation exists in Scandinavia

---

[1] Quimby later shifted the proposal to a national monument, which can be created by presidential proclamation under the Antiquities Act. In 2016 Elliotsville Plantation and the Quimby Family Foundation donated 87,563 acres of land to the National Park Service, and it was proclaimed as the Katahdin Woods and Waters National Monument by President Barack Obama (Sambides Jr., 2016). Local opposition still continues.

(Kaltenborn et al. 2001). Ostrom has noted (2003, p. 240) that common-pool resources are not automatically associated with common property regimes—or any other type of property regime. The Maine forest land case suggests that the situation is even more complicated. It is possible that all kinds of goods might be produced by all kinds of property regimes.

Sea Tenure, Land Tenure, and the Commons

In recent years, there has been increasing interest in the origin of property rights. Much of the work on property rights stems from the insight that property rights are generated in situations of conflict for resources. Yet this insight ignores several important points: (1) It says nothing about the type of property that will be developed (e.g., common property, private property); (2) it says nothing about whether property rights will be developed at sea or in estuarine areas, as well as on land; and (3) it says nothing about costs or benefits of developing property rights. Recent work begins to fill these gaps.

My case studies support the idea that development of common property or private property depends on economic defendability. That is, when the costs of protecting an area are high relative to the value of the goods on that area, a commons will develop. If the value of the goods in the area is high relative to costs of exclusion, then private property will likely evolve (Acheson 2015, p. 29). The only thing that influences whether property rights develop at sea or not is economic defendability. As we shall see, the mix of variables influencing economic defendability at sea is apt to be different than those on land, but the same factors are involved.

Economic defendability involves the worth of defending an area—not just the value of the goods in an area. An area producing a small amount of goods might be worth defending if those goods are worth a good deal (Dyson-Hudson and Smith 1978). By the same token, an area producing a huge volume of goods may not be worth defending if the cost of defense is prohibitively high. Many factors influence economic defendability including abundance of product, market, predictability, economic density, costs of exclusion, costs of labor, etc. Obviously, the costs of producing agricultural goods are very different from costs of producing fish, but "costs of production" are involved in both cases. Such costs can differ from case to case. In order to study the effects of economic defendability on property rights, a large number of cases were examined. Cases were selected for this study when they met two criteria: (1) There was or is a common property regime and (2) when the ethnography contained enough data to determine economic defendability.

The sample contained six types of cases: (1) Cases in which land held as commons was transformed to private property, (2) cases where land held as common property remains as common property, (3) a case where commonly held land morphed into private property for one type of resource and open access for another, (4) a case where land tenure changed from open access to common property, (5) cases where ocean area remained as common area, and (6) cases in which ocean area is held as private property. Table 1 (Acheson 2015, pp. 32–33) shows all of the cases used in this study.

In 14 of 21 land cases, there was increasing pressure on the resource due to population increase. In these cases, economic defendability increased leading to a change from common property to private property. Five cases are presented to show the exact changes involved leading to increased economic defendability and private property. In the case of US western rangelands, population rose due to migration from the eastern part of the country, and by organizing, stock growers' associations were able to control grazing on public lands (Anderson and Hill 1998). Among the Samburu (Lesorogol 2008) the government instituted a policy of private ownership, which combined with the advent of wheat farming, increased land values, and the change to private property. In six cases land began as common property and continued as common property. This occurred in the highland Mesoamerican Indian communities' case (Wolf 1955). Even though resources were put under competitive pressure, the economic value of land is low because of low technology, and exclusion costs are high due to pressure from powerful mestizos who want to acquire land. Holding land in common helps to lower exclusion costs by making it impossible to sell land.

In general, it is correct to say that marine resources put under competitive pressure will be held as common property regimes. Of 15 marine cases in our sample, 13 are held as common property regimes. The reasons are various. There is one general factor involved: the economic defendability of ocean area is not high enough to warrant holding ocean privately, but the reasons vary considerably (Acheson 2015). In the case of the Maine lobster industry (Acheson 2003), ocean area on bays is valuable enough for a group to warrant defense as commons. Further offshore, traps become less competitive, making it less worthwhile to hold ocean area. The result is an open-access area.

In one village described by Aswani (2002), population growth, in combination with poor enforcement of fishing rules and ease with which foreigners are permitted to fish locally, makes it less worthwhile to hold ocean area. The result is a common property regime.

The case studies give a good deal of evidence that economic defendability correlates with property rights. High economic defendability is linked with the advent of private property. What is surprising is the number of variables affecting the value of resources or the cost of defending them. Virtually each case has a different set of factors influencing economic defendability.

Several general conclusions are warranted about common property. First, it is an error to think common property can be studied as a single phenomenon. Conditions producing a commons do not have to change much to produce a private property regime. Second, land tenure and sea tenure are the result of the same variables. What distinguishes them is the difference in factors influencing the cost of defense. It is more costly to defend the ocean area as fish are more mobile and less visible and thus more difficult to quantify and monitoring fishing gear far from shore is very costly. But a piece of ocean can be held as a commons or privately, if economic defendability is high enough.

It is notable in studying landholding patterns in Third World countries that there are many cases where arable land is privatized under competitive pressure, while ocean and large lakes are held as a commons (Pinkerton and Weinstein 1995). This suggests that privatization is a rational and efficient use for land but may be less so for oceans. Holding oceans as a commons may help to solve the problem of defense. The value of resources may not be high enough to be worth holding privately, but they may be valuable enough to be worthy of defense costs if those costs are shared. In addition, holding land as a commons may avoid expensive policing and administrative costs (Baland and Platteau 1996, pp. 196, 173). Also, holding resources as a commons is more equitable and avoids the potential for conflicts that come with privatization. It is also a way of pooling user risks (Baland and Platteau 1996, p. 174). Holding ocean areas as a commons may have the value of ensuring that people have access to resources a high percentage of the time.

Theory of Cooperation and the Commons

According to the classic theory of the commons, people do not cooperate where common property resources are concerned because it is rational not to do so. These are cases where rational action by individuals brings disaster for the group. They are best modelled as prisoner's dilemma games, which are notoriously difficult to solve. All common property resources including marine fisheries can be modelled as a prisoner's dilemma. The basic logic of the prisoner's dilemma dictates that both players have a dominant strategy to defect even though the equilibrium outcome that results is worse for both than if they played their dominated strategy. That is, if both players cooperate in a PD game, both players get a high reward. If both defect, both get low payoffs. If one defects and the other does not, the defector gets a big reward, while the other gets a low payoff. Unfortunately, the high reward for defection motivates both to defect, with the result that they get the worst of all payoffs. Defection dominates cooperation even though cooperation by both would bring higher payoffs and a more efficient equilibrium (Elster 1989; Taylor 1990).

There are several standard ways of producing cooperation in a prisoner's dilemma. The first is a norm or rule which outlaws defection. It is logical for fishermen to overfish. Thus, rules are passed making it impossible or costly to overharvest. In the parlance of game theory, these rules outlaw the use of the dominant strategy by both players.

The second is repeated play over an iterated game. If a game is played once, then it is rational to defect (Axelrod 1984). But if the game has no certain ending and is played many times, cooperation can be maintained with the use of the correct strategy (e.g., tit for tat).

The third is leadership (Dixit and Skeath 2004). In these cases, players obtain so much from these public goods they are willing to produce them even though others free ride off their efforts.

However, there are increasing numbers of cases showing that people are far more cooperative than would be predicted on the basis of game theory (Ostrom 1990, 2000; Baland and Platteau 1996; Fehr and Gächter 2000; Henrich 2000; Camerer 2003). Henrich and colleagues state "researchers from across the social sciences have found consistent deviations from the canonical model of self interest in hundreds of experiments around the world" (Henrich et al. 2005, p. 795). They are cooperating in cases where this behavior appears irrational.

There is growing work on cooperation that gives a variety of insights on the reasons people might cooperate in the face of a prisoner's dilemma (Agrawal 2002). Axelrod argues that two phenomena can lead to such cooperation: One is altruism in which people are motivated to put the interests of others' ahead of their own selfish goals. Nowak and Sigmund (2005) make a distinction between direct reciprocity (you help me and I will help you) and indirect reciprocity where there is no necessary reward between the help one gives and what one receives (I help you and you help someone else). They stress that indirect reciprocity is rewarded by less tangible factors—especially reputation.

Axelrod (1984) also points out that the discount rate or the future value of investments can influence the willingness to cooperate. He notes that mutual cooperation can be stable if the future is sufficiently important relative to the present (Axelrod 1984, p. 109). Dixit and Skeath (2004, p. 372) write: "In a prisoner's dilemma a player has a short run incentive to defect but can do better in the long run by developing a pattern of cooperation with the other. But the player will only do this if he is sure the discounted benefits of cooperation over time outweigh the onetime benefits to be had from defection."

Another set of ideas coming from "social preferences" also promotes cooperation (Charness and Rabin 2002). In game theory social preferences refer to a situation in which a player's payoff no longer depends solely on his or her economic reward but more broadly to a concern (or lack thereof) that people have for each other's welfare. Social preferences include everything from altruism, reciprocity, a concern with justice, and a willingness to punish violators of the law.

The Maine Lobster V-Notch Practice

Maine fishermen's practice of V-notching lobsters is a good example of cooperation where it is difficult to understand why participants do what they do. If a Maine lobster fisherman catches a female lobster with eggs, he may cut a small notch in her tail. Maine law protects such lobsters from being taken again as they are proven breeding stock. Fishermen throw such lobsters overboard by the thousands, convinced such lobsters play an essential role in replenishing the stock. In the view of fishermen, the two laws that ensure the future of the industry are (a) the V-notch and (b) the oversize law. The rest of the conservation laws are of far less importance (see Acheson 2003; Acheson and Gardner 2010).

The key question is: Why should a fisherman V-notch? There is little evidence that the V-notch is beneficial—especially in the local area. There is no evidence if a fisherman has V-notched a lobster. Nor is there evidence a lobster contributes to the pool of eggs in the water column. Once a lobster is stripped of eggs, there is no indication where its eggs went or where eggs in the water came from. Nevertheless, Maine fishermen do protect such lobsters by the thousands in the belief this augments the stock generally. V-notching essentially involves fishermen—presumably acting with others—sacrificing some time to mark gravid females to increase the breeding stock to the benefit of all, with little evidence such rewards will materialize.

We believe there are several disparate threads in the new literature on cooperation which provide an explanation for the V-notch.

First, lobster fishermen have a low discount rate. It is important that the industry persists and that families of fishermen have an opportunity to earn their living in the fishery (Acheson 2003, pp. 160–64). In their view, V-notching provides a path to this end.

Second, it is noteworthy that fishermen who are V-notching brag about it and that those who do not say little. In fishing circles, reputation is determined by being known as a person who helps the industry. Some of the most successful fishermen were known as prolific V-notchers, and fishermen want to advertise that fact. V-notching can best be considered as a case of indirect reciprocity. It is typical in such cases that rewards are intangible. Most lobstering communities have a long history. They are small, homogenous places where people know each other well. If the work of Fehr and Gächter (2000) is correct, it is exactly in such communities that having a reputation could result in less free riding and more cooperation.

Third, the horrible history of the lobster bust in the early 1930s when 40% of lobstermen went broke reinforces the idea that lack of conservation rules, or failure to observe existing rules, can be very dangerous.

Fourth, all of these are connected to the idea that cooperation to ensure the stock is good policy and profitable.

The Knowledge Commons

In the past 20 years or so, the concept of the commons has been applied to knowledge, defined broadly. This conception shares a good deal with the older theory of common property resources, but there are some major differences. The theory of common property resources refers to physical resources or physical property. The information commons "refers to shared knowledge base and the processes that facilitate or hinder its use. It also refers to a physical space, usually an academic library, where any and all can participate in the process of information research, gathering and production" (Wikipedia—Information Commons). From this perspective, knowledge is all useful ideas, information, and data in whatever form. Hess (2012, p. 40) says that she and her colleagues agreed on the following definition: commons is a resource shared by a group of people that is subject to social dilemmas (Hess

2012, p. 140). This seemingly straightforward definition has been used to describe work in a wide variety of different fields. One is the launching of the open access journal, *International Journal of the Commons*. The *Cornell Law Review* devoted an issue to the information commons in 2010 which explored "constructed" knowledge and cultural commons. An international effort made astounding headway in establishing a microbiological scientific commons. A conference on the knowledge commons in Belgium in 2012 published articles on a variety of topics ranging from the innovation commons and digital information commons to genetic resource commons and cultural commons. These topics give only a cursory idea of the breadth of research on the information commons (see Hess 2012, pp. 18–20). The "unifying thread in all commons resources is that they are jointly used, managed by groups of varying sizes and interests" (Hess and Ostrom 2012, p. 5). The knowledge commons is subject to similar behavior and conditions that had long been identified with other types of commons, e.g., congestion, free riding, conflict, overuse, and "pollution" (Hess and Ostrom 2012, p. 4). Hess and Ostrom note that "there is continual challenge to identify the similarities between knowledge commons and traditional commons such as forests or fisheries, all the while exploring the ways knowledge as a resource is fundamentally different from natural—resource commons" (2012, p. 5). The similarities and differences are still not all obvious.

Much more research needs to be done, however. McCay and Delaney point out that we do not understand any kind of global commons very well (Hess 2012). Hess (2012, pp. 29–31) notes the need for good case studies is especially acute; I will make no pretense of covering this vast and continually changing field, except to note that this topic will occupy us for many years to come.

Still Other Directions in the Study of the Commons

This article has covered a number of ways in which the study of the commons has been expanded and pushed in new directions since Hardin's time. There are others I have not had the time to develop here in any detail:

1. A large number of psychological variables have been shown to influence cooperation in the solution of commons problems, including social motives and personality type (Kopelman et al. 2002).
2. Studies in complexity show how actors or agents interacting at one level of analysis can affect behavior and events at another (Poteete et al. 2010).
3. Experimental games are being applied in laboratory settings to understand the conditions under which people are willing to cooperate to solve commons dilemmas, e.g., Fehr and Gächter (2000) and Ostrom et al. (1994).
4. Richerson et al. (2002) discuss other ways of viewing a commons from an evolutionary perspective.

References

Acheson, J. M. (1989). Management of common property resources. In S. Plattner (Ed.), *Economic anthropology* (pp. 351–378). Stanford, CA: Stanford University Press.

Acheson, J. M. (2003). *Capturing the commons: Devising institutions to manage the Maine lobster industry*. Hanover, NH: University Press of New England.

Acheson, J. M. (2015). Private land and common oceans: A cross-cultural analysis of the evolution of property rights. *Current Anthropology, 56*(1), 28–55.

Acheson, J. M., & Acheson, J. (2010). Maine land: Private property and hunting commons. *International Journal of the Commons, 4*(1), 552–570.

Acheson, J. M., & Gardner, R. (2010). Evolution of conservation rules and norms in the Maine lobster fishery. *Ocean and Coastal Management, 53*(9), 524–534.

Agrawal, A. (2002). Common resources and institutional sustainability. In E. Ostrom, T. Dietz, N. Dolsak, P. Stern, S. Stonich, & E. U. Weber (Eds.), *The drama of the commons* (pp. 41–85). Washington, DC: National Academy Press.

Anderson, T., & Hill, P. J. (1998). From free grass to fences: Transforming the commons of the American west. In J. Baden & D. Noonan (Eds.), *Managing the commons* (2nd ed., pp. 119–134). Bloomington, IN: Indiana University Press.

Aswani, S. (2002). Assessing the effects of changing demographic and consumption patterns on sea tenure regimes in Roviana Lagoon, Solomon Islands. *Ambio, 31*(4), 272–284.

Austin, P. (2003). Roxanne Quimby purchases high priority 24,000 acre township east of Baxter park. *Maine Environmental News* (24 November).

Axelrod, R. (1984). *The evolution of cooperation*. New York: Basic Books.

Baland, J.-M., & Platteau, J.-P. (1996). *Halting degradation of natural resources: Is there a role for rural communities?* New York: Oxford University Press.

Berkes, F. (1985). Fishermen and the 'tragedy of the commons'. *Environmental Conservation, 12*, 199–206.

Berkes, F., & Farver, M. (1989). Introduction and overview of common property resources. In F. Berkes (Ed.), *Common property resources: Ecology and community-based sustainable development*. London: Belhaven Press.

Camerer, C. F. (2003). *Behavioral game theory: Experiments in strategic interaction*. Princeton, NJ: Princeton University Press.

Charness, G., & Rabin, M. (2002). Understanding social preferences with simple tests. *Quarterly Journal of Economics, 117*(3), 817–869.

Ciriacy-Wantrup, S. V., & Bishop, R. C. (1975). Common property as a concept. *Natural Resources Journal, 15*, 713–727.

Cornell Law Review. 2010. *Cornell Law Review 95*(4). Retrieved September 12, 2017, from http://cornelllawreview.org/issue/volume-95-issue-4/

Dixit, A. K., & Skeath, S. (2004). *Games of strategy*. New York: Norton.

Dyson-Hudson, R., & Smith, E. A. (1978). Human territoriality: An ecological reassessment. *American Anthropologist, 80*(1), 21–41.

Edwards, V. M., & Steins, N. A. (1996). Developing an analytical framework for a multiple use commons. *Journal of Theoretical Politics, 10*(3), 347–383.

Elster, J. (1989). *The cement of society: A survey of social order*. Cambridge: Cambridge University Press.

Feeny, D., Berkes, F., McCay, B., & Acheson, J. (1990). The tragedy of the commons 22 years later. *Human Ecology, 18*(1), 1–19.

Fehr, E., & Gächter, S. (2000). Cooperation and punishment in public goods experiments. *American Economic Review, 90*, 980–994.

Hagen, J., Irland, L., & Whitman, A. (2005). *Changing timberland ownership in the northern forests and implications for biodiversity* (Report #MCCS-FCP2005-1). Brunswick, ME: Manomet Center for Conservation Sciences.

Hardin, G., & Baden, J. (Eds.). (1977). *Managing the commons*. New York: W.H. Freeman.

Hardin, G. (1968). The tragedy of the commons. *Science, 162*, 1243–1248.

Henrich, J., Boyd, R., Bowles, S., Camerer, C., Fehr, E., Gintis, H., et al. (2005). 'Economic Man' in cross-cultural perspective: Behavioral experiments in 15 small-scale societies. *Behavioral and Brain Sciences, 28*, 795–855.

Henrich, J. (2000). Decision making, cultural transmission and adaptation in economic anthropology. In J. Ensminger (Ed.), *Theory in economic anthropology* (pp. 251–295). Walnut Creek, CA: Altamira Press.

Hess, C. (2012). The unfolding of the knowledge commons. *St Antony's International Review, 1*, 13–24.

Hess, C., & Ostrom, E. (Eds.). (2012). *Understanding knowledge as a commons: From theory to practice*. Cambridge, MA: MIT Press.

Kaltenborn, B., Haaland, H., & Sandell, K. (2001). The public right of access: Some challenges to sustainable tourism development in Scandinavia. *Journal of Sustainable Tourism, 9*(5), 417–433.

Kopelman, S., Weber, M., & Messick, D. (2002). Factors influencing cooperation in commons dilemmas: A review of experimental psychological research. In E. Ostrom, T. Dietz, N. Dolsak, P. Stern, S. Stonich, & E. U. Weber (Eds.), *The drama of the commons* (pp. 113–156). Washington, DC: National Academy Press.

Lesorogol, C. (2008). *Contesting the commons: Privatizing pastoral land in Kenya*. Ann Arbor, MI: University of Michigan Press.

Nowak, M., & Sigmund, K. (2005). Evolution of indirect reciprocity. *Nature, 437*, 1291–1297.

Ostrom, E. (1990). *Governing the commons: The evolution of institutions for collective action*. New York: Cambridge University Press.

Ostrom, E. (2000). Reformulating the commons. *Swiss Political Science Review, 6*(1), 29–52.

Ostrom, E. (2003). How types of goods and property right jointly affect collective action. *Journal of Theoretical Politics, 15*(3), 239–270.

Ostrom, E., Gardner, R., & Walker, J. (1994). *Rules, games and common-pool resources*. Ann Arbor, MI: University of Michigan Press.

Pinkerton, E., & Weinstein, M. (1995). *Fisheries that work: Sustainability through community based management*. Vancouver, BC: David Suzuki Foundation.

Poteete, A., Janssen, M., & Ostrom, E. (2010). *Working together: Collective action, the commons and multiple methods in practice*. Princeton, NJ: Princeton University Press.

Richerson, P., Boyd, R., & Paciotti, B. (2002). An evolutionary theory of commons management. In E. Ostrom, T. Dietz, N. Dolsak, P. Stern, S. Stonich, & E. U. Weber (Eds.), *The drama of the commons* (pp. 403–442). Washington, DC: National Academy Press.

Sambides, Jr., N. (2016). Roxanne Quimby transfers 87,000 acres planned for national monument to US government. *Bangor Daily News* (23 August).

Schlager, E., & Ostrom, E. (1992). Property rights regimes and natural resources: A conceptual analysis. *Land Economics, 68*(3), 249–262.

Short, C. (2008). The traditional commons of England and Wales in the 21st century: Meeting old and new challenges. *International Journal of the Commons, 2*(2), 191–221.

Taylor, M. (1990). Cooperation and rationality: Notes on the collective action problem and its solutions. In K. S. Cook & M. Levi (Eds.), *The limits of rationality* (pp. 222–249). Chicago: University of Chicago Press.

von Benda-Beckmann, F., von Benda-Beckmann, K., & Wiber, M. (2006). The properties of property. In F. von Benda-Beckmann, K. von Benda-Beckmann, & M. Wiber (Eds.), *Changing properties of property* (pp. 1–39). New York: Berghahn Books.

Wolf, E. (1955). Types of Latin American peasantry: A preliminary discussion. *American Anthropologist, 57*(3), 452–470.

Who Is in the Commons: Defining Community, Commons, and Time in Long-Term Natural Resource Management

Michael R. Dove, Amy Johnson, Manon Lefebvre, Paul Burow, Wen Zhou, and Lav Kanoi

Nearly 30 years after Ostrom's (1990) overturn of the "tragedy of the commons" hypothesis, community management of common pool resources—fisheries, water sources, grazing fields, forests, etc.—remains a compelling topic of study and investment for researchers, practitioners, states, and nongovernmental organizations. Criticism of the commons as ipso facto exclusionary cooperative partnerships (Block and Jankovic 2016) has not dampened the mystique of collective, community-oriented, natural resource management. As Agrawal (2003, p. 244) pointed out, by connecting forms of property to resource management outcomes, literature on the commons lends itself to broad theoretical and practical application as a method to influence politics of collective action. Social and natural scientists have, in this way, converged around common desires to enable sustainable environments, environmental knowledge, and practices that promote cultural diversity, biodiversity, and democracy. With these lofty goals, it is easy to forget to look down at the semantic grounds that frame our interventions: community, commons, and time.

We present here case studies that invite reflection on the enterprise of long-term commons management. These studies emerge from ethnographic and historical research into commons management appearing in Madagascar, the USA, Gabon, India, and Southeast Asia. Divided into three thematic sections, we discuss (1) the boundaries of community, (2) the significance of extra-local state and non-state actors in constructing and managing commons, and (3) the delay in recognizing time as essential to validating "what counts" as commons management. Our five case studies provide a critical reading of commons in order to inspire more reflexive, locally attuned, and enduring management of natural resources.

M. R. Dove · A. Johnson (✉) · M. Lefebvre · P. Burow · W. Zhou · L. Kanoi
Department of Anthropology, School of Forestry and Environmental Studies, Yale University, New Haven, CT, USA
e-mail: amy.l.johnson@yale.edu

Community: Who Belongs?

Madagascar Mangrove Restoration and the Problem of the "Stranger"

As scholars have argued, no "community" is monolithic. Rather, communities exist within particular contexts, histories, and politics, entangled in overlapping and complex power dynamics of gender, race and ethnicity, sexuality, religion, age, and beyond. Thus, to critically think through the efficacy of community resource management, we must always begin by interrogating the politics and power differentials within the "community" of which we speak. In this case study, we interrogate the gendered politics of reforestation in a mangrove forest in Madagascar in order to trouble the myth of homogeneity in community resource management.

In 2017, one of us conducted research in a village (with a population of approximately 5000 people) within Madagascar's largest mangrove forest, the Ambanja-Ambaro bay mangrove.[1] In 2000, members of this community created the Communauté Locale de Base (CLB), a community resource management body, to protect and manage their mangrove forest. The CLB has over 200 members in its Assemblé Générale and works with the state and local conservation organizations to enact community resource management policies and monitor community use of the mangrove. In recent years, the CLB has undertaken a series of community reforestation projects as a key part of its conservation efforts. Notably, it is the women of the community who are responsible for reforestation. Over the last five years, women have carried out a series of paid reforestation projects. However, not all of the women participate evenly in reforestation. In reality, deep-rooted social divisions often determined who could or could not take part in community conservation. This case study explores the hierarchy of power in this community that allows for the exclusion of certain women from community reforestation.

In investigating mangrove reforestation, a discourse of blame for deforestation against women seen as social outsiders becomes apparent, which in turn contributes to an uneven participation of women in community reforestation. This blaming of social outsiders is part of a larger social hierarchy rooted in competing identities around homeland, especially the important division of *tompon-tany* and *vahiny* identities in Madagascar. *Tompon-tany* are masters or children of the land, social insiders, and occupy positions of leadership in the community and in conservation; *vahiny* are visitors to the region, outsiders, and often do not participate in conservation activities. This division of *tompon-tany* and *vahiny*, of insiders and outsiders, had profound consequences for uneven community participation in mangrove reforestation.

Many of the *tompon-tany* women encountered through the restoration project felt that the *vahiny* women had no stake in the land on which they had settled and therefore had no respect for the forest. As one *tompon-tany* woman said: "The prob-

---

[1] The island's largest mangrove forest; it measures at over 45,000 ha.

lem is people not from here. They come here to make money before going back home."[2] This sentiment was echoed by a number of other *tompon-tany* women, as seen in the words of another *tompon-tany* woman: "People who come from here understand the importance of the mangrove and know that cutting the mangrove will cause sea level rise."[3] Or yet another *tompon-tany* woman, who said: "People from here respect the mangrove forest, as they are their source of livelihood. People from the South do not respect the mangrove forest, so they do not care. They cut wood in secret and make charcoal. They destroy the forest."[4] By positioning themselves as insiders, *tompon-tany* women placed themselves in contrast with "outsiders": women belonging to other ethnic groups who come from different places. The common narrative is that while the *tompon-tany* protect and respect the mangrove, *vahiny* disrespect and exploit the mangrove.

The social divisions in the conservation of this mangrove forest hinge on *tompon-tany* women's belief that *vahiny* women do not care about the mangrove forest and therefore are responsible for its destruction. Yet, the narrative of blame is largely a mischaracterization of *vahiny* women. In interviews and conversations, many *vahiny* women shared the same connection to the mangrove and visions for its future to those of *tompon-tany* women. They spoke of seeing a decrease in mangrove forest over time. They also spoke of their fears of the future and their dependence upon the mangrove forest for survival. Their stories reveal a tension: while the women understand the mangrove's importance and have a subsequent desire to protect it, they also feel disconnected from, or even resentful toward, mangrove forest conservation restrictions.

Although many of the women in this mangrove share common visions and care for their forest, they remain divided by a deep-rooted social tension that fosters this narrative of blame. It was a *tompon-tany* woman who said: "Only those who do not need the mangrove to survive would find the rules unjust."[5] And yet, *vahiny* women depend on the mangrove for survival just as much as *tompon-tany* women. The central factor in explaining this opposition in community resource management is the insider/outsider division in this community. This social division and the *vahiny* exclusion from conservation are co-constituted: while *vahiny* women who are outsiders may care about the mangrove forest, they are excluded from conservation because of their status as outsiders. The exclusion then reifies them as outsiders, prevents their participation in community reforestation, and upholds the narrative of *vahiny* as outsiders who do not care about the mangrove forest. This logic has consequences for conservation, as it shapes the way that women understand their environment and the importance of conservation. When *vahiny* women who might otherwise be more invested in conservation activities feel excluded from conservation, such exclusion fosters resentment toward conservation and forecloses solidarity among all women.

---

[2] Interview with Anja on June 23, 2017.
[3] Interview with Antsa on June 21, 2017.
[4] Interview with Mialy on June 24, 2017.
[5] Interview with Anja on June 18, 2017.

In this mangrove, women are implicated in a social hierarchy of power that results in the exclusion of certain women marked as strange in the landscape, the *vahiny*. In order to untangle the politics of community reforestation, it is important to recognize the ways in which *tompon-tany* understand *vahiny* women and to do the difficult work of considering the ways institutions and women themselves uphold structures of exclusionary power. Conservation discourses that fail to disentangle the power relations inherent to any community resource management project risk obscuring the lived realities of these communities. Too often, such a discourse reproduces communities, especially those in the Third World, as universal victims of environmental degradation. Rendering the "community" as a homogeneous entity can obscure the politics of inequity within community resource management projects.

Managing Bison Kin in the American West

If the social difference among women is concealed in the desire to produce a women-centric management of mangroves in Madagascar, how might the recognition of bison as kin to the Salish trouble the boundaries of community in the management of a common bison herd in the American West? This case examines long-term community resource management through the long-running conflict over the creation and existence of the National Bison Range, a US-federal wildlife refuge inholding within the Flathead Reservation in western Montana. Wildlife conservation is commonly viewed as a state-led resource management activity. But this case shows a different mode of care located in indigenous efforts to protect the bison. This history of "saving the bison" is a co-production of two different visions and practices—one rooted in Salish beliefs and practices that were tested by the onslaught of white settlement and another in the nascent wildlife conservation movement that emerged nationwide in the late nineteenth century. The conventional narrative of the protection of bison tends to obscure the important part Salish efforts played in the story of bison conservation. Also obscured is how their efforts were undermined by the federal policy of allotment that saw reservation lands opened to white settlement.

Bison sit at the center of Salish lifeways. Elders' stories relay a sense of "respect for the buffalo, of how much the people relied upon them, both spiritually and materially" (Whealdon 2001). Yearly buffalo hunts were and are an important practice to Salish communities. With the decline of buffalo populations in the late nineteenth century, the hunt became increasingly difficult. The absence of buffalo threatened the relationships between Salish people and animal kin. Furthermore, it undermined territorial claims under threat by an expanding settler state. The declining yields during annual buffalo hunts collapsed to close to zero by the late 1880s (Whealdon 2001). Market hunting brought on by demand for consumer and industrial leather products, an active US military campaign to destroy the buffalo as a means of undermining the economy of Plains tribes, and a changing rangeland ecology, all played a role in the rapid decline of the bison (Isenberg 2000). Over a period of years, Salish leaders sanctioned bringing home a small number of orphaned calves to raise a herd that came to be known as the Pablo-Allard herd (Coder 1975).[6] Using land proximate to the Flathead River affording ample water and a valley floor for good pasture, the herd was left on the open range. At the same time, leaders of the emergent conservation movement in metropolitan cities sought to secure wildlife for the future, developing a model for wildlife conservation still used today: the game refuge.

Leaders of the nascent conservation movement, including William T. Hornaday, the first director of the New York Zoological Park and founder of the American Bison Society (ABS), came to ultimately believe secure public parks would be necessary to provide a sufficiently large range when herds began to outgrow their owners' private lands (Hornaday 1887). This emergent model called for a public-private partnership to protect the bison, with the organization raising funds to support the purchase and sourcing of the bison, and the government providing the requisite land and infrastructure to support it (Trefethen 1961; Coder 1975; Jacoby 2001). The first use of this model was the dispossession of lands on the Apache-Comanche-Kiowa Indian Reservation to become a forest reserve that was then turned into a game refuge. When President Roosevelt signed the Flathead Allotment Act in 1904, it changed access to land dramatically in the Salish and Kootenai Nation. The legislation called for "the sale and disposal of all surplus lands after allotment" (Statutes, V. 33: 302). A new threat emerged for Pablo: How would he acquire additional grassland for his bison or even maintain his existing land use under a new federal policy of allotment? It was not long before someone recommended such a practice on the soon-to-be allotted Flathead Reservation. Pablo was eventually forced to sell his herd, and it was purchased by the Canadian government which was setting up its own bison refuge in northern Alberta. With private fundraising, Hornaday suggested the society find and purchase a "nucleus herd" for the government in return for their support providing land and fencing. He outlined the key attributes of a game preserve: accessibility for animal transport and public visitation, suitable range for all seasons with plenty of water, good terrain for fencing, and a good space for caretaking staff.[7] Indigenous lands were key targets for prospective refuge locations.[8]

---

[6] See Charles Aubrey, "The Edmonton Buffalo Herd," Forest and Stream, Vol. 59, July 5, 1902, p. 6; D.J. Benham; see Charles Aubrey, "The Edmonton Buffalo Herd," Forest and Stream, Vol. 59, July 5, 1902, p. 6; D.J. Benham, "The Round-up of the Second Herd of Pablo's Buffalo." Edmonton Bulletin, November 8, 1907, pp. 9–11; W.A. Bartlett, Bon I. Whealdon, "I Will Be Meat for My Salish." Salish Kootenai College Press, 2001, p. 69–82; John Kidder "Montana Miracle: It Saved the Buffalo," Montana: The Magazine of Western History, 15(2):52–67, Spring, 1965; see letter from Malcolm McLeod to Martin S. Garretson dated May 12, 1926, in American Bison Society Papers, Collection 1010, Wildlife Conservation Society Archives, New York.

[7] Whealdon, 2001; Letters between William T. Hornaday and Dr. Morton J. Elrod, American Bison Society Papers. Collection 1010. Wildlife Conservation Society Archives, New York; Daily Missoulian, May 29, 1907.

[8] Fourth Annual Report of the American Bison Society, 1991, pp. 1–8.

It is clear that Salish efforts to protect the bison were operating successfully before the opening of the reservation through allotment. Allotment forced Pablo to sell his herd. The usefulness of a national campaign under the auspices of the ABS at that time only became necessary in the context of an allotment policy that make these indigenous efforts untenable. Many local people do not endorse this centralized vision of conservation planning and find their own lifeways endangered when national governments undertake conservation projects through dispossession and centralized control. Salish efforts to protect kin relations with bison were rendered invisible and were erased by the actions of the settler government to manage wildlife populations as a duty of the nation. The National Bison Range is still operated by the US government today through the Fish and Wildlife Service. The Salish and Kootenai nation continues to advocate for the return of this land and the role of caring for the herd, much like their forbears' generations ago.

This erasure of indigenous political claims and practices is elemental in the emergence of long-term resource management regimes around threatened animals like the American bison. Invisibility works its way into the contemporary system of wildlife management, obscuring indigenous practices of care and maintaining relations with kin and replacing them with a technoscientific regime of managerial control of nature that serve to reinforce state institutions and the national prerogative to "save" nature for settler publics. This exclusion of community management offers a counter-story to case studies that presuppose recognized political claims distinct from settler communities, clear community boundedness, and analogous interests among groups. Recuperating the history of indigenous efforts to sustain important human-animal relationships offers a different approach to caring for wildlife that troubles the boundaries of a "management" paradigm that foregrounds the control and heavy intervention common to scientific wildlife management. Strengthening indigenous sovereignty by returning lands dispossessed for the purpose of state wildlife conservation is a way to address the political claims of indigenous nations while also enabling greater human and other-than-human flourishing through indigenous modes of care and resurgence.

The above two studies confirm that community is a social construct rather than pre-given entity. Members of the defined "community," such as *tompon-tany* women in Madagascar, can work to exclude others from inclusion in management of common natural resources, like mangroves. In doing so, a universal category, "women," is shown to mask deeply entrenched social hierarchies among Madagascar women and in some sense to reproduce them. Similarly, the dispossession of bison from Salish peoples of the American West, through the imposition of settler-colonial law (e.g., the Allotment Act) and metropolitan visions of game refuge conservation, flattens the Salish worldview to accept bison as kin, thus removing bison from their human relations and making relations between Salish and Bison invisible to settler-colonial wildlife managers. As kin, bison push the boundaries of community to incorporate the other-than-human while also blurring the distinction of bison as the object of long-term management: can you manage a commons of kin? The historical exegesis of indigenous and federal bison management illustrates that new conceptions of community and commons are required if our aim is to facilitate locally meaningful and sustainable forms of conservation. Our depiction of social hierarchies among women in Madagascar likewise serves as a caution to apolitical concepts of community, imploring practitioners to think critically about who is valorized as part of community and who is excluded in the design and execution of commons management. From these studies of community, we shift our attention to the extra-local actors impacting the delineation of commons in Gabon and India.

Extra-Local Controls: Defining Commons and Management Techniques

Constructing the "Rural Forest Domain" in Gabon

In response to global calls for the decentralization of forest management over the past 30 years, the Central African country of Gabon created a new land use category (the "rural forest domain") in its 2001 Forestry Code, which permitted the legal establishment of community forests. With a reported forest cover of nearly 90% (FAO 2015), Gabon has long seen commercial logging interests lay claim to its extensive tropical forests that constitute the western edge of the Congo Basin, beginning under French colonization in the late nineteenth century with the wholesale delegation of the forest interior to European logging companies (Coquery-Vidrovitch 2001 [1972]). While industrial forest concessions continue to occupy the vast majority of Gabon's forests, this tentative opening for villagers to benefit from the proceeds of small-scale forestry has seen formal project support from the European Union and the World Wildlife Fund (Meunier et al. 2011; WWF 2014). The prospects of these newly established community forests, however, are not only challenged by the limited durations of donor project cycles (with funding and institutional support having already ceased) but by the very assumption of "community" units that possess a shared history, identity, and tenurial claims on surrounding forests. Instead, the long-standing forest claims of private logging concerns pose concrete limits to the expansion of community forests in Gabon and further challenge the aims of community forestry for sustainable and decentralized forest governance.

In the forests of Central Africa, present-day communities can be understood as the products of colonial interventions. Emphasizing the essential mobility of peoples and settlements in pre-colonial societies, Vansina (1990) has argued that historical relations between the fundamental units of household, village, and district were imminently flexible, such that individual households could choose to join and leave villages, and villages leave and join districts as political alliances waxed and waned. This independence of movement, premised on low population densities and seemingly limitless forests for swidden cultivation and subsistence hunting, was forcibly curtailed by colonial and postcolonial policies of "regroupment" in French Equatorial Africa, which relocated seminomadic forest peoples into fixed settlements along the banks of rivers and roads (Pourtier 1989). New administrative structures were overlaid onto these diverse assemblages of households, formally recategorized as villages and cantons administered by government-appointed officials. As resettlement continued into the 1970s, residents in rural Gabon are still able to identify themselves by the different clan and lineage groups that have been compressed into the space of these immobilized villages. Such identifications formerly served as the basis of strictly controlled forest management units. However, regroupement and the external appointment of administrative heads greatly weakened customary forest governance, with non-lineage members appropriating local forest resources under emergent conditions of open access (Walters et al. 2015).

Colonial and postcolonial governments took advantage of regroupment to reinscribe forests as logging concessions and protected areas, such that customary claims to the forest were further effaced by the new state and private proprietors of land. Indeed, the resettlement of villages from the forest interior enabled the intensified exploitation of forest resources by concessionary companies, while further easing the recruitment of forced labor among these stabilized villagers (Giles-Vernick 2002). Thus, the 2001 creation of the "rural forest domain" requires a reappropriation of forestland from concessionary land regimes, and the designation of community forests entails a number of conditions that must be met by private corporations rather than state or local actors. Logging companies must first map the sites of customary forest use as part of the socioeconomic surveys required for their applications for long-term forest concession permits (CFADs). Should a company not have conducted socioeconomic studies while operating under their initial temporary forest management permits (CPAETs), or never intended to acquire their permanent forest management permits due to the costs of the application process, such a zone of customary use would not have been defined, and a formal community forest would be technically impossible to designate.[9]

While some villagers thus see their ability to claim community forests denied from the outset, certain logging investors see community forests as an opportunity to access timber at a greatly reduced cost. As the nominal beneficiaries of the "rural forest domain", villagers in marginal locations are far removed from the wealth of urban centers, thus there are much lower barriers to obtain a community forest permit in comparison to a formal forest concession: only a simplified management plan is required of the applicant community, and no taxes are levied on their forest harvests. Nonetheless, as most rural communities do not have the funding or technical knowledge to draft even a simplified management plan, logging companies and individual entrepreneurs have sought to apply for forest permits on their behalf in exchange for timber exploitation rights in the designated community forest and so pay nominal rents, if any, on the volumes of wood harvested.[10] As harvesting can begin before permits are received and can occur on the basis of informal agreements with villagers alone, investors have found this to be an efficient means of expanding their effective logging domains at low cost. In recent years a number of foreign log-

---

[9] Interview, Makokou, August 2, 2017.
[10] Interview, Libreville, July 4, 2017.

gers and sawmill operators have specialized solely in harvesting timber from the rural forest domain, where they do not have the capital to obtain a formal forest concession permit nor the desire to submit to greater government oversight under a strict harvesting regime. Thus, the promise of community forests, whether for the repatriation of customary land claims or improved rural incomes, sees its reclamation by private interests as a new land opportunity.

Water Management Across Community and State in Pre-colonial and Colonial India

The state and private partners, as we read in the case of Gabon, are actively engaged in delineating commons and structuring their use by communities. Looking back to the pre-colonial period of India, it is possible to discern the *longue duree* of state investment in commons management. As such, the premise of community management as distinctive from state management becomes difficult to maintain. Communities do not exist in isolation. Even if the state does not directly support community resources, it still mediates access and control to them and influences their management. Here we examine how water commons in India (lakes, ponds, and *jhors*[11]), and associated knowledge about their construction and maintenance, suffered destruction with the advent of the colonial government and technological modernity.

Up until colonial India, lakes and ponds were, as part of an older tradition, built communally and maintained collectively. The Indian sociologist and environmentalist Anupam Mishra (1993) wrote about the eventual fall and demise of India's traditional water management systems during the colonial period in his seminal work *Aaj Bhi Khare Hain Talab*[12]; Mishra's work describes that once the colonial government took control of India, its traditional and local systems of water management fell apart. Mishra (1993, p. 82) writes about the Kingdom of Mysore and that around the year 1800 (just after the Anglo-Mysore wars), there were almost 40,000 lakes, reservoirs, or tanks in the state and that watershed management systems would maximize water harvests from the monsoons. The Mysore Kingdom also contributed to the maintenance of these water-harvesting structures. Around 1839, under the colonial regime, the British halved what they thought was *fizoolkharchi* (or wasteful expenditure) on water bodies. This deficit in state-sponsorship was initially covered by local communities for over 30 years, when the Public Works Department (PWD) was constituted and ownership of these ponds was taken away from the community (Mishra 1993, p. 82).[13] Thereafter, the British government

---

[11] Over ground rainwater ducts.
[12] Title translation, "The Ponds are Still Relevant".
[13] The Central Public Works Department of India was instituted in 1854 CE. The Karnataka (erstwhile Mysore) PWD came into being in 1856 CE, although Mishra writes that it came into being in 1863 CE. However, the exact year of the PWD's creation is not, from our perspective, as impor-

replaced the traditional arrangements with new rules for use of these water structures and in effect they fell into disrepair.

Contrary to Mishra's account, other writers have maintained that while the British tried to appropriate traditional irrigation tank systems when they failed to set up large-scale irrigation systems in the 1830s in some parts of the country, they did not have the "budget or the staff to take care of such widely scattered independent systems of tanks" (Naz and Subramanian 2010, pp. 3–4). Consequently, they believed in what Naz and Subramaniam call the "Colonial Myth of Kudlmaramat" that village communities would undertake "voluntary labor to maintain these tanks as a tradition" (Naz and Subramanian 2010). We are reminded immediately, however, that in pre-colonial times, individuals did not provide labor for the maintenance of the tanks for free "but were paid from the funds mobilized at the village level" (Naz and Subramanian 2010).

Part of the reason the British government did not have funds for tank maintenance was that they were spending their budgets on large-scale irrigation systems, as exemplified by the case of the Ali Mardan canal (near the city of Delhi), which had been revived in 1821. The canal was supposed to provide healthy drinking water for city-dwellers, but farmers used more water than administrators anticipated and in result "the quantity flowing into the city decreased and the canal finally dried up again" (Gupta 1981, p. 19). More importantly, "during the eighteen-twenties and eighteen-thirties, when the canal did provide potable water, the wells were neglected" (Gupta 1981). The canal was restored once again by 1867, but the wells continued to decline (Dasgupta 2012, p. 59). The Ali Mardan canal was not the only one being revived at that time. The Jumna canals were reopened around this period, the western Jumna canal in 1819 (the Ali Mardan canal was an extension of this canal) and the eastern Jumna canal in 1830, with improvements being made to both in the 1840s (Brown 1978, p. 40).

However, the conditions of these wells and other community-developed water resources declined not just because of negative impact of government intervention but also because of newer and more convenient technologies. In a book that seeks to trace the history of Delhi through its ruins, Anand Vivek Taneja (2018) recounts his conversation with the Delhi-based artist-researcher, Bhagwati Prasad,[14] who works on water. Taneja reports that, according to Prasad, till the introduction of centralized pipe water, there were primarily two sources of water: the Yamuna river and wells. In addition to these two, "the third was the rainwater collected in *jhors*" which required maintenance by local users. According to Prasad, the *jhors* were always built on village common lands and were controlled by the *panchayat* responsible for their maintenance and for ensuring that the water thus collected was clean (Prasad 2018, p. 198). *Panchayat* is an ancient form of local self-governance in the Indian

---

tant as the historical trend it represents.

[14] See, for example, http://indiaifa.org/grants-projects/bhagwati-prasad.html (accessed: October 27, 2018). Bhagwati Prasad has recently published an incredibly graphic account of water-related conflict in contemporary peri-urban Delhi, *The Water Cookbook* Prasad (2011), http://sarai.net/the-water-cookbook/ (accessed: October 10, 2018).

subcontinent with an expectedly complex history. Suffice to say that while this institution had suffered during the colonial British dispensation (see, e.g., Dharampal 2000, pp. 249–56), it has regained relevance in Independent India, especially after the 1990s.

In the villages where *jhors* were properly maintained, they could, as Prasad argues, provide for a year's worth of water for agriculture. However, "in villages that have come within the perimeter of Delhi's urbanization… these old ways are going… [T]he government made promises of a centralized system of water: there will be taps and running water in your homes and you will drink straight from them" (Taneja 2018, p. 198). However, where there was inadequate centralized water supply (either due to lack of supply or unclean supply), people were able to pump up groundwater using new and affordable techniques, particularly tube wells. Consequently, the people's relationships with these traditional water sources began to decline. "The panchayat's relationship with the wells also slowly finished. When the wells started drying up, which happened because people started pumping the groundwater and hence water levels went down, the panchayats didn't try to dig the wells deeper. And the wells died" (Taneja 2018, p. 199). As a result, the common lands where the *jhors* were built, and the watersheds which fed into *jhors*, also ceased to be useful in the old way. "People slowly started occupying the land of the *jhors*, incorporating them into their individual fields till there was nothing left. Today in a village no one knows on what land the *jhor* was, how big it was…" And now, with the wells gone, the river destroyed, and the *jhors* finished, people have begun to draw clean water from deeper and deeper within the ground (Taneja 2018).

Something else died along with the wells, invaluable indigenous technical knowledge of how these water structures were built and maintained. Mishra (1993, p. 10) attempted to re-present this knowledge, but he wrote unambiguously that no "full description of how lakes are built is available." In related way, Scott (1998, p. 316) argued that metis (Greek μῆτις, meaning practical wisdom, skill, craft) is a kind of practicable knowledge or skill that resists codification and "simplification into deductive principles." It requires an alert and continuous engagement with one's immediate environs rather than the indiscriminate application of general precepts or rules-of-thumb outside of context. However, when authoritarian states have sought to indiscriminately impose "high-modernist schemes" upon peoples "in the grip of a self-evident (and usually half-baked) social theory," through scientific planning or otherwise they have ignored metis and ended up doing "irreparable damage to human communities and individual livelihoods" (Mishra 1993, pp. 340–341). We see this destruction playing out in the common water histories of India that we have traced, in the shallows, above.

Metis, in the case of Indian *jhors*, can be lost as the technologies and skills of commons management become devalued by changing political regimes. Can the same be true of changing regimes of resource management? In this final section, we consider how practices of commons management become valorized as such and what the temporality of this representation tells us about the shifting values of natural resource management.

Time in the Commons

Teleology and Historiography of Natural Resource Management: The Case of Swidden Agriculture in Southeast Asia

A little examined dimension of the history of natural resource management is the historiography of such management. A case in point is swidden agriculture in Southeast Asia and popular perceptions of its historical trajectory. Nothing has been more salient in the history of this system of agriculture, from colonial times to the present, than predictions of its imminent collapse. Swidden has been characterized by a peculiar focus not on its past or present, thus, but on its future. Swidden has been characterized by a ubiquitous "discourse of waning," which has been central to its critique by central state actors (Fig. 1).

Historic attention to swidden agriculture by state actors in Southeast Asia has been episodic. Swidden cultivators appear in the historical record, then disappear, then reappear, etc. (cf. Stoll 2017). One of the reasons for its appearance is political. Scholars characterize swidden agriculture as a "fugitive" form of agriculture, which

Fig. 1 American painter George Harvey's 1841 mournful painting of a swidden on the frontier

can be practiced in upland forests beyond the reach of lowland states—swidden agriculture being not only difficult for central states to govern but also difficult to extract from (Scott 2009; Dove 2011). When national governments in the region have been troubled by rural insurgencies, this has brought to the fore beliefs that swidden agriculture is not merely primitive but opposed to civilized governance. For example, in the mid-1970s, in the wake of the Indonesian "emergency" with Malaysia, maps in police stations on the coast of Kalimantan labeled the entire swiddening interior of the island as "komunis." Even the official label given by the Indonesian government to the indigenous peoples of Borneo and the other islands beyond Java was *suku terasing* "ethnic group most strange/foreign/alien" (Echols and Shadily 1992, p. 32, 531).

The other factors that highlight swidden agriculture in historic accounts are economic competition. When a logging boom began in the 1970s in Indonesia and Malaysia, placing swidden cultivation in direct competition with timber companies for the lowland dipterocarp rain forest, anti-swidden sentiments in government offices were fanned into a flame. National governments, echoing colonial Dutch references to swidden agriculture as *roofbouw* "robber agriculture," attacked forest-clearing in swidden agriculture as "wasteful destruction," notwithstanding the fact that the timber exported during this period to Japan went into single-use concrete forms in building construction. The critique of "waste" elided an important political dimension: customary tenure to the forests being logged was generally held by local ethnic minorities, whereas it was national elites—Muslim Malays in Malaysia and Javanese (and Chinese) in Indonesia—who profited from the timber extraction.

The critique of swidden agriculture as destructive was embedded in an overarching discourse of development—the national government of Indonesia from the 1960s to the 1990s called itself the *pemerintah pembangunan* "development government"—within which swidden agriculture was found wanting. Swidden agriculture fell short with respect to both the western "stage of growth" model of Rostow (1960) and the native state model that valorized intensive irrigated rice agriculture over extensive swidden agriculture. The historic and countervailing involvement of swidden agriculture in commodity production and trade was simply ignored (Dove 2011). In addition, a Malthusian argument was levied against swidden agriculture: it was argued that whatever its merits or demerits, population growth would ultimately doom these systems. Much effort was devoted to calculating "carrying capacities" of territories for swidden agriculture—marking the limits of these agricultural systems, and no others, in time and space— the illogic of which was eventually exposed by anthropologists (Carneiro 1960).[15]

This teleological dismissal of swidden agriculture, in effect this dark historiography of swidden agriculture, served well the colonial and postcolonial state policy in the Southeast Asian region. If systems of swidden agriculture were doomed by their own inherent dynamics, if they literally had no future, then there was no reason for

---

[15] Historical-ecological studies of swidden agriculture communities have been rare, but when carried out, they have documented the practice of this system of agriculture for decades, even centuries, with no noticeable degradation of the environment (Lawrence and Schlesinger 2001).

the state to support them, tolerate them, or indeed not sanction them. Inherent to this historiography was amnesia regarding the place of swidden agriculture in the history of the colonial powers themselves, in which no Malthusian collapse was to be seen. Swiddening was common in Sweden in the mid-eighteenth century according to Linnaeus (Weimarck 1968; Dove 2015); it thrived in parts of France until the end of the nineteenth century; pockets remained in Germany, Austria, and northern Russia until the mid-twentieth century (Sigaut 1979); and it probably survived longest in the less-populated and less-industrialized parts of Scandinavia (Myllyntaus et al. 2002; Kunnas 2005). Scandinavian immigrants brought its technology to the USA, beginning in the seventeenth century, where it was integral to clearing forests and pushing the frontier ever westward (Otto and Anderson 1982; Stoll 2017).

Linnaeus' study of swidden agriculture was politically controversial, which is characteristic of this topic not only in Europe but also Southeast Asia. The teleological character of the popular discourse on swidden agriculture has been prejudicial to its study: if it was disappearing, its study mattered little, and the nature of its disappearance mattered equally little. As a result, the persistence of swidden agriculture throughout the colonial period, and through much of the postcolonial period, was a source of unfailing surprise to outside observers.

A series of canonical studies in the mid-twentieth century explained the actual dynamics and strengths of swidden agriculture, demonstrating that it is a sustainable adaptation to forest environments in which labor is scarcer than land; population/land balances allow for fallow periods long enough to restore forest cover between periods of cropping, and resource appropriation by external actors is minimal (e.g., Izikowitz 1951; Condominas 1957; Freeman 1970 [1955]; Conklin 1977 [1957]). Swidden agriculture gradually waned in scholarly interest until the turn of the twentieth century, when new questions began to be studied, concerning fallow management and environmental change (Cairns 2007, 2015), the politics of upland-lowland relations (Scott 2009), and the role of forest peoples in global trade (Dove 2011).

While the public discourse on swidden agriculture depicted it as a resource system on its last legs, swidden agriculture continued to expand—supporting by the end of the twentieth century as many as one billion people—22% of the population of the developing world in tropical and subtropical zones (Thrupp et al. 1997). By the beginning of the twenty-first century, however, while swidden agriculture continued to be important in Africa and Latin America, its practice began to contract in one of its historic territories, Southeast Asia. Scholars today are examining the factors responsible for this decline, the first time this long-imagined dynamic has actually been studied (Mertz et al. 2009; Padoch et al. 2010; Heinimann et al. 2017). Ironically, the actual versus imagined waning of swidden agriculture has been accompanied by a new appreciation of its virtues. Scholars are asking, for example, in the face of environmental change, what role swidden agriculture might be able to play in reducing farmer risk and preserving biodiversity (Van Vliet et al. 2012; Mertz et al. 2013). Once tarred with the brush of being "anti-state," now swidden agriculture is associated with biodiversity and human resilience. Today there is another teleological narrative of doom regarding farming, but its specter is climate change not Malthus, and its focus is on modern, intensive, market-oriented cultivation. Ironically, swidden agriculture is seen—in part because of its traditional and once-critiqued character—as possible insurance against this new teleological dynamic.

Swidden agriculture is a uniquely evocative system of agriculture: its mere existence seems to pose questions about the self and the other. Views of swidden agriculture have historically reflected wider clashes of worldviews between political elites and ethnic minorities in Southeast Asia. A temporal dimension has been central to this confrontation: imbricated in judgments about the other have been assumptions about their future histories—or lack thereof—about their historiography. One lesson of the actual history of swidden agriculture is that its teleology has been overly hasty and misdirected: there are no final stories, only final stories as a political tactic.

Conclusions

Throughout this chapter, we have attended to the challenge of defining communities, commons, and indeed what are valued as appropriate techniques of natural resource management. We raise the important question of how natural resource management initiatives frame the parameters of community practices for commons management, excluding traditional practices at one time and validating them at another. In historical perspective, our discussion of *jhors* and common water management in India reveals the dangers of disenfranchising community access to commons: loss of metis or cultural ecological knowledge. We show that the state of Gabon, in consortium with private concessionaires, is presently delimiting access to commons through channels that privilege private interests over community interests. Yet, as we read in the cases of Madagascar and the Western USA, who is included in community is itself a fraught question, requiring scrutiny and flexible locally specific definitions.

Our analysis navigates a tension between metropolitan, nationalist, scientific, universal initiatives to conserve commons and local circumstances that are frequently at odds with the technoscientific paradigm of contemporary natural resource management. Practitioners of long-term natural resource management mediate these divides as part of their everyday work. But, this everyday work itself can inscribe values that surreptitiously disenfranchise, exclude, and dispossess groups gathered in commons (Li 2007). They may furthermore, by upholding resources as passive nature to be manipulated for human concern, undermine non-Western ontological commitments, as well as subvert the "active participation" of animals and other-than-humans in extant common pool resource management (Schmidt and Dowsley 2010). In this messy praxis, how can long-term community resource management proceed?

Our analysis joins others in suggesting change in the paradigm and structure of long-term community resource management is necessary. This change begins with working out for ourselves the grounds of our engagement in this particular type of intervention—that is, being simultaneously reflexive, historical, and sociological about our work. Pragmatically, this may consist of three broad points: firstly, attending to locally meaningful forms of community—including the recognition of other-than-human kin and kith—and locating ourselves as participants in community-driven programs that assure equity and inclusion for all members; secondly, acknowledging the historical processes leading to the delineation of the common in question and its parameters of access, i.e., denaturalizing the common; and thirdly, highlighting the temporality of management practices and their historiographies, evaluating why some practices become emblematic of natural resource management and others maligned as detrimental to it. Taken together, these starting points can aid practitioners in conceptualizing long-term natural resource management projects responsive to diverse ways of engaging environments collectively.

References

Agrawal, A. (2003). Sustainable governance of common-pool resources: Context, methods, and politics. *Annual Review of Anthropology, 32*, 243–262.

Block, W., & Jankovic, I. (2016). Tragedy of the partnership: A critique of elinor ostrom. *American Journal of Economics and Sociology, 75*(2), 289–318.

Brown, J. (1978). Sir Proby Cautley (1802–1871), a pioneer of Indian irrigation. In A. R. Hall & N. Smith (Eds.), *History of technology* (Vol. III). London: Mansell.

Cairns, M. (Ed.). (2007). *Voices from the forest: Integrating indigenous knowledge into sustainable upland farming*. Washington, DC: Resources for the Future.

Cairns, M. (Ed.). (2015). *Shifting cultivation and environmental change: Indigenous people, agriculture and forest conservation*. London: Earthscan.

Carneiro, R. L. (1960). Slash-and-burn agriculture: A closer look at its implications for settlement patterns. In A. F. C. Wallace (Ed.), *Men and cultures* (pp. 229–234). Philadelphia, PA: University of Pennsylvania Press.

Coder, G. D. (1975). *The national movement to preserve the American buffalo in the United States and Canada between 1880 and 1920*. PhD Dissertation. The Ohio State University.

Condominas, G. (1957). In A. Foulke (Ed.), *We have eaten the forest: The story of a Montagnard Village in the central highlands of Vietnam*. New York: Hill and Wang.

Conklin, H. (1977 [1957]). *Hanuno'o agriculture*. Rome: Food and Agriculture Organization of the United Nations.

Coquery-Vidrovitch, C. (2001 [1972]). Le Congo au temps des grandes compagnies concessionnaires 1898–1930. Tome 1. In *Editions de l'Ecole des Hautes Etudes en Sciences Sociales* (Vol. 1).

Dasgupta, R. (2012). *Urbanising cholera: The social determinants of its re-emergence*. New Delhi: Orient Blackswan.

Dharampal. (2000). *Collected writings, volume IV: Panchayat Raj and India's polity*. Goa: Other India Press.

Dove, M. R. (2011). The banana tree at the gate: The history of marginal peoples and global markets in Borneo. In J. C. Scott (Ed.), *Yale agrarian studies series*. New Haven, CT: Yale University Press.

Dove, M. R. (2015). Linnaeus' study of Swedish swidden cultivation: Pioneering ethnographic work on the 'economy of nature'. *Ambio, 44*(3), 239–248.

Echols, J. M., & Shadily, H. (1992). *Kamus Indonesia-Inggris: An Indonesian-English dictionary* (3rd ed.). Jakarta: P. T. Gramedia.

FAO. (2015). *Global forest resources assessment 2015: How are the world's forests changing?* Rome: Food and Agriculture Organization of the United Nations.

Freeman, D. (1970 [1955]). *Report on the Iban*. New York: The Athlone Press.

Giles-Vernick, T. (2002). *Cutting the vines of the past: Environmental histories of the central African rain forest*. Charlottesville: University Press of Virginia.

Gupta, N. (1981). Delhi between two empires 1803–1931: Society, government and urban growth. In *The Delhi omnibus*. New Delhi: Oxford University Press.

Heinimann, A., Mertz, O., Frolking, S., Christensen, A. E., Hurni, K., Sedano, F., et al. (2017). A global view of shifting cultivation: Recent, current, and future extent. *PLoS One, 12*(9), e0184479.

Hornaday, W. T. (1887). *The passing of the buffalo*. Rochester, NY: Schlicht & Field.

Isenberg, A. (2000). *The destruction of the bison: An environmental history, 1750–1920*. Cambridge: Cambridge University Press.

Izikowitz, K. G. (1951). *Lamet: Hill peasants in French Indochina*. Göteborg: Etnografiska Museet.

Jacoby, K. (2001). *Crimes against nature: Squatters, poachers, thieves, and the hidden history of American conservation*. Berkeley: University of California Press.

Kunnas, J. (2005). A dense and sickly mist from thousands of bog fires: An attempt to compare the energy consumption in slash-and-burn cultivation and burning cultivation of peatlands in Finland in 1820–1920. *Environment and History, 11*, 431–446.

Lawrence, D., & Schlesinger, W. H. (2001). Changes in soil phosphorus during 200 years of shifting cultivation in Indonesia. *Ecology, 82*(10), 2769–2780.

Li, T. M. (2007). *The will to improve: Governmentality, development, and the practice of politics*. Chapel Hill, NC: Duke University Press.

Mertz, O., Egay, K., Bruun, T. B., & Colding, T. S. (2013). The last swiddens of Sarawak, Malaysia. *Human Ecology, 41*(1), 109–118.

Mertz, O., Padoch, C., Fox, J., Cramb, R. A., Leisz, S. J., Lam, N. T., et al. (2009). Swidden change in Southeast Asia: Understanding causes and consequences. *Human Ecology, 37*(3), 259–264.

Meunier, Q., Federspiel, M., Moumbogou, C., Grégoire, B., Doucet, J.-L., & Vermeulen, C. (2011). The first community forests of Gabon: Towards sustainable local forest management? *Nature et Faune, 25*(2), 40–45.

Mishra, A. (1993). *Aaj bhi khare hai talaab [The ponds are still relevant]*. New Delhi: Gandhi Shanti Pratishthan.

Myllyntaus, T. & Mattila, T. (2002). Decline or increase? The standing timber stock in Finland, 1800–1997. *Ecological Economics, 41*(2), 271–288.

Naz, F., & Subramanian, S. V. (2010). *Water management across space and time in India* (ZEF working paper series) (Vol. 61). Bonn: Center for Development Research. Retrieved October 27, 2018, from https://www.econstor.eu/bitstream/10419/88305/1/639006426.pdf

Ostrom, E. (1990). *Governing the commons: The evolution of institutions for collective action*. Cambridge, MA: Cambridge University Press.

Otto, J. S., & Anderson, N. E. (1982). Slash-and-burn cultivation in the highlands south: A problem in comparative agricultural history. *Comparative Study of Society and History, 24*, 131–147.

Padoch, C., Coffey, K., Mertz, O., Leisz, S. J., Fox, J., & Wadley, R. L. (2010). The demise of swidden in Southeast Asia? Local realities and regional ambiguities. *Geografisk Tidsskrift, Danish Journal of Geography, 107*(1), 29–41.

Pourtier, R. (1989). *Le Gabon: Etat et developpement* (Vol. 2). Paris: Harmattan.

Prasad, B. (2018). *India foundation for the arts*. Website: Retrieved October 27, 2018, from http://indiaifa.org/grants-projects/bhagwati-prasad.html

Prasad, B. (2011). *The water cookbook*. Delhi: The Sarai Programme, CSDS. Available online: Retrieved October 10, 2018, from http://sarai.net/the-water-cookbook/

Rostow, W. W. (1960). *Stages of economic growth, a non-communist manifesto*. Cambridge: Cambridge University Press.

Schmidt, J. J., & Dowsley, M. (2010). Hunting with polar bears: Problems with the passive properties of the commons. *Human Ecology, 38*, 377–387.
Scott, J. C. (1998). *Seeing like a state: How certain schemes to improve the human condition have failed*. New Haven, CT: Yale University Press.
Scott, J. C. (2009). *The art of not being governed: An anarchist history of upland Southeast Asia*. New Haven, CT: Yale University Press.
Sigaut, F. (1979). Swidden cultivation in Europe: A question for tropical anthropologists. *Social Science Information, 18*(4/5), 679–694.
Stoll, S. (2017). *Ramp hollow: The ordeal of appalachia*. New York: Hill and Wang.
Taneja, A. (2018). *Jinnealogy: Time, islam, and ecological thought in the medieval ruins of Delhi*. California: Stanford University Press.
Thrupp, L. A., Hecht, S., & Browder, J. (1997). *The diversity and dynamics of shifting cultivation: Myths, realities, and policy implications*. Washington, D.C.: World Resources Institute.
Trefethen, J. (1961). *Crusade for wildlife: Highlights in conservation progress*. Mechanicsburg, PA: Stackpole Books.
Van Vliet, N., Mertz, O., Heinimann, A., Langanke, T., Pascual, U., Schmook, B., et al. (2012). Trends, drivers and impacts of changes in swidden cultivation in tropical forest-agriculture frontiers: A global assessment. *Global Environmental Change, 22*(2), 418–429.
Vansina, J. M. (1990). *Paths in the rainforests: Toward a history of political tradition in equatorial Africa*. Madison, WI: University of Wisconsin Press.
Walters, G., Schleicher, J., Hymas, O., & Coad, L. (2015). Evolving hunting practices in Gabon: Lessons for community-based conservation interventions. *Ecology and Society, 20*(4), 31.
Weimarck, G. (1968). *Ulfshult: Investigations concerning the use of soil and forest in Ulfshult, Parish of Örkened, during the last 250 years*. Lund: C.W.K. Gleerup.
Whealdon, B. I. (2001). In R. Bigart (Ed.), *'I will be meat for my salish': The buffalo and the Montana writers project interviews on the flathead Indian reservation*. Pablo, MT: Salish Kootenai College Press.
WWF. (2014). *Community forestry, Gabon*. http://wwf.panda.org/wwf_news/?235851/Community-Forestry-Gabon

Managing Risk Through Cooperation: Need-Based Transfers and Risk Pooling Among the Societies of the Human Generosity Project

Lee Cronk, Colette Berbesque, Thomas Conte, Matthew Gervais, Padmini Iyer, Brighid McCarthy, Dennis Sonkoi, Cathryn Townsend, and Athena Aktipis

Introduction

Making a living often involves risks. Whether you are a Hadza hunter who often comes home empty-handed; a Maasai herder facing the prospect of losses due to drought, disease, and theft; or a modern-day cowboy in the American Southwest using potentially dangerous heavy machinery on a day-to-day basis, risk is an integral and inevitable part of life. Given risk's inevitability, managing it is an important component of both individual and community strategies to adapt to local conditions. Social risk management strategies are diverse. They include, for example, Hadza sharing food with camp members who do not have enough to eat, Maasai herders agreeing to help each other when disaster strikes, and American ranchers coming to the aid of their injured neighbors. The Human Generosity Project, a transdisciplinary effort to examine both biological and cultural influences on human cooperation, has documented and analyzed these and many other examples of social risk management.

What do these three examples of social risk management have in common? In every case they are characterized by people who have the capacity to help giving aid to others who are in need as a result of risk and uncertainty. Because these instances

---

L. Cronk (✉) · T. Conte · P. Iyer · B. McCarthy · D. Sonkoi · C. Townsend
Department of Anthropology, Rutgers University, New Brunswick, NJ, USA
e-mail: lcronk@anthropology.rutgers.edu

C. Berbesque
Department of Life Sciences, University of Roehampton, London, UK

M. Gervais
Department of Psychology, University of British Columbia, Vancouver, BC, Canada

A. Aktipis
Department of Psychology, Arizona State University, Tempe, AZ, USA

of sharing and helping are based on recipient need, we refer to them as *need-based transfers* (Aktipis et al. 2016; Cronk and Aktipis 2016a, b). As shown in Table 1, the societies included in the Human Generosity Project (http://humangenerosity.org) provide abundant evidence that need-based transfers are a common strategy for the social management of risk. Our field sites span three continents (Fig. 1; Table 1) and

Table 1 Summary of major characteristics of the eight Human Generosity Project field sites and the individual and social risk management strategies used at each site

Name (location)	Subsistence	Major risks and hazards	Individual risk management strategies	Social risk management strategies
Maasai (Kenya/ Tanzania)	Pastoralism	Drought, disease, theft	Livelihood diversification, veterinary care, herd accumulation	*Osotua* stock friend relationships for risk pooling and risk retention[a] Group defense
Yasawa Island (Fiji)	Fishing and horticulture	Cyclones, droughts, illness, injury	Livelihood diversification, relocation, lifestyle changes	Demand sharing within households, *kerekere* need-based sharing norm, ritual exchange between clans and villages[a]
Hadza (Tanzania)	Hunting and gathering	Variable hunting returns, wild animals, diseases, droughts, floods, and witchcraft	Consumption of a wide range of wild foods, development of foraging skills over lifetime	Central place food sharing with those in need[a]
Darhad (Mongolia)	Pastoralism	Severe winter storms	Cutting and storing hay, repairing livestock shelters, short-term migrations	Providing assistance to reduce risk including building shelters and other preparations[b]
American ranchers (Cochise County, AZ and Hidalgo County, NM)	Commercial ranching augmented by small businesses and wage employment	Droughts, floods, injuries, and illness	Livelihood diversification, herd accumulation, veterinary care, wells and stock tanks	*Neighboring* ethic, help given freely to those experiencing unexpected needs, chiefly from injuries and illnesses[a]
Ik (Uganda)	Horticulture, hunting, gathering, and beekeeping	Drought, variable hunting returns, resource raiding by outsiders	Livelihood diversification	Widespread sharing *(tomor)* norm, with supernatural enforcement of sharing norm[a] Group defense

(continued)

Table 1 (continued)

Name (location)	Subsistence	Major risks and hazards	Individual risk management strategies	Social risk management strategies
Karamoja (Uganda)	Pastoralism and agriculture	Drought, disease, theft	Livelihood diversification, livestock movement, herd accumulation, agricultural intensification, food storage	*Akoneo* stock friend relationships; aid given to relatives, neighbors, acquaintances, and friends[a]
Kijenge (Tanzania)	Casual labor	Chronic unemployment	Livelihood diversification	*Kushirikiana* sharing ethic[a]

Across societies, need-based transfer systems are key components of social risk management (indicated by [a]). Among Mongolian herders, providing need-based assistance in real time (for the purpose of pooling risk) is often impossible due to ecological constraints, yet they assist one another with risk-reduction activities (indicated by [b])

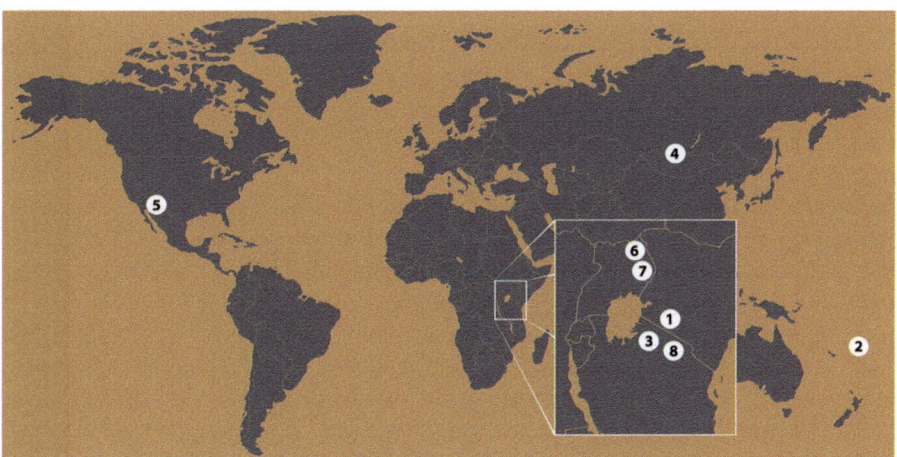

Fig. 1 A map of the world with a detailed inset for East Africa showing the approximate locations of our eight field sites: (1) Maasai, Kenya, and Tanzania; (2) Yasawa Island, Fiji; (3) Hadza, Tanzania; (4) Darhad Depression, Mongolia; (5) Cochise County, Arizona, and Hidalgo County, New Mexico; (6) Ik, Uganda; (7) Karamoja, Uganda; and (8) Kijenge, Arusha, Tanzania. Map image courtesy of Wikicommons

include many different subsistence strategies, from hunter-gatherers to fisher-horticulturalists to pastoralists to market-integrated societies. In this chapter we will provide an overview of the risk management framework we are using and describe how each society manages risk socially, focusing especially on the use of need-based transfers to buffer the effects of disasters and ecological uncertainty.

Risk Management as a Social Enterprise

From the very beginning of life, organisms who effectively managed risk were the most evolutionarily successful, surviving better and leaving more descendants than their competitors. This includes all life forms from simple such as early bacteria to biologically complex modern-day humans. If we look across life, we see that it is rife with risk management strategies. Everything from the accumulation of body fat for buffering against starvation to the building of structures such as dens and nests is a biological example of risk management. Many of these risk management strategies can be employed by individuals. They do not require cooperation or coordination to achieve the risk management benefits. Others, however, do require social action—for example, the creation of complex hives and honey storage in some bees or the biofilm structures created by bacteria that help them survive exposure to toxins. Humans, of course, engage in many risk management practices that are fundamentally social. And compared to other species, humans have a (perhaps unique) capacity to flexibly respond to challenges, incorporate new information, and share information with one another to solve problems including the management of risk.

Humans have colonized diverse environments throughout the globe, each one characterized by unique challenges and hazards. Dealing effectively with these risks requires the application of risk management practices that are well suited to the risks that individuals and communities face. In our work, we adopt the risk management framework proposed by Dorfman (2007). In his scheme, risk management practices fall into four main categories: risk retention, risk avoidance, risk reduction, and risk transfer (Dorfman 2007). *Risk retention* consists of accepting risk and absorbing any resulting losses and includes storing resources (either individually or as a group) and institutional self-insurance. Risk retention may be most appropriate when losses occur frequently but are not very severe (Rejda 2011). *Risk avoidance* involves the reduction of dependence on high variability outcomes. For example, pastoralists sometimes avoid risk by reducing their reliance upon herds and practicing other forms of subsistence, such as farming (e.g., Little et al. 2001). Risk avoidance can either be an individual strategy or a coordinated group strategy, as with social and institutional restrictions on risky practices (e.g., gambling). Risk avoidance can be a hard strategy to commit to and/or enforce socially because avoiding risks can also mean giving up on potentially high rewards. *Risk reduction* refers to efforts to lower the probability of loss or to reduce the size of losses. For example, investors may buy bonds as well as stocks, and pastoralists often diversify their livestock holdings among different species and divide their herds among different ecological areas (Dahl and Hjort 1976, p. 114; King et al. 1984; Mace and Houston 1989; Mace 1990, 1993). Building of shelters for oneself or for livestock is another example of risk reduction. Across the societies we study in the Human Generosity Project, we see many examples of shelter building as both an individual and social risk management strategy (e.g., see the description of our Mongolian field site). *Risk transfer* is the exchange of risk from one individual or group to another. Although all four risk management strategies may involve social interactions, only risk transfer *requires* sociality: risk transfer simply cannot occur unless there is someone to whom to transfer the risk. One common way to transfer risk is to pool it, i.e., to agree to take on some of another party's risk in exchange for their willingness to take on some of one's own, as occurs in formal and informal insurance systems (Wiessner 1982; Cashdan 1985; Levy 2012; Aktipis et al. 2011). Risk pooling decreases the size and severity of losses, though it is accompanied by a higher likelihood of those losses. Need-based transfer relationships, where individuals agree to help one another during times of need if they are able to do so, result in a form of limited risk pooling.

The focus of our work is on need-based transfers as a strategy for limited risk pooling. As with many social strategies, there is a potential for individuals to cheat and take advantage of each other's generosity. In the case of need-based transfer systems, there are two primary ways to cheat: the first is to ask when one is not in need, and the second is to refuse to give even if one has sufficient resources. If cheating is frequent, a system of risk pooling through need-based transfers—like any cooperative system—will collapse. Thus, solving the problem of risk management socially can introduce new problems that must then get solved, such as monitoring, enforcing, and coordinating around the rules of engagement in need-based transfer systems. Our goal with the Human Generosity Project is to better understand the implicit and explicit rules that are used in need-based transfer systems across societies and identify mechanisms that stabilize, maintain, and enhance the effectiveness of these need-based transfer systems for risk management.

In the Human Generosity Project, we use a combination of fieldwork, computational modeling, and laboratory experiments to understand the nature and evolution of human generosity. Each of these approaches is complementary to the others, and our goal is to create constructive, creative synergies among the three methods. The focus of this article is on the fieldwork that Human Generosity Project team members have conducted, or are currently conducting, at eight field sites around the world. When appropriate we will also refer to our modeling and laboratory work. The members of the Human Generosity Project are by no means the first scholars to study community risk management. We build upon a large body of existing scholarship, most notably work by economists on systems of risk sharing (e.g., Fafchamps and Lund 2003; Barr and Genicot 2008; Fafchamps 2011) and by human behavioral ecologists and economic anthropologists on risk management strategies in small-scale communities (e.g., Wiessner 1982; Cashdan 1985; Winterhalder 1986; Cashdan 1990; Bird and Bird 1997; Gurven et al. 2000; Bliege Bird et al. 2002; Gurven and Hill 2009, 2010).

Our Field Sites

Our eight field sites are ecologically, culturally, and economically diverse. They include pastoralists, horticulturalists, hunter-gatherers, fisher/farmers, urban poor, and commercial ranchers. Although five are clustered near each other in East Africa, they are quite different from one another, ranging from very isolated groups such as the Hadza and Ik to the urban dwellers of Kijenge. We apply the same theoretical framework to all our sites, but we adjust our methods to suit local conditions. Beyond such standard and universal methods as participant observation and ethnographic interviews, each field site supervisor tailors his or her approach to the specific local circumstances. Other methods we employ include experimental economic games, focus group interviews, risk preference surveys, social network analysis, wealth inventories, cultural domain analysis, and mail surveys.

At each of these sites, we are investigating the resource sharing and helping systems that are used among members of each community. We are particularly interested in documenting how these sharing systems help individuals and communities manage risk. In every society that we have examined to date, we see evidence of need-based transfer systems: sharing that is characterized by helping based on the need of the recipient. Below we provide brief overviews of each of our field sites and the resource sharing systems we have documented at them.

Maasai (Dennis Sonkoi and Lee Cronk)

Maasai and other Maa-speaking pastoralists live in a swath running from Lake Turkana in northern Kenya south through the Great Rift Valley to central Tanzania. An important precursor to the Human Generosity Project was Cronk's fieldwork among the Mukogodo Maasai (Cronk 2004) on the Maasai system of risk pooling based on need-based transfers (Cronk 2007). Maasai refer to this system as *osotua*, which literally means a human umbilical cord. *Osotua* relationships usually begin with a request for a gift or a favor. Such requests arise from genuine need and are limited to the amount actually needed or less if that is all that the donor can afford to give. Gifts given in response to such requests are given freely (*pesho*) and from the heart (*ol-tau*) but, like the requests, are limited to what is actually needed (see also Perlov 1987, p. 169). Because the economy is based on livestock, many *osotua* gifts take that form, but virtually any good or service may serve as an *osotua* gift. Once *osotua* is established, it is pervasive and eternal. It cannot be destroyed, even if the individuals who established the relationship die. In that case, it is passed on to their children (see also Spencer 1965, p. 59). *Osotua* does not follow a schedule. It will not go away even if much time passes between gifts. Although *osotua* involves a reciprocal obligation to help if asked to do so, actual *osotua* gifts are not necessarily reciprocal or even roughly equal over long periods of time. The flow of goods and services in a particular relationship might be mostly or entirely one way, if that is where the need is greatest. Not all gift-giving involves or results in *osotua*. For example, some gift-giving results instead in debt (*esile*). *Osotua* and debt are not at all the same. While *osotua* partners have an obligation to help each other in time of need, this is not at all the same as the debt one has when one has been lent something and must pay it back (see also Spencer 1965, p. 27; Perlov 1987, p. 169). Going along with the idea that *osotua* gifts do not repay debt, *osotua* gifts are not payments at all, and it is inappropriate to use the verb "to pay" (*alak*) when referring to them. *Osotua* is imbued with respect (*enkanyit*), restraint, and a sense of responsibility in a way that non-*osotua* economic relationships are not. In the words of one interviewee, "*keiroshi*": It is heavy.

To learn more about *osotua*, Cronk used it to frame trust games played by Maasai. In the trust game, two players, who are anonymous to each other, are given an initial endowment. The first player can then give none, some, or all of his endowment to the second player. The experimenter triples that amount and then passes it on to the second player. The second player can then give some, none, or all of the funds in his control to the first player. A total of 50 games were played. All players were given standard instructions, in Maa, on how to play the trust game. Half of the games were played with no framing beyond the instructions themselves. The other half were played with a single additional framing sentence: "This is an *osotua* game." That minimal framing resulted in several contrasts between *osotua*-framed games and unframed games. In keeping with the emphasis in *osotua* relationships on restraint, respect, and responsibility, amounts given by both players as well as the amounts that first players expected to receive in return were all lower in the framed than in the unframed games. In games played without *osotua* framing, a positive correlation was found between amounts given and amounts expected in return, suggesting that players were invoking such common principles of exchange as trust, investment, and tit-for-tat reciprocity. In the *osotua*-framed games, in contrast, no relationship was found between amounts given and amounts expected in return. In *osotua*-framed games, but not in unframed games, amounts given by the first player and proportional amounts returned by the second player were *negatively* correlated, suggesting that the *osotua* framing shifts game play away from the logic of investment and toward the mutual obligation of *osotua* partners to respond to one another's genuine needs but only with what is genuinely needed.

Osotua differs greatly from *esile* (debt). In *esile*, repayment is expected in the form of an animal at least as valuable if not more so than the one given. The repayment is referred to as *elaata*, which means to set free or untie a knot (Perlov 1987, p. 184). If a debtor fails to repay, his creditor has the option of forgiving the debt but then referring to him henceforth as "*Pasile*": One whose debt I have forgiven. This type of construction, in which the prefix "pa" is used to indicate what a person has given or received, is common in Maa, but it is normally used in a positive way. For example, a man refers to his father-in-law as "*Pakiteng*," meaning "cow receiver," in recognition of the bridewealth that was paid. The use of the term "*Pasile*" essentially serves as a mild public reproach to those who fail to repay their debts.

Our current work on the *osotua* system is being conducted by Dennis Sonkoi, who is focusing his efforts not on the impoverished Mukogodo but rather among the relatively wealthy Loita Maasai, whose territory straddles the Kenya-Tanzania border. His attention is focused primarily on how *osotua* partners are chosen and how *osotua* relationships develop over time. The process of instilling *osotua* values begins in childhood. Children are encouraged to form childhood friendships known as *isirito* (singular: *esirit*). These are developed mainly within neighborhood settlement clusters. Children share food and exchange small gifts. Friendships formed during childhood eventually lead to adulthood exchanges of much more valuable gifts, which may lead to the formation of *osotua* partnerships. The overall process is somewhat similar to courtship, with prospective *osotua* partners getting to know each other and giving small gifts over a period of years. When a degree of trust has been established, the relationship may then be recognized as *osotua*. People often make some effort to establish *osotua* relationships with people in different ecological zones and, thus, complementary risk profiles. For example, people living in the drought-prone lowlands seek *osotua* partners in the wetter highlands, and vice versa, which then provides both parties with access not only to food but also to pasture when their own is either too dry or too wet. A similar pattern has also been observed among both Maasai in north central Kenya and the Turkana of northern Kenya (Gulliver 1955; Dixit et al. 2013).

One interesting contrast between the Mukogodo and Loita Maasai stems from the large differences between the two areas in average livestock wealth. While the Loita Maasai have long had livestock and maintain large herds of cattle supplemented by some sheep and goats, most Maasai in the Mukogodo area obtained livestock relatively recently and have herds dominated by sheep and goats with only a few cattle. The wealth of the Loita Maasai enables them to use their *osotua* relationships not only as sources of support after disasters occur but also to help each other build up herds during good times so that they can engage in risk retention. The relative poverty of people in the Mukogodo area, in contrast, means that they have little opportunity to engage in risk retention and must use their *osotua* ties solely for risk pooling.

In addition to fieldwork, our team has also developed three computer simulations based on the *osotua* system (Aktipis et al. 2011; Hao et al. 2015a, b; Aktipis et al. 2016). We have found that *osotua*-style need-based transfers increase survivorship and decrease wealth inequalities compared to no transfers and to transfers that follow the rules of *esile* (debt). Another research team (Hao et al. 2015a, b) independently developed a computer simulation to examine the effects of spatial and temporal correlations of disasters on survival in an *osotua* network. Their main finding that synchronous disasters reduce survivorship is in line with our model described above.

Yasawa Island, Fiji (Matthew Gervais)

Yasawa Island is the northwestern-most island in the Republic of Fiji in the South Pacific (Figs. 2 and 3). Twenty kilometers long and rarely more than 1 kilometer wide, Yasawa Island is home to six villages averaging around 200 people each. Transport between villages is primarily by foot, horse, or motorboat. Travel between Yasawa and the port of Lautoka on Fiji's largest island (Viti Levu) takes from 5 to 15 h. Among the least economically developed islands in Fiji, subsistence is based primarily on marine foraging and slash-and-burn horticulture, with approximately 25% of calories coming from purchased foodstuffs such as flour, sugar, and cooking oil. Yasawans face a number of hazards for which there are few management options beyond risk transfer through mutual aid. These include injuries, illnesses, droughts, and cyclones. While Yasawans believe that some risks can be avoided or reduced by

Fig. 2 The matanivanua ("mouth of the chief") from a nearby village presents a tabua during the funeral of the Tui Yasawa or regional chief of the Yasawa Islands. The tabua, a polished sperm whale tooth on a braided cord, symbolizes and reaffirms the heavy weight of the social ties connecting clans across villages. Photo credit: Matthew Gervais

relocation to town or by lifestyle choices related to diet, exercise, and piety, limited economic resources and deep attachments to place and tradition mean that much risk is retained (see also Nolet 2012). Social relationships are explicitly viewed as essential to survival among interdependent Yasawan villagers, with extensive time and energy devoted to building and preserving social capital. As one villager succinctly stated, *keda leqa kece*, "we all have problems" such that no one can survive on their own. In open-ended queries about the problems, risks, or fears of villagers, the topic nominated most often is "village responsibilities"—underscoring social relationships as the most proximate concern of villagers and ecological risks as almost-taken-for-granted facts of life.

Yasawan villages are normatively patrilocal, with patrilineal descent groups organized hierarchically from extended households (*itokatoka*) to ranked landowning clans (*mataqali*) composing village-level *yavusa*. Universal kinship ties are the backbone of Yasawan village life. Four types of resource transfers are noteworthy in Yasawa. The first is a system of demand sharing among members of extended households, in which property is shared and can be used or taken with little more than a notification. The second is a system of ad hoc need-based requests known as *kerekere* (Sahlins 1962). Villagers respectfully use *kerekere* among extended kin when in need of a resource, and the target of the request is expected to give the

Fig. 3 In the foreground sit roofs of thatched houses (bure) that collapsed during a tropical storm in 2010; behind them sit several new bure built to replace them. All such houses on Yasawa Island fell during Cyclone Evan in 2012, but the central government replaced them with wooden houses, undercutting the practice-based knowledge of traditional house building in these villages. Photo credit: Matthew Gervais

resource if able. Clans and villages as corporate units also use *kerekere* to acquire resources such as land for gardens or labor help on large projects or on special occasions. A *kerekere* request creates no expectation of short-term repayment, but it does engender expectations of reciprocal help if fortunes reverse. Gossip against those who are "stingy" or "bad-hearted" is the principal means of sanctioning violations of *kerekere* etiquette, while falling into bad standing compromises one's ability to use *kerekere* when in need. Third, there is a system of ritual exchanges (*veiqaravi vakavanua*) that attend numerous life-course ceremonies in Yasawa such as births, marriages, and funerals, as well as special occasions such as visitations of chiefs, first visits from matrilineal kin, completed house construction, or formal apologies (Ravuvu 1987). These exchanges are showings of respect among clans and villages and involve the reciprocal presentation of valued goods (*iyau*) such as kava roots, woven mats, yams, pigs, and kerosene. While the initiators usually present a greater quantity of goods, the receivers reciprocally present not-insubstantial "appreciations" that clear them of debt and strengthen the relationship. The "lead" objects in these reciprocal exchanges are *tabua*, whale's teeth with large woven cords braided from end to end. *Tabua* carry explicit symbolism: the braided cord is the tie among the exchanging parties, while the weight of the tooth is the "heaviness" or visceral significance of the relationship (unpublished data; also Ravuvu 1987). Such ritual exchanges across clans and villages may help to scale up kinship networks in the service of mutual aid during shocks that affect a large portion of the village or island population. The fourth type of resource transfer is a system of collective fund raising (*soli*) for clans, churches, schools, and sometimes the *vanua* (village). These usually involve a feast, kava drinking, and turn-taking donations with public announcements of the amount given.

Yasawans do not consider all types of resources as being appropriate for *kerekere* requests. Data from a card-sorting task conducted in 2015 indicate that Yasawans distinguish between two kinds of resources. The first group consists of subsistence foodstuffs, tools, land, and labor, all of which are often *kerekere*'d, given without question, and which do not create debt. The second group consists of ritual exchange goods and monetized resources (e.g., fuel, cash itself) that are not often *kerekere*'d and that create debt and are expected to be reciprocated in kind based on an informal agreement. Violating the terms of this agreement puts the relationship into bad standing, compromising future sharing within it. One villager clearly summarized the distinction in exchange types: "Debt and *kerekere* are different."

Interviews with randomly selected informants indicate that Yasawans do routinely provide aid to one another in response to the unpredictable hazards that they all face. For each of the four often-mentioned hazards (debilitating injuries and illnesses, droughts, and cyclones), ten villagers were interviewed, and each answered questions about two or three hazards. All ten interviewees reported that villagers help one another in dealing with injuries. Nine reported having given help to an injured person, while eight reported having received such help recently. Similarly, nine reported that villagers do help one another in dealing with illnesses, with eight reporting having given help recently to the sick and eight reporting having received such help while recently sick. Eight out of ten interviewees reported that villagers do help one another in dealing with drought, with seven reporting having helped someone recently and the same number reporting having been helped recently. Yasawans also reported extensive helping among villagers, and even among villages on the island, before and after a cyclone hit. Eight out of ten interviewees said that villagers help one another in dealing with cyclones, with seven reporting having given help in a recent cyclone and seven of ten reporting having received help. This help included food sharing, equipment sharing, and sharing of supplies such as kerosene and, more so than for any other shock, collective house building and collective farming directed at those most in need (cf. Takasaki 2011).

The hazards that Yasawans face—injury, illness, drought, and cyclones—differ considerably from one another in terms of the synchronicity with which they strike their victims. While Yasawans tend to report that injuries and illnesses only affect one or a few villagers at a time, droughts and cyclones are thought to influence everyone at once. During synchronous shocks such as droughts and cyclones, Yasawans appear to scale up and out of their social networks by seeking help from and giving help to a more far-flung network of social ties. This is qualitatively the case in our data, in that Yasawans mention other villages and relatives in town and abroad more often as helping partners during droughts and cyclones than during injuries and illnesses. It is also the case quantitatively. Looking at the relative frequencies of close kin (nuclear families + $r \geq 0.25$) vs. distant kin (e.g., classificatory fathers or mothers, classificatory cousins) among people nominated as having helped or having been helped by interviewees during low-synchrony (injuries + illnesses) vs. high-synchrony (droughts + cyclones) shocks, we find that close kin are overrepresented in low-synchrony helping (16/44) compared to high-synchrony helping (7/47) (χ^2 = 5.55, p = 0.019). Although this result is tentative because it is derived from a small sample (ten interviewees for each type of shock), the pattern is encouraging. This result supports the thesis that ritual exchanges (*veiqaravi vakavanua*) across clans and villages help scale up kinship networks in the service of mutual aid during shocks that affect a large portion of the village or island population. Currently we are collecting comprehensive helping network data for these four risks across multiple Yasawan villages.

Experimental economic game data collected in 2012 (Gervais 2016) reinforce that need-based transfers are important determinants of Yasawan generosity. In an allocation game similar to an *N*-recipient dictator game, a subject was presented with a grid of photographs of 53 people in their community alongside a picture of himself and the opportunity to distribute money among the photographs. Only one of 51 subjects kept all the money for himself. Twenty-two subjects (43%) kept nothing for themselves, while 39 (76%) kept 10% or less. Perceived need was by far the most important reason that subjects gave for their allocation decisions, with 47 subjects (92%) citing the recipients' weakness (*malumalumu*), old age, lack of income, financial troubles, many dependents, widower status, general problems, or desire to help them. Similarly, a lack of need was the overwhelming reason given for not allocating to particular individuals, with 37 subjects (72.5%) mentioning a potential recipient's strength (*kaukauwa*), sources of income, or support from a large family. Compassion (*kauwai*), love (*loloma*), and thinking of others (*veinanumi*) are central tenets of Yasawan village life.

Hadza (Colette Berbesque)

The Hadza are a group of hunter-gatherers who live in savannah/woodland areas in northern Tanzania. They live in mobile camps, which average 30 individuals (Marlowe 2010) (Figs. 4 and 5). Camp membership often changes as people move in and out of camps (Jones et al. 2005). These camps move about every six weeks on average. Hadza men usually go foraging alone. They hunt birds and mammals using bow and arrows. While on walkabout they often feed themselves (Berbesque et al. 2016), but routinely bring meat, honey, and baobab fruit back to camp to share with others. Hadza women go foraging in groups of three to eight adults plus nurslings and often some older children. They mainly collect baobab fruit, berries, and tubers of several species.

Unpredictability shapes Hadza life in many ways, including positive ones. Hadza acquire large game approximately 1.4 days per hunter per month (Berbesque et al. 2016). These kills are fairly infrequent and unpredictable, and certainly months can go in a given camp without any large game kills. However, a large game kill can

Fig. 4 Hadza men carrying a dead antelope to be butchered and shared. Photo credit: Frank Marlowe

easily yield 50 kg of meat and fat or more, which is a very large number of calories for a camp of 30 adults on average. Because a hunter must get help from others to process the carcass and carry it back to camp, he must also share it. Large game carcasses are shared widely in camp with both kin and nonkin. There are occasionally disputes over parts of large game carcasses and their distribution in camp. These disputes can involve shouting and may be resolved by changing the distribution. However, if the distribution is not changed, anger often remains. In such cases it is common for the offended family to move out of that camp and avoid the person they feel has shortchanged them for a period of time.

When asked about the risks and hazards they face, Hadza produce a long list, most of which they see as being very rare. For example, although most Hadza listed animal attacks as the foremost danger they face, they also said that although such attacks can be lethal, they are also quite rare. Among most commonly listed diseases were malaria and AIDS, but both were agreed to be rare. Also feared are droughts, floods, and witchcraft, which they think is sometimes used by other ethnic groups against them. Droughts and floods are associated not only with food shortages but also with increased numbers of snakes in the case of droughts and increased numbers of mosquitoes in the case of floods. Despite all of these hazards, most Hadza agree that deaths from starvation are extremely rare or nonexistent. A few said that these food shortages only seriously affected people that were very old or very ill.

Fig. 5 Hadza women roasting and sharing//ekwa (Vigna frutescens) roots that they had just dug up. Photo credit: Athena Aktipis

Most of these risks are both asynchronous and unpredictable, making them good candidates for risk pooling, an outcome the Hadza achieve routinely through food sharing. Droughts and floods, which affect large swaths of the Hadza population simultaneously, are notable exceptions to this pattern. Like many other warm-climate hunter-gatherers, the Hadza do not store food or attempt to buffer themselves with other contingency measures against food shortages caused by floods and droughts. This is likely because of the unpredictable nature of these risks in warmer climates. Hunter-gatherer groups with predictable and frequent food shortages, in contrast, very often do have contingency measures (Berbesque et al. 2014). Other risk management strategies available to the Hadza include risk avoidance through the acquisition of foods with predictable, reliable yields such as tubers, fruits, and other plant foods. In keeping with the sex-based division of foraging labor found in almost all documented hunter-gatherer societies, these reliable foods are primarily targeted by Hadza women, while Hadza men tend to focus on foods with more variable return rates. Another way Hadza reduce their exposure to risks is through the refinement of their foraging skills. Because Hadza do not accumulate wealth, risk retention is not a viable strategy for them.

Mongolian Pastoralists (Thomas Conte)

Roughly one third of the Republic of Mongolia's population of slightly fewer than three million is employed in nomadic or seminomadic animal husbandry (Endicott 2012). These herders make use of Mongolia's diverse steppe, desert, forest, and mountain ecosystems to sustain herds of horses, sheep, goats, cattle, and camels (Humphrey and Sneath 1999). Because the Inner Asian steppes are subject to an extreme continental climate with periodic temperature and precipitation fluctuations, Mongolian herders have developed flexible nomadic land use strategies based on livestock's seasonal nutritional and hydrological needs (Fernandez-Gimenez 2000; Pederson et al. 2014; Conte 2015).

Over the last two decades, the Mongolian Plateau has experienced a rise in unpredictable severe weather conditions known as *zud*. In the winter, *zud* occur when snowstorms are followed by severely cold temperatures that cause a thick layer of ice to form over the ground (Begzsuren et al. 2004). When these conditions occur, livestock cannot access the forage beneath the ice, and many die of starvation or exposure (Fernandez-Gimenez et al. 2012). As climate change affects the Mongolian steppes, *zud* conditions are becoming both increasingly severe and more unpredictable. Current estimates indicate that the Mongolian pastoral economy suffered the loss of over 21 million livestock as a result of *zud* between 1990 and 2010 (UNDP 2010). *Zud* have been identified as a major driver of rural poverty in Mongolia and have forced many of the nation's pastoral nomads to abandon herding and seek alternative sources of income (Vernooy 2011; Endicott 2012).

Previous ethnographic research on Mongolian pastoralists indicates that herders often rely on cooperative networks with other families to effectively manage daily herding tasks and seasonal migrations (Cooper 1993; Bold 1996; Conte and Tilt 2014). However, *zud* conditions present herders with seasonal risks that are both unpredictable and affect entire communities simultaneously. The synchronous nature of winter *zud* often renders herders unable to engage in patterns of mutual assistance and labor sharing with other families (Templer et al. 1993; Thrift and Byambabaatar 2015). To effectively manage *zud*, herders often rely on cooperative risk-reduction strategies that aim to both prepare families for *zud* and reduce the severity of the effects of severe winter weather conditions when they occur (Swift and Siurua 2002). These strategies include pooling labor to build and repair winter livestock shelters, cutting and storing supplementary forage for times of scarcity, and making short-term migrations to reserve pastures where herders can fatten livestock in preparation for winter (Humphrey and Sneath 1996). Thus, while the unpredictable and synchronous nature of winter *zud* make herders unable to use cooperation to overcome *zud* when they occur, many herders rely on cooperative networks of extended kin and neighbors to reduce the severity of *zud* through preparatory risk management strategies.

In order to assess the effects of *zud* on Mongolian herders' willingness to cooperate with one another, in June 2015, Human Generosity Project team member

Thomas Conte ran a series of common-pool-resource games in Mongolia's Bulgan province. In common-pool-resource games, two anonymous players are each given access to a hypothetical envelope containing a sum of money. Each is then allowed to remove from the envelope whatever sum of money he or she wishes (Sosis and Ruffle 2003; Gelcich et al. 2013). If anything remains in the envelope after each of the two players has made his or her decision, then it is multiplied by a factor greater than one and divided evenly between the two players. However, if the two players collectively choose to extract an amount of money greater than the total amount in the envelope, then neither player gets anything. These games aim to simulate the problem of subtractability that is inherent in common-pool-resource management systems (Messick et al. 1988; Gardner et al. 1990).

Conte ran three versions of the game with a sample of 60 pastoralists (20 per version). The first version was a standard common-pool-resource game with a certain, unchanging amount of money in the hypothetical common envelope. The second version introduced uncertainty and stochasticity into the game in which participants were unsure if the total sum of money in the hypothetical envelope would be reduced by 20% after they made their decisions on how much money to remove. The third version of the game presented participants with the exact same uncertainty as the second version, but the reduction was framed as a *zud*. Participants were asked both how much money they would like to remove from the common envelope and how much they expected their partners to remove from the envelope. A comparison of mean taking for each of the three scenarios revealed no significant difference in average taking among the three versions. However, a comparison of mean expected taking revealed a statistically significant difference between the stochastic and *zud*-framed game versions: participants expected their partners to take significantly more from the common envelope in the *zud*-framed version. When interviewed regarding this difference, participants cited the needs of their partners as the reason why they expected greater taking in the *zud*-framed games.

Conte is currently establishing a site for his dissertation research in the Darhad Depression in northern Mongolia. Conte will again play common-pool-resource games, with one added wrinkle: He will run them both during a season of abundance and during a season of scarcity. This was inspired by a study in Afghanistan that found lower rates of enforcement of sharing norms in a third-party punishment game during lean times than immediately following a harvest (Bartos 2015), which suggests that people become more sensitive to one another's needs during times of scarcity. In addition, Conte will use social network analysis to better understand patterns of mutual support and run allocation games like those played by Gervais at his site in Fiji (see above) to find out whether Mongolians, like Fijians, donate more to people that they perceive as needy.

Ranchers in the American Southwest (Lee Cronk and Athena Aktipis)

Cochise and Hidalgo counties are located adjacent to each other along the US-Mexico border in southeastern Arizona and southwestern New Mexico, respectively (Fig. 6). Although the two counties together cover an area larger than six of the United States, they are home to only about 130,000 people. We were initially drawn to this region by the notoriety of the Malpai Borderlands Group, an organization of ranchers who work with each other, the Nature Conservancy, and federal and state authorities to sustainably manage the region's rangelands (Sayre 2005). They have also engaged in international exchanges, including one with Maasai that included Human Generosity Project team member Dennis Sonkoi (Curtin and Western 2008). Because the Malpai Borderlands Group has too few members to provide statistically valid results, our focus in this project is not on the Malpai group itself but on the region and the ranchers that live in the general area, all of whom face roughly similar environmental, economic, and political challenges.

Most ranches in the area are family operations, but few families find that they can make a living solely from ranching. To make ends meet, people do a wide variety of things including horse breeding, commercial hunting, renting out land to quail and deer hunters, owning small businesses, and a wide variety of jobs in nearby towns. Ranches vary in terms of the degree of control they have over the land on which they run livestock. A few have deeds to all the land they use, but more often a ranch is a

Fig. 6 Cowboys roping steers in Hidalgo County, New Mexico. Photo credit: Lee Cronk

combination of deeded land and land owned by the federal and state governments to which the rancher has limited access. Some ranches are on contiguous tracts of land, but many of them are broken up into multiple physically separated holdings.

When asked about the risks and hazards they face, almost all ranchers in this area first mention the weather. They are particularly wary of droughts, but heavy rains can also cause a variety of problems including washed out roads and drowned cattle. After the weather, interviewees brought up a variety of different problems including unpredictable market forces, government regulation, estate taxes, predators, and the scarcity of people who really know how to work with cattle. Injuries were also frequently mentioned. Many injuries occur while people are working with livestock and arise from the inherent unpredictability of cattle and horses. Others involve various pieces of heavy equipment that are often used on modern ranches. One retired rancher described it this way: "There are a lot of opportunities to injure yourself." Another put it even more succinctly: "It is a very dangerous business."

Because most ranches are family-run, few of them have enough skilled people on hand to deal with such large chores as branding and shipping cattle. Although some do hire cowboys, many complain about the difficulty of finding people who still have the skills necessary to do the work efficiently and safely. Having an unskilled person around, rather than being helpful, is actually a detriment, an idea colorfully expressed in this common saying: "A person that don't know cattle is like two good cowboys gone." However, one source of skilled labor is readily available: neighbors. Not only do neighbors have the skills, they also have the same need. This creates a perfect situation for a regular, steady exchange of labor. Ranchers refer to this as "trading out work" or "neighboring," as in this quote from one rancher: "I've been neighboring with the Millers since I don't know when." Neighbors, who may live as much as 2h drive apart from each other, negotiate with each other regarding the dates certain types of work will be done, and then they show up and help out. In such situations, there are two unstated expectations: first, that they will be fed and, second, that they will receive similar help when they need it on their ranch.

When needs are not so predictable—say, when a rancher is injured or when equipment suddenly and unexpectedly fails—all interviewees agreed that neighbors would come to that person's aid with no questions asked and no expectation of any return apart from a similar generosity should they ever be in a similar bind. This kind of behavior is simply seen as being neighborly, and no accounts are kept or debts created. A few quotes capture the spirit of this kind of neighborliness:

> If there's any major occurrence that happens these little communities all come together to take care of those left behind, clean their houses, feed them, really amazing.

> I don't think anybody keeps track. If you kept track it would become a headache .... If somebody needs help, you help them .... My family's never worked that way and we never will .... It all comes out in the wash.

> It's a solidarity-type world out here.

The next step for the Human Generosity Project at this site is to administer a mail survey regarding patterns of risk, need, and generosity among the ranchers in

Cochise and Hidalgo counties. The data we gain from the survey will enable us to test our ideas about the role that the predictability of need plays in determining patterns of cooperation as well as a variety of other ideas.

Karamoja (Padmini Iyer)

The Karamoja region in northeastern Uganda is home to over one million pastoralists who subsist on a mixed economy of livestock production and opportunistic agriculture. Our study population includes members of two similar but distinct ethnic groups, the Matheniko Karimojong and the Tepeth. For simplicity, we will refer to everyone in our study population as residents of Karamoja. The greatest risk in Karamoja is drought, which typically occurs in 4-year cycles and which creates chronic food insecurity. Other major risks in the environment include unchecked livestock disease, small-scale animal theft, human illness, and variable cash incomes from alternative livelihoods. Further compounding these risks is the overall low livestock base of the majority of households in Karamoja, which is the result of decades of violent intercommunity livestock raiding and subsequent state-imposed interventions (Mamdani et al. 1992; Gray et al. 2003; Stites et al. 2007). To sustain livestock and crop production under these circumstances, residents of Karamoja use a variety of strategies. These include the movement of livestock and people for the exploitation of key productive patches, herd accumulation, agricultural intensification and storage, livelihood diversification, and the use of informal systems of mutual insurance.

One particularly important risk management strategy is the formation of livestock sharing relationships among men known as stock friendships or associations (*akoneo*) (Dyson-Hudson 1966; see also Gulliver 1955 and Bollig 2006). These relationships are formed between an individual and others from his extensive kin and nonkin networks through the exchange of gifts ranging from small favors to cattle. In founding a network of stock friends (sing., *ekone*; pl., *ngikonei*), an individual herder establishes a network of mutual insurance unique to him. The networks can range in size from three to thirty individuals, with an average of eight *ngikonei*. During a time of need, *ngikonei* are expected to assist each other under an assumption of mutual obligation created through livestock transfers. However, *ngikonei* are chosen not on the basis of their asset wealth, which would be sound from a purely economic perspective, but rather on account of their peace-loving and genial personalities as well as the chemistry between the two potential friends.

Ngikonei share livestock with each other for a number of reasons. These include animals given to assist in bridewealth accumulation, for dispute resolution, during rituals such as initiation, during periods of food insecurity or urgent cash needs, and simply as gifts. Once an animal is transferred to a friend, the giver ceases to have property rights over it, and such transfers also do not create debt. A few categories of livestock transfers, such as animals given for fertilization and milking, create symbolic debt in that the giver continues to retain property rights over the transferred animal but never actually reclaims his property. By placing livestock in each other's herds, *ngikonei* establish, maintain, and strengthen ties of mutual obligation that stretch over generations.

Women herders in Karamoja also maintain similar risk-pooling relationships with other women and men who constitute the category of "close friends" (*ngikonei ke etau*—"friends of the heart"; see also Pollard et al. (2015) for a description of risk-pooling friendships among Marakwet and Pokot women). While the circle of close friends tends to be small (between two and three friends per individual) and there is less ceremony associated with friendship formation, women's friendships serve some of the same purposes as men's stock associations. For example, in a time of food insecurity, women approach their friends for help with fulfilling the household's nutritional needs. Women with extra money or those who receive food aid may circulate the surplus in their friendship and kinship networks not only to help those in need but also to reinforce pre-existing relationships. Contrary to established beliefs about gendered sharing within the Karamoja economy (Quam 1976), women also transfer livestock to their male and female friends as gifts, for bridewealth accumulation, and for survival.

As important as *akoneo* relationships may be, *ngikonei* constitute only one part of a herder's multifaceted, wide-ranging need-based transfer network. This is illustrated by data on mutual aid during a prolonged drought in 2015. Help flowed in various networks including agnatic and affinal relatives, neighbors, acquaintances, and friends. Whereas nearly half of all exchanges were between "friends" (45%), less than 15% of the individuals listed as "friends" were *ngikonei*. Thus, the flow of help in Karamoja communities during crises may be influenced as much or more by people's immediate need and ability to help as by profound and long-lasting contractual relationships such as those between *ngikonei*. This exchange system based on need is necessary in an environment where a herder's luck may change overnight due to devastating raids or livestock disease that can render those who were previously sufficient suddenly destitute.

Ik (Cathryn Townsend)

The Ik people of northeastern Uganda are former hunter-gatherers who speak a peripheral isolate Nilo-Saharan language, which distinguishes them from neighboring pastoralist peoples such as the Karimojong and the Turkana. The Ik people became notorious in anthropology following Colin Turnbull's ethnography *The Mountain People*, in which he described them as "unfriendly, uncharitable, inhospitable and generally mean as any people can be" (Turnbull 1972, p. 32). We included them in the Human Generosity Project precisely because of that controversial description, and our interest in including a society purported to be ungenerous.

Today the Ik practice a mixed subsistence strategy involving the seasonal cultivation of maize, sorghum, and millet alongside year-round gathering and hunting within a semiarid environment subject to intermittent droughts and fluctuating wet seasons and beekeeping. Contrary to Turnbull's account, sharing between Ik people is both rigorous and extensive, as is typical for hunter-gatherer peoples. Beneficiaries are typically close relatives, friends, and those in need. Both foraging and the small-scale cultivation that Ik people engage in have unpredictable, stochastic outcomes at the individual level but are adequate in providing for the group so long as food is shared. Another factor that adds to the asynchronous nature of the risks that Ik people face is that individuals may become the victims of sporadic violence and resource raiding from neighboring groups.

The risk-pooling networks of Ik people are maintained by cultural norms. Ik people have extensive kinship practices and terminology of the empirically universal kind (Barnard 1978). Nurturing circles of sharing and trust beyond close relatives create important social obligations. If it is noticed that an Ik person is not sharing, they will quickly gain the reputation of being stingy, which will jeopardize their chances of getting help from others in the future. Ik conventional wisdom says that even if a household stores all its farm produce for itself, it will still finish it all before the dry season is through. By the time the dry season comes, when the Ik must survive from wild foods alone, a household must rely on others for help in the event that their own hunting or gathering luck is poor. This wisdom is summed up in the Ik saying *maranga tomora* ("it's good to share"). Moreover, those who do not share incur the wrath of others. The Ik also believe that nature spirits of the earth (*kijawikå*, literally "children of the earth") will pick up these negative emotions and bring misfortune to those who do not share. Also, one should give freely and with good will. *Kijawikå* can sense antisocial feelings of annoyance or resentment on the part of a donor, and so such emotions are suppressed lest the *kijawikå* react badly to them. Conversely, the more one shares, the luckier one will be, as the *kijawikå* feed off the positive emotions of both the donor and the receiver.

Given the widespread sharing norms of the Ik, how, then, did Turnbull (1972) come to form such a negative impression of Ik generosity? The answer no doubt lies in that his fieldwork with Ik people fell within the years of 1965–1966, a period of drought and famine during which many people starved to death and raids from Kenyan pastoralists increased. Today the year of 1966 is remembered in northeastern Uganda by the Karimojong name *lopei kopo*, the utterance of which is inevitably accompanied by a chuckle of characteristically dark humor. It means "year of one cup," which refers to the fact that the government aid for the entire year amounted to one cup of ground maize per person. For the Ik, that was also a time when they were adapting to life on top of Mount Morungole after having been pushed out of their previously large and transnational foraging area. Two factors led to sedentarization. Firstly, the creation of the Kidepo Valley National Park by the British colonial authorities in 1958 excluded the Ik from one of their prime hunting grounds. Secondly, they retreated to the highlands to escape an upsurge in interethnic violence. This combination of drought and an enforced shift of subsistence strategy from mobile foraging to sedentary cultivation created a synchronous shock. Ik were all suffering such severe caloric restriction that nobody was in a position to help anybody else, even if they had had the desire to do so. It is perhaps no wonder, then, that traditional social ties and practices broke down to the point of societal collapse during *lopei kopo*. The fact that the Ik, though still poor, have rebounded and recovered their strong ethic of sharing is a testament to the importance of need-based sharing systems in subsistence economies.

Kijenge, Tanzania (Brighid McCarthy)

Kijenge is a diverse and densely populated slum in the city of Arusha, Tanzania. Most of its residents live in chronic economic precarity, with unpredictable and intermittent employment, high food insecurity, and little money for long-term investments in property or human capital. The most common source of wage income for men is temporary day labor, such as construction, seasonal agricultural labor, or transporting goods on foot. Some people, particularly women, have small businesses such as selling vegetables, street vending, or brewing banana beer. Some families also keep small livestock such as chickens, ducks, and rabbits. Nearly all income comes from the informal sector, and purchased staples typically make up the large majority of calories. Household composition is variable and flexible. For example, it is common for children to change residence or caretakers, and men may move if they are unable to support their families. Adults in a household may or may not be employed, for short or long periods, with no job security or income predictability. As a result, household income is subject to large unpredictable variations over time. Most of the shocks that affect household income are asynchronous, even between close neighbors. Shocks may be positive or negative, and the prevailing condition of precarity makes it difficult to define any baseline for income. These conditions are well suited to risk pooling through need-based transfers, and the people of Kijenge do indeed engage in such transfers extensively. They refer to this practice as *kushirikiana*, a multivalent Swahili word that may be translated as "cooperation," "collaboration," "participation," "partnership," or "sharing." Kushirikiana creates social networks based on mutual interdependence that are the backbone of the community.

According to preliminary fieldwork based on focus group discussions and participant observation, the people of Kijenge have three categories of cooperative giving, each with a different social script for asking and receiving and different expectations about repayment. The first category includes predictable needs that require labor sharing or financial contributions. Examples mentioned included weddings, other life cycle ceremonies, and building new houses. The family requesting help is expected to host a gathering, inviting neighbors and paying for a communal meal. After the guests have eaten, the head of household will discuss the project and ask for help. This sequence explicitly frames this kind of cooperation as reciprocal, and large contributions create a debt obligation. The second category of helping governs public goods provisioning, including contributions to community development and maintaining common spaces. Public goods provisioning improves one's reputation but is not explicitly repaid.

The final category of helping corresponds to need-based transfers and involves urgent needs that result from misfortune, especially sickness and acute hunger. In this case, the affected family will selectively make calls to close friends, who contribute according to their ability. Helping in these circumstances does not create debt, but it results in a special kind of relationship in which both the donor and recipient can call on each other in times of future need. At the first such need-based request, donors are not under an obligation to give, and they go through a complex decision-making process evaluating the potential recipient's history. If the requester has demonstrated generosity in the past to others, even with very small financial contributions, she will likely receive help without debt. Interviewees viewed this kind of helping as a prudent investment for this reason: "Even if you give a hundred shillings when they have a problem, they can give you much more if you need it." Notably, this statement explicitly frames participation in need-based transfers as a choice involving time and risk and specifically risk for which an expected value cannot be easily calculated. If the recipient has not helped others in need in the past, donors look for a history of signals of empathy. They report that they are more likely to give to those who "feel pain at the pain of others." They believe this kind of generosity is proximately motivated by sorrow (*uchungu*), and donors may help recipients who have never helped others in the past if they have displayed visible signs of empathy.

Not all need-based transfers in Kijenge begin with a request. In many instances, respected community members in need are offered assistance before they ask, when others suspect they might be in need. Similarly, not all need leads immediately to requests for help. Several people said they had severely reduced their own food consumption for several days before making a serious and formal request for a need-based transfer. Such delays in making requests for help serve as honest signals of need. Another way to cheat is to hide resources in order to avoid requests from others. While livestock and large game animals are difficult to hide, cash is easy to conceal. Yet, with remarkable reliability and speed, others do find out and gossip about who has recently come into money. As one interviewee put it, "Everyone knows who has money—how he walks, what clothes he wears."

Discussion

Need-Based vs. Debt-Based Transfers

As we have seen, Maasai make a distinction between *osotua* relationships, in which transfers are made to partners in need with no expectation of repayment and *esile* transactions, which do create debt and which must be repaid. Similarly, Yasawans distinguish between resources that are appropriate for *kerekere* requests and whose transfer does not create debt and others that are inappropriate for *kerekere* requests and that do create debt. The same distinction can be found in labor-sharing arrangements among ranchers in the American Southwest: If a need arises unexpectedly, as in the case of an injury or a sudden equipment failure, aid is given with no expectation of repayment other than a similar kindness should the donor ever be in similar straits. But if a need is one that arises predictably, as when it is time to brand cattle or ship them off to market, then the ranchers make arrangements for a balanced exchange of favors.

These three examples demonstrate a distinction that may be useful to generalize. On the one hand, we have need-based transfers, which do not create debt and which may lead to long-lasting relationships even when the flow of resources is solely or predominantly one way. On the other, we have situations in which debt is a crucial element and gifts must be repaid or the relationship will end. We refer to gifts that create debt as "debt-based transfers." Our agent-based models have shown that, when environmental conditions are volatile, need-based transfers lead to more risk pooling and longer survival than do debt-based transfers (Aktipis et al. 2016). The reason is that the unpredictability of need applies not only to the party that happens to be in need at the moment but to everyone. Given that the future is unpredictable, it makes sense to exchange the low probability of a catastrophic loss for a high probability of small, manageable losses. But when needs occur regularly and predictably, as in the case of branding time for our ranchers, debt-based transfers may work better to maintain cooperative networks over time (Fig. 7).

We use the terms "need-based transfers" and "debt-based transfers" rather than other existing terms because no current terms used in the literature capture the underlying logic of need-based transfers (Cronk and Aktipis 2016a, b). "Sharing," for example, is a broad concept that does not by itself capture the idea that the giving is to those in need. One can, after all, share with someone who is wealthy as easily as with someone who is poor. Similarly, while Fiske's (1991) "communal

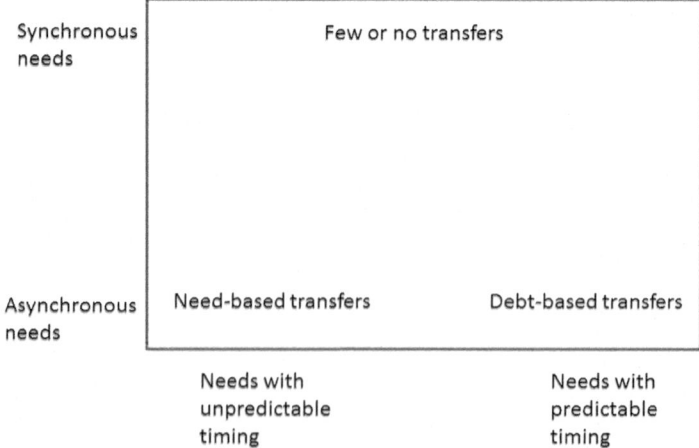

Fig. 7 Risk pooling through need-based transfers is most appropriate and feasible when needs occur unpredictably and asynchronously

sharing" and Sahlins' (1965) "generalized reciprocity" overlap with some cases of need-based transfers, they do not describe the kinds of formal, contractual risk-pooling arrangements found at some of our field sites. Why not "risk-reduction reciprocity," a term used by some human behavioral ecologists (e.g., Bliege Bird et al. 2002)? In this instance, our objection is logical. The risk pooling that results from need-based transfers does not actually *reduce* risk but simply redistributes it; hence "risk-reduction reciprocity" is a misnomer. It is also tempting to refer to need-based transfers simply as "risk pooling." However, our computer simulations have shown that some limited risk pooling can be achieved even when agents are limited to debt-based transfers (Aktipis et al. 2016). Risk pooling is best seen as an outcome of certain kinds of transfers rather than as a particular kind of transfer. As for "debt-based transfers," we could instead say "balanced reciprocity" (Sahlins 1965) or "tit-for-tat reciprocity" (Axelrod 1984), both of which capture the same basic idea. We choose instead to avoid the word "reciprocity" because of the way that it has come to mean so many different things, including many things that are not reciprocity at all (e.g., negative reciprocity, indirect reciprocity, and strong reciprocity; Cronk and Leech 2013).

One thing that need-based and debt-based transfers do have in common is that neither will work unless the people involved have a high likelihood of future interactions with each other (Axelrod 1984). Although this is usually the case in the kinds of small-scale societies where anthropologists often work, it may not be in large-scale societies. Large-scale systems may be made stable by a variety of mechanisms including institutional frameworks, impersonal ways of assessing the qualities of potential cooperative partners (e.g., background checks and credit scores), and actuarial databases, which make it possible to remain ignorant about the likelihood of any particular individual suffering a loss while being quite confident about the likelihood that a category of people will suffer one (Levy 2012).

A comparison of debt-based and need-based transfers, respectively, to the analogous systems of lending by banks and insurance markets found in modern, large-scale societies may be enlightening. Debt-based transfers are like bank loans: If you don't repay your current loan, you will not receive any more loans. Just as debt-based transfers work well if the two parties to the agreement can set up a tit-for-tat exchange of favors, bank loans work well if lenders have good reasons to believe that borrowers will have the means to repay. Need-based transfer systems, in contrast, are similar to insurance policies purchased on the market. When you pay your insurance premiums, you are not giving a loan to the insurance company and hoping that they will one day repay you. On the contrary, you hope that you are so fortunate as to never have to file a claim and that, as a result of your good fortune, all of your premiums end up being a complete waste of money. But the future is unpredictable and you are prudent, so you buy an insurance policy and pay your premiums, anyway. Similarly, when fortunate people give to those in need in a risk-pooling system, they are hoping that their good fortune will continue and that they themselves will never be in need. But they, too, are prudent, and so they enter into risk-pooling relationships even as they hope that they will never need to call upon them.

However, market insurance differs from social risk pooling in interesting and important ways. For example, insurance products are very specific, insuring against a single risk or a narrowly defined set of risks (e.g., flood, legal liability, medical expenses) and cover a single asset or a narrowly defined set of assets (e.g., home, business property, health). In contrast, social risk pooling is typically much more flexible. A single relationship can cover a wide range of risks and a wide range of assets. Instead of having separate insurance products for each source of risk, the same social networks can insure against shocks resulting from many different causes. Furthermore, in systems of risk pooling based on need-based transfers, the risks covered do not always need to be fully specified in advance. If unforeseen risks emerge, the same social networks are often able to absorb them.

Synchronous Needs, Asynchronous Needs, and the Question of Scale

When everyone in a community experiences the same need simultaneously, neither need-based nor debt-based transfers may be feasible, and resource transfers and other forms of helping may occur only for other reasons, such as parenting and kinship (Fig. 7). The Mongolian herders provide a good example of a group that relies mainly on means of risk management other than risk pooling for precisely this reason: When disaster strikes, no one is in a position to help anyone else. They still cooperate and provide assistance to each other to manage risks, but before the disaster strikes rather than during the disaster. Turnbull's fieldwork during the Ik's disastrous *lopei kopo* famine shows how completely social support networks can fall apart when disasters are both severe and simultaneous. On the other hand, Cathryn Townsend's current work shows that even in a group that has undergone such extraordinary stress, sharing norms and the beliefs that support them can re-emerge when conditions improve.

Despite the dramatic examples of simultaneous needs provided by our Mongolian and Ik field sites, the simultaneity of needs may need to be quite extreme before systems of risk pooling become nonviable. This is because when a community is hit by a disaster, its impact may not be felt equally by everyone in the community. For example, when drought and disease struck livestock herds owned by Pokot in western Kenya in 1991 and 1992, some herders lost about 50% of their cattle, while others lost only a few head. Losses among goat herds were similarly variable, with some herds dropping by as much as 30%, while one actually grew by 11% (Bollig 1998, p. 145). To take an example closer to home, when Superstorm Sandy hit New Jersey and New York in October, 2012, its impact on communities was quite uneven. Some were devastated, while others suffered only minor damage and power outages. Even within hard-hit communities, the extent of damage varied from block to block and house to house. As a result, people were able to help each other even in very hard-hit communities.

The example of Superstorm Sandy highlights another important issue regarding synchronicity of needs: Whether people experience needs simultaneously is really a matter of spatial scale. While parts of New Jersey and New York were hit hard by the storm, most of the rest of the United States was untouched by it. Thus, one way to change the nature of the risk management game is to find ways to scale up, which decreases the odds that everyone in the risk-pooling system will suffer a loss simultaneously. In the United States, this is made possible by large institutions (the government, churches, Red Cross, etc.) and by high-quality and large-scale infrastructures for communication and transportation. However, our Yasawa Island field site, where aid comes mainly from close kin in the event of very local events such as illnesses and injuries but from distant kin when widespread disasters such as droughts and cyclones strike, shows that some limited scaling up may be both possible and helpful even in small-scale communities.

Cheating, Cooperative Partner Choice, and Moral Hazard

Whenever people cooperate at some cost to themselves, there is the potential for cheating. Risk-pooling arrangements are no exception to this rule. At some of our sites, cheating may be difficult for a simple, practical reason: The resource in question is highly visible. Large dead animals and livestock are difficult things to hide. Despite the visibility of livestock, it would in principle be possible to hide one's wealth by taking advantage of practices such as *enkitaaroto*, a Maasai system in which animals are put in someone else's herd but without a transfer of ownership. We have livestock census data from both Mukogodo Maasai (Cronk 1989, 2004) and Karamoja. In both cases, the correlation between herders' apparent wealth, defined as the numbers of animals in their herds regardless of who really owns them, and actual wealth, defined as the number of animals that they actually own regardless of whose herd they happen to be in, is too high for this kind of cheating to be a real problem (Mukogodo Maasai, Pearson's $r = 0.984$, $p < 0.01$, $N = 183$; Karamoja, Pearson's $r = 0.968$, $p < 0.01$, $N = 44$). In need-based transfer systems where resources can be hidden or individuals are otherwise unable to evaluate the resource holdings of others, cheating is likely to be a larger problem.

Maasai also discourage cheating by imbuing their *osotua* relationships with a deep sense of sacredness and responsibility that is captured by the very term the use to describe such relationships: umbilical cord. Given how tempting and, at least in some circumstances, how easy it might be to cheat in need-based transfer systems, it makes sense that cheating may be guarded against by a threat of supernatural punishment. In the Maasai case, that threat is rather vague. However, among the Ik, the threat of supernatural punishment and the complementary possibility of supernatural reward are quite explicit, with the *kijawikå* earth spirits monitoring everyone's generosity and stinginess and rewarding or punishing them accordingly.

It may also not be coincidental that the kinds of situations that give rise to systems of risk pooling based on need-based transfers are also the kinds of situations where one is most likely to find extreme religiosity, superstition, and magical thinking. When events are out of one's control, it is common for people to imagine that they are in the control of forces that can be influenced through such means as prayer and magic. This "uncertainty hypothesis" was first inspired by Malinowski's (1922) observation that, in the Trobriand Islands, magic was more often associated with dangerous activities such as open ocean fishing than with safe activities such as lagoon fishing. Gmelch (1971, 1992; see also Burger and Lynn 2005) provided an entertaining example of this phenomenon among professional baseball players: Superstitions regarding rituals, routines, and magical charms are frequently related to activities that have high rates of failure, such as pitching and hitting, and are rarely associated with activities with high rates of success, such as fielding. Somewhat similarly, people who feel that they are in danger are more likely to engage in religious rituals (Sosis 2007). Perhaps the sacredness with which need-based transfers are often imbued is enhanced by their association with high-risk situations and thus with religion, superstition, and magical thinking (Cronk and Aktipis 2016a, b).

Another way of suppressing cheating is for individuals to carefully choose partners with whom they enter into need-based transfer relationships. Partner choice is one way of enhancing assortment of cooperators with one another, and it can be realized through both simple and complex rules for choosing and maintaining relationships (Noë and Hammerstein 1994; Aktipis 2004, 2006, 2011; Barclay and Willer 2007; Nesse 2009; Barclay 2013). Careful partner choice may be particularly important in societies like the Maasai and in Karamoja where such relationships are formal, clear, and long-lasting obligations. As we have seen, in both societies stock friends are chosen carefully and with great attention to trust, congeniality, and compatibility. Among the Maasai and in Karamoja, this process is somewhat like courtship and involves the exchange of small gifts and favors over time. Such gifts serve as signals of each party's commitment to the relationship. This is reminiscent of the *hxaro* gift-giving system found among the Ju/'hoansi hunter-gatherers of the Kalahari. In the hxaro system, partners exchange small gifts, most of which are of little economic consequence, in order to maintain relationships that become vital when one partner has a serious need, such as an unexpected shortage of food or water (Wiessner 1977, 1982). In this way, reciprocal gift-giving serves as a signal of commitment to a system that is ultimately about the management of unpredictable risks through need-based transfers. These systems of signaling commitment may serve to help solve the problem of cheating by requiring ongoing mutual investment and engagement in order to maintain relationships that can then be called on during times of need. In Yasawa, Fiji, such exchanges among households, clans, and villages may enable the scaling up of social support networks to be drawn on in times of locally synchronous need.

We are also exploring the issue of cheating through laboratory experiments. Our preliminary findings indicate that, in a standard test of cheater detection ability called the Wason selection task (Cosmides 1989), people are quite good at identifying cheaters in need-based transfers, particularly those who ask when they are not actually in need (Chang et al. 2015; Muñoz et al. 2016). We are currently adapting this method for use at some of our field sites, as well. Vigilance about need-based transfer cheating may help explain a recent finding in political science that people in both the United States and Denmark support welfare payments to people who find themselves in need through no fault of their own while opposing such payments to people perceived as lazy (Petersen 2012). In short, those who receive help without actually being in need are perceived as cheaters regardless of whether the help is provided by the government or a friend.

In addition to outright cheating, need-based transfer systems may be undermined by another deleterious outcome: the "moral hazard." This refers to the possibility that people who know that they will be taken care of if they suffer a loss may then take on additional risk. When all of the risks people face are negative, this can be a serious problem. But what if risks can also be positive? In that case, people should encourage their risk-pooling partners to take risks because they might receive part of the resulting windfall. At some of our field sites, this simply is not possible. Apart from possibly high yields from livestock raiding (which obviously come with their own set of risks), pastoralists do not experience sudden windfalls. Livestock reproduce at particular rates, and that is that. But at two of our sites, both coincidentally in Tanzania but worlds apart in most other ways, people do experience occasional windfalls. Among the Hadza, big game are seldom obtained, but when they are they are shared widely. Similarly, residents of Kijenge occasionally get lucky, perhaps by finding a job. When that happens, the proceeds are often shared within networks of *kushirikiana*. Thus, the system of risk pooling simultaneously provides support in the event of loss and encourages people to take positive risks, which in the long run increases the health, wealth, and well-being of the community as a whole. These observations fit well with findings from experiments and computer simulations that strong sharing norms are most likely to emerge when resource acquisition is uncertain (Kameda et al. 2002, 2003).

Social vs. Individual Risk Management

The vulnerability of need-based transfer systems to cheating highlights the fact that the social management of risk can, in itself, be a risky prospect. Relying purely on risk pooling or other social forms of risk management may be unwise. If risks can be avoided, reduced, or absorbed, then people may be able to reduce their dependence on their social networks for help and, thus, their exposure to the problems of cheating and the moral hazard. Thus, individual-based risk management strategies are important across the societies that we study as well. Pastoralists guard their livestock, have them vaccinated, engage in other forms of subsistence, and maintain large herds. Foragers develop their hunting and gathering skills and rely not only on unreliable large game but reliable foods such as plants, small game, and honey. Ranchers vaccinate their livestock, kill predators, get jobs as teachers, open bed-and-breakfasts, and so on. Sometimes, one risk management strategy may do double duty. This is exemplified by the way that Loita Maasai use *osotua* relationships not only to help each other after losses have occurred but also to build up herds before disaster strikes so that losses can simply be absorbed. In other situations, need-based transfers at the moment of need are simply not feasible. In Mongolia's Darhad Depression, for example, when a disaster strikes, it strikes everyone. Rather than pooling risk after the fact, Mongolian herders cooperate with each other to reduce their exposure to risks by gathering hay and building livestock shelters.

Across the societies of the Human Generosity Project, we see a diversity of individual and social risk management strategies that are well suited to the particular challenges and opportunities of each local ecology and subsistence practice. Across all our sites, we find social risk management systems, most notably systems of risk pooling via need-based transfers. However, this social risk management comes with risks including the possibility of cheating and moral hazard. Interestingly, many need-based transfer systems encourage individual-level risk management practices to reduce the reliance on need-based transfer systems. For example, among the Maasai, *osotua* partners are expected to manage their own risk through being responsible and restrained in their herding practices. Cowboys in the Malpai borderlands of the southwestern United States expect themselves and their neighbors to be self-reliant, managing their own risks effectively and not taking unnecessary ones. Yasawan horticulturalists expect one another to work hard in their own gardens throughout the year to reduce seasonal shortfalls. Similar patterns are emerging at our other field sites as well: We find that norms of self-reliance coexist with a strong ethic of helping others in need. This suggests that norms of self-reliance and responsibility about managing risk as an individual can actually be an important part of a larger social risk management system by reducing the risk of cheating and moral hazard. Norms of self-reliance may also help limit the reverberation of negative events in a network, increasing the resilience of the system to catastrophic events. The interplay between individual and social risk management strategies and the norms underlying them is an important topic that we are continuing to explore at our field sites and in The Human Generosity Project more generally.

Conclusion

Risk management is an evolutionarily ancient and widespread problem that all humans face. Members of the Human Generosity Project are working together in a highly interdisciplinary team to understand both individual and social risk management strategies employed by societies around the world. Every society we have studied to date utilizes social forms of risk management, most notably systems of risk pooling through need-based transfers. Need-based transfers are often characterized by giving "from the heart" to individuals who are in need. These need-based transfer systems differ in important ways from society to society, with some based on dyadic relationships and others based on group membership, and some based on small transfers, while others are based on large gifts. These differences across need-based transfer systems appear to be suited to the spatial and temporal patterning of local risks. We suggest that risk pooling through need-based transfers is an important and flexible strategy that communities can and do use to manage risk and maintain a sustainable way of life across diverse ecologies.

Acknowledgments The Human Generosity Project is supported primarily by a grant from the John Templeton Foundation titled "Generous by nature: Need-based transfers and the origins of human cooperation." Any opinions, findings, conclusions, or recommendations expressed in this chapter are those of the authors and do not necessarily reflect the views of the John Templeton Foundation. Work by Human Generosity Project team members has also been supported by the National Science Foundation, American Center for Mongolian Studies, Fulbright IIE, and Rutgers' Center for Human Evolutionary Studies.

References

Aktipis, C. A. (2004). Know when to walk away: Contingent movement and the evolution of cooperation. *Journal of Theoretical Biology, 231*(2), 249–260.
Aktipis, C. A. (2006). Recognition memory and the evolution of cooperation: How simple strategies succeed in an agent-based world. *Adaptive Behavior, 14*, 239–247.
Aktipis, C. A. (2011). Is cooperation viable in mobile organisms? Simple walk away strategy favors the evolution of cooperation in groups. *Evolution and Human Behavior, 32*(4), 263–276.
Aktipis, C. A., Cronk, L., & de Aguiar, R. (2011). Risk-pooling and herd survival: An agent-based model of a Maasai gift-giving system. *Human Ecology, 39*(2), 131–140.
Aktipis, C. A., de Aguiar, R., Flaherty, A., Iyer, P., Sonkoi, D., & Cronk, L. (2016). Cooperation in an uncertain world: For the Maasai of East Africa, need-based transfers outperform account keeping in volatile environments. *Human Ecology, 44*(3), 353–364.
Axelrod, R. (1984). *The evolution of cooperation*. New York: Basic Books.
Barclay, P. (2013). Strategies for cooperation in biological markets, especially for humans. *Evolution and Human Behavior, 34*(3), 164–175. https://doi.org/10.1016/J.Evolhumbehav.2013.02.002
Barclay, P., & Willer, R. (2007). Partner choice creates competitive altruism in humans. *Proceedings of the Royal Society B: Biological Sciences, 274*(1610), 749–753.
Barnard, A. (1978). Universal systems of kin categorization. *African Studies, 37*(1), 69–82.
Barr, A., & Genicot, G. (2008). Risk sharing, commitment, and information: An experimental analysis. *Journal of the European Economic Association, 6*(6), 1151–1185.
Bartos, V. (2015). *Seasonal scarcity and sharing norms*. http://vojtechbartos.net/wp-content/uploads/Bartos-AFG-Seasonality.pdf
Begzsuren, S., Ellis, J. E., Ojima, D. S., Coughenour, M. B., & Chuluun, T. (2004). Livestock responses to droughts and severe winter weather in the Gobi Three Beauty National Park, Mongolia. *Journal of Arid Environments, 59*(4), 785–796.
Berbesque, J. C., Marlowe, F. W., Shaw, P., & Thompson, P. (2014). Hunter–gatherers have less famine than agriculturalists. *Biology Letters, 10*(1), 20130853.
Berbesque, J. C., Wood, B. M., Crittenden, A. N., Mabulla, A., & Marlowe, F. W. (2016). Eat first, share later: Hadza Hunter–Gatherer men consume more while foraging than in central places. *Evolution and Human Behavior, 37*(4), 281–286.
Bird, R. L. B., & Bird, D. W. (1997). Delayed reciprocity and tolerated theft: The behavioral ecology of food-sharing strategies. *Current Anthropology, 38*(1), 49–78. https://doi.org/10.1086/204581
Bliege Bird, R., Bird, D. W., Smith, E. A., & Kushnick, G. C. (2002). Risk and reciprocity in Meriam food sharing. *Evolution and Human Behavior, 23*(4), 297–321.
Bold, B. (1996). Socio-economic segmentation – Khot-ail in nomadic livestock keeping of Mongolia. *Nomadic Peoples, 33*, 153–162.

Bollig, M. (1998). Moral economy and self-interest: Kinship, friendship, and exchange among the Pokot (NW Kenya). In T. Schweizer & D. White (Eds.), *Kinship, networks, and exchange* (pp. 137–157). Cambridge: Cambridge University Press.

Bollig, M. (2006). *Risk management in a hazardous environment: A comparative study of two pastoral societies* (Vol. 2). New York: Springer.

Burger, J. M., & Lynn, A. L. (2005). Superstitious behavior among American and Japanese professional baseball players. *Basic and Applied Social Psychology, 27*(1), 71–76.

Cashdan, E. A. (1985). Coping with risk: Reciprocity among the Basarwa of Northern Botswana. *Man, 20*, 454–474.

Cashdan, E. A. (Ed.). (1990). *Risk and uncertainty in tribal and peasant economies.* Boulder, CO: Westview.

Chang, A., Cronk, L., & Aktipis, C. A. (2015). *Cheater detection in need-based transfer systems.* Columbia, CO: Human Behavior and Evolution Society.

Conte, T. J. (2015). The effects of China's Grassland contract policy on Mongolian Herders' attitudes towards grassland management in Northeastern Inner Mongolia. *Journal of Political Ecology, 22*(1), 79–97.

Conte, T. J., & Tilt, B. (2014). The effects of China's Grassland contract policy on pastoralist attitudes towards cooperation in an Inner Mongolian banner. *Human Ecology, 42*(6), 837–846.

Cooper, L. (1993). Patterns of mutual assistance in the Mongolian pastoral economy. *Nomadic Peoples, 33*, 153–162.

Cosmides, L. (1989). The logic of social exchange: Has natural selection shaped how humans reason? Studies with the Wason selection task. *Cognition, 31*(3), 187–276.

Cronk, L. (1989). *The behavioral ecology of change among the Mukogodo of Kenya.* Ph.D. dissertation, anthropology, Northwestern University.

Cronk, L. (2004). *From Mukogodo to Maasai: Ethnicity and cultural change in Kenya.* Boulder, CO: Westview.

Cronk, L. (2007). The influence of cultural framing on play in the trust game: A Maasai example. *Evolution and Human Behavior, 28*, 352–358.

Cronk, L., & Aktipis, C. A. (2016a). *What are "Need-Based Transfers"?* Human generosity project blog post. http://humangenerosity.org

Cronk, L., & Aktipis, C. A. (2016b). Sacredness as an implied threat of supernatural punishment: The case of need-based transfers. *Religion, Brain, and Behavior, 8*, 282–285.

Cronk, L., & Leech, B. L. (2013). *Meeting at grand central: Understanding the social and evolutionary roots of cooperation.* Princeton, NJ: Princeton University Press.

Curtin, C., & Western, D. (2008). Grasslands, people, and conservation: Over-the-horizon learning exchanges between African and American Pastoralists. *Conservation Biology, 22*(4), 870–877.

Dahl, G., & Hjort, A. (1976). *Having herds: Pastoral herd growth and household economy.* Stockholm: Dept. of Social Anthropology, University of Stockholm.

Dixit, A. K., Levin, S. A., & Rubenstein, D. I. (2013). Reciprocal insurance among Kenyan pastoralists. *Theoretical Ecology, 6*(2), 173–187.

Dorfman, M. S. (2007). *Introduction to risk management and insurance.* London: Prentice Hall.

Dyson-Hudson, N. (1966). *Karimojong politics.* Oxford: Clarendon Press.

Endicott, E. (2012). *A history of land use in Mongolia: The thirteenth century to the present.* New York: Palgrave Macmillan.

Fafchamps, M. (2011). Risk sharing between households. In J. Benhabib, A. Bisin, & M. O. Jackson (Eds.), *Handbook of social economics.* San Diego/Amsterdam: North-Holland.

Fafchamps, M., & Lund, S. (2003). Risk-sharing networks in rural Philippines. *Journal of Development Economics, 71*, 261–287.

Fernandez-Gimenez, M. E. (2000). The role of Mongolian nomadic pastoralists' ecological knowledge in grassland management. *Ecological Applications, 10*(5), 1318–1326.

Fernandez-Gimenez, M. E., Batkhishig, B., & Batbuyan, B. (2012). Cross-boundary and cross-level dynamics increase vulnerability to severe winter disasters (dzud) in Mongolia. *Global Environmental Change, 22*, 836–851.

Fiske, A. P. (1991). *Structures of social life: The four elementary forms of human relations.* New York: Free Press.

Gardner, R., Ostrom, E., & Walker, J. M. (1990). The nature of common-pool resource problems. *Rationality and Society, 2*(3), 335–358.

Gelcich, S., Guzman, R., Rodriguez-Sickert, C., Castilla, J. C., & Cardenas, J. C. (2013). Exploring external validity of common pool resource experiments: Insights from artisanal benthic fisheries in Chile. *Ecology and Society, 18*(3), 2.

Gervais, M. M. (2016). RICH economic games for networked relationships and communities: Development and preliminary validation in Yasawa, Fiji. *Field Methods, 29*, 113–129. https://doi.org/10.1177/1525822X16643709

Gmelch, G. (1971). Baseball magic. *Society, 8*(8), 39–41.

Gmelch, G. (1992). Superstition and ritual in American baseball. *Elysian Fields Quarterly, 11*(3), 25–36.

Gray, S., Sundal, M., Wiebusch, B., Little, M. A., Leslie, P. W., & Pike, I. L. (2003). Cattle raiding, cultural survival, and adaptability of East African pastoralists. *Current Anthropology, 44*(55), S3–S30.

Gulliver, P. H. (1955). *The family herds: A study of two pastoral tribes in East Africa, the Jie and Turkana.* London: Routledge & Kegan Paul.

Gurven, M., & Hill, K. (2009). Why do men hunt? *Current Anthropology, 50*(1), 51–74.

Gurven, M., & Hill, K. (2010). Moving beyond stereotypes of men's foraging goals. *Current Anthropology, 51*(2), 265–267.

Gurven, M., Allen-Arave, W., Hill, K., & Hurtado, M. (2000). "It's a wonderful life": Signaling generosity among the ache of Paraguay. *Evolution and Human Behavior, 21*(4), 263–282.

Hao, Y., Armbruster, D., & Hütt, M.-C. (2015a). Node survival in networks under correlated attacks. *PLOS One., 10*(5), e0125467. https://doi.org/10.1371/journal.pone.0125467

Hao, Y., Aktipis, C. A., Armbruster, D., & Cronk, L. (2015b). Need-based transfers on a network: A model of risk-pooling in ecologically volatile environments. *Evolution and Human Behavior, 36*(4), 265–273.

Humphrey, C., & Sneath, D. (1996). *Culture and environment in inner Asia 1: The pastoral economy and the environment.* Cambridge: White Horse Press.

Humphrey, C., & Sneath, D. (1999). *The end of nomadism? Society, state, and the environment in inner Asia.* Cambridge: White Horse Press.

Jones, B., Hawkes, K., & O'Connell, J. F. (2005). Older Hadza men and women as helpers: Residence data. In B. S. Hewlett & M. E. Lamb (Eds.), *Hunter-Gatherer childhoods: Evolutionary, developmental and cultural perspectives* (pp. 214–236). New Brunswick: Transaction.

Kameda, T., Takezawa, M., Tindale, R. S., & Smith, C. (2002). Social sharing and risk reduction: Exploring a computational algorithm for the psychology of windfall gains. *Evolution and Human Behavior, 23*, 11–33.

Kameda, T., Takezawa, M., & Hastie, R. (2003). The logic of social sharing: An evolutionary game analysis of adaptive norm development. *Personality and Social Psychology Review, 7*(1), 2–19.

King, J. M., Sayers, A. R., Peacock, C. P., & Kontrohr, E. (1984). Maasai herd and flock structures in relation to livestock wealth, climate, and development. *Agricultural Systems, 13*, 21–56.

Levy, J. (2012). *Freaks of fortune: The emerging world of capitalism and risk in America.* Cambridge, MA: Harvard University Press.

Little, P. D., Smith, K., Cellarius, B. A., Coppock, D. L., & Barrett, C. (2001). Avoiding disaster: Diversification and risk management among East African Herders. *Development and Change, 32*(3), 401–433.

Mace, R. (1990). Pastoralist herd compositions in unpredictable environments: A comparison of model predictions and data from camel-keeping groups. *Agricultural Systems, 33*, 1–11.

Mace, R. (1993). Nomadic pastoralists adopt subsistence strategies that maximise long-term household survival. *Behavioral Ecology and Sociobiology, 33*(5), 329–334.

Mace, R., & Houston, A. I. (1989). Pastoralist strategies for survival in unpredictable environments: A model of herd composition that maximises household viability. *Agricultural Systems, 31*(2), 185–204.

Malinowski, B. (1922). *Argonauts of the Western Pacific*. London: Routledge & Kegan Paul.

Mamdani, M., Kasoma, P. M. B., & Katende, A. B. (1992). *Karamoja: Ecology and history*. Kampala: Centre for Basic Research.

Marlowe, F. (2010). *The Hadza: Hunter–gatherers of Tanzania*. Berkeley: University of California Press.

Messick, M., Allison, S. T., & Samuelson, C. D. (1988). Framing and communication effects on group members' responses to environmental and social uncertainty. In S. Maital (Ed.), *Applied behavioral economics* (Vol. II). New York: New York University Press.

Muñoz, A. E., Sznycer, D., Chang, A., Cronk, L., & Aktipis, C. A. (2016). *Cheater detection for need-based transfers: Beyond account-keeping*. Chicago: Association for Psychological Science.

Nesse, R. M. (2009). Runaway social selection for displays of partner value and altruism. In *The moral brain* (pp. 211–231). Amsterdam: Springer.

Noë, R., & Hammerstein, P. (1994). Biological markets: Supply and demand determine the effect of partner choice in cooperation, mutualism and mating. *Behavioral Ecology and Sociobiology, 35*, 1–11.

Nolet, E. (2012). *Are you prepared? Representations and management of floods in Lomanikoro, Rewa (Fiji). Disasters*. In Uncertainty and Disquiet, 12ème Biennale de l'European Association of Social Anthropologists, Université de Nanterre, 10–13 July 2012.

Pederson, N., Hessl, A. E., Baatarbileg, N., Anchukaitis, K. J., & Di Cosmo, N. (2014). Pluvials, droughts, the Mongol empire, and modern Mongolia. *Proceedings of the National Academy of Sciences, 111*(12), 4375–4379.

Perlov, D. C. (1987). *Trading for influence: The social and cultural economics of livestock marketing among the Highland Samburu of Northern Kenya*. Ph.D. dissertation, anthropology, University of California, Los Angeles.

Petersen, M. B. (2012). Social welfare as small-scale help: Evolutionary psychology and the deservingness heuristic. *American Journal of Political Science, 56*(1), 1–16.

Pollard, G., Davies, M. I. J., & Moore, H. L. (2015). Women, marketplaces and exchange partners amongst the Marakwet of Northwest Kenya. *Journal of Eastern African Studies, 9*(3), 412–439. https://doi.org/10.1080/17531055.2015.1089699

Quam, M. D. (1976). *Pastoral economy and cattle marketing in Karamoja, Uganda*. Ph.D. dissertation, Indiana University.

Ravuvu, A. D. (1987). *The Fijian ethos*. Suva: Institute of Pacific Studies.

Rejda, G. E. (2011). *Principles of risk management and insurance*. Bengaluru: Pearson Education India.

Sahlins, M. D. (1962). *Moala: Culture and nature on a Fijian island*. Ann Arbor: University of Michigan Press.

Sahlins, M. D. (1965). On the sociology of primitive exchange. In Banton, M. (ed.), *The relevance of models for social anthropology*. Tavistock. Reprinted in Stone Age Economics, London (1972, Transaction).

Sayre, N. F. (2005). *Working wilderness: The Malpai Borderlands group and the future of the American range*. Tucson, AZ: Rio Nuevo.

Sosis, R. (2007). Psalms for safety. *Current Anthropology, 48*(6), 903–911.

Sosis, R., & Ruffle, B. (2003). Religious ritual and cooperation: Testing for a relationship on Israeli religious and secular kibbutzim. *Current Anthropology, 44*(5), 713–722.

Spencer, P. (1965). *The Samburu: A study of gerontocracy in a nomadic tribe*. Berkeley: University of California Press.

Stites, E., Akabwai, D., Mazurana, D., & Ateyo, P. (2007). *Angering Akujů: Survival and suffering in Karamoja -a report on livelihoods and human security in the Karamoja Region of Uganda* (p. 33). Boston: Feinstein International Center.

Swift, J., & Siurua, H. (2002). Drought and Zud but no famine (yet) in the Mongolian herding economy. *IDS Bulletin, 33*(4), 88–97.

Takasaki, Y. (2011). Do the commons help augment mutual insurance among the poor? *World Development, 39*, 429–438.

Templer, G., Swift, J., & Payne, P. (1993). The changing significance of risk in the Mongolian pastoral economy. *Nomadic Peoples, 33*, 105–122.

Thrift, E. D., & Byambabaatar, I. (2015). *Management of Dzud risk in Mongolia: Mutual aid and institutional interventions*. In Proceedings of the Trans-disciplinary Research Conference: Building Resilience of Mongolian Rangelands, Ulaanbaatar, Mongolia, June 9–10, 2015.

Turnbull, C. M. (1972). *The mountain people*. New York: Simon & Schuster.

UNDP. (2010). *UNDP on early recovery: 2009–2010 Mongolian Dzud*. http://www.undp.mn/publications/Early_recovery.pdf

Vernooy, R. (2011). *How Mongolian herders are transforming nomadic pastoralism*. Solutions. http://www.thesolutionsjournal.com

Wiessner, P. (1977) *Hxaro: A regional system of reciprocity for reducing risk among the! Kung San*. Ph.D. dissertation, anthropology, University of Michigan.

Wiessner, P. (1982). Risk, reciprocity and social influences on! Kung San economics. In E. Leacock & R. Lee (Eds.), *Politics and history in band societies* (Vol. 61, pp. 61–84). Cambridge: Cambridge University Press.

Winterhalder, B. (1986). Diet choice, risk, and food sharing in a stochastic environment. *Journal of Anthropological Archaeology, 5*(4), 369–392.

Trolls, Water, Time, and Community: Resource Management in the Mývatn District of Northeast Iceland

Ragnhildur Sigurðardóttir, Anthony J. Newton, Megan T. Hicks, Andrew J. Dugmore, Viðar Hreinsson, A. E. J. Ogilvie, Árni Daníel Júlíusson, Árni Einarsson, Steven Hartman, I. A. Simpson, Orri Vésteinsson, and Thomas H. McGovern

R. Sigurðardóttir
Reykjavík Academy, Reykjavík, Iceland

A. J. Newton · A. J. Dugmore
School of GeoSciences, University of Edinburgh, Edinburgh, UK

M. T. Hicks
Hunter College, CUNY, New York, NY, USA

V. Hreinsson
Reykjavík Academy, Reykjavík, Iceland

Stefansson Arctic Institute, Akureyri, Iceland

Natural History Museum of Iceland, Reykjavik, Iceland

A. E. J. Ogilvie
Stefansson Arctic Institute, Akureyri, Iceland

Institute of Arctic and Alpine Research (INSTAAR), Boulder, CO, USA

Á. D. Júlíusson
Reykjavík Academy, Reykjavík, Iceland

National Museum of Iceland, Reykjavík, Iceland

University of Iceland, Reykjavík, Iceland

Á. Einarsson
University of Iceland, Reykjavík, Iceland

Mývatn Research Station, Myvatn, Iceland

S. Hartman
Stefansson Arctic Institute, Akureyri, Iceland

Mälardalen University, Västerås, Sweden

I. A. Simpson
Stirling University, Stirling, UK

O. Vésteinsson
University of Iceland, Reykjavík, Iceland

Institute of Archaeology, Iceland, Reykjavík, Iceland

© Springer Nature Switzerland AG 2019
L. R. Lozny, T. H. McGovern (eds.), *Global Perspectives on Long Term Community Resource Management*, Studies in Human Ecology and Adaptation 11, https://doi.org/10.1007/978-3-030-15800-2_5

T. H. McGovern (✉)
Hunter College, CUNY, New York, NY, USA

> In olden days there was a troll woman named Kráka who lived in Bláhvammur by Bláfjall. She lived in a cave the remains of which can still be seen. It is so high up in the crags of Bláhvammur that it is inaccessible to all human beings. Kráka was extremely evil, and she constantly attacked the sheep belonging to the people of Mývatn and did great damage in the form of seizing sheep and killing humans (Kráka tröllskessa in Þjóðsagnabókin Sýnisbók íslenzkra þjóðsagnasafna. Sigurður Nordal tók saman. Translation Astrid Ogilvie) (Nordal 1971–1973).

Introduction

This paper draws on an unusually productive research partnership that involved representatives of geoscience, archaeology, environmental and climatic history, and environmental humanities as well as the residents of the Mývatn lake basin who offered their traditional knowledge accumulated within the last millennium. This collaborative approach produced knowledge regarding the management of upland subarctic floodplains and rivers that supported animal husbandry through the cultural manipulation of wetlands on the millennial time scale.

This case study focuses on the Mývatn highland lake basin in Iceland. It integrates local cultural records and academic science and scholarship and draws upon several decades of international interdisciplinary research projects of the lake area, sponsored by the North Atlantic Biocultural Organization (NABO) cooperative (www.nabohome.org). This integrated approach to human-environmental studies spearheaded in these collaborations involves scholars from different disciplines and countries: primarily from Iceland, Greenland, Scandinavia, the UK, Canada, and the USA. Anchored in NABO's long-standing research engagement in the region, this work has recently generated many affiliated projects and field studies strengthened by international collaborative efforts and undertaken together with local partners and international organizations. Local partners include the Barðárdalur-based project Svartárkot Culture-Nature active in the contiguous Eyjarfjarðarsýsla and Thingeyarsýsla counties of northern Iceland; the Mývatn Research Station; the *Fornleifastofnun Íslands* (the Institute of Archaeology, Iceland); and the Stefansson Arctic Institute (SAI). Closely collaborating international partner organizations include the Nordic Network for Interdisciplinary Environmental Studies (NIES, https://www.nordforsk.org/en/programmes-and-projects/projects/nordic-network-for-interdisciplinary-environmental-studies-nies), the Integrated History and Future of People on Earth (IHOPE)—in particular the Circumpolar Networks sub-project of IHOPE (http://ihopenet.org/circumpolarnetworks/)—and the Humanities for the Environment (HfE) network of global observatories (https://hfe-observatories.org),

---

The Icelandic language contains the letters ð (upper case Ð) pronounced like the "th" in "clothe" and þ (upper case Þ) pronounced like the "th" in "thing". Unless in a quotation or a personal name, the letter "Þ" is transliterated to "Th" here.

in particular the newly established HfE Circumpolar Observatory, which also connects to the northern Icelandic locality framed in this case study through its anchoring hub of SAI in Akureyri, the northern capital of Iceland in Eyjafjarðarsýsla. The research collaboration undertaken through these coalescing networks and interconnected projects are defined by openness to disciplinary border crossing that aligns physical environmental studies with historical and cultural modes of inquiry. Such an approach opens up new possibilities for multidisciplinary crowdsourcing of data, expertise, and local knowledge concerning questions of common interest while working to realize genuinely transdisciplinary ambitions of codesign, co-execution, and co-dissemination of research findings, thereby gaining new knowledge as the current research conditions allow.

Evidence of the human dimensions of long-term environmental change over centuries in Iceland, as compiled from different sources, evaluated through a diversity of methods and shared across specialized disciplinary divides, has significant potential to improve understanding of human ecodynamics at different spatial and temporal scales, from the annual to the decadal to the centennial and even the millennial. The development of local communities over the 1000 years of Icelandic history raises a great many interesting questions concerning the interdependency of social and environmental factors. Some communities provide fascinating case studies for comparing anthropogenic and non-anthropogenic environmental change on various scales, both spatial and temporal.

Iceland's remarkably well-preserved indigenous record of local human responses to social-environmental changes is in some key ways unique in the circumpolar north for its historical depth and archive of written observations and oral traditions recording the stories of specific localities at close hand by those who were born, lived, worked, and died in these places. Storytelling sources (written and oral) provide us with windows through which it is possible to capture intriguing and sometimes highly telling glimpses of 1000 years of documented history and then compare the information derived with other bodies of evidence that rely primarily on the scientific method, such as the environmental and life sciences. Such storytelling provides insights concerning local ecological knowledge transmitted over many generations and is referred to as "environmental memory".[1] Whether in the form of highly achieved and highly regarded world literature (as in the renowned *Sagas of Icelanders*) or as recorded in homelier forms such as farmer's diaries, letters, or orally circulated folk tales, storytelling resources offer immensely valuable contex-

---

[1] This is encapsulated specifically in the initiative entitled *Inscribing Environmental Memory in the Icelandic Sagas* (IEM). This is one of several projects that have unfolded through the integrated network collaboration described above. IEM is a major cross-cutting initiative of the Nordic Network for Interdisciplinary Environmental Studies (NIES), the North Atlantic Biocultural Organization (NABO), and the Global Human Ecodynamics Alliance (GHEA). See http://ihopenet.org/circumpolarnetworks. Other recent and new projects include the National Science Foundation (USA) funded award 1,446,308, *Investigations of the Long-Term Sustainability of Human Ecodynamic Systems in Northern Iceland* (MYCHANGE); the RANNÍS (Icelandic Centre for Research) funded award 163133-051, *The Mývatn District of Iceland: Sustainability, Environment and Change ca. AD 1700–1950* (MYSEAC); and the Riksbankens Jubileumsfond (Sweden) award P16-06051, *Reflections of Change: The Natural World in Literary and Historical Sources from Iceland ca. AD 800–1800* (ICECHANGE).

tual information concerning communities embedded in their landscapes and "timescapes", narratives that both contain and transmit vital cultural and environmental knowledge across generations (National Library 1960; Benediktsson 1968; Hartman et al. 2017).

This paper also engages with the legend of Kráka, the troll woman presented as the enemy of the human community in Mývatn, who stole sheep, abducted shepherds (sometimes for sex, sometimes for consumption), and ultimately turned the Kráká river into an agent intended to destroy the pastures and livelihood of the human residents. The troll legend is only a part of rich and many-stranded body of local traditional knowledge that has provided the basis for a sustained community-level effort to conserve key resources in the face of changing climate and geomorphology. The story of Kráka and the river Kráká that bears her name serves as more than just a fanciful and humorous tale. It provides a striking metaphor for the case study considered here that focuses on the themes suggested in the chapter title: the all-important water resources of the Mývatn district, environmental changes through time, the farming community who sought to manage these fragile resources, and also the community of researchers from both Iceland and elsewhere, who, together with local community informants and leaders, have pooled their complementary interdisciplinary knowledge in the best collaborative spirit to understand the key elements that contribute to successful sustainability of natural resources over time. While cross-disciplinary research that combines all of the disciplines noted above, together with local knowledge and the insight it provides, is required to understand how people adapted and promoted sustainability on the local level, the specific analytical perspective of historical ecology is adopted here to better understand how these environmental systems have been manipulated over multigenerational time scales, as well as the motivations behind shifting human interventions through time.

The Case Study

Limited attention has been paid to the ways in which communities who do not grow arable crops manipulate river systems to manage vegetation and surface processes. These activities may leave very subtle direct traces of intervention as the structures used to manage river flow may be built of wood, earth, and stone and last for only a few seasons. Yet while they are used and maintained, key processes such as seasonal inundations, floodplain alluviation, riverbank erosion, and channel migration may be encouraged, inhibited, or prevented. Because physical traces of direct interventions are subtle or ephemeral, even though the consequences for the floodplain and its ecology may be profound and enduring, folk history, including oral and written testimonies, is vital to gain an understanding of how people manage these environments and how they have mobilized community responses across generations.

This study has wider implications for the understanding of other past long-term floodplain management strategies and to enrich and improve scenario building efforts to adapt to future environmental changes by productively integrating environmental science, humanities, and local knowledge. The Mývatn case study provides an example of applied co-production of knowledge (disciplinary and traditional) to document and disseminate centuries of accumulated expertise that may have broad practical applications in other floodplains present and future, underlining the practical value of past knowledge for more sustainable adaptive responses to changing climate and geomorphology.

The Lake Mývatn Region, the River Kráká, and *Framengjar* Wetlands

The Lake Mývatn region (Icelandic *Mývatnssveit)* is located in subarctic northeast Iceland. The lake itself is situated about 280 m above sea level (a.s.l.) at about 65.5° north and represents one of the highest continually occupied parts of Iceland. The catchment supports a farming community focused on animal husbandry. Climatic limitations have meant that, historically, grass and hay production for domestic animal fodder has been the only viable crop, though limited barley production may have taken place in the Viking Age settlement period (Ogilvie 1992, 2001; Ogilvie et al. 2015; Sigurðardóttir et al. 2016). In recent decades, with a warming climate, local farmers have again begun to experiment with crops such as barley. Close to the southern margin of Lake Mývatn, the river Kráká has created a rich wetland system, named *Framengjar* in Icelandic, meaning "outer meadows" (Fig. 1). This has been

Fig. 1 View across the Framengjar wetlands to the mountain lair of the troll woman (Photo T. H. McGovern)

a vital resource for the local community, providing wetland fodder and grazing for livestock for hundreds of years and playing a key role in the persistence of the only upland community in Iceland that has existed continuously since settlement in the late ninth century AD.

Farming activity was traditionally supplemented by fishing in lakes and streams, large-scale collection of eggs from migratory waterfowl, and the hunting of non-migratory ptarmigan and arctic fox (McGovern et al. 2007; Hicks et al. 2016). The egg-collecting tradition is notable as an example of sustainably managed resources. The people of Mývatn refrained from hunting the tens of thousands of waterfowl that nest and breed in the region. Instead, they collected their eggs in a specific, limited fashion—usually less than half of the eggs in any given nest. Nest desertion is a common reaction of ground-nesting waterfowl when they detect significant predator activity, and the communities' practice was carefully designed to respect the birds' tolerance for limited predation. While the community protected waterfowl in their nesting habitats by waterways, they avidly hunted the ptarmigan (*Lagopus mutus*) with traps and guns in the heathlands. This collective, complementary birding tradition, which seems to have been followed closely, ensured that waterfowl populations would always return in numbers to nest in the communities' lands, providing hundreds of eggs per household each year.

The River Kráká catchment spans key environmental gradients between its headwaters which lie at over 400 m a.s.l. to the *Framengjar* wetlands that lie at under 300 m (Fig. 2). In these areas, soil cover developed slowly in the aftermath of early Holocene deglaciation. It was not until the mid-Holocene that an extensive shallow andosol developed (Ólafsdóttir and Guðmundsson 2002). The lower Kráká catchment would have been fully vegetated in prehistory with birch woodlands on the well-drained slopes, but higher levels would have had a sparser vegetation cover of moss and heath. Currently, patches of woodland survive on inaccessible but favourable slopes up to about 400 m a.s.l., and this indicates woodland limits in prehistory, which probably included the lower western slopes of Sellandafjall, the isolated table mountain that rises to a height of 988 m and lies on the eastern margins of the Kráká catchment. The river Kráká originates from a number of springs within thick deposits of volcanic ash (tephra) in the southern communal rangeland grazing area (*Suðurafréttur*) of the Lake Mývatn community. The upper reaches meander, but once the upper tributaries flowing from the springs combine into a single channel, it follows a sinuous course to the north; series of small islands and bars characterize some reaches. Before the river reaches the farmhouses at Baldursheimur, it is joined by a major tributary system that drains the summit and western slopes of Sellandafjall, capped by semi-permanent snow fields and with steep flanks that presently are heavily gullied.

A few kilometres south of the farmhouses at Baldursheimur, the Kráká enters a level plain and flows north following the western margin of the floodplain towards Lake Mývatn. The floodplain supports the 15–20 km^2 *Framengjar* wetland system. According to written sources, the *Framengjar* once extended further to the south than they do today, but that area is now sparsely vegetated and eroded. Distributaries from the Kráká meander across the floodplain to the north, and a major palaeochannel

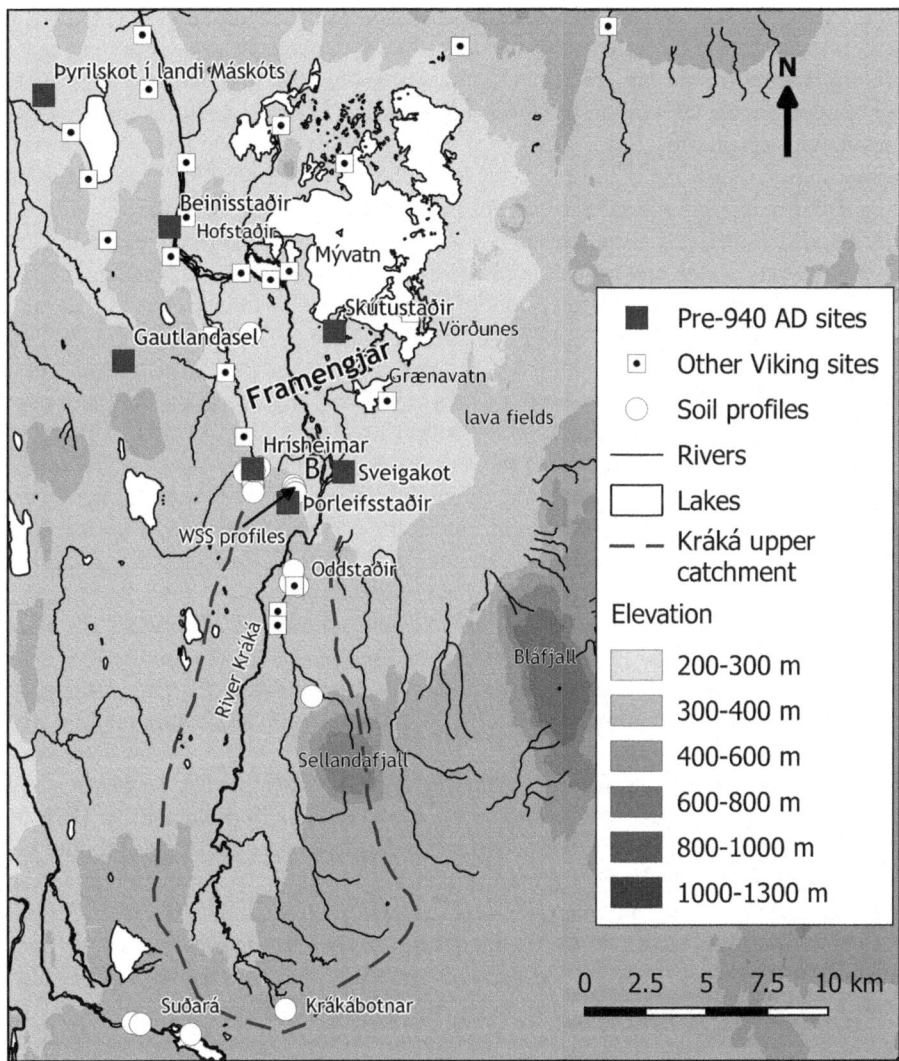

Fig. 2 Location map showing place names and early sites. Note that the Viking Age settlements, including multiple sites pre-dating the V-Sv 938 ± 6 volcanic tephra, were widespread

system extends from the course of the Kráká towards Lake Grænavatn. At various times in the past, these channels have carried water and sediment into Grænavatn and Mývatn (Fig. 2). At its northern (downslope) limit, the floodplain banks up against the barrier formed by presettlement old lava formations and pseudo craters around Skútustaðir. These formations separate the wetlands to the south from Lake Mývatn to the north and created the initial conditions for their build up. The river Kráká enters Mývatn just to the east of the Laxá river. Today, Kráká carries a noticeably high suspended sediment load compared to other spring-fed rivers in the region, and locally this has been attributed to the extensive soil erosion on both the eastern side of the river and in the highland desert to the south. An additional source of sediment is where the emerging river erodes the tephra deposits from which it springs. It is not known what the current proportion of the river's sediment load is due to wind erosion of surrounding slopes, erosion of the riverbanks, or erosion of spring portal, nor is it known how these contributions have changed through time, but the lack of channel braiding today and in the recent past indicates that the amount of sediment carried as bed load has always been low. According to local knowledge, the largest amounts of riverbank erosion are connected with rapid melting and breakup of ice on the river. Under normal winter conditions of the late twentieth century, the surface of the river was frozen, and the thickness of ice was sufficient for the river to support motor vehicles. Before the current road system was developed and serviced with snow removal, the frozen river formed a key winter route in the southern part of the Mývatn district, utilized by trucks collecting milk from the farms.

Despite the lack of meanders in the lower reaches, a sign of geomorphological stability, there has been some natural channel change. Around Vörðunes, the channel has encroached upon the wetlands, and in the nineteenth century, a Viking Age burial site was exposed by riverbank erosion. In the upper reaches, changes in fluvial processes have been driven by climate fluctuations, episodic volcanic impacts, and variations in runoff. Here, human impacts have tended to be indirect and generally a result of landscape modifications by grazing domesticated animals to vegetation patterns and soil erosion. The lower reaches are very different as local people have managed the river flow over multigenerational time scales producing long-term change in the wetlands.

The wetland ecosystem formed by the rivers Kráká, Laxá, and Lake Mývatn has international importance, and since 1973 it has been legally protected. In 1978, it was the first site in Iceland to be added to the Ramsar list of wetlands of international importance (https://www.ramsar.org/). In 2011, Mývatn was recommended as a protected World Heritage Site due to its singular geology and biodiversity. While the ecological significance of the area has been the key rationale for its protection, the wetlands exemplify the difficulty in separating ecological conditions from cultural because of the way they have been subject to long-term floodplain management strategies (Ogilvie and Pálsson 2006; Sigurðardóttir et al. 2016).

Catchment Changes After Settlement

Settlers first came to Iceland in the late ninth century in a colonizing effort that is known in Icelandic as *Landnám*, literally "land taking". Although it is no longer regarded as a completely reliable historical account, the *Landnámabók* or *Book of Settlements*, which lists some 400 of the early settlers and their land claims, is still the most important documentary source regarding this settlement. The colonizers found an uninhabited island but soon created a complex cultural landscape in one of the "last settled places on earth" (Vésteinsson and McGovern 2012). The early

Icelanders were already a hybrid society, with a substantial human genetic component coming from Ireland and the northern British Isles, and much of their adaptive tool kit (seabird hunting, use of peat for fuel, turf and stone construction methods) derived from the Celtic North Atlantic island communities to the east (Keller 2010). Some of the chiefly first settlers were probably already Christian (as were their Celtic slaves), and Celtic personal names survived until present in Iceland. However, perhaps most significantly for cultural landscape formation, almost all place names are Nordic, and the elite material culture (as reflected in pagan burials, Vésteinsson and Gestsdóttir 2015) is also Scandinavian in character (Gestsdóttir 2014). The first settlers brought a mix of imported plants and animals widespread in the mixed farming/fishing/marine hunting economies of northwest Europe (cattle, sheep, goats, pigs, horses, dogs, cats, barley, flax, possibly rye) and made use of wild birds, freshwater and marine fish, and sea mammals (Perdikaris and McGovern 2007, 2008). They accidentally imported mice, probably both *Mus musculus* and *Apodemus sylvaticus*, though only *Mus musculus*, the house mouse, is known from archaeological contexts (Jones et al. 2012) and a range of unintentionally introduced weedy plants and insects (Dugmore et al. 2004).

While recent research has revealed a far more complex pattern of short-term and long-term human impact of first settlement in Iceland than assumed by early research (e.g., McGovern et al. 1988, McGovern 1990 vs. Vésteinsson 2014; Dugmore et al. 2014), it remains clear that the introduction of large numbers of herbivorous mammals triggered a shift island-wide from a system generally characterized by more extensive woodlands and low rates of aeolian sediment accumulation (SeAR) to low levels of birch and high SeAR (Streeter et al. 2015). SeAR reflects both local and regional rates of soil erosion, because the wind can effectively mobilize exposed andisols, and erosion proceeds by a loss of area. Soil erosion typically begins with the formation of erosion spots within vegetated areas that grow into deflation patches, and their margins form erosion fronts (rofabards) that then eat into the surviving areas of soils and vegetation; eroded areas expand, and the surviving areas of soil thicken, and SeAR gives a proxy record of soil erosion that can be dated with tephrochronology (Dugmore et al. 2009; Dugmore and Newton 2012).

The timing and pace of this change varied across Iceland. There is evidence of landscape disturbance around the time of settlement (the *Landnám* and V-Sv tephra layers) in many of the soil profiles throughout the Kráká catchment. However, Figs. 3 and 4 show that SeAR, away from the river (i.e. away from the fluvial sedimentation shown in SvGeo1), remained similar to pre-settlement times, although there have been areas where more localized soil erosion occurred. Trees close to settlement sites were rapidly removed, but in areas away from the farms, significant areas of woodland persisted into the fourteenth century. Lawson et al. (2007) found a slow decline in birch between the late ninth century and around 1300. Today woodland survives east of the Kráká catchment on isolated western facing slopes, north of Bláfjall (Fig. 2). In early settlement times, this remnant would have been part of a much more extensive tree cover within the Kráká catchment on well-drained slopes below 400 m. The extensive lava fields of Bláfjall that define the eastern margins of the catchment are, however, not likely to have supported any significant soil or woodland cover. The headwaters of the catchment are also likely to have always had areas lacking in vegetation, but here the early settlers would have also found upland heaths that would have provided rangeland grazing. Across Iceland as a whole, these upland areas were impacted by grazing from early settlement times, and soil erosion soon developed. As they are characterized by shallow pre-settlement soils, this erosion would have produced comparatively limited regional increases in regional SeAR (Fig. 4) but would have impacted the hydrological regime, runoff, and drainage.

More than 30 soil profiles have been dug to establish patterns of SeAR throughout the Kráká catchment (Fig. 2). These reinforce and amplify previous studies in this area (e.g., Einarsson et al. 1988; Sigurgeirsson et al. 2013). Significant changes occurred after AD 1717 where there was a dramatic shift in SeAR across all sites, which is a reflection of a massive increase in soil erosion and the related environmental flux of sediment (Figs. 3 and 4). The deposition of large volumes of tephra to the south of the Kráká catchment, after the Veiðivötn eruptions of 1477 and 1717, would have boosted regional SeAR due to winnowing out of fine-grained sediment from this unconsolidated material. Figures 3 and 4 show that the highest rates of SeAR actually occur post-1717, with the biggest increases seen at Krákábotnar (Fig. 4b) at the headwaters of the Kráká; here SeARs increase 30–40 times the pre-twelfth century rates (0.01–0.02 cm/year to 0.6 cm/year). The profiles further north (Fig. 4a, labelled WSS and H on the map, Fig. 2) show post-1717 SeAR up 20–30 times that of pre- and post-settlement times (0.01–0.02 cm/year to 0.2–0.4 cm/year). Many of the post-1717 profiles contain a very significant proportion of small pumice pieces diffused through the sediment profile, which were remobilized over many decades from the tephra deposits produced from the Askja eruption of 1875, only 40 km south of the source of Kráká.

Soil erosion in Iceland since *Landnám* has been driven by climate changes as well as land management and volcanic impacts (Streeter and Dugmore 2014). Iceland's maritime, subpolar climate has always been characterized by variability, and this was particularly so in the eighteenth century. The early decades of the 1700s were relatively mild in comparison with the very cold 1690s, 1730s, 1740s, and 1750s. The 1760s and 1770s show a return to a milder regime in comparison. The 1780s are likely to have been the coldest decade of the century, but this was compounded by volcanic activity (Ogilvie 1992, 2005, 2010; Ogilvie and Jónsson 2001). There is also evidence of heightened storminess during this period (Dugmore et al. 2007). The variability of the climate is likely to have caused more difficulties than continuous periods of cold and would have depressed biomass production at a time when animals would also have needed to be supported through long winter periods (Simpson et al. 2001). All these elements—humans, climate, and volcanic activity—emphasizes the complexity of factors which have influenced the ecology of the Kráká catchment.

Fig. 3 (continued) Hv tephra is from the eruption of Hverfjall approximately 2500 years ago, and the Hekla 3 tephra was erupted just over 3000 years ago

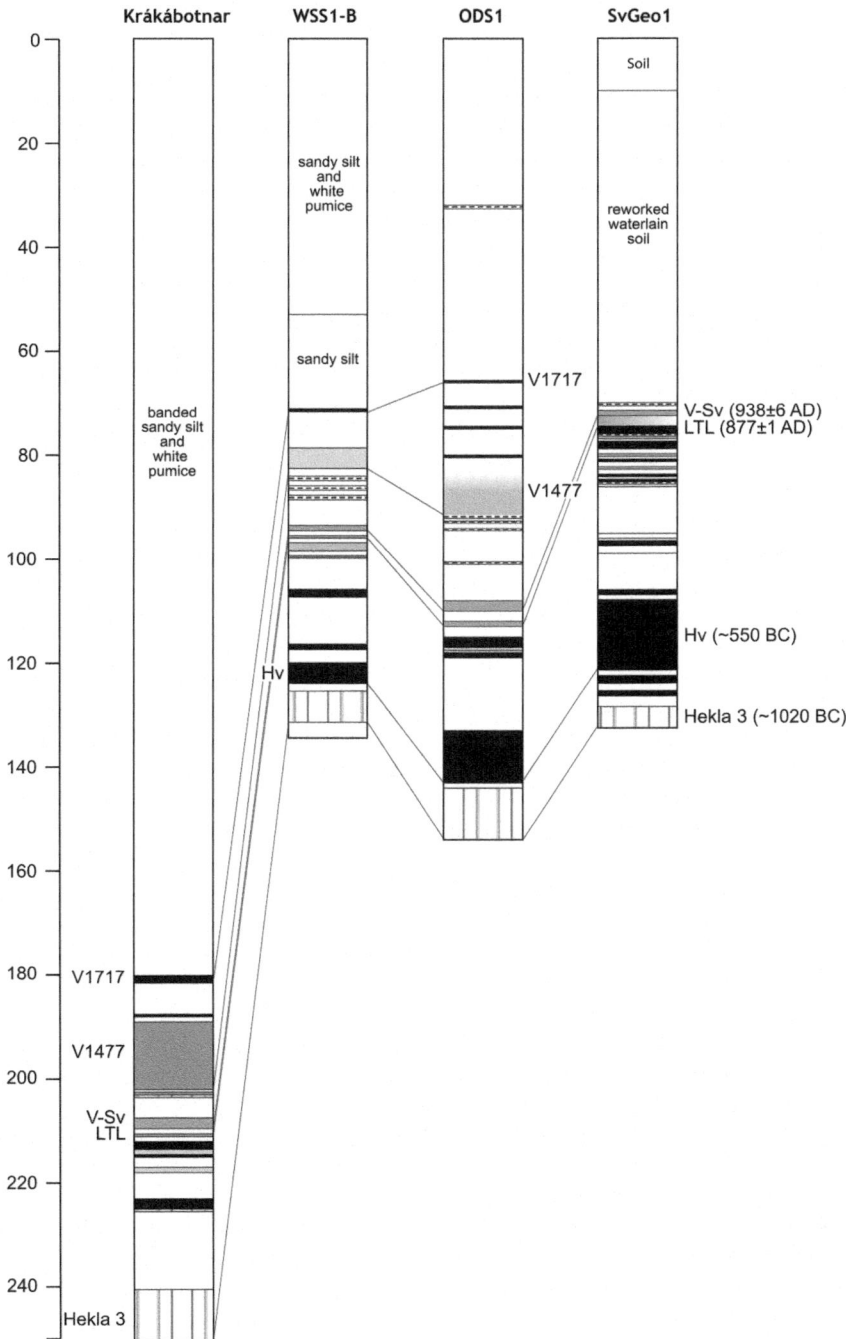

Fig. 3 Four sediment profiles from the headwaters of the Kráká (Krákárbotnar), east of the Kráká (ODS1 at Oddstaðir), to the west of the Kráká (WSS1-B), and the geo-trench at Sveigakot (SvGeo1).

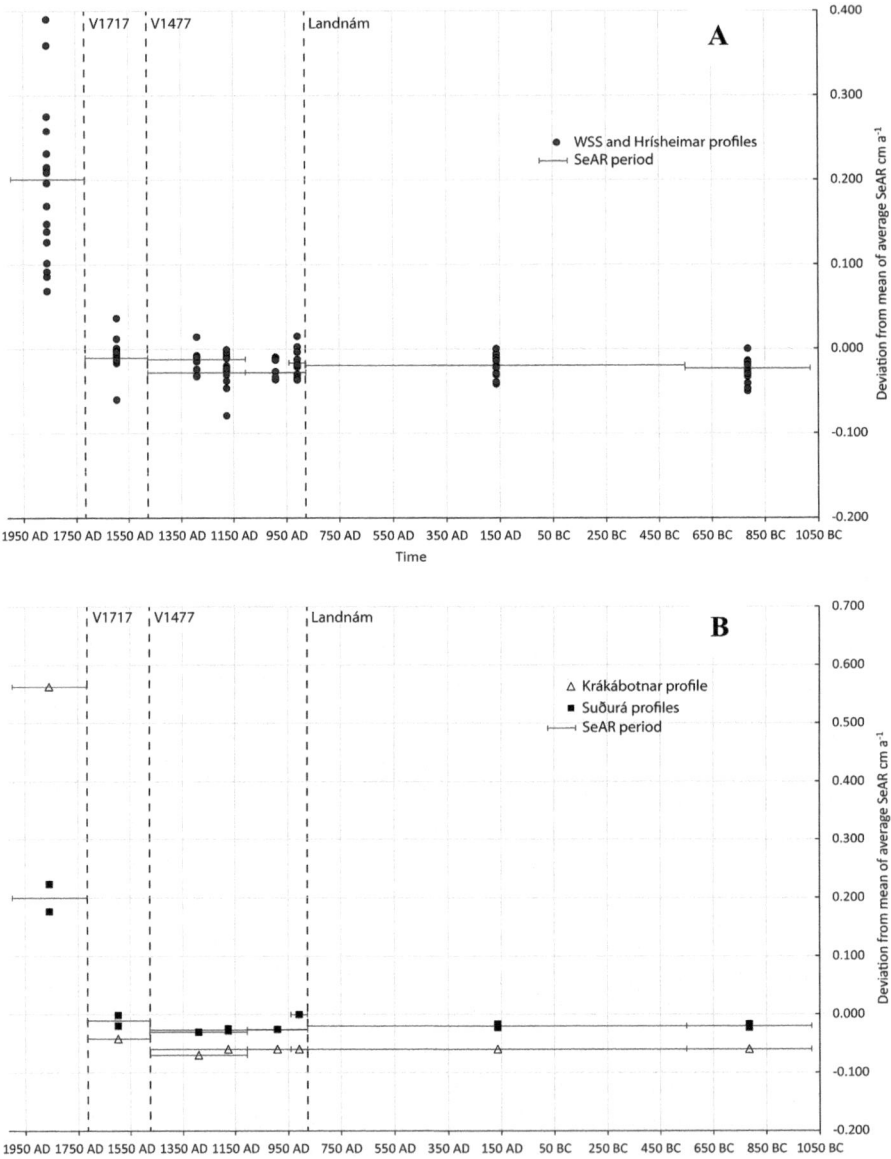

Fig. 4 (a) Deviations from the mean SeAR from profiles in the northern part of the Kráká catchment and to the west of the river. This large number of profiles demonstrates the range of variation there is in SeAR between profiles and how this increases post-1717. (b) Deviations from the mean SeAR from profiles to the south of the Kráká. The highest post-1717 increases in SeAR are found at Krákábotnar, although there is no long-term change after settlement in either Krákábotnar *or* Suðurá profiles. The horizontal lines on the graphs represent the mean SeAR for all profiles for periods defined by tephra layers

Archaeology of the Lake Mývatn Region and the River Kráká Catchment

The archaeological record of the region provides a long-term perspective on settlement and human ecodynamics that effectively complements environmental history, environmental humanities, folklore, and local and traditional knowledge. Archaeological research in the Mývatn region began with the pioneering excavation work of Daniel Bruun and Finnur Jónsson at Hofstaðir in 1908 (Bruun and Jónsson, 1908, 1909, 1910, 1911). The Hofstaðir excavations were remarkable for their era and began a long-standing controversy on the role of pagan temples or temple farms in Nordic archaeology (Roussell 1943; Olsen 1965; Lucas 2009). In 1992 the Mývatn region became the centre of a set of long-running international interdisciplinary collaborative projects led by *Fornleifastofnun Íslands* (the Institute of Archaeology, Iceland) and supported by the North Atlantic Biocultural Organization (NABO) research and education cooperative that continues to the present. (see, e.g. Lawson et al. 2004; Simpson et al. 2004; Price and Gestsdóttir 2006; Thomson and Simpson 2007; Lucas and McGovern 2008; Lucas 2009; Brown 2010; Colquhoun et al., 2010; Hicks 2014; Einarsson 2015; Hicks et al. 2016; McGovern et al. 2006, 2014, 2017; Sigurðardóttir et al. 2016; see also www.nabohome.org). Major excavations at the sites of Hofstaðir, Hrísheimar, Sveigakot, and Skútustaðir, combined with smaller-scale surveys and testing at sites across the lake basin, have produced a fully landscape-scaled perspective on human settlement and land use in this part of Iceland (McGovern et al. 2007, 2017; Vésteinsson 2008). One major finding is the apparently rapid spread of settlement across the basin following the deposit of the Landnám (877 ± 1) tephra layer and before the fall of the V-Sv (938 ± 6) tephra (Sigurgeirsson et al. 2013; Schmid et al. 2017). The unusually complete archaeological record for the Mývatn area indicates that initial Norse settlement in the late ninth century was more of a "torrent than trickle" with a substantial community apparently colonizing multiple sites in both prime farm land and more marginal locations within the first generation of the Icelandic settlement (Vésteinsson and McGovern 2012).

The site of Sveigakot was fully excavated during 1998–2006 and proved to date to the first phase of settlement, with pit houses and associated sheet-midden deposits directly associated with the Landnám (877 ± 1) tephra (Vésteinsson 2008; Batt et al. 2015). This was apparently always a small site and appears to have undergone periods of abandonment and reoccupation, with the last small hall and byre structure being finally abandoned ca. AD 1200. Sveigakot today is located between a barren prehistoric lava field and what is now a dry heath extending westwards to the Kráká river. Both the archaeology teams and local farmers were initially at a loss to explain the attraction of this now long-abandoned site for early settlers. The animal bone collection (archaeofauna) produced from the two major phases at Sveigakot (Phase I ca. 871–938, Phase III ca. 938–1080) may hint at different local conditions in the Viking Age (McGovern et al. 2017). Both phases contain many cattle and pig as well as sheep and goat bones, indicating that this was a small farm rather than a specialized seasonal herding station. Both phases also contain substantial amounts of freshwater fish bones from both Arctic Char (*Salvelinus alpinus*) associated with lakes and ponds, and trout (*Salmo trutta*) usually found in clear streams, and some bones from migratory waterfowl (ducks, geese, divers, grebes) today found nesting closer to the lake and in the *Framengjar* wetlands to the northwest.

In the 2000 season of excavation at Sveigakot, a 10-metre-long geo-trench (SvGeo1—Fig. 3) was dug to the west of the site area by University of Edinburgh geographers Andrew Dugmore and Anthony Newton. This trench revealed that the modern land surface was 1–1.5 m above the medieval ground surface and that multiple layers of water-lain sediment had accumulated before and after the V 1477 tephra fall (Fig. 3). The exact dating of this is not clear, however, but probably reflects a combination of erosion and deposition. In the Viking Age, the Sveigakot site apparently sat upon a low ridge overlooking what was likely to have been an extensive wetland similar to the modern *Framengjar* area with rich grazing and access to freshwater fish and water birds. Today, the ridge in the landscape is in the midst of eroded swaths of land, no longer rich enough to sustain a farmstead, and the Sveigakótot land is used instead for upland summer grazing by the Grænavatn farm closer to the lakeshore. The Sveigakot site thus suggests that major changes in local geomorphology since the Viking Age may have drastically altered the farming potential of this part of the Kráká valley.

On the northern end of the *Framengjar* sits a settlement that experienced none of the depletion that Sveigakot did. Skútustaðir is a long-term higher status farm that seems to have maintained access to resources from the rivers, lake, and *Framengjar* wetland over 1100 years, while later written records indicate it was one of the two most productive farmsteads in its municipality, securing the most hay from the wetlands (Hicks 2014). Additionally, the archaeofauna demonstrates continual access to a diversity of birds' eggs and an abundance of freshwater fish from the lake and rivers (Hicks et al. 2016). Just a few kilometres away from the Sveigakot ruin, Skútustaðir prospered at a safe distance from the eroding southern edge of the settlement. The sustained biodiversity in the Skútustaðir farm environs puts the abandoned southern farmstead of Sveigakot into context as perhaps a risky, short-lived settlement in the volatile environment of the eroding Kráká catchment.

Historical Floodplain Management

The *Framengjar* wetlands have provided key resources for inhabitants of the Lake Mývatn district since the earliest times of settlement. They form the most extensive and productive wetland area in the community, as all other wetlands are small or fragmented or relatively unproductive. Their importance, and the intensity and type of land use, has changed through time, from being harvested for outfield fodder during times of subsistence farming in the area, to becoming a major resource for increased agricultural production in the nineteenth and early twentieth centuries (Hicks et al. 2016), through to being abandoned for fodder production in the mid-twentieth century and to the current use which is solely for grazing. It is of note that when Hjálmar Stefánsson, a legendary poet and fiddler, built the new farm, Vagnbrekka, north of the lake in 1922, there were no meadows or hayfields, and he had to harvest all the hay for his sheep in *Framengjar* (see manuscript sources under National Library, Iceland). Most likely, he transported much of the hay across the lake during the winter.

Historically, significant effort was needed to both maintain and exploit these essential wetlands. The main objectives in managing the productivity of the wetlands were to keep the river flowing in the westernmost channel into river Laxá and to protect the wetlands from both marginal erosion and being smothered by too much sediment. This continued effort is reflected in written accounts (letters and manuscripts), local myths, folktales (notably the story of the troll woman, Kráka), and the traditional ecological knowledge of people in the area. Current local knowledge attributes the destructive forces of the river to climate, such as the mass of snow cover, the frequency and intensity of snow melts, and the amount of ice in the channel prior to the melting event. According to local informants, the winters for the last 30 years have been mild enough for those erosion events to be less frequent and thus the related intensive management of the river to be less important.

It is unclear precisely when people first began to manage the Kráká river and the *Framengjar* floodplain, but some sort of management strategies are likely to have existed from early settlement times. The earliest known Icelandic law texts are known as *Grágás*, literally meaning "Grey Goose", and were formally written down in the years AD 1117–1118 (*Grágás* 2001). They detail the legalities and protocols of moving and managing river systems and waterways in Iceland as a whole (Foote and Wilson 1970). Certain of the *Sagas of Icelanders* (Hreinsson 1997) and the *Sturlunga Sagas* (1970, 1974) mention the permanent re-routing of some river channels, perhaps most famously the alteration of the course of the Öxará, which was diverted to bring freshwater supplies to the assembly area of the Althing at the Thingvellir site and also create the "drowning pool". Later written sources, such as the extremely valuable *Jarðabók*, originally from 1712, a detailed register of land values and human and livestock populations (Magnússon 1913–1943), as well as the rich folklore and myths from the Mývatn area indicate that direct channel management of the Kráká river and the *Framengjar* wetlands has occurred for at least 200 years.

Within living memory, the floodplain wetlands have been managed by making temporary dams in, or on, the banks of the river Kráka. These temporary structures have been used to variously increase or decrease the water level in the wetlands, enrich the wetland soils with mineral nutrients, or minimize the sediment accumulation; they have also served to direct water deeper into the wetlands via a system of artificial channels. The emphasis and intensity of management has varied through time, as the local community responded to environmental changes. Overall, a changing mix of short-term actions have been used to deliver a long-term goal of preventing degradation of the wetland system.

Before the middle of the nineteenth century, the temporary dams used to modify the river Kráká were created by the collective efforts of seven to eight farms that bordered the *Framengjar* wetlands. In the second half of the nineteenth century, more farms from the Lake Mývatn region acquired a stake in the *Framengjar* harvest, and so the number of people involved increased. The damming process was abandoned by most of these farms in the 1970s when mechanized hay harvesting from dry, flattened, fertilized fields became the preferred method of fodder collection in the area. The farm Baldursheimur (B on Fig. 2) continued direct channel management, and a limited amount of river damming happened annually until around 1980, but this intervention ceased completely in the early twenty-first century.

According to the *Jarðabók* (Magnússon 1913–1943), the main management strategy was to keep the river in its western channel by damming its banks to prevent it from flooding into the *Framengjar* or the eastern channels. Also, according to this source, high water levels in the Kráká had the tendency to flood the *Framengjar* wetlands all the way to the lava dam that formed its northern margin. During the winter, these flood waters would freeze over and result in long periods of ice cover across the wetlands which prevented the farmers from using the *Framengjar* for winter grazing. The *Jarðabók* (Magnússon 1913–1943) also describes the major effort involved in the dam making to constrain the Kráká and states that the *Framengjar* wetlands could not have been harvested without this effort. For the farm Sveinströnd, the channel management was particularly time consuming and labour intensive because the largest dam or levee needed to be 40 *faðmar* or fathoms (a fathom is approximately 6 ft or 1.82 m) in length. This was a particularly challenging task given the limited labour available and the demands of other essential tasks. For the farm Arnarvatn, for example, dams and levees were essential to prevent its outfields from being smothered with sand deposits from the river and structures, and channel management had to be renewed or replaced annually using new construction material.

Millennial Management and the Struggle for Sustainability

In the early nineteenth century, as international markets for sheep products developed, the economic focus of the Mývatn district and farmers of the *Framengjar* wetlands changed, and the long effort to manage the Kráká river altered in response to a need to increase fodder production (Hicks 2014; Hicks et al. 2016). Instead of managing the river to limit the flow of water and sediments into the wetlands as had been the practice in the eighteenth century, by the mid-nineteenth century, the managerial aim was to enhance the flow of water into the wetlands and use the sediment load as fertilizer while still keeping the river channel to the western margin of the floodplain. This coincides with the period when severely cold years beginning in the 1850s and culminating in the 1880s increased the need for fodder and reduced the biological productivity of the wetlands through shorter growing seasons (Ponzi 1995; Ogilvie 2010; Sigurðardóttir et al. 2016). Instead of building their temporary dams on the banks of the wetlands to restrict flow, the farmers now needed to invent a way to divert the river itself, which created new challenges. The wetlands became more intensely managed as dykes and waterways were created to enable the water from the river to carry sediment deeper into the wetlands. The construction of these waterways is documented in annual farm reports from the mid-nineteenth century onwards. In the farm evaluation and description *Jarðamat* (1849–1850), river management is noted to be very demanding and costly in terms of labour and the need to maintain extra horses to accomplish the task of dam making. Close cooperation between farms was needed to selectively divert flow into the wetlands. The result was a legal agreement that defined the proportional share or rights each farm had to the river flow, including when the flow could be dammed, and the length of time each farm had a right to keep the dam standing. During the damming period, the water from the river flowed into the waterways/channels in the wetlands. When these occurred close to the bank of the river Kráká, they were closely constrained to prevent uncontrolled flooding from the river.

During the mid-nineteenth century intensification of the use of wetlands, more farms in the district leased or bought the rights to participate in its harvesting. The farm Reykjahlíð, which lies to the northeast of Lake Mývatn, transported outfield hay from the *Framengjar* across the lake during the winter freeze using horse-drawn sledges. The farming account *Jarðamat* (1849–1850) reports that the outfield hay harvest increased from the mid-nineteenth century to 1930, when a collapse in international markets for sheep products hit farming production in the Mývatn district and thus reduced the demand for the *Framengjar* wetland harvest. Although markets recovered, dependence on the wetlands declined through the mid-twentieth century as farms began to rely more heavily on the fodder yield from cultivated hayfields and the use of chemical fertilizers to improve soils and expand dry hayfields in the region.

While river flow was selectively diverted into the wetlands, the main course of the Kráká still needed to be contained in its westerly channel at the south end of the *Framengjar* on the east side of the farm of Grænavatn. This major task needed a collaborative effort. The *Jarðamat* (1849–1850) records that the farm Garður assisted with the necessary construction work in return for the use of some of the wetlands owned by Grænavatn. In addition to labour, substantial amounts of wood, turf, and stone were needed to maintain the Grænavatn dam and keep the main river out of a palaeochannel named Randaskarð. Raw materials included between 50 and 80 horse loads of dry wood per year, equalling around 5000–8000 kg of timber. Birch wood came from the distant slopes of the mountain Bláfjall and was transported about 8 km over a lava field. Willow wood was collected from closer sites in the Sellönd/Sellandasel shieling area. Many large rocks were collected all year round but transported on ice to close to the dam site during the winter. Turf also needed to be transported to the site. The routine, annual renewal of this dam ceased around 1970, and since then infrequent maintenance has been sufficient to prevent the river from changing course into the eastern channels. According to local knowledge, the river has been carrying less sediment than before, the channel has deepened, and there has been limited overbank flow in the upstream reaches. In addition to this, the relatively mild winters during the last 30 to 35 years have decreased the frequency and intensity of winter and spring floods with ice activity.

The Parallel World of Folklore and Myths

Trolls and giants may be said to have been in Iceland at least since the time of the settlement and belong to a great variety of beings that later times have termed "supernatural". In early times, it is likely that people viewed them as being embedded in the natural world and closely connected with natural forces. One of the *Sagas of Icelanders*, *Bárðar saga* ("Bard's Saga") (Hreinsson 1997 II, p. 237–266) may be regarded as a parallel to the *Landnámabók* but concerns the settlement of trolls and giants rather than humans. The settler Bard was described as being descended from the Norwegian giant Dofri (who notably appears in Ibsen's *Peer Gynt*), and his saga describes the settlement of a number of other giants and their society inside certain mountains. Some of these beings were closely and often ambiguously related to humans, for example, in romantic entanglements between an ogress and a male human (Jakobsson 1998–2001). The acceptance of Christianity in Iceland in AD 1000 made life somewhat difficult for many of these beings, as reflected in the words of a man relating his dream in a saga narrative. Just before the arrival of the first Christian missionary to Iceland, Thorhall the Prophet woke up smiling and was asked why he was smiling: "Thorhall answered 'I am smiling because many hills have opened and every living creature, both great and small, is preparing its burden, and making ready to change its abode' And a little later, those events which shall now be related came to pass" (Hreinsson 1997 II, p. 461–462).

Nonetheless, these many different kinds of beings did survive over the centuries, through folklore. However, the folktales concerning them were not formally collected until the nineteenth century. There are, nevertheless, sporadic appearances in earlier sources, not the least the writings of Jón lærði or Jón the Learned (1574–1658). He was a self-educated farmer, fisherman, artist, poet, and writer who fought ghosts by means of sorcery poems and wrote about elves, but he also considered giants who may still be regarded as guardian spirits in his renowned description of Iceland's nature from around 1647:

> In our old Icelandic books of settlement, a lot is written about the country's varied nature, also about the wise, heathen leaders who came here from Halgoland, Finnmark and Gandvík's boundaries while Iceland was being settled, and some came later. Among them were some who learned the giant Dofri's tricks. They knew how to open the earth and rocks, how to close them again, and how to walk in and out as Bárður of the glacier, Hámundur of Hámundur's cave, Bergþór of Bláfell, Ármann of Ármannsfell, and Skeggávaldi, who found the Demon Valleys and became a god there. Thus, the people there pray like this: "Skeggávaldi, shade your country so nobody can find the Valleys of Demons." Such old leaders chose to live in such hideouts, caves or hills, to be free from attacks by the inhabitants of the country. Otherwise they could not be at ease with their magic stones, masses of silver and other metals from the earth, with the good intoxicating grapes, and mineral springs that naïve people have found both in ancient and recent times and which they truly cannot deny. Now the countrymen pay no heed to anything, although there is in many places, here in the ground, plenty of silver, copper, lead, or more kinds of metals, and also sulphur, mercury, enough iron ore, stone coals, lignite, and peat of many kinds, colours and natures, all kinds and varieties of rocks, both hard and soft. (Hermannsson 1924, p. 1–2, translation by Viðar Hreinsson)

Jón lærði's *Natural History* was written as an account of natural resources in the country, in fact among the first such work to be written (Hreinsson 2016, p. 573–609). He also composed *rímur* (long, narrative poems) about one of the guardian spirits he mentions in the *Natural History*, Ármann of Ármannsfell. There he mentions soil erosion in Thingvellir and reveals remarkable ideas concerning the relations between humans and nature, underlining the delicate semantic universe of the giants and nature spirits (Hreinsson 2016, p. 477–488). The troll woman Kráka belongs to this category of trolls or giants, as do an abundance of other nature beings and outlaws in Icelandic folklore, and it may be noted that she is not the only amorous troll woman in Icelandic folktales. There is actually more than one tale of Kráka and other monstrous and evil beings in the Bláfjall mountain, and one of these beings is reported to have killed the shepherd Brandur Andrésson as late as 1755, although the tale was first written down in 1907 (Björnsson 1977, p. 140–144). The sexual craving for mortal men by these creatures reveals ambiguity in the relations between humans and nature, an ongoing struggle between approximation and distance from earth or nature (Lévi-Strauss 1955). Kráka created the river Kráká by using earthly material, wood, stones, and turf. These stories may thus represent a kind of instruction concerning the materials out of which dams could be made and at the same time expressing a kind of ecological anxiety, the fear that the scarcity of these materials would eventually lead to destruction. In general, legends and folktales of this kind invite a variety of interpretations of folklore as traditional ecological knowledge.

The lives of the farmers of the *Framengjar* wetlands have been marked by their struggle with the Kráká river to protect the resources they needed for survival. This struggle is symbolically and expressively reflected in the myth of the troll woman Kráká. Her purpose was to wreak revenge on the human population for resisting her romantic advances and culinary tastes. According to the legend, she created and animated the river to make life difficult for the local people. Having been outwitted by the human population more than once, in a fit of rage, she decreed that the river could not be managed except by using the same materials, trees, turf, and rocks, that she had used to carve a channel for the Kráká river. Her intention was to cut off the farms of its west bank from the *Framengjar*, thus making it more difficult for them to access their outfield hay resources. Her ultimate goal was to destroy all human habitation in the Mývatn community, which she expected to happen when the people finally lost the battle with the river. The challenges involved in the management of the river were thus twofold, relating both to the struggle of people to be able to survive in this system—a challenge of farming in marginal environments with natural processes but also the challenge of not being beaten by the curse of the troll.

Summary and Conclusions

The resource management decisions of the farmers in the Lake Mývatn region show an understanding of ecological processes, as they have effectively maintained the biodiversity and managed the density of plants in the system. Favoured species such as *Carex lyngbyei* have been nurtured and demonstrate a sustainable resource management for an extended period of time (Sigurðardóttir et al. 2016). These management strategies have been adaptive, altering with changes in the character of the river, its catchment, and the technical and economical social structure of the community. The time-consuming, labour-intensive annual management effort needed both significant material resources in the form of wood, stone, and turf and close coordination, and this was sustained through cultural memory and included in myths and tales.

The present wetlands with their internationally recognized conservation significance are a result of a sustained multigenerational management strategy which evolved to meet the changing needs of the community. Over the centuries the overarching aim has been to promote the use of the wetlands to support animal husbandry through fodder production either by minimizing damage to the wetlands or boosting their productivity. In the twentieth century, a very different management strategy for the Kráká waters orientated towards power generation developed, driven by demands from outside the local community. In the 1930s, the power development in Laxá river began with a small hydropower station downstream from Lake Mývatn. During the mid-1960s, much larger plans for a hydropower dam emerged, some of which included re-routing drainage from the highlands to the Kráká River, denuding much of the upper river valley of Laxá, and increasing the water level of Lake Mývatn. These plans created intense local opposition, which culminated in the removal of a dam using stolen explosives. In the wake of this conflict, special conservation laws for the lake and river system were created. In the twenty-first century, tensions resurfaced as the National Power Company and the Icelandic government revisited some of the older plans. The age-old problem of sand carried by the Kráká river re-emerged, but this time not in relation to the management of the wetland biota, but with the desire to minimize wear to the turbines of hydropower stations and to protect the breeding grounds for salmon further downstream. Today, most of these plans have been shelved—at least for the time being. The old friend and foe, the sediments carried by the river Kráká, still affect the decisions and management of the whole river system. Historically, local management of the river Kráká and the *Framengjar* wetlands has managed to boost biomass production and support long-term human settlement while maintaining and promoting ecosystem diversity and stability. Its value for agriculture may have decreased, but its greater value for the community and nature conservation has remained the same and now forms an essential part of the draw for international tourists.

Beyond positioning human triumph against unruly and difficult nature—embodied by the troll woman Kráka—the myth was a device that united people by asserting a common goal in a common landscape. In doing so it transcended the fact of boundaries, private land, and separate households just as the people of Mývatn collectivized their efforts in channelling and distributing the Kráká flow among several wet meadow plots and farms. This relates to another example of commons-making in Mývatnssveit, the 1100-year-old tradition of rule-guided bird hunting and egg collection noted above (Hicks et al. 2016). By this tradition, the people of Mývatn collectively refrained from hunting the tens of thousands of waterfowl that nest and breed in the region and instead only collected the eggs, but also in a specific, limited fashion—usually taking less than half of the eggs in any given nest. Today the Mývatn region is recognized for the biodiversity of waterfowl that nest there; for example, 15 species of ducks regularly breed there, migrating annually from Eurasia and North America. Tourists also flock to see the birds, and so they have become a different kind of economic resource. These examples of long-term commons management in the region demonstrate not simply a mastery of difficult nature; they demonstrate the knowledge, intimacy, and collaboration required to maintain biota, biodiversity, and human livelihood in a potentially vulnerable assemblage.

For centuries, the management of the Kráká river has certainly been the challenge that the disgruntled troll Kráka wanted it to be. Controlling the river was one of the most demanding annual tasks of the farmer, one that could not be shirked and that required communal cooperation. Even when the river was managed, harvesting the wetlands themselves was another major challenge, as the wet fodder needed to be transported from the *Framengjar* over the river Kráká and then dried. In the past, the imperatives and scales of management have been local, but over the last 80 years, this has changed as national attention has been drawn to the potential for energy generation. Large-scale alteration of the rivers and related lake systems through hydropower development would fundamentally alter the ecological and geomorphological characteristics of the system and its landscape and perhaps finally realize the Troll's ambition to destroy the farms along the river.

Acknowledgements This research was made possible by generous grants from the National Geographic Society, the Social Sciences and Humanities Research Council of Canada, the Leverhulme Trust, the Wenner-Gren Foundation for Anthropological Research, the Leifur Eiriksson Fellowship Program, the American Scandinavian Foundation, and the US National Science Foundation (awards: 0732327; 1140106; 1119354; 1203823; 1203268; 1202692; 1249313; 0527732; 0638897; 0629500; 0947862; 1446308). Also funding from RANNIS (Icelandic Research Council award 163133-051) and from Riksbankens Jubileumsfond of Sweden (award P16-0605:1) is gratefully acknowledged. We would also like to extend our warmest thanks to our host communities in Iceland who have supported this work and partnered in the investigation of their own rich heritage as a source for education for sustainability.

References

Manuscript Sources

Jarðamat. (1849–1850). S.- og N.-þingeyjarsýsla. National Archives of Iceland. Available online at https://myndir.handrit.is/doShowDocument.jsp?lang=is&source=ICDB&sourceId=Jar%F0 amat+1849-1850+S-+og+N-%DEingeyjars%FDsla&style=&navpanes=0&view=Fit
National Library. Lbs (the manuscript archives of The National and University Library of Iceland): Not registered: 27. maí 1960. Helgi Jónsson frá Þverá í Dalsmynni.

Published Works

Batt, C. M., Schmid, M. M. E., & Vésteinsson, O. (2015). Constructing chronologies in Viking age Iceland: Increasing dating resolution using Bayesian approaches. *Journal of Archaeological Science, 62*, 164–174.

Benediktsson, J., 1968. Íslendingabók. Landnámabók. Reykjavík: Íslenzk Fornrit I.

Brown, J. L. (2010). *Human responses, resilience and vulnerability: An interdisciplinary approach to understanding past farm success and failure in Mývatnssveit, northern Iceland*. Unðublished PhD thesis, University of Stirling.

Bruun, D., & Jónsson, F. (1908). Kaptajn Daniel Bruuns og Professor Finnur Jónssons Undersøgelser og Udgravninger paa Island 1907-1909. *Geografisk Tidsskrift, 19*, 302–315.

Bruun, D., & Jónsson, F. (1909). Om hove og hovudgravninger paa Island. In *Aarbøger for nordisk Oldkyndighed og Historie* (pp. 245–316). København: I Commission i den Gyldendalske Boghandel.

Bruun, D., & Jónsson, F. (1910). Undersøgelser og Udgravninger paa Island 1907-09. *Geografisk Tidsskrift, 20*, 303–315.

Bruun, D., & Jónsson, F. (1911). Finds and excavations of heathen temples in Iceland. *Saga Book of the Viking Society, 7*, 25–37.

Björnsson, Oddur (1977, 1st edi. 1908) Þjóðtrú og þjóðsagnir. Safnað hefir Oddur Björnsson, Jónas Jónasson frá Hrafnagili bjó undir prentun (Collected by Oddur Björnsson, Jónas Jónasson from Hrafnagil prepared for publication) Bókaforlag Odds Björnssonar (Oddur Björnsson Publishing) Akureyri 1977 [1. edition 1908].

Colquhoun, L., Tisdall, E. Smith, H. & Simpson, I. (2010). *Historical resilience of landcapes to cultural and natural stresses Grænavatn farm estate Mývatnssveit NE Iceland*. Field report to NABO CIE project 2010.

Dugmore, A. J., & Newton, A. (2012). Isochrons and beyond- maximising the use of tephrochronology. *Jökull: The Icelandic Journal of the Earth Sciences, 62*, 39–52.

Dugmore, A. J., Larsen, L., & Newton, A. J. (2004). Tephrochronology and its application to late quaternary environmental reconstruction, with special reference to the North Atlantic islands. In C. E. Buck & A. R. Millard (Eds.), *Tools for constructing chronologies* (pp. 173–188). London: Springer.

Dugmore, A. J., Borthwick, D. M., Church, M. J., Dawson, A., Edwards, K. J., Keller, C., et al. (2007). The role of climate in settlement and landscape change in the North Atlantic islands: An assessment of cumulative deviations in high-resolution proxy climate records. *Human Ecology, 35*(2), 169–178.

Dugmore, A. J., Gísladóttir, G., Simpson, I. A., & Newton, A. J. (2009). Conceptual models of 1,200 years of Icelandic soil erosion reconstructed using tephrochronology. *Journal of the North Atlantic, 2*, 1–18.

Dugmore, A. J., McGovern, T. H., & Streeter, R. (2014). Landscape legacies of Landnám in Iceland: What has happened to the environment as a result of settlement, why did it happen and what have been some of the consequences. In R. Harrison & R. Maher (Eds.), *Long-term human ecodynamics in the North Atlantic: An archaeological study*. Lanham, MD: Lexington Publishers.

Einarsson, Á. (2015). Viking age fences and early settlement dynamics in Iceland. *Journal of the North Atlantic, 27*, 1–21.

Einarsson, Á., Hafliðason, H., & Óskarsson, H. (1988). Mývatn: Saga lífríkis og gjóskutímatal í Syðriflóa. ("Mývatn: palaeolimnology and tephrochronology of the Sydriflói basin"). In *Mývatn Research Station, report no. 4*. Reykjavik: Náttúruverndarráð. 96 pp.

Foote, P., & Wilson, D. M. (1970). *The Viking achievement: The society and culture of early medieval Scandinavia*. London: Sidgwick and Jackson.

Gestsdóttir, H. (2014). Themes in Icelandic bioarchaeological research. In B. O'Donnabhain & M. Lozada (Eds.), *Archaeological human remains. SpringerBriefs in archaeology*. Cham: Springer.

Grágás. (2001). In G. Karlsson, K. Sveinsson, & M. Árnason (Eds.), *Lagasafn íslenska þjóðveldisins*. Reykjavík: Mál og menning.
Hartman, S., Ogilvie, A. E. J., Ingimundarson, J. H., Dugmore, A. J., Hambrecht, G., & McGovern, T. H. (2017). Medieval Iceland, Greenland, and the new human condition: A case study in integrated environmental humanities. *Global and Planetary Change, 156*, 123–139. https://doi.org/10.1016/j.gloplacha.2017.04.007
Hermannsson, H. (1924). Jón Guðmundsson and his natural history of Iceland. In *Islandica* (Vol. XV). Ithaca, NY: Cornell University Library.
Hicks, M. (2014). Losing sleep counting sheep: Early modern dynamics of hazardous husbandry in Mývatn, Iceland. In R. Harrison & R. Maher (Eds.), *Human ecodynamics in the North Atlantic: A collaborative model of humans and nature through space and time*. Lanham, MD: Lexington Publishers.
Hicks, M., Einarsson, Á., Anamthawat-Jónsson, K., Edwald, Á., Friðriksson, A., Þórsson, Æ. Þ., et al. (2016). Community and conservation: Documenting millennial scale sustainable resource use at Lake Mývatn Iceland. In C. Isendahl & D. Stump (Eds.), *Handbook of historical ecology and applied archaeology*. Oxford: Oxford University Press.
Hreinsson, V. (Ed.). (1997). *The sagas of Icelanders, Vols. I–V*. Reykjavik: Leif Eiríksson Press.
Hreinsson, V. (2016). *Jón lærði og náttúrur náttúrunnar*. Reykjavík: Lesstofan.
Jakobsson, Á. (1998–2001). History of the trolls? Barðar saga as an historical narrative. In *Saga-Book* (Vol. XXV, pp. 53–71). London: Viking Society for Northern Research, University College London.
Jones, E. P., Skinisson, K., McGovern, T. H., Gilbert, M. Y. P., Willerslev, E., & Searle, J. B. (2012). Fellow travelers: A concordance of colonization patterns between mice and men in the North Atlantic region. *BMC Evolutionary Biology, 12*, 35.
Keller, C. (2010). Furs, fish and ivory: Medieval Norsemen at the Arctic fringe. *Journal of the North Atlantic, 3*(1), 1–23. https://doi.org/10.3721/037.003.0105
Lawson, I. T., Gathorne-Hardy, F. J., Church, M. J., Einarsson, Á., Edwards, K., Perdikaris, S., et al. (2004). Human impact on freshwater environments in Norse and Early Medieval Mývatnssveit. Iceland. In J. Arneborg & B. Grønnow (Eds.), *Dynamics of northern societies, proceedings of the SILA/NABO conference on Arctic and North Atlantic archaeology 2004* (pp. 375–383). Copenhagen: National Museum of Denmark.
Lawson, I. T., Gathorne-Hardy, F. J., Church, M. J., et al. (2007). Environmental impacts of the Norse settlement: Palaeoenvironmental data from Myvatnssveit, northern Iceland. *Boreas, 36*, 1–19.
Lévi-Strauss, C. (1955). The structural study of myth. *The Journal of American Folklore, 68*(270), 428–444.
Lucas, G. (2009). *Hofstaðir: Excavations of a Viking age feasting hall in north-eastern Iceland* (Institute of Archaeology monograph series – 1) (p. 8). Reykjavik: Fornleifastofnun Íslands.
Lucas, G., & McGovern, T. H. (2008). Bloody slaughter: Ritual decapitation and display at Viking age Hofstaðir N. Iceland. *Journal of European Archaeology, 10*(1), 7–30.
Magnússon, Á. (1913–1943). Jarðabók Árna Magnússonar og Páls Vídalín, I-V, Hinu Íslenska fræðjafjelagi í Kaupmannahöfn (Copenhagen).
McGovern, T. H. (1990). The archaeology of the Norse North Atlantic. *Annual Review of Anthropology, 19*, 331–351.
McGovern, T. H., Bigelow, G. F., Amorosi, T., & Russell, D. (1988). Northern Islands, human error, & environmental degradation: A preliminary model for social and ecological change in the medieval North Atlantic. *Human Ecology, 16*(3), 45–105.
McGovern, T. H., Perdikaris, S., Einarsson, Á., & Sidell, J. (2006). Coastal connections, local fishing, and sustainable egg harvesting, patterns of Viking age inland wild resource use in Mývatn district, northern Iceland. *Environmental Archaeology, 11*(1), 102–128.
McGovern, T. H., Vésteinsson, O., Friðriksson, A., Church, M. J., Lawson, I. T., Simpson, I. A., et al. (2007). Landscapes of settlement in northern Iceland: Historical ecology of human impact and climate fluctuation on the millennial scale. *American Anthropologist, 109*(1), 27–51.

McGovern, T. H., Harrison, R., & Smiarowski, K. (2014). Sorting sheep and goats in medieval Iceland and Greenland: Local subsistence or world system? In R. Harrison & R. Maher (Eds.), *Long-term human ecodynamics in the North Atlantic: An archaeological study*. Lanham, MD: Lexington Publishers.

McGovern, T. H., Smiarowski, K., Hambrecht, G., Brewington, S., Harrison, R., Hicks, M., et al. (2017). Zooarchaeology of the Scandinavian settlements in Iceland and Greenland: Diverging pathways. In *The Oxford handbook of zooarchaeology*. Oxford: Oxford University Press. https://doi.org/10.1093/oxfordhb/9780199686476.013.9

Nordal, S. (1971–1973). *Þjóðsagnabókin Sýnisbók íslenzkra þjóðsagnasafna. Sigurður Nordal tók saman*. Reykjavík: Almenna.

Ogilvie, A. E. J. (1992). Documentary evidence for changes in the climate of Iceland, A.D. 1500 to 1800. In R. S. Bradley & P. D. Jones (Eds.), *Climate Since A. D. 1500* (pp. 92–117). London/New York: Routledge.

Ogilvie, A. E. J. (2001). Climate and farming in northern Iceland, ca. 1700-1850. In I. Sigurðsson & J. Skaptason (Eds.), *Aspects of Arctic and sub-Arctic history* (pp. 289–299). Reykjavík: University of Iceland Press.

Ogilvie, A. E. J. (2005). Local knowledge and travellers' tales: A selection of climatic observations in Iceland. In C. Caseldine, A. Russell, J. Harðardóttir, O. Knudsen, & Jim Rose (Series Editor) (Eds.), *Iceland - modern processes and past environments, developments in quaternary science* (Vol. 5, pp. 257–287). Amsterdam: Elsevier.

Ogilvie, A. E. J. (2010). Historical climatology, *Climatic Change*, and implications for climate science in the 21st century. *Climatic Change, 100*, 33–47.

Ogilvie, A. E. J., & Jónsson, T. (2001). "Little Ice Age" research: A perspective from Iceland. *Climatic Change, 48*, 9–52.

Ogilvie, A. E. J., & Pálsson, G. (2006). Reflections on wetlands in Iceland. In P. Huse (Ed.), *Intimate absence* (pp. 99–101). Høvikodden: Henie Onstad Art Center/Delta Press.

Ogilvie, A. E. J., Sigurðardóttir, R., Júlíusson, Á. D., Hreinsson, V., & Hicks, M. (2015). Climate, grass growth, and hay yield in northeastern Iceland A.D. 1700 to 1950. *Program and Abstracts, 45th International Arctic Workshop, Bergen, Norway, 10–13 May 2015* (pp. 80–81).

Ólafsdóttir, R., & Guðmundsson, H. J. (2002). Holocene land degradation and climatic change in northeastern Iceland. *The Holocene, 12*(2), 159–167.

Olsen, O. (1965). Hørg, hov og kirke. Historiske og arkeologiske vikingetidsstudier. In *Aarbøger for nordisk Oldkyndighed og Historie* (pp. 5–307). København: Kongelige Nordiske Oldskriftselskab.

Perdikaris, S., & McGovern, T. H. (2007). Walrus, cod fish, and chieftains: Intensification in the Norse North Atlantic. In T. L. Thurston & C. T. Fisher (Eds.), *Seeking a richer harvest: The archaeology of subsistence intensification, innovation, and change* (pp. 193–216). New York, NY: Springer.

Perdikaris, S., & McGovern, T. H. (2008). Codfish and kings, seals and subsistence: Norse marine resource use in the North Atlantic. In T. Rick & J. Erlandson (Eds.), *Human impacts on marine environments* (UCLA press historical ecology series) (pp. 157–190). Berkeley, LA: UC Press.

Ponzi, F. (1995). *Ísland fyrir aldamót harðindaárin 1882–1882. Iceland the dire years: 1882–1888. From the photographs and diaries of Maitland James Burnett and Walter H. Trevelyan*. Mossfellsbær: Brennholt.

Price, T., & Gestsdóttir, H. (2006). The first settlers of Iceland: An isotopic approach to colonisation. *Antiquity, 80*(307), 130–144. https://doi.org/10.1017/S0003598X00093315

Roussell, A. (1943). Komparativ avdelning. In M. Stenberger (Ed.), *Forntida gårdar i Island* (pp. 191–223). Copenhagen: Ejnar Munksgaard.

Schmid, M. M. E., Dugmore, A. J., Vésteinsson, O., & Newton, A. J. (2017). Tephra isochrons and chronologies of colonisation. *Quaternary Geochronology, 40*, 56–66.

Sigurðardóttir, R., Ogilvie, A. E. J., Júlíusson, Á. D., Hreinsson, V., & Hicks, M. T. (2016). Water and sustainability in the Lake Mývatn region of Iceland: Historical perspectives and current concerns. In J. F. Shroder & G. B. Greenwood (Eds.), *Mountain ice and water: Investigations of the hydrological cycle in alpine environments* (pp. 155–192). Amsterdam: Elsevier.

Sigurgeirsson, M. Á., Hauptfleisch, U., Newton, A., & Einarsson, Á. (2013). Dating of the Viking Age landnám tephra sequence in Lake Myvatn sediment, North Iceland. *Journal of the North Atlantic, 21*, 1–11.

Simpson, I., Dugmore, A. J., Thomson, A., & Vésteinsson, O. (2001). Crossing the thresholds: Historical patterns of landscape degradation in Iceland. *Catena, 42*, 175–192.

Simpson, I. A., et al. (2004). Assessing the role of winter grazing in historic land degradation in Myvatnssveit, Northeast Iceland. *Geoarchaeology, 19*(5), 151–168.

Streeter, R. T., & Dugmore, A. J. (2014). Late-Holocene land surface change in a coupled social-ecological system, southern Iceland: A cross-scale tephrochronology approach. *Quaternary Science Reviews, 86*, 99–114.

Streeter, R., Dugmore, A. J., Lawson, I. T., Erlendsson, E., & Edwards, K. J. (2015). The onset of the palaeoanthropocene in Iceland: Changes in complex natural systems. *The Holocene, 25*(10), 1662–1675.

Sturlunga Saga I-II. (1970, 1974). *The library of Scandinavian literature* (Vols. 9–10, translated from the old Icelandic by McGrew, J. H. & Thomas, R.). New York, NY: Twayne Publishers.

Thomson, A. M., & Simpson, I. A. (2007). Modeling historic rangeland management and grazing pressures in lanscapes of settlement. *Human Ecology, 35*(2), 151–168.

Vésteinsson, O. (2008). *Archaeological investigations in Mývatnssveit*. Reykjavík: Fornleifastofnun Íslands, FS386-02263.

Vésteinsson, O. (2014). Shopping for identities: Norse and Christian in the Viking Age North Atlantic. In I. Garipzanov & R. Bonté (Eds.), *Conversion and identity in the Viking Age, MISCS 5* (pp. 75–91). Turnhout: Brepols.

Vésteinsson, O., & Gestdóttir, H. (2015). The colonization of Iceland in light of isotope analyses. Viking settlers of the North Atlantic: An isotopic approach. T. Douglas Price. *Journal of the North Atlantic, 7*, 137–145.

Vésteinsson, O., & McGovern, T. H. (2012). The peopling of Iceland. *Norwegian Archaeological Review, 45*, 206–218. https://doi.org/10.1080/00293652.2012.721792

The Organizational Scheme of High-Altitude Summer Pastures: The Dialectics of Conflict and Cooperation

Ludomir R. Lozny

In Brief

When I observed the use of water by the San of the Kalahari Desert, or native groups of the American Southwest, I wondered how they regulate access to this scarce resource in a highly arid environment. In one case, access seems to be open while in the other communally controlled. In neither case, however, the local users attempted to enclose such highly demanded and critical to local wellbeing resource in order to exclude others and profit from restricting access to its potential users. This observation invoked several questions. Is controlling access to a vital resource the best strategy to use such resource? If yes, how should its control be designed? In fact, in both cases people control access to water. The Kalahari San's approach is regulated by their indigenous knowledge[1] based on such observable and fully comprehended factors as seasonality, distance to waterholes, density of human groups, oral history, human physiology, etc. Despite the source being open, access to it is not institutionalized but regimented, and the two key rules of use are clear: share and do not overuse. The communally controlled system of the American Southwest is more rigid, regulated by folkways and customs. Neither is centrally controlled or privately owned. The high cost of its defendability demands community-controlled access.

---

[1] Indigenous knowledge (IK) has been recognized as a source of ideas that should be included in all programs dealing with resource management (see the contributions in Sillitoe 2017) and environmental stewardship. It contributes, among other things, to promoting sustainable practices in resource use and to outline an agenda for future work.

I dedicate this paper to the memory of Stéphane Lévêque, a Parisian who loved the Pyrenees, the feeling I share.

L. R. Lozny (✉)
Hunter College, CUNY, New York, NY, USA
e-mail: llozny@hunter.cuny.edu

No exclusion of others applies. What are the political and economic gains behind such arrangements? Private controllers might initially benefit, but overtime problems will rise. The controlled will not likely engage in reciprocal relationship, instead would try to regain access to the resource. Escalation of conflict becomes inevitable. On the other hand, there are strong economic incentives that favor sharing (community-controlled use). In the Kalahari Desert, people share waterholes with animals, which are significant part of their subsistence. Different groups interact at several levels: social, by engaging in interpersonal relations including exchange of mates, and political, by ensuring amicable intergroup relationship. Sharing thus is not a gesture of goodwill; it becomes an agreed form of control, premeditated strategy to ensure social sustainability and to minimize risk.[2]

Here I discuss managerial rationale represented by institutions[3] for collective actions under specific ecological conditions. Private ownership arrangements are, logically, not institutionalized. I discuss specific regulations designed to control access to scarce resources for all interested. The significance of the existence of institutionalized collective access to commons, as oppose to open access, is in the fact that regulations in principle mitigate overuse and depletion of the resource, although a level of free riding should always be anticipated. Collectivization may produce severe economic and political repercussions as such rules hinder economic growth and obscure political competition. Nevertheless, some authors argue (for instance, Bollier 2017) that the commons paradigm will replace the traditional economic thinking whether left or right. Current climate changes impact natural resources critical to human wellbeing such as land, water, air, etc., and we must learn how to manage these scarce resources to avoid (unavoidable) conflicts.

I focus on a case of rational cooperation under forced conditions to share a limited resource, high-altitude pastures. In my attempt, I subscribe to a softer version of Hobbes' view to suggest that people engage in cooperation due to rational self-interest. Rational cooperation is not morally motivated; it is based on economic calculations (sort of cost-effect approach). Simply put, people do not need to be nice to each other to engage in rational cooperation.

Historically, the Pyrenean valleys comprised independent political and economic territorial units with their own rules to manage pastures. Differences in high-altitude architecture and other characteristics of pastoral lifestyle exist from valley to valley, and each is represented by idiosyncratic cultural signature to identify the "ownership" or rights to use high-altitude pastures. Localized diversities in transhumance-related material culture and social arrangements to use high-altitude pastures have been noticed in medieval texts. Access to pastures and their use was traditionally organized and managed in a collective/cooperative manner that persisted for hundreds of years until present. The current fast-paced socioeconomic changes cause serious threats to local sustainable development and wellbeing. Centralization of decision-making weakens communal cooperatives and contributes to local economic

---

[2] Empirical studies show that people display cognitive capacity for cooperation (Brosnan et al. 2010; Gärdenfors 2012).

[3] Institutionalization of commons means that resources are managed in organized manner and controlled by a collective body such as village board, etc.

and social crisis. Participatory, polycentric scheme of governance of scarce resources seems a viable alternative. I thus briefly theorize on the relevance of a bifurcated governance system to regulate access to scarce resources in complex, (post)industrial societies: centralized and local.

Historical Context[4]

This chapter is, among others, about durability of traditional boundaries and identities defined by the jurisdictional limits of villages, customs, and traditions still followed despite the current political context. The Treaty of the Pyrenees of 1659 (Sahlins 1991) defined the mountains as the administrative division between France and Spain, but did not define a clear boundary. It was established after 1866 (Treaty of Bayonne of 26 May 1866). The political split into two nations artificially divided the common culture of the Pyrenean communities. Such administrative division, however, did not affect the practice of sharing high-altitude pastures, coded in local customs and traditions through language.

In this section, I briefly review the historical evidence of conflicts, some of which endured into the twentieth century. These historical events confirm perennial conflict conditions between owners and users of pastures and other critical resources.

In 850, the first count of Bigorre created the baronetcy of Tourmalet (high mountain zone) at the upstream end of the Campan Valley and gave it to the town of Tarbes, thus inducing, for centuries to come, a long series of lawsuits for the possession and/or usage of forests and grazing lands. In 1328, a conflict arose between the Campan people and the Lord of Asté concerning primarily the access to mountain summer pasture areas. This dispute came to an end in 1950. In 1524, the monks of the Escaladieu donated some of their land in Cabadur to the communities of Campan and Cieutat. This donation instituted an interweaving of terrains that became a source of conflict. In 1602, people from Campan demolished huts of the shepherds from Ancizan and slit the throats of their ewes. In 1610, a conflict concerning the passage of herds was mediated by the Lord of Beaudéan. In 1615, the consuls of Campan imprisoned a resident for nine days for constructing a hut without authorization. In 1628, Campan and Asté sealed an agreement stipulating the rights of herd passage. In 1737, about 100 armed people from Campan stopped the passage of livestock from Bagnères toward the mountain summer pastures in Arizes, which belonged to the people of Bagnèrais. In 1739, more problems regarding hospitality, threats, and improper treatment of people from Campan against foreign shepherds erupted. In 1761, after a violent brawl between shepherds from Cieutat and Campan, two people from Campan were killed. In the nineteenth and twentieth centuries, these conflicts continued, although in a more legal context. In the early 2000s, yet another dispute occurred on the public forum with regard to a pasture of which Campan claimed full and complete ownership, whereas three nearby villages

---
[4] For detailed historical data, see Lévêque (2013), who also provides literature on the subject.

claimed joint ownership shared by them and Campan. Each side used historic texts in an attempt to prove its rights, and the dispute has not been resolved yet.

These events, and the list is much longer, show the scale of tensions that existed with regard to access and use of high-altitude summer pasture. The tensions are strong because many summer pastures, are communally owned by villages located at the foot of the mountain and even in the lowland, and some areas have been "conquered" by the Aurois, the Barègeois, and certain communities in the Argelès Valley.

Data

The history of the communal (collective) use of high-altitude pastures in the Hautes-Pyrenees is supported by the ethnographic (landscape archaeology), linguistic, and historic data.

Although historically each big valley was a separate political and economic unit, all were linked through an exchange network with big towns located at the opening of large valleys to lowlands, where regional market places were located (for instance, Aucun, Argelès-Gazost, and Lourdes, the biggest towns of Val d'Azun, my project area) (Fig. 1).

Presently, pastures in the Labas Valley, Bouleste, and Les Artigues (Fig. 2) are not in danger of immediate human-related alterations. They are not going to be converted to a peripheral urban zone with secondary residential homes, as many other regions in the Pyrenees, because they are located in the created in 1967 National Park of the Pyrenees (Parc National des Pyrénées) and therefore offer access to a fairly preserved cultural landscape. By contrast, regions neighboring the project area face the consequences of enduring and fast-moving socioeconomic processes, including industrialization and depopulation (due to out-migration), posing serious threats to local sustainable development and wellbeing.

Transhumance is still of critical importance to Pyrenean herders as taking the animals to higher elevations for 4–5 months allows for preparation of hay and forage for the winter. In some provinces up to 50% of farms still practice transhumance (Fig. 3). In 2006, herders of the eastern Pyrenees had moved 18,000 sheep between the summer and winter pastures. The agropastoral system still accounts for a sizable local job market (25–30%).

Currently, the rules regulating access to high-altitude pastures vary, but in most cases the grazing lands are owned [used] collectively either publicly (open access) or by group of owners (cooperatives), and the users [participants] pay an amount per head for the livestock they graze. Besides its obvious economic significance, transhumance also serves as a form of displaying prestige and reputation. Recently, the region is also a scene of conflict between traditionalists and progressivists epitomized in the decline of the traditional transhumance-based culture and the emergence of a new, service-oriented postindustrial economy with tourism being its most significant local component.

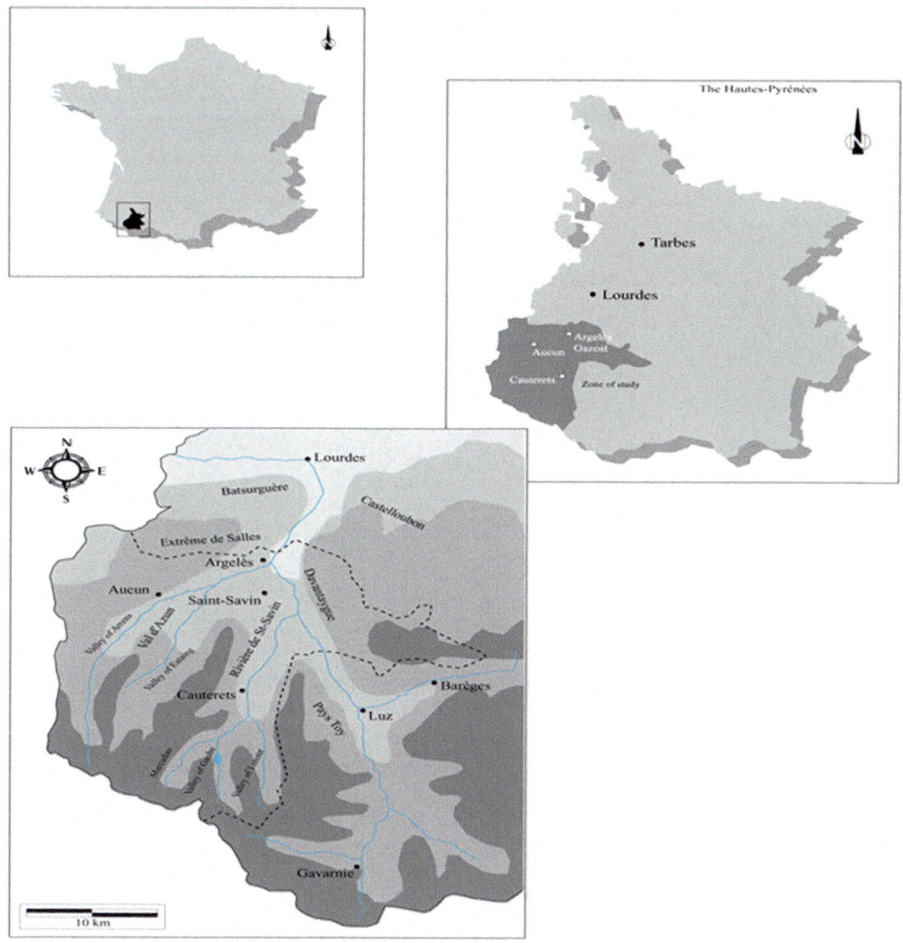

Fig. 1 Project area

Toponymy Related to High-Altitude Commons

The Pyrenees do not constitute a boundary. They are a frontier, permeable zone that separates two nations but unites mountain communities that speak common to a larger region Occitan language and its Pyrenean dialects (Edelmayer 2012). This unification is laid out by the rules to collectively manage high-altitude pastures. Villagers on both sides of the modern nation-state border still respect and follow those historical rules. They graze their livestock in communal pastures, access to which is coded through the local language. Here are some examples:

Cuyéou—this term is widely present in the toponymy of the study area. It is the equivalent of *cuyéla* in Aspois, of *cujala* in the Ossau dialect, or of *courtau* from the valley of Adour (Figs. 4 and 5). It appears in historic texts of the eleventh century

Fig. 2 Pastures: (**a**, **b**) Bouleste and (**c**, **d**) Les Artigues. Photo L. Lozny

Fig. 3 Bouleste, modern shepherd. Photo L. Lozny

Fig. 4 Les Artigues, two structures (*courteous*). Photo L. Lozny

Fig. 5 Les Artigues, *courtau*. Photo L. Lozny

and in the thirteenth century, as evidenced by the 1290 settlement regarding a tract of land in the Cauterets Valley. It is presently used in Val d'Azun and Cauterets, but in Davantaygue, this term has been used interchangeably with *cuyéla* since the fourteenth century and with *courtau* for about the same time. In fact, it would seem that all these terms are interchangeable even if the last two are used jointly in the context of high-elevation pastures.

What the word means precisely remains debatable. Overall it appears that the *cuyéou* designates a hut and its immediate surroundings with enclosed areas for livestock, but also a part of the mountain and pasture in which these various structures are established. The award of 1290 lists 37 *cuyéous* in Cauterets and other areas. Thus, *cuyéou/cuyela/courtau* define a space where essential pastoral activities, including corralling, were conducted. When the historic writers designated huts to shepherds, they often used just the word "hut," (*acabanar*), whereas *cuyéla* was used in the context when livestock was present. In the settlement of 1301 concerning the forests above Saint-Pastous, the right to "make a hut" is clearly pointed out in such meaning as well as the need for the livestock to stay in the *cuyéla*. Thus, multiple huts, and of course multiple shepherds, may be present in the same *cuyéou*, sometimes with a number of enclosures and associated structures. In an assessment of 1533 concerning Houscaou Mountain in Davantaygue, it has been established that this mountain consists of several *courteous*, two of which, the Lhens and Tournaboup *courteous*, were used by at least four communities. In the Napoleonic cadaster concerning the mountain summer pastures in Cot de Bo at Villelongue, the *cuyéou* contains from two to five huts and that corresponds to "partitioning" of this mountain first mentioned around 870 in the assessment of the properties belonging to the abbey at Saint-Orens.

Communal spatial arrangements are known in Ossau, where, since the late fourteenth or early fifteenth centuries, the Jurade has been setting up a distribution of pastures into three Toques, which are themselves divided into 14 *cujalas*. The Souletine Mountain is divided into numerous *cayolards* (about 60), which have the same number of pastoral units shared by several livestock keepers. In Ariège and up to Catalogne, the term *orri* designates a space[5] that is intended for the corralling of ovine, as well as an area of the pasture that may contain several *barracas*. Thus, *cuyéou/cuyela/courtau* identifies a spatial unit defined by a distribution of structures. In fact, these terms identify a mountain district.

Formadgere is translated as "dairy" or "cheese maker." A 1384 document mentions systematic levying of cheeses per *formadgere* located in summer pastures of the Davantaygue and Castelloubon. Sometimes, as presented in a document form in 1612, the levying has been done by huts. In all cases, however, several shepherds appear to have been able to use the same *formadgere*. *Formadgere* could also involve structures intended to accommodate men and herds and focused on the production of chesses as well as their temporary storage. Therefore, the term incorporates one or more huts and all related structures such as *leytés* (Fig. 6). In this context, it can

---

[5] Presently it also means dry-stone hut.

also be a term that is interchangeable with that of the *cuyéou* but with a marked specialization (the *cuyéou* where cheese is manufactured).

Dairies did not have the same status; some belonged to single families while others were communal. A document from 1339 states that communal dairies were managed by religious or military authorities and certain communities; local lords could have also managed them although under certain conditions. The same document also states that a *formadgere* consists of livestock belonging to a single owner, whereas the communal dairy includes mixed livestock, local and foreign. Thus, *formadgere* might also indicate a herd of dairy animals. The term is not easy to pin down, but it mostly relates to a fiscal unit at the base of the levying manorial system (*casadure*).

The survey of the Labas Valley revealed 44 structures, material correlates of the cultural codes how to use and manage hight altitude pastures, which I discuss in the next section. Generally, the structures are of three functions:

- Human shelters related to transhumance
- Animal enclosures (sheep and cattle)
- Pastoral amenities, *leytés*

Human shelters are of three different types:

- Small, single-person shelters
- Cabanas
- Human shelters constructed around erratic boulders or toues

Fig. 6 Les Artigues, *leyté*. Photo L. Lozny

One *cabana* may have been occupied by five to six men (Figs. 7 and 8). The effort put in the construction of such structures in comparison with other structures where opportunistic economic behavior is clearly represented (structures with erratic boulders or *toues*) suggests that they represent a significant group effort in both construction and maintenance and therefore correspond to the communal organization of animal husbandry and the use of high-altitude pastures.

Leytés are constructions built over a source of water (spring, stream, etc.) (Fig. 6), or a diverted stream, and used to keep milk fresh. Generally small, but some can reach respectable dimensions (more than 1m high), and made of dry-stone walls, sometimes with great care, located alone or in groups. They are often present in Azun and also in the Cauterets Valley, where they are called *cabanère* or simply *houn* (spring). Single *leyté* could also be used as a cheese-salting tub associated mostly with the ovine but also mixed livestock.

Structural Elements of the High-Altitude Commons

Spatial analysis of all structures ($N = 44$) reveals grouping in three clusters (Figs. 9 and 10):

Fig. 7 Les Artigues, remains of *cabana*. Photo L. Lozny

The Organizational Scheme of High-Altitude Summer Pastures: The Dialectics… 113

Fig. 8 Bouleste, modern *cabana* and remains of *courteous*. Photo L. Lozny

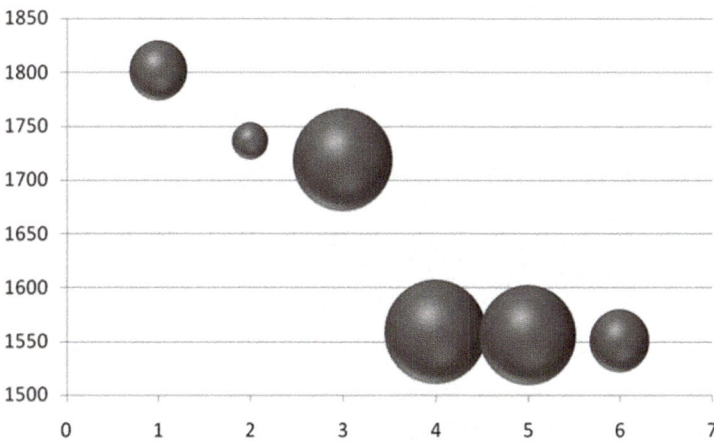

Fig. 9 Six large-area structures: 200 m² at 1801 m (Upper Bouleste); 77 m² and 600 m² between 1700 m and 1750 m (Bouleste); 620 m², 560 m², and 221 m² at or above 1550 m (Les Artigues). All represent courteous and the three from les Artigues also formadgeres

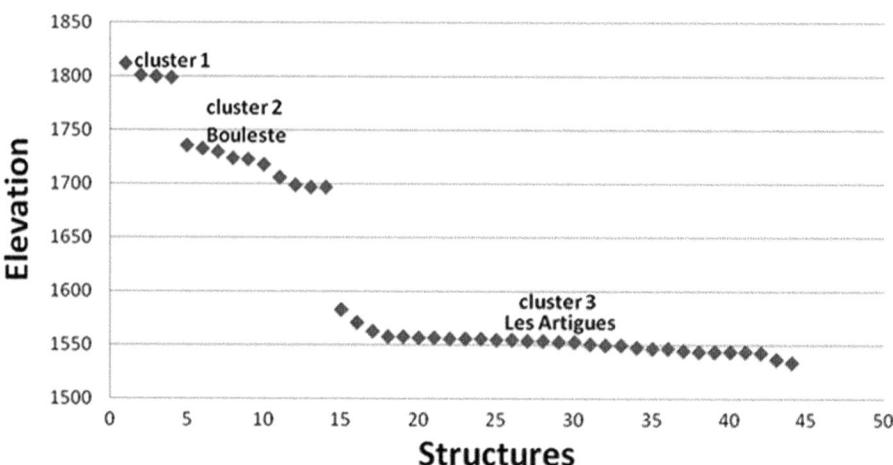

Fig. 10 Three clusters of structures ($N = 44$) starting from the highest elevation to the lowest: cluster 1, Upper Bouleste cluster consists of 4 structures; cluster 2, the Bouleste plateau consists of 10 structures; cluster 3, Les Artigues consists of 30 structures. Each cluster is composed of structures of different sizes, complexities, and functions

- Cluster 1, elevation 1812–1799 masl, ~2.5 ha, Upper Bouleste, consists of four structures
- Cluster 2, Bouleste, elevation 1736–1697 masl, ~10 ha, consists of ten structures
- Cluster 3, Les Artigues, elevation 1583–1534 masl, ~28 ha, consists of 30 structures

Large-Area Structures (Six)

Six structures represent large-area structures, ranging from 77 to 620 m^2. One, 200 m^2 is at 1801 m (above Bouleste); two, 77 m^2 and 600 m^2 are between 1700 m and 1750 m (Bouleste); and three, 620 m^2, 560 m^2, and 221 m^2 are at almost the same elevation at or above 1550 m (Les Artigues). Large structures are also present in cluster 2 (Bouleste) and cluster 3 (one is over 200 m^2). The large-area structures probably represent local communal (cooperative) arrangements to use the commons. Whether they represent different chronological phases or communities will be determined in the upcoming research.

Discussion

Collective use of high-altitude pastures has been confirmed by the medieval sources for the Alps and currently researched by Robert McC. Netting, Elinor Ostrom, and others. As discussed above, the Pyrenean high-altitude summer pastures represent a territorial resource that is indispensable for the survival of human groups who practice animal husbandry, which appears to be the best adaptational choice under local ecological conditions. Its primary and secondary products (meat, wool, leather, milk, butter, and cheese) comprise an exchange currency that allows for compensation of the deficit in cereal grains. Through another of its products, animal droppings, animal husbandry is essential to the improvement of high-altitude soils and flora.

The Pyrenean pastures have traditionally been used and managed in a collective/cooperative manner. The Basques created cooperative neighborhood work parties (*auzolan*), and resilience of such management pattern suggests its significant contribution to sustainable existence and wellbeing. Meredith Welch-Devine (2010, p. 44) described the ownership structure for the Basque in Xiberoa and pointed out that the common-pool grazing lands are collectively owned and open to all the residence and animal risers in the province.

In the Hautes-Pyrenees, the idea of the commons is represented in vernacular terms such as *cuyéou cuyéla*, *courtau*, *courteous*, etc. identifiable in local toponymy. Some of the Pyrenean common property regimes date to the Middle Ages (such as Basque Coutume de Soule). The French law of 1837 authorized the creation of syndicates to facilitate inter-communal cooperation and to manage the common-pool resources owned by multiple communes.

The organization of the commons of the Pyrenees contributed to the emergence of special conditions to regulate inter- and intragroup interactions and to diffuse conflicts. Recently introduced changes in herd management and the use of common-pool resources are mostly caused by local factors (family disputes) and national and supranational policies, such as Natura 2000. Disputes and local conflicts regarding grazing lands have been traditionally mitigated by, for instance, cross-boundary treaties (*facerías*), transborder agreements called *lies* and *passerines* in Hautes-Pyrenees, and arbitration by the pasture police (institution in decline) and mediation, as evidence in the Aragon Pyrenees (Carbonell 2010, pp. 76–78).

The Labas Valley is a good example of enduring common property regimes which date to the Middle Ages and are well-structured through the established rules. The rules are based on customs, norms, and traditions which regulate access to resources and also sanction abusers. Common property regimes thus provide a framework for social organization and interactions, and their governing bodies, such as the *Cour Générale* of the Basque region of the Kingdom of Navarre, which seemed an incipient democratic institution (Murray 2010, p. 31), gain power to organize larger groups. Management of common-pool resources might be organized in a complex structure with cooperating villages, clans, families, or other groups requesting access to summer pastures in high altitudes. Rules of cooperation involve payments or various reciprocal arrangements. Although Pyrenean transhumance alters local biodiversity, it remains significant to the livelihood of people and their cultural identity. In their effort to manage common resources, diverse groups create common identity, which signifies more than just a community of practice. Its importance declined recently due to policies imposed through centralized decision-making by the French government and the EU. The point exemplified by the modern history of the Pyrenean transhumance is that the increase of centralization in decision-making weakens communal cooperative organizations by imposing new rules and enforcing these rules through governmental agencies. Such political activities contribute in effect to local, social, and economic crisis but not necessarily to governmental crisis.

Certain terms of the local language and its dialects still used by local residents point out to the collective arrangements in the use high-altitude pastures and to the fact that their cultural [social] designation change over time. *Cuyéou* or *couéyla* or *cujala* and *cortau* are vernacular designations of not well-defined territorial units, which changed as new arrangements to use high-altitude pastures are made in the village or among villages (which may also include linguistic change as terms for territorial units change from valley to valley). They represent places with new physical provisions and filled with new meanings as people see fit at the time. For instance, *courtau*, which in fact is a territorial district without well-defined boundaries, may change depending on such social arrangements. The district typically incorporates a *cabana* and animal enclosures but also immediate pasture. Several cabanas and shepherds might use the same territorial unit such as *cuyéla*, as recorded in some cadasters, where a *cuyéou*, another term for territorial unit, includes two to five cabanas. Above the beech grove zone, there are summer shelters that are locally called *courteous*, sometimes gallicized to *curtail*. Local terms used to describe mountain summer pasture shelters vary depending on the Pyrenean region. From east to west, we find terms such as *jasse*, *orry*, *courtaou*, *cujala*, and *cayolar*. Depending on the valley, these terms may have slightly different meanings.

The name *courtaous*, used in the Haut-Adour (i.e., in Campan and Lesponne) for pastoral shelters in summer pastures, implies the idea of an enclosure, a primordial component of mountain pastoralism, but also suggests the social and economic organization. *Courtaous* are located in high-altitude areas above 1200/1300 m and can be defined as groups of pastoral exploitation units of summer pastures. One of the particularities of the huts from the Haut-Adour as compared to neighboring valleys lies in the fact that the summer pasture huts constitute a family asset. Each house in the valley is inseparable from its barns and from its high-altitude hut. On the other hand, the areas of summer pasture are collective assets. However, it appears that a part of the summer pastures located in the geographic area of one valley belongs to outside communities. Such is the case in Campan and Lesponne where villages and even a city in the lowland or piedmont are either specific or undivided owners of high-altitude summer pastures. In such cases, the use of pastures was and still remains subject (for herds that were foreign to the valley and whose masters did not have their own high-altitude grasslands) to a fee payable either for single livestock, or by *baccade* a group of ten heads of large livestock or 20 heads of small livestock. The construction and occupation of the mountain hut by the inhabitants from the valley and others were also subject to taxation.

In the Napoleonic land registry carried out in 1825 in Campan, all of the *courtaous* that existed at the time were indicated there. Each hut is represented by a small red rectangle to which a parcel number is assigned. No associated structures were mentioned, which is confirmed by the matrix accounting for only the surface area of the huts. However, and very curiously, the huts were assigned a surface area that is most often 24 m^2, more rarely 20 m^2 or 18 m^2. A few surface areas may be larger or smaller. It appears that these huts, or more frequently their ruins, have a surface area that is often less than the one indicated above. It is probable, but still needs to be verified, that the mapped surface is a fictional surface area that refers to a different method of formation than the actual surface of the hut.

The economic significance of summer pastures relies in the possibility of having access to vast pastures in the mountain hay meadows, necessary for obtaining winter forage and temporarily ease the animal feeding pressure. Access to pastures appears, therefore, in the history of the Pyrenean populations as determining element in their survival, and the existing archives constantly refer to endless conflicts and disputes that result from the use of the high-altitude grasslands. In fact, the story of the Pyrenean valleys is inseparable from the many disputes associated with the possession or the use of summer pastures. These conflicts, which sometimes appear as legal battles and sometimes take a form that could, without exaggeration, qualify as warfare, and occasionally become both, seem to have been continuous and are documented as far back as the oldest archives go, i.e., around the twelfth century. The permanence, multiplicity, and intensity of these conflicts confirm that the mountain summer pastures represent a vital economic domain. It is essential, therefore, to allow livestock to feed there, and in practice it does not matter much whether the access is controlled by full ownership of the pasture or simply by possessing the right to use it; this latter appears to be a means that allows the owner to limit free availability of his assets. The main cause of these conflicts concerning the use of mountain summer pastures should certainly find its origin in demographic pressures, which consequently induced an increase of livestock in relation to pasture areas, which are not extensible despite, in some cases, deforestations for the creation of high-altitude clearings which were turned to pastures. There was, of course, a time when such demographic pressure did not exist. However, a few valley communities had more mountain summer pasture space than they needed. In these favorable situations, some of the high-altitude grazing lands have been rented out to villages at the foot of the mountain, or in the lowland, or to Spanish communities. These "rentals" allowed the beneficiary community to take advantage of additional resources, but also caused conflict. Such strong and constant tensions regarding the use of territories that are, a priori, hostile to human occupation indisputably indicate the vital importance that they represent for the local populations.

Irrigation projects in form of canals in Campan Valley are another example of collective arrangements. These canals, which are shallow and about 0.60 m wide, are sometimes more than 16 km long. They start in a torrent that is sometimes at more than 1500 m elevation. Their function is to bring water to the base of the valley for irrigation of arable areas that have no aquatic resources. The management of these canals has given rise to an original system with communal stewards who were responsible for controlling that everyone respects their irrigation time as the users frequently violated the scheduling. The same canals, sometimes supported by specific constructions, were used to bring manure mixed with water down from the hut in the summer pastures to the valley grasslands to fertilize the fields.

In fact, management and uses of the mountain summer pastures differed from one valley to another. Sometimes, as in the Haut-Adour, the huts belonged to families recognized by name. In other cases, the first person to arrive after the snow had melted took the possession of it. Some huts have also been auctioned off, etc. The huts were also used collectively by several shepherds, but sometimes belonged to just one. Every valley, or almost every valley, has established a set of rules that were built around the production of milk, meat, etc., but also the legal nature of the summer pastures (whether they were subject to lordly rights or not, whether or not they were shared among multiple villages including those from the Spanish side, etc.), and social organizations that were extremely varied.

The concept of "territory" is thus perfectly applicable to mountain summer pasture areas. Territories are well organized. Since the establishment of the land registry in the early nineteenth century, parcels of land reflect and defined earlier division of land not by its relief but by "custom," i.e., "usage." But here we find a great deal of ambivalence between ownership and usage. Despite the appearance of a territory without limits, the customary boundaries are, however, quite real, proven, among other things, by the murder of a Campan shepherd by the people from Bagnères in 1490 as a result of a dispute over a summer pasture. These high-altitude territories are more defined on a psychological plane than they are materialized in the physical outline of summer pastures, the fact which does not make them any less real.

Areas of mountain summer pasture do indeed correspond to the concept of "high-altitude territory," which sometimes overlapped each other and required rites of passage and a strict monitoring of the animals' paths. The ease of access from the valley, quality of grasslands, slopes with northern exposure, the presence of springs or brooks, all these components, which are eminently variable, constituted and still constitute the stakes considered to be vital.

Ownership is represented by the architecture and organization of structures. In other situations, which are also rather frequent, hut, cowshed, and shed are spread out on different sides of the enclosure. Sometimes, although less frequently, the hut is outside the enclosure, which encloses the cowshed and shed. Finally, but much more rarely, the hut, cowshed, and shed may be outside the enclosure.

These different types of structure organization may coexist in the same *courtaou*, which is not a rare occurrence. A chronological distinction of the organization of structures does not appear to be an issue. There are, therefore, typical layouts in the distribution of constructions, consisting of a base structure, just as there are typical layouts in the permanent valley shelter. Beyond the need to arrange architectural components that are required for the practice of high-altitude pastoralism, these typical layouts are also the expression of a cultural identity, supported by the ways in which high-altitude pastures are used. In fact, the manner in which the summer pastures are used is, of course, dependent upon the way they are inhabited. The same architectural forms are not required for a visit by a family's herd as they are for the presence of a communal and therefore larger herd with several herders. Likewise, the owner of a summer shelter will behave differently than one that is granted different places from year to year. In the Campan and Lesponne Valleys, the use of the mountain is very much individualized and a specific hut on the mountain is associated with a specific house in the valley. This form of assignment, not to say "privatization" of summer pasture, is a phenomenon that is not recurrent from one valley to another. The basic structures that comprise the *courtaous* are not, of course, fixed constructions. Their reconstruction, enlargements, and reorganizations have taken place over the years.

These temporary high-altitude shelters are not just indicative of agropastoral practices, but they also indirectly reflect on a specific way of adaptation of human groups to an environment that is, apparently, not very favorable to them. Thus, they allow us to examine a range of social practices through the community management of high-elevation grazing lands and the various ways in which huts have been used. The very variable dimensions of the base units of the *courtaous* show the social differentiations, which are sometimes very clear, within communities that are often thought of as being egalitarian. Through the established architectural selections, through the organization of structures associated with specific production, and through inventiveness of which the *leytés* are a proof, they testify of multiple adaptational skills, translating to us the energy of a culture that abruptly collapsed not long after it reached its technological apogee.

Incentives of Cooperation: Why Do People Cooperate?

Voluntary vs Instrumental Motivation for Cooperation

Communal involvement is critical in solving variety of social problems. Centrally organized administrative agencies, including law enforcement, become inefficient without communal involvement. In fact, communal participation is critical in building civic societies. Individuals engage in collective action either under pressure or voluntarily. Cooperation allows a form of opposition toward conditions or issues that may not satisfy groups. They create new rules which might contradict official policies of state administrations or other forms of political decision-making.

The key question is how to motivate people to cooperate beyond family/kinship level knowing that their action will benefit the group and not just selected individuals (see Binmore 2006 for discussion). Even more problematic is the voluntary context of cooperation, although it may be illusionary, for people recognize personal gains in group success. This is to say that successful cooperation happens in organized manner (it is rarely spontaneous) and operates under specific rules and conditions. In the case presented here, resolution of pernicious conflict in the context of scarce resources was a strong motivation for cooperative group behavior that persisted for centuries.

Social motivations can be examined by analyzing organizational policies and practices (rules, customs) and dispositions (personalities, attitudes). This is the approach presented in this chapter. It indirectly tests the hypothesis that social motivations based on cognitive ability to recognize incentives work better than instrumental motivation to engage people beyond family/kinship level in cooperative behavior. Cooperation is a goal-oriented activity. The ultimate goal is well-defined and has long-term objective, while proximate goals may frequently change. The key question remains, however: Is maximization of gains or minimazition of risks the best strategy in achieving the ultimate or proximate goals?

Cooperation is the field studied by social psychologists who examine motivations behind voluntary cooperation (for discussion on psychology of cooperation, see Jaeggi et al. 2010). Central to understand cooperation is to study motivations; how to convince and manage people to cooperate are central to successful governance. In the discussion regarding social vs instrumental motivations for cooperation, social means voluntary cooperation, whether instrumental relate to codes, norms, and laws of conduct to force (coerce) cooperation. The case discussed in this chapter relates to instrumental motivation to cooperate.

I consider cooperation through analysis of intersection between psychology and economy, to identify motivations and decision-making. A comparative study by experimental economists (Henrich et al. 2005) suggests that motivations for cooperative behavior are shaped by social expectation and not personal material payoffs. Among such expectations are fairness and reciprocity over material self-interest. The argument is that people accept personal costs to maintain social cohesion through ruling that indicates fairness (Gürerk et al. 2006). Thus, people engage in cooperative behavior because they follow rules (adherence) or voluntarily engage in solving group needs (performance) to ensure group's viability.

Economic or Political Rationale Behind Collective Action (Communal Arrangements to Use Scarce Resources)

There is, no doubt, an economic rationale behind collective action toward high-altitude pastures. The communal ownership of high-elevation pastures is advantageous over private ownership. Surely, the users of the pastures discussed here must have found the communal system more appealing. Eggertsson (1992, p. 429) suggested that "the joint use of the mountain pastures (rather than individual plots) is consistent with the minimization of costs, particularly if the farm communities can overcome the problems of collective action and establish effective institutions for internal governance and the control of spillover effects." Distribution of wealth might not, however, be the most significant component of such communal arrangements, but its political gains that mitigate potential conflict.

Cooperation as Negotiation to Mitigate Conflict: The Dialectics of Conflict and Cooperation

Conflict is a dynamic process that initiates with an awareness of difference or contrasting goals, thoughts, attitude, beliefs, norms, cultural values, principles, and opinions. In the case presented here, conflict arises due to the inadequate pasture-sharing system among the herders, improper availability of inputs, and improper use that contributes to less output. If crimes are committed (killings, robbery), conflicts extend in time and escalate. Conflicts adversely impact local economy and development.[6]

In conflict resolution unconditional surrender is a rare exception. Barraging over resources contribute to successful dissolution of a problem, especially if negotiations are between parties of compatible political structure and economic organization. Policies regarding sharing of a commons involve a cycle of conflict and negotiations to impose cooperation and mitigate conflict. Simply put, conflict helps to design strategies for cooperation.

How to mitigate conflict through cooperation? Conflict affects the opposite thoughts and actions and thus contributes to ideas and strategies to mitigate (minimize) risk rather than to maximize gains. In terms of game theory, if such game is played, the players watch each other, and no defection is expected, unless some outliers decide not to play, which is possible but not likely. The key goal is to maintain local economy that benefits a larger group, presumably all, but not necessarily in the same way. Eggertsson (1992) demonstrated that such logic has been practiced by Icelandic farmers and that "(a) joint utilization of the mountain pastures is economically rational when allowance is made for transaction costs (costs of exclusion and internal governance), (b) that the social and economic environment of Icelandic farm districts was suitable for collective action, and there is evidence, extending back through the entire history of the country, of elaborate rules for preserving the jointly used *afrettir* and (c) that open access problems in the common mountain pastures are not an important explanation of centuries of economic decline in Iceland."

Decision-Making and Bifurcated Political Structure to Govern Commons

The structure of a bifurcated political system involves two levels of decision-making: local communities and centralized state agencies. The commons discussed here are excellent examples of institutionalized self-governance in the context of centralized nation-state.

---

[6] See Tilly (1990) for examples.

The communal level consisted of villages organized as corporate groups in a similar way as other Pyrenean communities (see Sahlins 1991, pp. 10–16). Such associations appointed judicial officers to enforce rules of sharing and settle disputes. These communities were autonomous in their political decision-making as neither state, France or Spain, interfered with their ruling. Communities formed federations of valley throughout Central and Western Pyrenees. Whether such decision-making scheme is optimal under the existing political and economic context remains the key theme of this paper.

One of the characteristics of the Pyrenean pastoral resource is the fact that more than 80% of the land concerned is still in public ownership, belonging to the state, communes, or syndicates (joint ownership by several communes). This is why the definition of the beneficiaries of the resource is still based today on the rights inherited from the *Ancien Régime* (before the French Revolution of 1789), which resisted various assaults on ownership and collective management throughout the nineteenth century (Eychenne and Lazaro 2014).

Despite their historical longevity, the strength of the customary rights of the use of pastures in the Pyrenean massif is, above all, related to a social and political consensus through which the local authorities (or the state) confirm the legitimacy of the local farmers to use the pastoral resource.

In this model, local authorities, which are owners of grazing land, manage the resource themselves. This is particularly the case in the western part of the range (Pyrenees-Atlantiques and the western part of the Hautes-Pyrenees), where, like the communities of the *Ancien Régime*, inter-communal commissions manage jointly-held property (pasture, forest, water, tourism infrastructure if applicable). The rules governing the use of pastures, as well as the mechanisms for verifying such use and possibly applying sanctions, are thus decided and implemented by local authority representatives.

In any case, the diversity of management methods from one valley to another testifies to a strong adaptation of the traditional rules to the local context either physical (relief, altitude, nature of the resource, type of farming, etc.) or social (traditions and shared representations, degree of collective decision-making, presence of other users, etc.). Access to the pastures is still regulated by the rules imherited from the *Ancien Régime* (Eychenne and Lazaro 2014), most of which relate to customs and traditions.

While a number of scholars have examined how polycentric and nested institutions contribute to common-pool resources management (cf. McGinnis 1999; Ostrom 1999), a few have examined how the success of sustainable common-pool resources institutions is affected by disturbances in nested governance institutions. Undoubtedly, certain regulations are necessary, but central government ruling limits individual access to common resources. Participatory polycentric governance seems a feasible alternative. "Polycentricity" is a normative approach to governance, which stresses the degree to which higher levels of government should not crowd out self-organization at lower levels. It points out that local people know the local environment better than outsiders. The conventional wisdom that common property is poorly managed and should be either regulated by central authorities or privatized is thus challenged.

Conclusions

The case presented here contributes to better understanding of the interconnection between human decisions and environment in historical perspective. The typical pastoral set in Hautes-Pyrenees included *cabana*, sheep/cowshed, and enclosure. Since the eighteenth century, clusters of such sets were identified as *courtau*, collectively shared landscape structures usually populated by *cabana*, *bederat*, or *tiarat* (small cowshed for claves), *sès* (shed for milking cows), *barguerot* (enclosure), and *leyté* (milk storage amenity). These are the material evidence of cooperative behavior applied to the use of high-altitude pastures.

Cooperation is not a strategy of just the powerless. It becomes a viable approach to mitigate conflict in the context of scarcity of resources and to secure communal sustainable wellbeing. Such win-win scenario, even if it has not produced state-level societies, has been practiced by indigenous peoples of the Pyrenes who survived until the present, but have eventually been colonized by politically complex and centrally organized, more powerful societies.

References

Binmore, K. (2006). Why do people cooperate? *Politics, Philosophy, & Economics, 5*(1), 89–96.

Bollier, D. (2017). *What will replace outdated left and right economic thinking? The commons paradigm.* http://evonomics.com/will-replace-outdated-left-right-economic-thinking-commons-paradigm/

Brosnan, S. F., Salwiczek, L., & Bshary, R. (2010). The interplay of cognition and cooperation. *Philosophical Transactions of the Royal Society of London. Series B, Biological Sciences, 365*(1553), 2699–2710.

Carbonell, X. (2010). Social and environmental conflicts in the planning and management of natural resources in the Aragon's Pyrenees: The case of los Valles Occidentales. In I. Vaccaro & O. Beltran (Eds.), *Social and Ecological History of the Pyrenees. State, Market, and Landscape* (pp. 75–90). Walnut Creek, CA: Left Coast Press.

Edelmayer, F. (2012) *The Pyrenees Region.* European History Online. http://ieg-ego.eu/en/threads/crossroads/border-regions/friedrich-edelmayer-the-pyrenees-region

Eggertsson, T. (1992). Analyzing institutional successes and failures: A millennium of common mountain pastures in Iceland. *International Review of Law and Economics, 12,* 423–437.

Eychenne, C., & Lazaro, L. (2014). Summer pastures: Between "commons" and "public goods" representations of pastoral areas and forms of government intervention. *Journal of Alpine Research |Revue de géographie alpine [Online], 102–2.* https://doi.org/10.4000/rga.2303. Online since 23 May 2014, connection on 06 October 2016. URL: http://rga.revues.org/2303

Gärdenfors, P. (2012). The Cognitive and Communicative Demands of Cooperation. In J. van Eijck & R. Verbrugge (Eds.), *Games, actions and social software. Lecture notes in computer science* (Vol. 7010). Berlin: Springer.

Gürerk, O., Irlenbusch, B., & Rockenbach, B. (2006). The competitive advantage of sanctioning institutions. *Science, 312*(5770), 108–111.

Henrich, J., Boyd, R., Bowles, S., Camerer, C., Fehr, E., Gintis, H., et al. (2005). "Economic man" in cross-cultural perspective: Behavioral experiments in 15 small-scale societies. *Behavioral and Brain Sciences, 28,* 795–855.

Jaeggi, A. V., Burkart, J. M., & Van Schaik, C. P. (2010). On the psychology of cooperation in humans and other primates: Combining the natural history and experimental evidence of prosociality. *Philosophical Transactions of the Royal Society of London. Series B, Biological Sciences, 365*(1553), 2723–2735.

Lévêque, S. (2013). Mountain summer shelters in the haut Ador region of the central French Pyrenees. Examples from the Campan and Lesponne valleys (Hautes-Pyrenees). In L. Lozny (Ed.), *Continuity and change in cultural adaptation to mountain environments: From prehistory to contemporary threats* (pp. 97–122). New York: Springer.

McGinnis, M. D. (Ed.). (1999). *Polycentricity and local public economies. Readings from the workshop in political theory and policy analysis (paperback)*. Ann Arbor, MI: University of Michigan Press.

Murray, S. (2010). The presence of the past. In I. Vaccaro & O. Beltran (Eds.), *Social and ecological history of the Pyrenees. State, market, and landscape* (pp. 25–41). Walnut Creek, CA: Left Coast Press.

Ostrom, E. (1999). Coping with tragedies of the commons. *Annual Review of Political Science, 2*, 493–535.

Sahlins, P. (1991). *The making of France and Spain in the Pyrenees*. Berkeley, CA: University of California Press.

Sillitoe, P. (Ed.). (2017). *Indigenous knowledge. Enhancing its contribution to natural resources management*. Boston, MA: Centre for Agriculture and Biosciences International.

Tilly, C. (1990). *Coercion, capital, and European states, AD 990–1990*. Oxford: Blackwell.

Welch-Devine, M. (2010). Local places, global influences: Pastoralism in Xiberoa and EU regulation. In I. Vaccaro & O. Beltran (Eds.), *Social and ecological history of the Pyrenees. State, market, and landscape* (pp. 43–57). Walnut Creek, CA: Left Coast Press.

Large-Scale Land Acquisition as Commons Grabbing: A Comparative Analysis of Six African Case Studies

Tobias Haller, Timothy Adams, Desirée Gmür, Fabian Käser, Kristina Lanz, Franziska Marfurt, Sarah Ryser, Elisabeth Schubiger, Anna von Sury, and Jean-David Gerber

Introduction

Policies that underlie the practice of large-scale land acquisition (LSLA) in relation to marginalized groups in Africa contribute to the debate regarding *land grabbing* viewed as *commons grabbing* and the way local actors resist such practice. Land grabbing is an important topic discussed in academia and also addressed by NGOs (Cotula et al. 2009; de Schutter 2011; Behrman et al. 2012), but there are very few comparative case studies on the issue.

In 2013, FAO published the guidelines for gender equity in the context of LSLA, related to the mainstreaming of gender equity. The document outlined the principles for equal gender participation in land-related policies and highlighted the need to extend discussion beyond narrow gender topics to include governance as well as institutional and customary issues (i.e., access to resources and inheritance). This publication was followed by a debate regarding Sustainable Development Goals (SDG) 1, 2, 3, and 5 (see UN SDG homepage[1]), where gender issues were discussed in regard to sustainable development, but without focus on economic, political, and ecological contextualization, and essential to this debate bottom-up institution building processes (see Haller and Merten 2008; Jones and Chant 2009; Haller et al. 2016, 2018).

We fill this gap as this chapter examines how LSLA practices impact the existing power structure that governs local access to common pool resources, gender-based

---

[1] http://www.un.org/sustainabledevelopment.

T. Haller (✉) · D. Gmür · F. Käser · K. Lanz · F. Marfurt · S. Ryser · E. Schubiger
A. von Sury
Institute of Social Anthropology, University of Bern, Bern, Switzerland
e-mail: tobias.haller@anthro.unibe.ch

T. Adams · J.-D. Gerber
Institute of Geography, University of Bern, Bern, Switzerland

division of labor, and food security. We also address a larger issue of increased livelihood vulnerability that results in what we call *resilience grabbing*—limited capacity to resist external and internal shocks and hazards. We address commons grabbing in the context of investments that change and shape access to communal lands previously regulated by kinship and lineage rules, which for women in Africa relate to their marriage status. These are now challenged under LSLA policies.

The Neo-Marxist approaches of the 1980s and 1990s (see Meillassoux 1981) stimulated the discussion on gender in relation to local LSLA cases. Our project adopts the New Institutionalism perspective (see Ensminger 1992; Haller 2010, 2013) that provides a theoretical tool to discuss ideologies, discourses, and narratives of companies, governments, elites as well as local actors on community level and within and between households. Ideologies are used to justify strategies employed to cope with the new LSLA-related challenges and also includes emic perceptions of men and women in the context of newly organized gender relations linked to resilience grabbing. Our approach is actor-oriented, focuses on gender-based labor relations, and links these to the debate regarding access to land and related common pool resources. We discuss how external economy, legal context, natural environment, immigration, and technological change lead to change in relative prices for resources that impact the bargaining power of actors and also ideologies (legitimacy created by discourses and narratives) of power relations that stimulate institutional choice of actors regarding access to and distribution of resources. The actors find themselves in an institutional pluralism of customs accompanied by state and foreign company laws that provide context for selection, transformation, and innovation, which we call *institution shopping* (term inspired by the concept of *forum shopping* in legal anthropology (see von Benda-Beckmann 1981). The process is founded in precolonial institutions, colonially transformed customary rights, and modern state and private property rules. International regulations on environment and development of human rights constitute a multiplicity of institutional options from which actors select actions according to their bargaining power and strategic goals (see Haller 2010, 2016). Such selection must to be considered in relation to coercion and feasible opportunities, however.

In order to understand the impact of LSLA on gender and women's bargaining power, as well as the institutional settings that emerge, we need to know more about the effects on land tenure and inheritance issues. These are very much shaped by family, internal labor relations, and group membership and by unbalanced interactions and presence of men and women in the household (for instance, issues of polygamy in African contexts). Such an approach does not exclude single female-headed households.

Our findings show diversity in marginalized groups: the case from Morocco presents the context of women's reduced opportunities to articulate their will, while cases from Ghana and Sierra Leone illustrate traditional options to access the commons. Sections on Kenya, Tanzania, and Malawi outline strategies related to patri- and matrilineal kinship systems, which provide access to land and land-related commons for daughters of certain lineages. Such differences impact norms regarding women's workload and the degree of dependency/independency from men and the family. We argue that as female-related institutions of co-ownership of the commons and access to the commons increase the bargaining power of women and marginalized groups, the better they face the new challenges.

On the other hand, we show that the past is crucial to understand LSLA's impacts on local groups as it involves institutional, political, and economic changes that shaped gender relations that existed before LSLA. Thus, we compare six empirical cases and the way customary/common property-related institutions governing access to land and related resources have transformed during the colonial and postcolonial times and what circumstances legitimize the policies of new states and international institutions. We identify the impact of LSLA under the changed conditions, including household labor, reproduction and child care, inheritance issues, and access to marginal common pool resources that contribute to food production and secure cash flow, i.e., the conditions that enhance the household's resilience. We outline strategies men and women develop in households and groups to defend their interests under the new LSLA and the impact these changes make on food security and group resilience.

Since the food, finance, and fuel crisis—called the triple F crisis—started in 2005 (Toulmin 2008), scholars hint to the fact that interest in land acquisition has massively increased. International investors from Europe, the USA, China, and economically rising countries, such as India, Brazil, South Africa, and the Middle East (Saudi Arabia, Kuwait), buy or lease land in Africa. There—as the dominant discourse suggests—land is cheap and abundant, much of it apparently being wasteland, lying idle or underused by economically underdeveloped peoples. Discursive justifications relate the reasons for these investments to the need to intensify food production in order to increase food security of the investing countries, to adapt to stock fluctuations by looking for a secure harbor for capital, or to respond to the expected growing market for green production of energy in form of biofuels (see Borras et al. 2010; Hall 2011; de Schutter 2011; Zoomers 2011; Anseeuw et al. 2012, to name some authors of this growing body of literature). This amplified interest led to the "land rush" phenomenon that contributed to anticipated negative effects on local people due to loss of land and production facilities. It also made negative environmental impact due to large-scale agribusiness investments and infrastructure as more than half of the large-scale land investments of 32 million ha are in Africa and relate to communities living at the margins of their livelihoods, facing challenges in food security, health and sanitation, and environmental problems (International Land Coalition [ILC] media report June 2013; see land matrix of ILC, Geiger et al. 2019).

Turning land to the production of biofuels or food for export has led to major criticism by the media, politicians, and scholars. On the one hand, the critics representing other than Neo-Marxist positions (see Basu 2007; Baird 2011) argue that this process further undermines the ability and resilience to secure livelihoods in the Global South (see de Schutter 2011). Interestingly, this was the argument made by dependency theorists in the 1970s, namely, Frank (1975) and Wallerstein (1979). On the other hand, mainstream scholars, such as economists and scientists from the World Bank, focus on developmental gains stemming from new investments and argue that these "necessary" attainments cannot be made by smallholders (reiteration of Rostowian modernism since the 1960s; see Deininger 2011). Especially LSLAs that work through outgrower schemes are presented as win-win scenarios as farmers can stay on their land and are guaranteed income (Glover 1987; Porter and Phillips-Howard 1997; Coulter et al. 2009). However, some researchers argue that LSLAs undermine all efforts for sustainability and resilience on local scale. LSLA projects often involve large-scale modern technology that requires huge quantities of water and energy inputs that are detrimental to local developmental needs. As these resources are scarce, LSLA contribute to competition between new investors and local peasants.

Contrary to this position, modernist scholars argue that since more effective and efficient technologies are employed, these will save resources and reduce negative impacts (see summary by de Schutter 2011). This debate has now extended its focus on land in order to include water and other resources leading to introduction of other "grabbing" terms (water grabbing, green grabbing (for protected areas), etc.) but often ignored the vast literature on the commons.

Thus, one perspective is to focus on positive effects of investments in local scale (development discourse) or structural robbery (land-grabbing discourse) with its negative impacts, while another would be to discuss the conditions under which such activities take place. The latter implies a question related to the New Institutionalism theory and political ecology: *Who are the actors, what power they have, and what is the purpose of their actions?* (see Blaikie and Brookfield 1987; Biersack 1999; Blaikie 2006). In historical developments of countries from the Global South, there are two facts worth mentioning. First, neoliberal or mainstream economic policies have led to decentralization of strategies in order to reduce government expenditures in governance, especially related to the management of natural resources. Land reforms and participatory co-management schemes were pushed from above, often inspired by international actors such as the World Bank (see Blaikie 2006). These reforms form the *conditio sine qua non* for further actions enabling governments to provide debt services and thereby receiving further aid. Decentralization is then linked to the quest for participatory approaches, which do not contradict the neoliberal view at all. Such quest at the community level of the otherwise centralized and costly services is appealing because of two reasons: (1) it is thought to cut transaction costs and (2) it applies the discourse that the local people are aware and supportive of the "magic bullet" provided by capitalism, i.e., linking business with (sustainable) development through participatory process. The notion of land reforms leading to privatization gives the impression of local ownership of land. This is the very basis for participatory action and is precisely what has happened with investors who buy or lease privatized lands. Such investors then publicly argue that the developments are in line with code of conduct including Free Prior and Informed Consent (FPIC) (Franco 2016, Borras et al. 2013, Lanz et al. 2018).

The second point relates to the question of land tenure from historical and area study perspective. Numerous studies address Africa, Latin America, and Asia; however, information on African land tenure rules reveals specific differences (see Peters 2009, 2013; Haller 2013). In Africa, the colonial process took place much later than in Latin America. In the latter case, regions were colonized between the fifteenth and eighteenth centuries, and land was seen as belonging to the colonizing state. Through historical struggle, the notion of indigenous groups translates into their land rights and the context of immigration into their areas (for a debate on this issue, see Haller et al. 2007, Niederberger et al. 2016). These groups faced land grabbing as commons grabbing earlier and developed strategies to defend their claims (Wolf 1983; see Stocks 2005 for debate on indigenous peoples in the Americas).

Although in Africa white settlers have not invaded the lands with such a rigor and scale as in the Americas, land tenure issues still suffer from the colonial gaze: from the colonial viewpoint, "real" land rights—often perceived as private property—do not exist in these communities; land is open access resource with usufruct rights and therefore lying idle and ripe to be taken (see Chanock 1991, 2005; Peters 2009). The denial of ownership and hinting at the notion of the commons as open access outrules the possibility of collective ownership in a serious way. It entails the discourse that land and its related resources such as fisheries, grasslands, water, wildlife, and forests have to be managed by the state—a view that fits the tragedy of the commons narrative (Haller 2010). The discourse that African customary land tenure denies property rights underlies the ideology that the use and management of such resources is unstructured and not coordinated at the local level (see Chanock 1991; Peters 2009). Despite evidence that badly enforced state property encourages overuse of resources (see Ostrom 1990, 2005; Haller 2010, 2013, 2016), state ownership and subsequent privatization is the dominating strategy in Africa. Actors with high bargaining power encouraged by internationally pushed neoliberal concepts on land laws see privatization as an easy opportunity to obtain gains from the resources. Despite the evidence that such laws are never fully implemented (Bayart 1989), they provide guidelines for decentralization and privatization of land and related resources (see Brown 2005 for an illustrative example from Zambia; Haller 2013). Therefore, a closer look at African tenure and property systems with a critical gender lense is needed.

Property, Common Tenure, and Gender in Africa

Chanock (1991, 2005), Peters (2009), and Haller (2010, 2013) pointed out that local property ownership used to manage resources in Africa is a mixture of private and collective rights and often includes overlapping rights (strangely called primary and secondary rights). They are adapted to local cultural landscapes and are the result of conflicts, negotiations, and local management. While the notion of boundaries exists among different groups, these boundaries are permeable and allow for flexible fixes as response to changes in the man-made environment as well as climatic and disease constraints. One thus should not speak about pure nature but about cultural landscape ecosystems created by their institutionalized use and governance (Haller 2013, 2016; Haller et al. 2013). These rights are also not fragmented as in European systems, and we find interrelated rights to water, land, pasture fisheries, and wildlife resources, often based on reciprocal arrangements. There are leaders who gain more but who are accountable to a larger body of people and who can be challenged in case of unfair activities (see Haller 2010 for discussion on tenure systems and common property institutions, and the management of common pool resources in floodplains, and Haller et al. 2013 for discussion regarding pastures in floodplain areas). At this point, it is important to note that these rights are partially undermined by the colonial and postcolonial (state) administrations leading to institutional change from common to state and private property or open access (Haller 2010). And if they are not undermined by the state and its government, they are under severe pressure by immigrants from other areas who argue that as citizens of a state, they can claim access because of the fact that these are still state-controlled resources and therefore state property (see Haller and Merten 2008). The discourse of citizenship is crucial here and serves as ideological justification to secure free access as states have financial difficulties to enforce their laws (a paradox of the state being present and absent at the same time, see Haller 2010, 2016). The problem of local property is not solved by decentralizing governance for two reasons: first, state and local elites that have profited from this form of governance find the means (called repertoire of domination by Poteete and Ribot 2011) to use decentralization in order to recentralize governance while not paying for monitoring and sanctioning and, second, local actors have adapted to changing power structure and use decentralization policies to increase what in the New Institutionalism approach in social anthropology (see Ensminger 1992, Haller 2010) is called bargaining power (i.e., the power to have better options in negotiating control over other actors). These two groups (state agents and local elites, chiefs in the African contexts) then are keen to open up the local institutional setting to foreign investment. In this way, elite's decisions are seen as informed consent of the whole community (Brown 2005; Haller 2013).

Influenced by such land and resource tenure dynamics, local institutional settings have different impacts on women and men and shape their relations and strategies when facing LSLA. Generally, social anthropologists discuss gender relations from the point of view of the social construction of the way women and men interact. Both are assigned rights and obligations in a power specific and asymmetric way. In anthropology, male anthropologists saw women's role in society through the male lens. Women were perceived in the context of exchange systems (women circulating between different groups in exchange of bride wealth), functional for procreation and material as well as subsistence-based reproduction of the working forces of a household, a group, or a whole society. Since Annette Weiner's (1976) reexamination of Malinowski's male-oriented centricity, scholars have indicated that such biased view is not fully explanatory. However, current studies in social anthropology focus on women only and not on changing gender interactions in several domains such as institutional (matrimonial, kin related, legal, property, etc.), or economic (gender-specific division of labor), and political (control over assets and decisions) domains (see also for a critique Narotzki 1997; Wilk and Cliggett 2007).

Such a gap might be filled by taking into consideration older theoretical debates in the new context, for instance, the work by Claude Meillassoux merged with contributions from feminist political ecology and feminist economics. Claude

Meillassoux shaped the Neo-Marxist debate in the 1970s, as he reintroduced the focus on household economies and gender-specific divisions of labor, indicating that in the domestic mode of production, woman's role was similar to the factory worker or the farm worker being exploited for the surplus value she produces. In the African context, however, older men exploit younger men and women. The latter provide surplus production, especially reproductive work and care (Meillassoux 1981). This Neo-Marxist position led to a wave of new studies in gender relations that discuss institutional, economic, and power issues between the sexes within and outside the household. Women in this view play the role of cheap laborers reducing the cost for male and female labor. This debate was then linked with the discussion on subsistence-based production that was analyzed as not being separate or traditional, but a modern interrelated part of the capitalist system (Elwert 1980). However, the Neo-Marxist analysis suffers from the avoidance to discuss strategic interests of all actors in such a setting. This does not downplay power asymmetries—on the contrary, this view brings in power asymmetries. Such asymmetries can lead to more inter-household conflicts and violence between women and men and to increased pressure on women (Dolan 2001).

In further debates, feminist political ecology introduces gender as a critical variable in shaping resource access and control, interacting with class, caste, race, and ethnicity to shape processes of ecological change (Rocheleau 1996). In this tradition, environmental issues are approached from the lens of social, distribution, and knowledge conflicts. The focus is clearly on power structures and women's and men's strategic interests that determine access and control over resources. Studies in feminist political ecology also suggest that women are often at the forefront of movements fighting environmental changes (Rocheleau 2001). In feminist economics and development studies, the work of Ester Boserup (1970) had crucial impact in documenting women's productive roles in society, particularly in agriculture. It led to a change from seeing women as passive recipients to active agents of change and development. Feminist economists (e.g., Molyneux 1979) highlighted how the unpaid care work provided by women is crucial to the functioning of any economy and society and how women's ability to provide care is often stretched to the limit when new modes of production require their labor power (e.g., Cagatay and Ozler 1995; Orloff 2002,) or through changes in their institutional and environmental setting. Women, in most developing countries, are also in charge of household food security (see, e.g., De Schutter 2011)—a role, which also comes under stress during environmental and institutional change. A focus on care work, as one of the domains in which gender inequalities are the most pronounced and hardest to change, is therefore highly important for any study on gender relations (Razavi 2007).

A combination of these three theoretical strands of thinking (common property tenure approach, Neo-Marxism and feminist political ecology) aids the focus of this chapter to see exactly who and how shapes the bargaining power within the household and the community. Following the framework of New Institutionalism, we therefore analyze how land area and the resources linked to it increase in value, leading to LSLA, which thus adversely impacts local institutional change.

These changes are related to current globalization developmental schemes. Since the colonial era, which concern issues such as access to land, common property tenure gave women specific rights, shared temporal ownership, and usufruct rights to land and over common pool resources related to land. However, with globalization and subsequent institutional changes, women's rights to land are challenged by external actors and by males within the household, who try to gain access to the land and/or related resources, as prices for these resources are increasing (see Haller and Merten 2008; Veuthy and Gerber 2011; Haller 2013).

As the studies reporting on the commons in African floodplains suggest, such challenges lead to many different pathways of institutional change regarding access to land, which often, as state property, turns into open access regimes due to lack of governmental enforcement, or to closed-range land via privatization. The actual LSLA practice falls in such a context that has reconfigured access to resources and possibly adaptation strategies. The preliminary evidence from the literature on LSLA indicates that access to land by women and other marginalized groups, including common pool resources (i.e., fuel wood, water, wild foods), is threatened by these investments (Schoneveld et al. 2011; White and White 2012). Thus far, there is no literature reporting on broader institutional changes in gender relations due to LSLA and the strategies women adopt to cope with these changes. This chapter aims to outline the current developments in such contexts. It adopts a historic perspective with a focus on institutions together with bargaining power of the sexes at the household, extended household level, and possible higher scales. Here the issue of how to legitimize one's institutional choice and strategies or how is resistance shaped in line with the New Institutionalism approach used in social anthropology (see Ensminger 1992; Haller 2010) is of central interest.

In the next section, we present six case studies that illustrate the processes of commons and resilience grabbing while at the same time indicate that different local actors are not just victims of the tragedy of the commons but are engaged in dramas related to commons grabbing. They develop a wide range of strategies to cope with such pressures. We start with cases from Northern Africa (Morocco) and West Africa (Sierra Leone and Ghana) and then move to Eastern Africa (Kenya and Tanzania), before finally reaching the Southern-Central African context (Malawi). These are mixed cases of LSLAs focused on solar energy production (Morocco), biofuels or flex crops (Sierra Leone and Malawi), food crops such as rice (Ghana and Kenya), and timber production (Tanzania), all mostly for the international or national markets. All of these cases relate to investments by European companies, one US enterprise, and a joint venture of local state and European investors. There is a different degree of compensations and corporate social responsibility (CSR) policies involved and also a different degree of LSLA with either hidden or obvious land-grabbing practices. These studies also reveal that compensation payments and CSR programs were not efficient and resembled what Ferguson (1994) called antipolitics machine, hiding political processes of commons grabbing. Such activities subsequently lead to resilience grabbing, because the loss of the commons undermines the capacity to adapt to food and cash crisis for marginalized groups. All cases show that common property institutions existed but became state or private property with mixed responses from different local stakeholders, including local elites and state administrators.

Presentations are in geographical order from Northern to Southern Africa. The authors describe precolonial institutional settings of the commons and their colonial and postcolonial transformations and subsequently analyze the new land deals viewed as commons grabbing and the reactions by the local actors.

Green Energy Investment as Commons Grabbing in Morocco[2]

Morocco focuses on green energy transformation. It developed "Noor Ouarzazate" (the light of Ouarzazate), the largest solar project in the world, comprising an area of 3000 ha, situated in the arid and semiarid Anti-Atlas, containing lowlands and several rivers important for water use. The parastatal Moroccan Agency for Sustainable Energy (MASEN) runs the project with participation of international investors and technology providers from the European Union (EU), mainly Germany and Spain, and also Saudi Arabia (Fig. 1).

Fig. 1 Solar panels on common land by the Solar Project Noor II in Ouarzazate, Morocco. Photo by Tobias Haller

---

[2] Data based on PhD research by Sarah Ryser (funded by the Swiss National Science Foundation in the Project LSLA and Gender in Africa, Grant: 10001A_152773, see also Ryser 2019).

The land was a common property of the Berber subclan Aït Ougrour (part of the Imghrane clan), governed by local institutions that regulated access to wet season pasture and veld products such as plants used for fodder. The common property arrangements were vital for the marginalized groups and women as well as for herders from neighboring communities with whom the local groups have reciprocal arrangements of resource use. The local Berber group is organized in clans and subclans living in villages in which a council of the elders is the ruling body. Before European colonization, the monarchy of Morocco had little control over the area. Since the times of the French Protectorate, the area has experienced several land investments such as the construction of dams. The French administration and later the post-Protectorate state build infrastructure and controlled this area by establishing state administration at different levels, from sub-areas to the village level. The current solar project is not the first state-controlled project, but it is of particular interest as the investment followed the assessment of the area as wasteland, and thus payments for the commons were low.

The appropriation of land was organized as follows: common land had to be expropriated from the state's energy company (Office National de l'Electricité et de l'Eau potable (ONEE)), which then transferred the land to the MASEN because land in common property cannot be sold directly. The leaders of five village communities were invited to sign the contract. The price fixed by the state was based on the argument that it is a fair appraisal for a desert wasteland. The state and the MASEN justified their investment through green development discourse that included sustainable energy development, creation of jobs, activities in cooperatives, health and sanitation, education, and new infrastructure that will be brought to the area. The proceeds from the land sale did not go to the communities directly, but to a state-controlled fund managed by the Directorate of Rural Affairs (DAR). The fund supposed to pay for planned communal projects, and the communities were told that they could submit projects to the DAR. The MASEN set up a series of projects according to its corporate social responsibility (CSR) policies. These included the provision of sanitary infrastructure such as a mobile hospital stationed for two days a year in the principal village of Ghessate, school buses, dormitory for girls, stables for sheep and goats, welding courses, sponsorship of local marathon, vacation for children, and allocation of funds for NGOs that support rural agricultural development, etc.

Several issues arise from the used ideology rooted in the gendered and green development discourse and poverty alleviation narrative, which include the elements of a policy labeled as anti-politics machine (Ferguson 1994):

- First, the deal was heavily based on the discourse that the area is a wasteland. The state argued that it offers a fair price for a wasteland. However, research by Ryser (2019) showed that it includes 20 plants used by local herders for fodder, specifically goats. Keeping goats is the economic domain of women. The animals are sold on local markets for relatively high prices because of special taste of their meat due to the herbs they consume. Thus, the sold land was a pasture and source of cash for women and it was also used seasonally by neighboring pastoral

groups. Neither the women nor other interest groups were part of the sales arrangement.
- Second, the price of the land was fixed by the state and could not be negotiated. It was certainly not perceived as being fair because the leaders demanded a price ten times higher. Most puzzling is the fact that only the leaders of three villages signed the contract. The other two did not sign because they felt they lack knowledge of the implications of the sale.
- Third, the projects that could have been proposed by local communities and financed by the money from the payments did not materialize. The locals perceived disinterest from the DAR and MASEN regarding their involvement. This points out to local power relations with elites, among village-level and state authorities who control the funds and did not want bottom-up organization of local people. The discourse of having ideas and wanting to set up their own projects indicates the will to have local control over the funds and projects. Being unable to get involved and generate developmental ideas, which was the goal of the proceeds from the sales, led to the feeling that the funds were meant to be managed by the state department in the first place. Thus, many villagers felt that the fees offered by the officials are not accessible.
- Fourth, the project led to institutional change from a commons to state and company ownership of the land; it excluded women from direct decision-making, regardless its relatively liberal gender policies.
- Fifth, the subsequent CSR projects do not provide the promised direct benefits and are not accessible to all the people in the area.

The state's and the company's discourse of gender-sensitive development of CSR projects must be challenged as these are not participatory and disregard local views and women's wishes, but represent stereotypes and gender ideologies that influence the choice of CSR. The 38 CSR projects for the local population, including projects focusing on men and women, favor men by providing training and education needed for such jobs as welding courses available for men only. However, men will have little options to find employment as these projects generate very few jobs. Women are limited mostly to gender-biased type of support such as traditional handicraft. There is no local discussion whether women would like to be educated in this way or what form of education they want to profit from. Therefore, for rural woman, projects are focused on handicraft, which does not offer possibility to work in the project in the future. Access to medical and other educational training is not for all the people from the area, and many remain excluded. Similarly, the promised jobs in the project are few and mostly occupied by outsiders. Therefore, the benefits are not directly accessible especially to women and marginalized groups.

The state and the company's portrayal of the process as fully participatory resembles a practice named anti-politics machine (Ferguson 1994) as their high bargaining power is hidden behind compensation payments, CSR, and the green and gender-sensitive development identity. This is clearly reflected in statements, which indicate that the gains from the "new commons" do not seem to replace the loss of the old commons and lead to a loss of options for women and more marginalized groups as men and elites are the primary beneficiaries. What was stated on paper and in interviews did not materialize. The researcher was often asked by them to contact the MASEN representatives responsible for the implementation of the CSRs, so that they could tell what they need or wish for. Others asked whether there were possibilities to participate in decision-making regarding what projects to be initiated in order to offer gains as this was not clear to local people. At some point the local discourse turned from "not getting access to the funds" to "robbery by state officials" as the narrative of the money being used raised feelings of being robbed.

Therefore, women and other marginalized people, including pastoralists, lost ownership and access to land and land-related resources. This loss was not compensated for but linked to the promise of projects that did not materialize or from which they were excluded. Such policy removed the option of adapting to several environmental and economic changes in the area and being resilient regarding food and cash options. Thus, appropriations of the commons proceeded (a) without consultations of women, (b) without involving seminomadic groups from the Atlas Mountain, (c) without participation of local groups in discussions and decisions on projects, and (d) with CRS measures which are ineffective for women and minorities or exclude them because of gender and biases toward pastoral groups. Generally, the process is not perceived by local actors (with the exception of the elites) as being fair, and people now realize that they have lost the commons, presently fenced and no longer available but desperately needed to secure sustainable livelihood. Because the project involves the king, there is not much resistance. However, local actors clearly state that they perceive the project as not creating gains in the new commons, but losses of the vital old commons. While discontent is uttered in the way that Scott (1985) labeled as the "weapons of the weak," it might lead to more political action if the contrast between loss of the commons and promised gains will intensify.

Green Biofuel Investment, Development Discourses, and Bottom-Up Practices in Sierra Leone[3]

The international context of this project relates to the climate change and increase in fuel prices. Sustainable production of green energy via biofuels became an important strategy of the EU in the 2000s (Fig. 2).

Sierra Leone and the area of Makeni in the north came into the focus for the EU biofuel energy investment project because of topography, access to water (a dam upstream of the area enabled irrigation), soil conditions, and transport facilities to a nearby port. The area is sparsely populated and only used for subsistence production, and the government offered favorable conditions for foreign direct investments

---

[3] Data after Käser (2014), Marfurt et al. (2016), and Lustenberger (2014), presented in the project "Ethnography Land Deals," funded by the Institute of Social Anthropology and the Centre for Development and Environment (CDE), University of Bern, Switzerland.

Fig. 2 Irrigation of sugarcane fields for biofuel production, Swiss Bioenergy Project in Sierra Leone. Photo by Fabian Käser

after the 11-year devastating civil war. The Sierra Leone Investment and Export Promotion Agency was created and supported by the World Bank, IMF, WTO, and the British Government and financed by international investors such as the African Development Bank and the European Union. Under these conditions, the Geneva-based company ADDAX & ORYX Group established the ADDAX Bioenergy Sierra Leone in 2008 and conducted impact assessments until 2010. Talks with stakeholders included local chiefs as "landowners," government officials, and NGOs. The villagers were informed about the plan by the company representatives and local authorities who used development discourses. The land was mapped, and in 2010 a memorandum of understanding (MoU) was signed by the ADDAX and the government that regulated land lease of 57,000 hectares (ha) for 50 years (with the possibility of extension for another 21 years) by the ADDAX and the Paramount Chief of the three chiefdoms of the area. According to this agreement, $8.89 per ha per annum must be paid to different stakeholders: 50% to landowners, 20% to District Council, 20% to Chiefdom Council, and 10% to the government. In addition, the ADDAX signed individual Acknowledgment Agreements (AA) with landowners to ensure their support. The AAs added an extra annual payment of $3.46 per ha per annum for the landowners. The company compensated the owners of crops and palm trees cultivated on the leased land with a small lump-sum payment. Activities started in 2009 with building a plant nursery and infrastructure (roads, field preparations, and irrigation systems), and in 2011 the construction of ethanol factory began. It became operational in early 2014. In addition to the payment, the Farmer Development Program (FDP) initiated a food project to mitigate negative food crop impacts. It was co-designed by the UN Food and Agriculture Organization (FAO). The FDP consists of rice fields ploughed and harrowed by the ADDAX. Farmers are meant to weed the plots, harvest the rice, and provide seeds to the ADDAX for replanting. After three years, the company planned to ask the farmers to pay a charge for technical help such as plowing, etc. Another component of the FDP is the Farmer Field and Life School where farmers are trained in "modern farming techniques" believed to improve crop yields compared to traditional shifting cultivation farming methods.

In such context, the ADDAX project became a flagship for sustainable investments in green energy. However, the research conducted in a village close to the sugarcane factory and in a village at the outskirts of the project indicates that this is another case of commons grabbing in several ways. Firstly, the consultation and compensation schemes of the land deal involved only "landowners" and chiefs of the local Temne ethnic group but did not consider groups with secondary user rights such as migrants, women, etc. Hence, it did not establish sustainable development for all, but rather exacerbated differences between local groups and the institutional change they have been exposed to since colonial times. The Temne lived in chiefdoms when they became subject to the British colonial legislation that altered land tenure systems through the introduction of indirect rule in the Protectorate. The British used the customary institutions in the region but transformed the former rulers from political and military leader into Paramount Chief responsible primarily for the collection of taxes in their chiefdoms. Historically, the groups that cleared the bush and established villages in rural areas considered themselves as firstcomers (or landowners). These firstcomers are distinguished from latecomers, also called land users or strangers. They were accepted in the community through initiation into the local secret societies and established access to land and associated resources and therewith gained legitimacy and political power in the community. Under the British Protectorate, the firstcomers became landowners, and latecomers became land users. Landowners did not have exclusive property rights, but rather acted as stewards and were morally obliged to give part of the land to land users for subsistence farming. The seasonally flooded lowlands (boliland), land-related resources such as water, veld products such as fruits from naturally grown palm trees, and forestry land were a common good of the community. A complex body of rules stipulated access to this common land and resources without overusing it. The ADDAX titled the customary land and gave land titles to the heads of landowners.

Women and latecomers, or secondary user groups, were not part of the land lease agreement and lost access to the commons, while families of the firstcomers became private landowners through the formalization of customary land tenure. The compensation fees thus went to the hands of this new elite, previously responsible only for controlling access to resources. Although land was left for local cultivation, access to the best land and to water was limited considerably, especially in dry seasons. Social anthropological research conducted in 2014–2016 indicated that development promises did not materialize as planned. In the village close to the factory, the landowners hoped to compensate the loss of land and veld products of other land users from whom they received prestige and support, by setting up a list of potential workers to be employed by the ADDAX. That would have put them in the position of redistributing gains, while at the same time profiting from the compensation and lease payments.

Several challenges surfaced during the project that contributed to its failure:

- First, the management of the ADDAX did not consider this list, but employed workers mainly from outside the area.
- Second, the best land for cultivation was lost, and for marginal households stemming from the latecomer groups, access to fruit trees such as palm fruits became extremely scarce, leading to a loss of cash income from palm oil.
- Third, access to water was lost. The loss of water as a common pool resource triggered resistance: the ADDAX had fields acquired from local landowners in wet and swampy areas, which the company irrigated and used for sugarcane plantation. This affected small-scale production by local women, who used these fields to grow vegetables for their own consumption and also for cash-generating market sales, important option at times of food and financial crisis. After the water was no longer available, the women complained and asked the ADDAX to provide water for irrigation, which the company refused and only paid for a small water pump.
- Fourth, villagers perceived serious health and environmental impacts of the agroindustry biofuel production. The company used fertilizers and different chemicals that entered the food system and local water courses and thus had negative impacts during dry seasons but especially during low water level of the main river.
- Fifth, the rice development scheme did not produce good results due to technical and coordination problems with centralized plowing system and other reasons (land disputes, new method of farming requires fertilizers and herbicides that are not affordable for the farmers, land is used too intensively because there is no more shifting cultivation practiced). Thus, no additional food was produced.

Described occurrences identify the impact on the area as commons grabbing, where losses due to development were not adequately compensated. Thus, marginalized people and women undertook the option to gain financial means via access to the commons in order to buffer environmental shocks and cash household expenditures (health, education, etc.). It has been shown that cash-generating options only partially materialized due to the ADDAX's involvement.

Such commons grabbing triggered several local reactions and strategies, which are called institution shopping. In the village close to the factory, local people—elites as well as women and other marginalized groups—made use of the secret societies (Poro society), in which people gather to discuss problematic situations. This included public rituals performances reuniting elites and latecomers by dressing in traditional cloths and wearing masks of the society. Rituals consist of blocking or marking the area of contestation, which the male secret society did because of lack of jobs. A ritual stick (*Poro*) was put at the entrance of the factory indicating that entering the factory is a taboo and thus blocking the workers in protest against the employment strategy of the ADDAX. The South African manager, who removed the stick, was later kidnapped in order to underline the demands of the Temne. Later on, the conflict was diffused by the company and administration officials, but the incident illustrates the major grievance of local people irrespective of their gender or political positions. However, the protest did not result in increased employment of local people, who then applied the "weapons of the weak" (Scott 1985) strategies such as bad talks about the company's management and stealing items important for cane production. In the second village, the women who lost access to commonly used water for irrigation of vegetable gardens have organized in a more efficient way and used a triple institution shopping strategy to buffer the commons and resilience grabbing. They put the local landowner under pressure using the traditional communal land rights institutions claiming that he has the obligation to provide access to seasonally flooded fertile boliland (common property institution). They urged him to make use of his private land title received through the formalization of land tenure to withdraw the leasehold title from the ADDAX in order to prevent establishing of a second sugarcane field on fertile land. The state thus secured private property institution. The legal support of an NGO allowed them to demand their rights by making use of international human and gender-specific rights according to national and international regulations (international human rights institutions). This triple institution shopping strategy was successful as the women were able to prevent more loss of fertile land crucial for their subsistence and further deterioration of local livelihoods (Marfurt 2019).

These two examples show a much more active type of reaction toward commons and resilience grabbing and indicate that we are dealing with a drama rather than tragedy of the grabbed commons. Interestingly, in 2015 the ADDAX has stopped its operations. The Ebola crisis was officially named as the reason, but it might have been a combination of the lack of local involvement, the weapons of the weak strategy, and the changing view of the EU about biofuels considered now not sustainable, and thus their production does not contribute to mitigation of climate-related problems (for more details, see also Marfurt et al. 2016).

Investors and Chiefs: Commons Grabbing, Gendered Development Discourse, and Coping Strategies in Ghana's Volta Region[4]

While LSLAs for agricultural purposes are not new phenomena in Ghana, the difference between the colonial and postcolonial processes is that the country's current agricultural policy receives strong support from private sector industrial

---

[4] Data based on PhD research by Kristina Lanz, funded by SNIS in 2015–2016 and the Swiss National Science Foundation in the Project LSLA and Gender in Africa, Grant: 10001A_152773, see also Lanz et al. 2018.

agriculture, which creates a favorable investment climate with 36 and more foreign companies in agriculture and forestry of which 90% have majority overseas shareholders (Amanor 1999; Schoneveld et al. 2011). The majority of these deals were negotiated directly by the investors with traditional or customary authorities such as chiefs who represent local people and often bypass local state authorities and local institutional setting. In this context, the chiefs and Paramount Chief, formally installed by the British colonial administration for indirect ruling, not only legitimate their position through tradition but also make use of extensive modern-day state institutions, which grant them extensive powers, as their role as land administrators and investment promoters becomes evident for state actors and international investors alike. Customary authorities are able to navigate the plural institutional setting and select the institutional designs that suit them best to increase their bargaining power in the local context (performing institution shopping).

Local actors became formally less dependent on chiefs, after the first President Nkrumah had attempted to reduce their power until the 1980s. Later on, following structural adjustment programs that demanded downsizing of the state administration and decentralization, chiefs gained more power because of their control over large tracts of land since colonial times, which is currently being strengthened by the ongoing Land Administration Project (LAP). The constitution differentiates the land surface of the state between public land (20%) and stool land (80%). Most people in Ghana thus obtain land access via chieftaincy, lineage, and kinship, based on narratives of ancestry that continuously reestablish the traditional rights of the groups related to the first settlers on the land (Lenz 2006). The chiefs, earth priests, or family heads are said to hold the allodial rights over the land, whereas all members of the group enjoy usufruct rights (Kasanga and Kotey 2001). While this resembles common property institutions in precolonial times, in which leaders and religious office holders acted as coordinators and managers of land and land-related resources, colonial interventions considerably strengthened the powers of some chiefs and other selected traditional leaders over others. In 1930, the British established native authorities, recognizing what they called "precolonial political jurisdictions" and centralizing power in paramount chieftaincies, who were said to have the "allodial title" or "ultimate title" over land, which reinforced their authority to manage and allocate land (Boni 2008) and also to collect land tributes from strangers wishing to cultivate stool land. As a result, peasants were denied full and secure rights to the land and acknowledged to have only use rights as "subjects" of their respective chief (Amanor 2008; Boni 2008; Boone 2015). Land use rights were however embedded in hierarchical descent-based groups, whereby "insider-outsider distinctions" were made particularly salient and settlers were often considered as "politically subordinate" within communities (Boone 2015) (Fig. 3).

Since the 1980s, and increasingly in the 2000s, formal institutions and clearly demarcated individual land rights are demanded by investors in order to guarantee security. In 2003, the Ministry of Lands and Natural Resources initiated the Land Administration Project (LAP) in order to coordinate control over land management, registration, and mapping as well as dispute settlement. This process is vested in

Fig. 3 Local women in a large-scale rice plantation in the Volta Region of Ghana. Photo by Divine Harrison

customary land secretariats (CLSs), headed by the respective customary authorities whereby these colonial-stemming elites gained more power and legitimized more security for investors. This actually meant a de facto privatization option for local elites in the context of rising prices for land due to new foreign investment interests.

In this context, the Ghana's Global Agri-Development Company (GADCO)—an international land-based investment in rice production—started in 2011 to invest in the Fievie Traditional Area in the South Tongu District of Ghana's Volta Region. The GADCO was a consortium of British, Nigerian, and Indian investors and received funding from various international sources such as the Acumen Fund, AATIF Fund (sponsored by KfW, Deutsche Bank), and Summit Capital. It went bankrupt in 2014 and was taken over by the Swiss company RMG Concept, which restarted operations in 2015 (still using the name GADCO).

The Fievie Traditional Area, which covers about 160 km^2, is inhabited by four clans that subsist on agriculture, fishing, and pastoralism. Before colonization, the Fievie did not have a Paramount Chief but revered their spiritual leader, the hunter Akalo—who, it is said, led them to their current location—among a number of other historically important individuals. Colonization, however, completely changed the structure of leadership in the traditional area, which is now headed by a Paramount Chief, his Stoolfather, a Paramount Queen Mother, and the four clan heads. Both the Paramount Chief and the Stoolfather are highly educated lawyers who do not reside in the local area, but in Accra, 110 km away. All land in the Fievie Traditional Area is vested in four clans and "owned" by the families making up these clans. Before the land deal, large tracts of land within the Fievie Traditional Area were used under a common property regime. A portion of this land was allocated by the elders over a century ago to pastoralists from both within and outside the traditional area. In addition, there is uncertainty regarding the ownership of a neighboring area presently occupied by another ethnic group, the Bakpa, which were resettled to the area in the 1960s due to the construction of the Akosombo Dam, which led to flooding of their home areas. The Fievie chiefs argue that they provided the land for resettlement and that the Bakpa are only "settlers" or "migrants" on their land, while the Bakpa clans are divided on the issue with some claiming that it really was Fievie's land, while others argue that it was provided by the neighboring Mafi Traditional Area. The GADCO investment is furthermore the second occasion when Fievie chiefs have provided large tracts of Bakpa-used farmland to a foreign investor. In 2009, land was leased to the Israeli jatropha company Galten, which by the time of research had abandoned its plantation. Providing land to foreign investors is a means for the Fievie chiefs to strengthen their status as "landowners" in the various land litigation cases, as well as in the face of boosted interest in their land by investors, by making use of their increased recognition by the state. Through the CLS, transaction costs for investors are reduced as negotiation partners are clearly identifiable. Furthermore, as the discussion above highlights, customary authorities are happy to use their state-backed recognition to claim sole decision-making power over all of Fievie lands, in the process of increased relative prices for the land and changing the land tenure system. The GADCO investment thus takes place in a context of ongoing contestation and transformations of the customary system, which, through LAP, is now increasingly backed up and legitimized by the state.

The GADCO was interested in the land for large-scale rice production and initially only contacted the Paramount Chief of the Fievie Traditional Area to acquire land. Neither government representatives nor family heads were included in the negotiations concerning 2000 ha of land to be leased for 50 years to the GADCO. The signed agreement, which included the establishment of an outgrower scheme on parts of the land, was labeled to be a "community-private partnership" agreement, outlining that 2.5% of the company's sales revenue would be paid to a "community development fund," which is a customary state account administered by the customary land secretariat. However, the Paramount Stoolfather felt left out of the agreement and involved the district authorities to stall the investment. As a result, he became the main negotiation partner of the GADCO, and the contract was now officially signed at the District Assembly in the presence of the chiefs, elders, and government officials. However, no Bakpa chiefs or representatives were present, even though parts of the disputed Bakpa territory were included. Similarly, many of the actual family heads, whose lands were included in the deal, were not part of the negotiations. The conflict between the Paramount Stoolfather and the Paramount Chief and their respective clans was mitigated by the GADCO. The company provided funds for a large homecoming ceremony, which celebrated the unity of the Fievie state with many references to their ancestry and tradition. At the same time, notions of development and modernity were evoked to highlight the benefits of the investment to the community. References to "tradition," as an important bonding mechanism, were thus combined with appeals to people's aspirations for "development" by chiefs eager to get their decisions legitimized by their community. The money generated by the "community-private partnership agreement" (which according to one chief amounted to approximately $50,000 per year in the first few years) was supposed to be used for community development projects.

However, for various reasons these compensations did not match the cost of loss of the land and land-related common pool resources:

- First, the enclosure of large areas of communal land restricted access to several common-pool resources vital for local livelihoods such as pasture, water, and land for traditional shifting agriculture and gardening. The sharp decrease in land available for cattle grazing has made this activity less feasible.
- Second, the destruction of several water ponds used for human and animal consumption and the spraying of pesticides (which according to various interviewees has had significant health impacts) have especially affected the cattle-rearing communities living from these communal lands.
- Third, the destruction of many man-made fishponds led to lowering the level of nutrition and to loss of cash income for women who traded fish.
- Fourth, most trees, used by local women for fuel wood and to produce charcoal for sale, were uprooted and thus led to a loss of income, especially for the poorest members of affected communities, which relied the most on charcoal sales.
- Fifth, while the two pastoral communities evoke tradition and long-standing access rights to these pastures, traditional leaders claim that these communities have no rights to the land. Similarly, the Bakpa settlers are viewed as migrants with no rights to the land and are not consulted or informed about the acquisition of their farmland. Fievie chiefs often used community meetings to mobilize people against the Bakpa.
- Sixth, there was a common feeling of being cheated, voiced especially by the youth, as most people did not know where the money paid to the chiefs went to. The GADCO did not question the use of money and described the customary authorities as "business partners," who are used as an interface between them and the local community. Of the 30 households questioned about compensation for farmland, the majority didn't receive any payments (those who did receive compensation were all related to chiefs or belonged to other important local elite groups).
- Seventh, the outgrower scheme that was established by the company to compensate local people for their losses benefitted largely the elite (nobody from the Bakpa and only one person from the affected cattle-rearing communities—a brother of one of the local chiefs—was included in the scheme).

In result, the marginalized people and women not stemming from elite families lost various ways to use the commons to generate cash, while their ability to be resilient in times of crisis were reduced as only few were part of the outgrower scheme and jobs created were mostly casual and low-paid. The possibility for women to pick rice after harvests and sell it in order to make a small income turned out to be the only access to new resources. While this income in some cases surpassed the income previously made from the sale of charcoal, it was strongly linked to the company's operations and thus put women in a dependent and vulnerable position, as exemplified by the GADCO's bankruptcy in 2015 (it was taken over by RMG Concept in 2016). In reaction to these grabbing processes, people stopped attending community meetings and started engaging government authorities. Complaints were filed with the District Chief Executives, District Directorates of Agriculture, and individual members of parliament. Sporadic violent actions took place. In 2013, the affected Bakpa and their chiefs forcefully reoccupied their fields threatening to use physical force in defense of their territories. This escalation led to an intervention by the District Chief Executives and District Security Councils from South and Central Tongu—as a result nine people were compensated (although the independent evaluation of the crop loss among Bakpa communities indicated that 26 farmers should be compensated). This led to further divisions and conflict among Bakpa communities. The only evidence of successful resistance has been by a group of cattle herders who resisted the integration of the last remaining area of grazing land into plantation. Government authorities did not reply to their letter of complaint; rather it was through intense negotiation and threats of violence and public disobedience that they persuaded the customary elite to allocate another piece of land for the expansion of the outgrower scheme. Similarly, after the conclusion of the second field study, the local youth organized themselves and demanded to be integrated into the outgrower scheme. They also demanded accountability and challenged the chiefs regarding the use of funds and that corporate social responsibility be exercised (see also Lanz et al. 2018).

The Tragedy of Christian Development: Large-Scale Rice Plantation on the Yala Swamps, Western Kenya[5]

This case study focuses on the Yala Swamp region in Western Kenya, inhabited mostly by the Luo ethnic group of about 15,000–35,000 people who use the area and its common pool resources for grazing, fishing, and dry season agriculture. The US-based Dominion Farms Ltd. established a large rice plantation on that swampy land. This investment was possible due to historical changes since colonial times. Under the British rule, the people from the region served as wage laborers and were therefore pushed toward cash economy and wage labor in distant places. On the other hand, land in Kenya has been transformed into state property, and also resource rights have been fragmented by the colonial rules. The colonial government also appointed chiefs, a political structure which the postcolonial, independent government reinforced. Authority shifted from the local people to the national

---

[5] Data based on MA thesis by Schubiger (2016) and von Sury (2016) and the project "Ethnography Land Deals" funded by the Institute of Social Anthropology and the Centre for Development and Environment (CDE), University of Bern, Switzerland.

government, and its agencies and common-pool resources became state property. These changes developed uncertainty on the ground of a hegemonic development discourse. The anti-colonial struggle led to independence, but also to the creation of ethnically structured elite within the new built Kenyan State. After independence, the land was divided into government land, land held in trust by the government, and privately owned land, while under the new constitution, from 2010 the division included public, community, and private land. Such legal pluralism in terms of land tenure systems relates to market-oriented, neoliberal approach to development, enabling the investment in the Yala Swamp by the Dominion Company owned by Calvin Burgess, a US businessman who started the Dominion Farms as a subsidiary of his other businesses (e.g., high security prisons in the USA). Burgess came to the Yala Swamp area in 2003 to set up a large farm. According to his statement, this engagement in setting up a large-scale rice farm was not based on commercial but religious motivations. He holds the view that the area of his investment was a useless and idle swamp to be saved by God via his activity. The land he leased was at that time a trust land, converted to public land in 2010 and managed by the parastatal Lake Basin Development Authority and by the two concerned councils of two respective counties thus involving local authorities. The contract concerned 3700 ha to be used for 25 years with the renewal option for 20 more years, while in the memorandum of understanding (MoU), 6900 ha, i.e., 3200 ha more, are mentioned. The unclear size and rights of land and its fragmentation from other land-related resources are a central feature in this investment case.

However, the research by Elisabeth Schubiger and Anna von Sury revealed that local people label the Yala Swamp as a very fertile land, full of important common pool resources for livelihood diversification such as water, fisheries, wildlife, and pasture areas. The Luo had developed common property institution based on segmentary groups, including reciprocal economic access rules and legal arrangements coordinated by local leaders and elders as agents of redistribution. The commons were used in combination with notions of private family property of land and related resources, which allowed them a flexible and seasonally adapted use of the commons. As a matter of fact, the swamp is not just purely natural, but a culturally designed landscape of multiple uses, governed through locally developed rules that allow its flexible use. Very fertile and moist land was used all year round for cultivation, and all families had small "private" plots in the land before the Dominion entered the area. Another important use of this common property was cattle grazing, which created wealth important for social and other obligations and is today very important to secure cash flow. Fisheries in the swamp and in adjacent lakes were also of central importance, as well as collection of veld products for housing constructions and other uses. While the fields were private, other common pool resources were held in common property regimes. Thus, the swamp could not be called idle, unused land. Most importantly, Schubiger and von Sury show that the swamp was currently considered as a means to generate cash in order to meet monetary subsistence needs. Thus, the Yala Swamp have to be seen as a cultural landscape, an ecosystem managed by a mixture of private and common property institutions that regulated access to its resources and created conditions for the Luo resilience.

The investor profited from the classification of the swamp as public land held in trust by the government. He addressed state officials in order to get access to the former commons, but also engaged local churches, where he argued that God brought him here in order to bring development. However, the people perceived him with doubt: "He arrived in the name of God to bring development and employment, but he hid the size of the land he wanted." Initially, Burgess addressed the grassroots level via church networks, which gave him credibility while excluding the elders and chiefs.

Politically motivated ethnicity also played an important role as some leaders blamed the Kikuyu—the largest ethnic group in Kenya—for the deprivation of the lake region regarding its economic development. Thus, Burgess used the discourse that via the Dominion Farms, development also arrives in Luo lands. However, unfulfilled promises regarding jobs and compensations produced conflicts, while complaints by the local people created a view that promises were not kept and cash options grabbed, a context that relates to the situation we call "resilience grabbing." The locally adopted view is that: "…Dominion has the biggest *shamba* (field) now."

Problems related to the Dominion investment are manifold:

- First, the Dominion Farms did not provide the promised jobs, but reduced options for cash flow and thus made livelihood of local actors more vulnerable and less resilient.
- Second, access to pasture and thus to cattle-based livelihoods and ultimately generation of cash were no longer possible at the previous level. This has also implication for agriculture as cows were used for traction and served as capital reserve in order to mitigate food and other crises.
- Third, the loss of cash and other gains might have contributed to an increase in poaching activities by local people to make money from game and trophies.
- Fourth, access to fisheries and veld products was reduced; the swamp provided a cash-generating option managed by local institutions that regulated its use in a more sustainable way.
- Fifth, food security was severely diminished. Before the investment, the people were able to have three meals a day based on fish, milk, and maize. The Dominion's activity contributed to the reduction of meals to one a day (von Sury 2016). This is puzzling as the company legitimated its investments as hunger fighting.
- Sixth, if the losses are compared with the compensations of a "communal land" given by the investor to local people, it appears to be ridiculously low (loss of 6900 ha of land which was used by 15,000–35,000 people compared to 150 acres as communal land). In addition, the rules to access land are unclear and lead to conflicts.
- Seventh, the institutions that previously regulated access to the whole swamp area are no longer in use as the Dominion, as well as the state, do not control the

use of resources, and thus this cultural landscape became an open access prone to overuse and conflicts. In addition, the Dominion investment led to the view that land can be privatized and the local elites are able to get access to it, excluding other users.
- Eighth, with these losses one would expect at least some gains from wage labor. However, only about 600 jobs were created for a population of 15,000–35,000 people who previously profited from the swamps. Only 20% of these jobs were given to the locals, mainly women. These jobs are extremely insecure, low-paid, and dangerous because of long walking distances and possible wildlife and snake encounters. Research indicated that the salaries are very low compared to the gains from pastures, cattle, fisheries, and other uses of the wetland.
- Ninth, on top of these negative impacts are ecological deteriorations as the Dominion Farms use chemicals and pesticides contaminating water and still available pasture and fisheries, fruit trees, and domestic animals.

Local people developed strategies of resistance by trying to reappropriate grazing lands not used by the Dominion. They also developed institutions to organize and coordinate access to these grazing lands in order to prevent damage to cultivated fields that are on the way to the pastures. Similarly, collective action takes place after harvest when fields become a local commons for cattle grazing. There is an interesting twist in people's discourse, however. They argue that Burgess has a *shamba* (field) that is too big and thus reduces and limits the people's use of resources. Because he does not make use of all lands, they claim that he does not use the land properly and that it is now idle land. Therefore, the investors "repertoires of domination" (Poteete and Ribot 2011) are undermined by the "weapons of the weak" (Scott 1985) approach by making use of the same idle land discourse by which the investor legitimized his investment. It thus becomes the legitimate basis for the local people to "encroach" on the Dominion's *shamba*. Other strategies are emerging such as self-help groups in which financial and other problems stemming from the investment are discussed and mitigated. Especially women get organized in order to secure food and school fees. In addition, people try to reinstate access to pastures and set up new institutions to coordinate their use.

Despite the negative impacts and all the new strategies to secure well-being, people did not want the Dominion to leave, but hope for its improvement. This is astonishing considering the heavy negative impact the company had on the area. However, having the company in the area enabled different actors on the local level to hold the investor responsible for the situation and ask for change and higher compensations. Nevertheless, in early 2018, the Dominion Farms Ltd. stopped all activities on the ground and laid off all staff without clarifying whether further farming is going to take place in the future (further information see Schubiger 2016; von Sury 2016).

A Land Grab Proper: Forestry, Plantations, and Loss of Common Pool Resources in Iringa District, Tanzania[6]

In Tanzania, large-scale land acquisitions (or alienations) began in colonial times. Like many other agrarian-developing countries, Tanzania attracts land investors from all over the world, especially since the mid-1980s, when it changed to a neoliberal political and economic system after nearly 20 years of socialism. All these changes have impacted traditional land tenure and related common pool resource management. Precolonial land tenure was organized as common property in the form of clan land and related common pool resources (Bryceson 1995; Benschop 2002). The change is illustrated with the case of the Wahehe located in Kilolo district, Iringa region in the Southern Highlands of Tanzania whose livelihood was impacted by the investment of the New Forest Company (NFC) (Fig. 4).

The NFC's plantation was installed on land that the company acquired from nine villages of the Wahehe ethnic group and immigrant farmers from Wbena ethnic groups from Njombe area. Kilolo is a very hilly district; cultivation is practiced in

Fig. 4 Looking at the lost land in Iringa District, Tanzania. Photo by Désirée Gmür

---

[6] Data based on PhD research by Desirée Gmür, funded by the Swiss National Science Foundation in the Project LSLA and Gender in Africa, Grant: 10001A_152773, see also Gmür 2019.

valley bottoms known as *vinyungu* (a Kihehe word for valley and/or garden) in the dry season and in uphill slope farms during the rainy season. The *vinyungus* are more productive as they are permeated by different sizes of streams and fertile soils, are not flushed out like those on the hills, and are therefore preferred for agriculture. In between, on the agricultural plots, there are often small areas of communal forest with trees producing non-timber forest products (NTFPs) such as fruits or leaves used as food, medicinal wild mushrooms, wild fruits, and wild vegetables used for food, health-related issues, and income. The Wahehe also plant different kinds of fruit trees there. Some trees are left for water conservation purposes. In the context of climatic change, people in the area are increasingly relying on such NTFPs. In addition, hunting is also done in nearby forest reserves and bushes.

For three decades the government of Tanzania has been actively seeking foreign investors to support development and economic growth. This is reflected in various laws, policies, and initiatives as well as the establishment of the National Land Bank as the main state organization aiming to facilitate land acquisition for foreign investors. Welcoming the perceived new source of foreign currency income and other benefits, the present government has declared large areas of its land as lying idle or being underused. The recent investments focus on food and forestry production and the use of former common pool resources such as water, pastures, and forests for subsistence and cash. This is done in the context of village land that is legally held as a commons (according to the Village Land Act), but this can be changed by the president if needed. Thus, in reality the land is not a commons, but state property. Such situation exists since socialist times, when two thirds of the rural population of different "ethnic" origins were mixed up and (re)settled in uniformly structured villages. The aim was to modernize agriculture and increase agricultural productivity and access to education, water, and health services for everybody. However, the government installed resource management institutions similar to those in colonial times. Common property institutional regimes to manage CPRs were "legislated out of existence" and transformed by the government to conform to socialist policies and ideologies describing these lands as state property (see Gmür 2019 for an overview).

Since 1986, economic liberalization and donor demands for participatory development have heavily influenced the tenure and management systems of land and related CPR. The post-socialist governments have maintained ownership and control of most natural resources, including land, and the resource management system is still very fragmented. A new land policy was accepted by the Parliament in 1995, and two new land laws were enacted in 1999, the Land Act and the Village Land Act (URT 1999a, b). These laws divided land into three categories: reserved (ca. 30%), village (ca. 2/3 of the land), and general land (ca. 2%).

In 2009, the New Forests Company (NFC), a UK-based South African company, established six plantations and three pole plants in Uganda, Tanzania, Rwanda, and Mozambique, and a head office in Johannesburg (NFC 2014a, b). It mixes commercial plantation forestry with protection and regeneration of indigenous tree species (ibid.) and produces wooden feed material from hardwood species of eucalyptus and pine trees for sawmills, board factories and pole treatment plants, as well as energy-producing operations. It focuses on local and regional export markets (ibid.). By early 2013, the company had acquired land from seven villages and was still looking for more in the neighboring villages. The company representatives approached new landholders in villages where they already had acquired land in an attempt to consolidate the pieces of land (see Locher and Müller-Böker 2014). Since 2010, more than 6300 ha have been taken, and since 2013, many people in the studied villages sold land, family- or individually owned, because the investor was looking for more land after a first round of acquisition in 2009 that targeted mainly village reserves. Thus, the NFC acquired granted rights of use for 99 years to land from villagers that usually had a customary right of occupancy. The acquired land is located uphill and in valley bottoms. In several cases the clan or family heads sold the land without involving the rest of the clan. While many families and/or members claimed to not use land because it is far away from their settlements and therefore has become spare or reserve land, others claimed to have used it (Gmür 2019).

There are several negative impacts that contradict the investor's claim for sustainable development:

- First, this case provides evidence of direct land grabbing: when the investor received the land, land prices increased and different people claimed rights to the same land because they wanted to sell it. There were also conflicts within families, with some members claiming the land unused in order to have an argument to sell it, while others, very often women, claimed that it is used and they don't want to sell. Brothers legitimated the sale by denying the customary rule of Wahehe and Wabena daughters having the right to inherit land from their fathers. In many cases people were just told to accept the compensation and leave their plots with the district because there is an investor coming to plant trees. They largely legitimized the acquisition by using the Land Act of 1999 and the Village Land Act of 1999, which, even though they respect customary land rights, stipulate that all land in Tanzania is public, vested in the president who has the final decisive power.
- Second, there are several cases where people were forced to leave fields (*vinyungus*) in the very fertile and often used by women valley bottoms. The investor's activity here can be identified as institution shopping. The NFC activated Article 34 of the Water Resources Management Act of 2009, which stipulates prohibition of human activities near water resources. Technically, the land still belongs to the villagers, but de facto the investor took it and did not compensate the people, following the Water Resources Act to legitimize its activity and arguing that what people are doing is illegal. Such actions were backed by the district's officials. The investor used environmental discourse to argue that the water source needs to be protected and the villagers are cutting down water-friendly trees.
- Third, the NFC paid monetary compensation for the acquired land, even though there are still some disputes. The loss of the *vinyungus* were not compensated and probably will never be. Those who sold voluntarily regret their decisions saying that they were not aware of the drawbacks of selling their land and the

extent to which they would no longer be able to access it. They also realized that the amount they received is very little and used very quickly compared to the continous income they could get through their land. The New Forests has paid an average of 100,000 Tsh/acre in compensation, which is around $45. This is very little if compare to the income women generate through the use of *vinyungus*. For example, two acres of land produce three bags of beans, which are sold at 300,000 Tsh per season.

- Fourth, people lost access to a lot of agricultural land and produce they used for subsistence and cash flow. Especially the *vinyungus* are the most productive areas where they plant beans, the cash crop that brings most income. Many people depended on these *vinyungus* to get extra income to pay school fees, buy extra food in cases of food scarcity when the harvests on subsistence plots were bad, and to buy fertilizers. Due to the loss of the *vinyungus*, food security is at risk. The LSLA also led to limitation of maize production that elevated maize price within the villages from 7000 Ths to 10,000–13,000 Ths for 18–20 kg. Another effect of this is that people started to brew beer with the remaining maize as this produces higher income than selling the pure maize or flour. With beans gone from the *vinyungus*, this is the only way to improve their income.
- Fifth, women were especially concerned about losing fruit trees such as lime trees, avocado trees, banana trees, and pear trees. Income from selling fruits is controlled by women and used to buy things for the household and the children. Fruits are also important for the children's nutrition. Loss of access to land-related common pool resources such as NTFP limited access to grasses for thatching houses.
- Sixth, false promises of job creation and CSR policies were made. When the investor approached the villages in 2006, the aims were presented as a long list of benefits, including a promise to "give better tree seedlings to villagers"; "create 10,000 jobs"; "give Tsh 300 million every year for social service" such as schools and health; "engage in the provision of education, health, water, etc."; and create infrastructure. The investor claims on its website that corporate social responsibility (CSR) is a fundamental aspect of their business model, mainly as a strategy to reduce risks because forest plantations are very vulnerable due to fire or illegal harvesting and long-term investments bring a return only after several years. The "new commons" created by the LSLA are mainly CSR or community development projects including income-generating projects and infrastructure investment, monetary compensation for the acquired land, jobs in the plantation, a planned outgrower scheme, and taxes and lease fees they pay to the district. However, access to these new commons is limited, especially for women. Furthermore, the company propagated that it will provide infrastructure, but people are disappointed as infrastructure development is slow and in lesser than expected scale, while the economic impact of the lost land is instant. Projects such as beehives produce low income, jobs in plantations are very few, on short term basis, and badly paid.

There is very little public reaction just some gossip and acts of limited civil disobedience, for example, cultivating the bottom valley land. However, there is no collective action against the investors reported from research (see Gmür 2019).

Privatizing Matrilineal Clan Commons: Creating Marginalization Through Sugarcane Outgrower Schemes in Malawi[7]

This research focused on the impact of large-scale sugarcane outgrower expansion on local communities' livelihoods and changing gender relations in the Dwangwa area of Nkhotakota District of Central Malawi. Sugarcane and tobacco plantations were established in early postcolonial times, when all lands were placed under the control of the President, indicating a shift from common to state property. This allowed the later postindependence governments to use the land previously held as a commons for cane growing, including an area of 48,750 ha along the lakeshores of Lake Malawi, which was confiscated through a series of presidential land orders in 1969 and 1975 for cane production. The remaining parts of these lands are again targeted for sugarcane under outgrower schemes. This is a clear change from common property control to state and private property regulations. Precolonial traditional institutions were based on kinship relations, making inheritance and marriage a key mechanism for access to land common to a lineage and clan. The people of the area are predominantly matrilineal Chewa, and land transfers are still based on matrilineal rules of inheritance. Men who are engaged in outgrower scheme have inherited land from their mothers, and therefore land was transmitted via matrilineal rule of inheritance as a common property of the larger matrilineage and clan.

The effects to local agrarian relations in the Dwangwa area had been less threatening as land was abundant and scarcity was not perceived as a problem, meaning that access to land was not an issue in agricultural production. More of an issue was adequate labor, which was the scarce resource and subject to slavery in precolonial times and control of the women's workforce in colonial and postcolonial times. But this was to change with the recent cane expansions, which changed relative prices of land, and thus access to land became scarce. Increase in the value of land for commercial reasons and scarcity of land and increasing population made the prices for land increase and plot sizes decrease.

In the last years, commercial agriculture and small-scale farming, coupled with increased population due to migration, led to reduction of farm sizes. In addition, traditional authorities (TAs) remained of central importance in land governance issues, in which these actors successfully combine the traditional notion of land

---

[7] Data based on PhD research by Timothy Adams, funded by the Swiss National Science Foundation in the Project LSLA and Gender in Africa, Grant: 10001A_152773, see also Adams et al 2018).

governance via customary laws (stemming from colonial times) with modern aspects of production under outgrower schemes. This gave the TA's room for institution shopping and facilitating outgrower schemes in the local communities. The Dwangwa Cane Growers Trust (DCGT) and Dwangwa Cane Growers Limited (DCGL), since its establishment in 1999, have assumed a facilitating role for sugarcane expansion, serving as state apparatus for implementing smallholder sugarcane projects at the local level (Adams et al.). In addition, DCGT received government and donor financial support (e.g., EU, AfDB) for expanding the outgrower scheme, in which smallholders would grow the cane and supply to the South-African-based, Associated British Foods sugar company, Illovo Sugar Limited. The smallholders do not have direct contract with the miller (Illovo), but have to bring the cane to Illovo through DCGL. In addition, the smallholders have to become members of the DCGT, which converts the smallholders' land into trust land.

This process has the following negative consequences:

- First, the land is no longer a commons of the matrilineage, but is out of their control. This can be seen as land alienation strategically planned by the DCGT that mobilizes relevant actors in customary land governance such as the TA to possess the customary land to the detriment and exclusion of many previous users of the land.
- Second, potential suitable land is identified for sugarcane cultivation. The DCGT then contacts the communities via the TAs, and if these farmers are not willing to hand in their plot for sugarcane production, the land is alienated with the argument that the TAs are the traditional owners and land must be put to development for the benefit of the entire community.
- Third, sugarcane cultivation requires some minimal technical requirement for commercial production such as irrigation, which create dependencies. Therefore, the small plots have to be pooled into larger plots. In Dwangwa, the dominant practice is that the smallholders' land is pooled into blocks of 40 ha and registered under titles held by the DCGT on behalf of the farmers (Chinsinga 2017; Adams et al. 2018).
- Fourth, long-enduring leasehold titles. According to the DCGT, though the lease agreement for the project area is 30 years, selected smallholders can only be given a license for five years, and the land is accrued to them after the first cane harvest. After the land is used, developed, and registered as trust land, it seizes to be regarded as customary land and can never be taken back. This means that the land is registered under a name and part of a block can no longer be demanded by members of the matrilineage. It is often the people selected by the TAs who are then part of the outgrower schemes, while other former commoners as well as women are left out and dispossessed.
- Fifth, concentration of providers. The Cane Supply Agreement (CSA) forces smallholders to supply their cane to Illovo as the only miller, yet Illovo does not recognize the individual farmers as contractual parties. Instead, DCGL signs the Cane Supply Agreement with Illovo, serving as a guarantor and mediator between

the DCGT farmers, i.e., Dwangwa Sugarcane Growers Association (DSGA) and the miller (Illovo). This gives Illovo indirect access to the smallholders' production without possibility for the smallholders to negotiate or hold the miller (Illovo) accountable. Furthermore, the smallholders do not have the possibility or power to discuss with the miller over the terms of the contract and, so, are placed at the receiving end of the relationship without a feedback loop. Another complexity stems from the fact that smallholders are bound in a contract in order to supply their cane to the miller. This license is valid for five years and subject to renewal upon the DCGT's approval and can terminate the licenses as it sees fit. If the contract is not renewed, the farmer hence loses his land as well. As such, outgrowers' rights to use their land are limited to the license they possess, which is conditioned to the DCGT membership.

- Sixth, conducive environment for exploitation by the miller. For instance, the contract entails a strict division of proceeds, allowing the miller to retain 40% of the total proceeds derived from the cane supplied by the outgrowers without justification on cost of milling (DCGL, Ass. General Manager, interview 23/11/2015). According to the DCGL, this 40% is "a take it or leave it" condition, and the farmers are informed with no choice but to accept it (Adams et al. 2018). Farmers reproduce the discourse of development—basically increased cash income to cope with cash expenditures (traditional and modern)—but also bring in arguments that they are better off than before and better off than their neighbors (Adams et al. 2018). In 36 outgrower households, the belief that outgrowers have money has resulted in the monetization of production relations now being measured in terms of cash, resulting in the monetization of household labor as against noncash reciprocal exchanges (ibid). Therefore, outgrowers use such redistributive obligations to justify for excluding other family members from their cash returns (ibid). However, outgrowers' decision to focus only on their immediate family leads to division and loss of trust among members in the broader family. Therefore, the outgrower scheme increases farmers dependency and potential loss of land and increased their dependence on the company and to some extent the TA.
- Seventh, increased monetization of production and exchange relations previously in the domain of reciprocal relation. The outgrowers face high cash demands within their communities, and all arrangements (material and nonmaterial), necessary for rural wealth development, suddenly become monetized as they are seen as the ones providing cash for larger groups while at the same time all social relations get monetized as well (mutual help, reciprocity rules, exchanges, etc.).
- Eighth, exclusive "private" property. In the legitimating ideology of modernity and inclusive discourse of individuality and entrepreneurial decision-making, the company introduces new labor relations (wage labor) and creates dependencies and disparities between the farmers through differentiation—a process which was buffered in the former system based on common lineage property.

Interestingly, more and more outgrower farmers seem to understand the dividing and unfair process, which takes place and discuss it as they come to an understanding of the value chain of sugarcane production that the company takes more profit than it should. This has led to intensive debates within and among the outgrowers who have now organized themselves into an organized body to fight for institutional change in the outgrower scheme and production arrangements toward more fair distribution of the gains and are addressing the company on these issues.

These struggles for institutional change could lead to better outcomes from the sugarcane and could help more people to benefit from sugarcane production beyond the few winners so far (see also Adams et al. 2018).

Discussion and Conclusion

All these cases describe LSLA's major impacts on the commons, a process called commons grabbing. The summative table below (Table 1) shows common property arrangements for land and land-related common pool resources and that leading actors were not individual private owners but had a more coordinating role to play for the governance of a common property system. These arrangements gave women and marginalized groups access to commons. The LSLA then did not change this situation immediately, but pre-LSLA changes since colonial and postcolonial times weakened the common property institutions giving more power to the elites, who were a part of the indirect rule arrangement. The neoliberal economy produces the ideology of development. This correlates with increasing prices for land and lowering bargaining power of the commoners, but increasing power of the elites who pursue the strategy of institution shopping in order to profit from the changes, first from commons via state property and then in the context of neoliberal order from state to private property. They are to be contacted and contracted by the companies. In all cases, the companies promise gender-oriented development and compensations as well as CSR. In effect, not just land but other common pool resources such as water, pastures, and fisheries, timber, and veld products were lost. These findings are analyzed within the New Institutionalism approach, which outlines historically occurring changes and fluctuations of relative prices of land and land-related resources that affect the bargaining power of local groups, the way different actors select institutions, and the way changes are legitimated ideologically and leading to distributional and strategic contexts.

However, as the model of institutional change shows, the privatization that follows the LSLA investments is not predetermined. The described situations develop in a drama rather than a tragedy of the grabbed commons as local actors react on several levels. We distinguish between the "weak weapons of the weak" strategies such as gossip in Morocco and Tanzania and more direct actions such as accessing the common lands not used by the company as act of civil disobedience (Kenya, Sierra Leone, Tanzania), or institution shopping on precolonial, state-based and international rules as users realize what they have lost (Sierra Leone with getting back access to water, also Malawi), and addressing the company and elites in meetings and court cases (Ghana) as well as violent strategies (Ghana, Sierra

Table 1 Comparison of institutional changes, discourses, company strategies, impacts, and local responses in LSLA on land and land-related commons in Morocco, Sierra Leone, Ghana, Kenya, Tanzania, and Malawi

Case/topic	Precolonial commons arrangement	Colonial/ postcolonial transformations	Major discourses/institution shopping	General impacts on gender marginal group	Local reactions
Morocco: Solar energy investor: Parastatal and EU financed company MASEN	*Common clan land (Berber) pastures and veld products, mobility*	State property but respect of customary land	Development of wasteland with compensations/CSR (jobs, infrastructure, projects)/*state resource ownership* for higher purpose (King), sustainable green energy development rules, rules of compensation and pricing of land	*Commons grabbing*, low compensations not accessible, loss of access to food and cash/workload increased as loss of cash income from loss of commons, compensations only for men and access to CRS not possible or not feasible	*Weak weapons of the weak*: development wanted by King and respected, however gossip and complaints as less jobs and no access to compensations and CSR
Sierra Leone: Biofuel-sugarcane plantations by ADDAX BIOENERGY (Swiss) funded by international donors/ development agencies (banks) Project renounce in 2016	*Communal land controlled by community, family land containing CPRs by firstcomers (Temne)* access to land, water and veld products available for latecomers, through management by firstcomers	*Customary including state property and precolonial land and CPR management*	Development of abundant land with compensation scheme and CSR (jobs, infrastructure projects, improvement of traditional agriculture). Development of rural areas, compliance with international rules for sustainable biofuel with environmental and social impact assessments. Consideration of state and customary land institutions	*Commons grabbing* with low direct compensations and only for landowning firstcomers. No substitution for lost access to land, CPR, and direct cash income opportunities of latecomers. Little job generation, mainly for landowners. CSR badly adapted to local conditions. Triple workload for women	*Traditional resistance, strong weapons of the weak, collaboration with external actors.* Local opposition by some elites and latecomers (demanding jobs, using traditional secret societies, stealing of goods, pressuring firstcomers), collaboration with legal NGO. Triple institution shopping by women for land and water

(continued)

Table 1 (continued)

Case/topic	Precolonial commons arrangement	Colonial/postcolonial transformations	Major discourses/institution shopping	General impacts on gender marginal group	Local reactions
Ghana: Rice production by GADCO (GB, Nigeria; India, taken over by Swiss) funded by international donors/development agencies on farm, pasture, and floodplain land	*Commons controlled by firstcomers (Ewe)* with institutions and rules membership of access to cultural landscapes	State property and indirect rule installment of chiefs/Paramount Chief as de facto private owners	*Development of abundant land* with compensations and CSR (jobs, infrastructure, projects)/*state territory for development based on customary land tenure* and chiefly rule, indirect rule arrangement	*Commons grabbing:* loss of access to land and CPRs (pasture, fuel wood, and fish) for food and cash, CSR and compensations unfairly distributed to chiefs)/loss of CPRs with little or no compensation means higher workload for cash, rice picking by women does not compensate	*All ranges of weapons of the weak to legal and violent actions:* from gossip, civil disobedience, court cases direct actions/rallies public meetings challenging chiefs
Kenya: Rice production by Dominion farms (USA): own capital and Christian mission orientation	Commons controlled by clan elders (*Luo*)	State property (land held in trust) and access for companies directly based on state rules of investment	*Bringing "Christian" faith and development of wasteland* (swamp wetland) with compensations and CSR (jobs, infrastructure, projects)/*state investment in land rules, development of remote area,* natural and social impact assessments	*Commons grabbing via loss of access to wetland* (pasture, food and cash, low compensation payments, marginal groups and women) and fish (revenues of women). Little opportunities for women badly paid and dangerous (snake bites)	Medium weapons of the weak and civil disobedience (gossip on investors fate and illegal use of the grazing and fishing grounds not used by company), new internal resource institutions

Tanzania: Forestry plantations by NFC (UK, SA)	Commons controlled by clan elders (Wahehe)	State property and access for companies directly based on state rules and village tenure	Development of abundant land with compensations and CSR (jobs, infrastructure, projects) on village level/state development rules for attracting investments, village rules, international and national assessments	Commons grabbing via direct and indirect loss of access to land and CPRs (water, veld products) for food and cash/grabbing and loss of most valuable land for women for farming loss of access to water, veld products for cash, eviction of women from most valuable land, sales without consulting women	Low level of weapons of the weak (gossip, gender-related conflicts, attempts for court cases, low level of collective actions
Malawi: Sugarcane in outgrower schemes by Illovo (UK, SA)	Commons controlled by matrilineal clans with institutions to defend resources	State property and indirect rule installment of chiefs/TAs as private owners	Development of abundant land with compensations and CSR via outgrowers schemes in block farming system and organization profiting TAs/state development rules based on state development rules for privatization (leases) and customary land ownership by TAs	Commons grabbing via direct loss of access to land for matriline by privatization for male elites and TAs/women and marginal groups in the matrilineal clans as belonging to clan no longer gives access (outgrowers land in long-term lease contracts)	Initially low levels of weapons of the weak but increasing awareness and collective as understanding contracts and value chains of Illovo

Leone). All the cases also show that women are denied access to the resources previously held as commons after they have been transformed into private property. Disenfranchisement of women increases their workload and decreases possibility to gain cash. In patrilineal systems, despite having lower status, women access the commons via their father's side. In Malawi the matrilineal system gives power to the women's lineage, which has been undermined during the LSLA process.

The following table summarizes the cases (Table 1).

Regarding the outcome of the drama of the grabbed commons, strategies to mitigate their adverse effects are successful if they address wider institutional and economic settings and the role of local elites. If new policies are backed by the state authority, they are not easily challenged. The case of the Temne women in Sierra Leone and outgrower farmers in Malawi indicate that these are successful strategies, while self-organization cannot be backed by institutions and alliances outside the local context. A combination of governing institutions seems to be a feasible solution.

Our comparative analysis highlights how the locally designed common property institutions for the management of common pool resources worked successfully before the new investments disabled sustainable well-being, including cash flow for local actors. Most of the actors who relied on the land-related commons have been excluded from resource use, while the promises of development, new jobs, and infrastructure were not fulfilled. Changes legitimized by international companies and elite groups as sustainable development and justified by legal claims ranging from transformed customs to state laws used by the powerful to justify their claims undermined resilience and food security for the most vulnerable actors. At the same time, women and marginalized groups do not have access to compensations, corporate social programs, and "new commons" such as funds, development schemes, etc. However, there is a potential as local actors, especially women, realize that the promise of corporate development is an anti-politics machine and that local bottom-up involvement as well as institution building is needed, in order to regain the commons. This, however, needs the backing from national and international organizations and law enforcement based on local participatory actions challenging the existing power relations (see the constitutionality approach by Haller et al. 2016, 2018).

References

Adams, T., Gerber, J.-D., & Haller, T. (2018). Who gains from contract farming? Dependencies, power relations, and institutional change. *Journal of Peasant Studies*. https://doi.org/10.1080/03066150.2018.1534100

Amanor, K.S. (1999). *Global restructuring and land rights in Ghana. Forest food chains, timber and rural livelihoods* (Research Rep. No. 108). Uppsala: Nordiska Afrikainstitutet.

Amanor, K. S. (2008). The changing face of customary land tenure. In J. M. Ubink & K. S. Amanor (Eds.), *Contesting land and custom in Ghana: State, chief and citizen* (pp. 55–81. Law, Governance and Development). Leiden: Leiden University Press.

Anseeuw, W., Boche, M., Breu, T., Giger, M., Lay, J., Messerli, P., et al. (2012). *Transnational land deals for agriculture in the global south. Analytical report based on the Land Matrix Database*. Bern/Montpellier/Hamburg: CDE/CIRAD/GIGA.

Baird, I. G. (2011). Turning land into capital, turning people into labour: Primitive accumulation and the arrival of large-scale economic land concessions in the Lao People's Democratic Republic. *New Proposals: Journal of Marxism and Interdisciplinary Inquiry, 5*(1), 10–12.

Basu, P. K. (2007). The political economy of land grab. *Economic and Political Weekly, 42*(14), 1281–1287.

Bayart, J. F. (1989). *L'État en Afrique. La politique du ventre*. Paris: Karthala.

Behrman, J., Meinzen-Dick, R., & Quisumbing, A. (2012). The gender implications of large-scale land deals. *Journal of Peasant Studies, 39*(1), 49–79. University of Agriculture.

Benschop, M. (2002). *Rights and reality: Are women's equal rights to land, housing and property implemented in East Africa?* Nairobi: Un-Habitat.

Biersack, A. (1999). Introduction: From the "new ecology" to the new ecologies. *American Anthropologist, 101*(1), 5–18.

Blaikie, P. (2006). Is small really beautiful? Community-based natural resource management in Malawi and Botswana. *World Development, 34*(11), 1942–1957.

Blaikie, P. M., & Brookfield, H. (1987). *Land degradation and society*. London: Methuen.

Boni, S. (2008). Traditional ambiguities and authoritarian interpretations in Sefwi land disputes. In J. M. Ubink & K. S. Amanor (Eds.), *Contesting land and custom in Ghana: State, chief and citizen* (pp. 81–112. Law, Governance and Development). Leiden: Leiden University Press.

Boone, C. (2015). Land tenure regimes and state structure in rural Africa: Implications for forms of resistance against large-scale land acquisitions by outsiders. *Journal of Contemporary African Studies, 33*(2), 171–190.

Borras, M. S., McMichael, P., & Scoones, I. (2010). The politics of biofuels, land and agrarian change: Editors' introduction. *Journal of Peasant Studies, 37*(4), 575–592.

Borras Jr., S. M., Franco, J. C., & Wang, C. (2013). The challenge of global governance of land grabbing: Changing international agricultural context and competing political views and strategies. *Globalizations, 10*(1), 161–179.

Boserup, E. (1970). *Women's role in economic development*. London: St. Martin's Press.

Brown, T. (2005). Contestation, confusion and corruption: Market-based land reform in Zambia. In *Competing jurisdictions: Settling land claims in Africa* (pp. 79–102). Leiden: Brill.

Bryceson, D. F. (1995). *Women wielding the hoe: Lessons from rural Africa for feminist theory and development practice*. Oxford: Berg Publisher Ltd.

Cagatay, N., & Ozler, S. (1995). Feminization of the labour force: The effects of long-term development and structural adjustment. *World Development, 23*(11), 1883–1894.

Chanock, M. (1991). Paradigms, policies and property: A review of the customary law of land tenure. In K. Mann & R. Roberts (Eds.), *Law in colonial Africa* (pp. 61–84). Portsmouth: Heinemann.

Chanock, M. (2005). Customary law, sustainable development and the failing state. In P. Oerebech, F. Bosselman, J. Bjarup, D. Callies, & M. Chanock (Eds.), *The role of customary law in sustainable development* (pp. 338–383). Cambridge: Cambridge University Press.

Chinsinga, B. (2017). The green belt initiative, politics and sugar production in Malawi. *Journal of Southern African Studies, 43*(3), 501–515.

Cotula, L. (2009). *Land grab or development opportunity? Agricultural investment and international land deals in Africa*. London/Rome: IIED/FAO/IFAD.

Coulter, J., Goodland, A., Tallontire, A., & Stringfellow, R. (2009). *Marrying farmer cooperation and contract farming for service provision in a liberalising sub-Saharan Africa*. London: Overseas Development Institute.

De Schutter, O. (2011). How not to think of land grabbing: Three critiques of large scale investments in farmland. *Journal of Peasant Studies, 38*(2), 249–280.

Deininger, K. (2011). Challenges posed by the new wave of farmland investment. *The Journal of Peasant Studies, 38*(2), 217–247.

Dolan, C. (2001). The 'good wife': Struggles over resources in the Kenyan horticultural sector. *Journal of Development Studies, 37*(3), 39–70.

Elwert, G. (1980). Überleben in Krisen, kapitalistische Entwicklung und traditionelle Solidarität. Zur Ökonomie und Sozialstruktur eines westafrikanischen Bauerndorfes. *Zeitschrift für Soziologie, 9*(4), 343–365.

Ensminger, J. (1992). *Making a market. The institutional transformation of an African society*. Cambridge: Cambridge University Press.

Ferguson, J. (1994). *The anti-politics machine. "Development" and bureaucratic power in Lesotho*. Minneapolis, MN: University of Minnesota Press.

Frank, A. G. (1975). *On capitalist underdevelopment*. Bombay: Oxford University Press.

Franco, J. (2016). *Reclaiming Free Prior and Informed Consent (FPIC) in the context of global land grabs*. Transnational Institute.

Geiger, M., Nolte, K., & Haller, T. (2019). Using evidence from the Land Matrix and other data repositories to investigate impacts of large-scale land investments on common pool resources. In T. Haller, T. Breu, T. de Moot, C. Rohr, & H. Znoj (Eds.), *The commons in a 'glocal' world: Global connections and local responses*. London: Routledge.

Glover, J. D. (1987). Increasing the benefits to smallholders from contract farming: Problems for farmers' organizations and policy makers. *World Development, 15*(2), 441–448.

Gmür, D. (2019). Grabbing the female commons: Large-scale land acquisitions for forest plantations and impacts on gender-relations in Kilolo District, Iringa Region, Tanzania. In T. Haller, T. De Moor, C. Rohr, & H. P. Znoj (Eds.), *The commons in a glocal world: Global connections and local responses* (pp. 301–317). London: Routledge. (in Press).

Hall, R. (2011). Land grabbing in Southern Africa: The many faces of the investor rush. *Review of African Political Economy, 38*(128), 193–214.

Haller, T. (Ed.). (2010). *Disputing the floodplains*. Leiden: Brill.

Haller, T. (2013). *The contested floodplain*. Lanham: Lexington.

Haller, T. (2016). Managing the commons with floods: The role of institutions and power relations for water governance and food resilience in African floodplains. In T. Ostegard (Ed.), *Water and Food – Africa in a Global Context* (pp. 369–397). Uppsala: The Nordic African Institute. I.B. Tauris.

Haller, T., & Merten, S. (2008). "We are Zambians – don't tell us how to fish!" institutional change, power relations and conflicts in the Kafue flats fisheries in Zambia. *Human Ecology, 36*(5), 699–715.

Haller, T., John, M., Bloenchlinger, A., Marthaler, E., & Ziegler, S. (Eds.). (2007). *Fossil fuels, oil companies, and indigenous peoples: Strategies of multinational oil companies, states, and ethnic minorities: Impact on environment, livelihoods, and cultural change* (Vol. 1). Münster: LIT Verlag.

Haller, T., Fokou, G., Mbeyale, G., & Meroka, P. (2013). How fit turns into misfit and back: Institutional transformations of pastoral commons in African floodplains. *Ecology and Society, 18*(1), 34. https://doi.org/10.5751/ES-05510-180134

Haller, T., Acciaioli, G., & Rist, S. (2016). Constitutionality: Conditions for crafting local ownership of institution-building processes. *Society & Natural Resources, 29*(1), 68–87.

Haller, T., Belsky, J. M., & Rist, S. (2018). The constitutionality approach: Conditions, opportunities, and challenges for bottom-up institution building. *Human Ecology, 46*(1), 1–2.

Jones, G. A., & Chant, S. (2009). Globalising initiatives for gender equality and poverty reduction: Exploring 'failure' with reference to education and work among urban youth in The Gambia and Ghana. *Geoforum, 40*(2), 184–196.

Kasanga, R. K., & Kotey, N. A. (2001). *Land management in Ghana: Building on tradition and modernity*. London: Eldis. http://www.eldis.org/document/A26335

Käser, F. (2014). Ethnography of a land-deal. A village perspective on the Addax Bioenergy project. MA-thesis. Institute of Social Anthropology, University Bern: Switzerland.

Lanz, K., Gerber, J. D., & Haller, T. (2018). Land Grabbing, the State and Chiefs: The Politics of Extending Commercial Agriculture in Ghana. *Development and Change, 49*(6), 1526–1552.

Lenz, K. (2006). First-comers and late comers: Indigenous theories of land ownership in the West Afrcan savanna. In R. Kuba & K. Lenz (Eds.), *Land and the politics of belonging* (pp. 34–57). Leiden: Brill.

Locher, M., & Müller-Böker, U. (2014). "Investors are good, if they follow the rules"–power relations and local perceptions in the case of two European forestry companies in Tanzania. *Geographica Helvetica, 69*(4), 249–258.

Lustenberger, S. (2014). Addax Bioenergy Sierra Leone: Analysis of the implementation process of a large scale land acquisition project from the perspective of assemblage theory. MA-thesis at the Institute of Geography, University of Bern: Switzerland.
Marfurt, F., Käser, F., & Lustenberger, S. (2016). Local perceptions and vertical perspectives of a large scale land acquisition project in Northern Sierra Leone. *Homo Oeconomicus, 33*(3), 1–19.
Marfurt, F. (2019). Gendered impacts and coping strategies in the case of a swiss bioenergy project in Sierra Leone. In T. Haller, T. De Moor, C. Rohr, & H. P. Znoj (Eds.), *The commons in a glocal world: Global connections and local responses* (pp. 318–335). London: Routledge.
Meillassoux, C. (1981). *Maiden meals and money*. Cambridge: Cambridge University Press.
Molyneux, M. (1979). Beyond the domestic labour debate. *New Left Review, 116*(3), 27.
Narotzki, S. (1997). *New directions in economic anthropology*. London: Pluto Press.
New Forests Company (NFC) (2014a). *Website.* http://www.newforests.net/ (accessed 10.10.2014).
New Forests Company (NFC) (2014b): *Sustainability Report FY 14*. http://www.newforests.net/wpcontent/uploads/pdf_docs/New%20Forests%20Co%20Sustainability%20Report_FY2014.pdf. (accessed 10.01.2015).
Niederberger, T., Haller, T., Gambon, H., Kobi, M., & Wenk, I. (2016). *The open cut: Mining, transnational corporations and local populations* (Vol. 2). Münster: Lit Verlag.
Orloff, A. S. (2002). Explaining US welfare reform: Power, gender, race and the US policy legacy. *Critical Social Policy, 22*(1), 96–118.
Ostrom, E. (1990). *Governing the commons. The evolution of institutions for collective action.* Cambridge: Cambridge University Press.
Ostrom, E. (2005). *Understanding institutional diversity*. Princeton, NJ: Princeton University Press.
Peters, P. S. (2009). Challenges in land tenure and land reform in Africa: Anthropological contributions. *World Development, 37*(8), 1317–1325.
Peters, P. E. (2013). Land appropriation, surplus people and a battle over visions of agrarian futures in Africa. *Journal of Peasant Studies, 40*(3), 537–562.
Porter, G., & Phillips-Howard, K. (1997). Comparing contracts: An evaluation of contract farming schemes in Africa. *World Development, 25*(2), 227–238.
Poteete, A. R., & Ribot, J. C. (2011). Repertoires of domination: Decentralization as process in Botswana and Senegal. *World Development, 39*(3), 439–449.
Razavi, S. (2007). *The political and social economy of care in a development context. Conceptual issues, research questions and policy options.* Geneva: UNRISD.
Rocheleau, D. (1996). *Feminist political ecology. Global issues and local experience.* London: Routledge.
Rocheleau, D. (2001). Complex communities and relational webs uncertainty, surprise and transformation in Machakos. *IDS Bulletin, 32*(4), 78–87.
Ryser, S. (2019). Are green energy investments levelled by the 'new commons'? Compensations, CSR measures and gendered impacts of a solar energy project in Morocco. In T. Haller, T. De Moor, C. Rohr, & H. P. Znoj (Eds.), *The commons in a glocal world: Global connections and local responses* (pp. 352–376). London: Routledge. (in Press).
Schoneveld, G., German, L., & Nutakor, E. (2011). Land-based investments for rural development? A grounded analysis of the local impacts of biofuel feedstock plantations in Ghana. *Ecology and Society, 16*(4), 10.
Schubiger, E. (2016). As much as the frog croaks, the cow still drinks the water: Ethnography of a large-scale land acquisition in West Kenya. MA-thesis. Institute of Social Anthropology, University Bern: Switzerland.
Scott, J. C. (1985). *Weapons of the weak: Everyday forms of peasant resistance*. New Haven, CT: Yale University Press.
Stocks, A. (2005). Too much for too few: Problems of indigenous land rights in Latin America. *Annual Review of Anthropology, 34*, 85–104.
Toulmin, C. (2008). Securing land and property rights in sub-Saharan Africa: The role of local institutions. *Land Use Policy, 26*, 10–19.
URT [United Republic of Tanzania]. (1999a). The land act no. 4. Dar es Salaam: Government Printers.

URT [United Republic of Tanzania]. (1999b). *The village land act no. 5*. Dar es Salaam: Government Printers.

Veuthy, S., & Gerber, J. F. (2011). Possession versus property in a tree plantation. Socioenvironmental conflict in Southern Cameroon. *Society and Natural Resources, 24*, 831–848.

Von Benda-Beckmann, K. (1981). Forum shopping and shopping forums: Dispute processing in a Minangkabau village in West Sumatra. *The Journal of Legal Pluralism and Unofficial Law, 13*(19), 117–159.

Von Sury, A. (2016). Ethnography of land deals: 'Dominion has the biggest shamba now': Local perceptions of the Dominion farms project in Western Kenya. MA-thesis. Institute of Social Anthropology, University Bern: Switzerland.

Wallerstein, I. (1979). *The capitalist world-economy* (Vol. 2). Cambridge: Cambridge University Press.

Weiner, A. (1976). *Women of value, men of renown: New perspectives in Trobriand exchange*. Austin, TX: University of Texas Press.

White, J., & White, B. (2012). Gendered experiences of dispossession: Oil palm expansion in a Dayak Hibun community in West Kalimantan. *The Journal of Peasant Studies, 39*, 995–1016.

Wilk, R., & Cliggett, L. (2007). *Economies and cultures. Foundations of economic anthropology*. Cambridge: Westview Press.

Wolf, E. R. (1983). *Europe and the people without history*. Berkeley, CA: University of California Press.

Zoomers, A. (2011). Introduction: Rushing for land: Equitable and sustainable development in Africa, Asia and Latin America. *Development, 54*(1), 12–20.

Open Access, Open Systems: Pastoral Resource Management in the Chad Basin

Mark Moritz, Paul Scholte, Ian M. Hamilton, and Saïdou Kari

Introduction

Is sustainable management of open access to common-pool grazing resources possible? A longitudinal study of mobile pastoralists in the Chad Basin suggests that management of open access is not an oxymoron, challenging long-held assumptions about the tragedy of the commons.

The discussion about the impact of pastoralists on ecosystems has been profoundly shaped by Hardin's (1968) tragedy of the commons that held pastoralists responsible for overgrazing the range. Hardin's argument focused on how population growth, in particular the freedom to breed, threatens our planet. Hardin gave an example of shepherds who keep their privately owned herds on pastures that are held in commons. He argued that it is in the economic interest of each individual

---

This chapter has been edited and reused with permission from Springer Publishers and was originally published in Human Ecology: Moritz, Mark, Paul Scholte, Ian M. Hamilton, Saïdou Kari. 2013. Open Access, Open Systems: Pastoral Management of Common-Pool Resources in the Chad Basin. Human Ecology. 41(3):351–365.

M. Moritz (✉)
Department of Anthropology, The Ohio State University, Columbus, OH, USA
e-mail: moritz.42@osu.edu

P. Scholte
Deutsche Gesellschaft für Internationale Zusammenarbeit, Bonn, Germany

I. M. Hamilton
Department of Evolution, Ecology and Organismal Biology, The Ohio State University, Columbus, OH, USA

Department of Mathematics, The Ohio State University, Columbus, OH, USA

S. Kari
Centre d'Appui a la Recherche et au Pastoralisme (CARPA), Maroua, Cameroon

herder to increase the size of the herd because they can gain all the benefits of additional animals while sharing the costs of using the pastures with other herders. When all herders follow this strategy, Hardin argued, it will inevitably lead to degradation, i.e., a tragedy of the commons.

Hardin's thesis that common-pool resources cannot be managed sustainably, unless it is governed by the state or transformed into private property, has been challenged by political scientists and anthropologists (McCay and Acheson 1987; Feeny et al. 1990; Ostrom 1990; Ostrom et al. 2002). One of the main critiques has been that Hardin confused commons with open access or unmanaged common-pool resources (McCay and Acheson 1987; Ostrom 1990). Common-pool resources are valued resources that are "available to more than one person and subject to degradation as a result of overuse. Common-pool resources are ones for which exclusion from the resource is costly and one person's use subtracts from what is available to others" (Dietz et al. 2002, p. 18). Four different types of property regimes of common-pool resources have been recognized: open access, public or state property, common property, and private property. In common property regimes, a specific user group has use rights over the resource, while in open access situations, no property rights are defined leading to a "free for all" (Dietz et al. 2002).

Ostrom (1990) has shown that common-pool resources can be managed sustainably as common property regimes. She also generated design principles for successful common property regimes that can be categorized as follows: (1) membership rules that define who can use the resources, their rights, and responsibilities; (2) appropriation rules that specify how much of what type of resources can be extracted, or the condition of the resource after extraction; and (3) procedural rules that empower monitoring, sanctioning, arbitration, and negotiation (Niamir-Fuller 1999b). Since Ostrom published the design principles, case studies, comparative studies, experiments, and meta-analyses have yielded more variables (Agrawal 2002; Ostrom et al. 2002; Poteete et al. 2010; Anderies and Janssen 2013), resulting in a more complex diagnostic framework for the study of social-ecological systems (Ostrom 2007). Despite a well-developed theoretical framework, it has been challenging to develop general explanations for successful commons that hold across resource systems, primarily because of the complexity of both social and ecological systems and the configurational nature of the multitude of multidimensional variables (Agrawal 2002; Ostrom 2007; Poteete et al. 2010). However, scholars continue to argue that open access to common-pool resources will lead to a tragedy (Berkes 2009).

The theoretical paradigms of both the tragedy of the commons and governing the commons have shaped our understanding of how pastoralists interact with common-pool grazing resources. Hardin's shepherds' parable forever linked pastoralists with the tragedy of the commons. In sub-Saharan Africa, for example, pastoralists have been held responsible for overgrazing the range, exacerbating the hardship they endured during the droughts of the early 1970s and 1980s (Lamprey 1983; Picardi and Seifert 1976; Sinclair and Fryxell 1985). In response, researchers of African pastoral systems have explained that often there is no evidence of a tragedy of the commons (Horowitz 1986; McCabe 1990) or that it is the result of outside interventions (Galaty 1994; Peters 1994; Ensminger and Knight 1997). McCabe (1990), for example, has shown how the Turkana in Kenya manage common-pool resources and avoid a tragedy of the commons through a combination of mobility, regulation of access to grazing resources through private ownership of wells, and environmental constraints on herd size. Longitudinal, interdisciplinary studies of pastoral systems have also shown that grazing ecosystems are more complex and dynamic than previously assumed and that they can be managed adaptively as commons (Behnke and Scoones 1993; Niamir-Fuller 1999a, b).

The current consensus in the literature on pastoral systems is that in most cases common-pool resources are managed as common property regimes but that open access leads to a tragedy of the commons (Homewood 2008; Galvin 2009). Others have argued that there are no pastoral systems that operated according to the open access paradigm (McCabe 1990; Lane 1998). However, this understanding is primarily based on research in East Africa, which has dominated the literature (Fratkin et al. 1994; Galvin 2009). Consequently, the East African commons model is assumed to be applicable to other pastoral systems in sub-Saharan Africa (Mwangi and Ostrom 2009).

West African pastoral systems do not necessarily fit this East African model of the commons. Instead it has been argued that in West African pastoral systems, access to common-pool grazing resources is regulated through a number of informal institutions, social networks, and norms of reciprocity that are characterized by flexibility, porosity, and malleability (Turner 1999; Fernández-Giménez and Le Febre 2006; Bassett and Turner 2007). However, it is not at all clear whether and how these norms, networks, and institutions regulate access to and use of common-pool resources. We think that in many cases these systems are best described as open access because there are de facto no restrictions on access and use but that researchers may (unconsciously) have been searching for some regulation as evidence of common property regimes where there is none and are afraid to use the label open access because of all its negative connotations.

Here we argue that the commons model may well describe many pastoral systems in East Africa, but not necessarily those in West and Central Africa, many of which have open access (Niamir-Fuller 1999a, b; Swallow 1990). Moreover, our longitudinal study of pastoral mobility and primary production in the Logone Floodplain in the Far North Region of Cameroon shows that open access does not have to lead to a tragedy of the commons (Scholte et al. 2006; Moritz et al. 2014a). In this chapter, we explain how this self-organizing system of management of open access works and discuss its implications for theories of management of common-pool resources and our understanding of pastoral systems.

Methods

This chapter is based on more than 20 years of research with pastoralists in the Far North Region of Cameroon, in particular on two long-term research projects of pastoral mobility in the Logone Floodplain as well as on parallel ecological studies conducted by the authors. The first study (1993–1999) focused on how the reflooding of the Logone Floodplain led to an increase in perennial grasses and thereby increase in rangeland production and quality (Scholte et al. 2006). We documented the responses of mobile pastoralists by studying their transhumance patterns in five different years between 1993 and 1999 using transhumance surveys in which we surveyed the whole population, i.e., all mobile pastoralists that used our study area at some point during the year, and asked them the names and number of days of all the sites they had stayed in the previous year. We also recorded the number of pastoral households and estimated the size of the herds.

In the second study (2008–2016), we examined how pastoralists coordinate their movements and avoid conflicts with each other using a combination of spatial and ethnographic analyses. We continued the transhumance surveys with the whole population of mobile pastoralists. In addition, we used GPS/GIS technology to map the locations of mobile pastoralists in the Logone Floodplain and beyond. Four times a year we took the geographic coordinates of pastoral households (February, May, August, November). We used a combination of participant observation and informal, semi-structured, and structured interviews to understand how pastoralists regulate access to and use of common-pool grazing resources in the Logone Floodplain. In this chapter, we focus our analysis on the ethnographic and ethnohistorical dataset.

Parallel to these studies, we have conducted extensive research on the vegetation of the Logone Floodplain between 1993 and 2003. A total of 199 plots, including 29 already studied in 1985 and 1986, were used to annually monitor changes in vegetation composition. Aboveground biomass has been measured as function of flooding depth in 32, 8, and 16 plots in, respectively, 1994, 1995, and 1996. In addition, forage quality and belowground biomass have been assessed in, respectively, 1996 and 1994 and 1995. The results of these studies, on which we build our argument regarding the lack of overgrazing, have been published elsewhere (Scholte 2007; Scholte et al. 2000).

Study Area and Population

Two phytogeographic zones characterize the Far North Region of Cameroon: Sudanian in the southern grades and Sahelian in the Logone Floodplain (Fig. 1). The Logone Floodplain, called *Yaayre* in Fulfulde, is flooded by the Logone River and its branches from September until November. After the water recedes in December, thousands of Arab and FulBe pastoralists from Cameroon, Nigeria, and

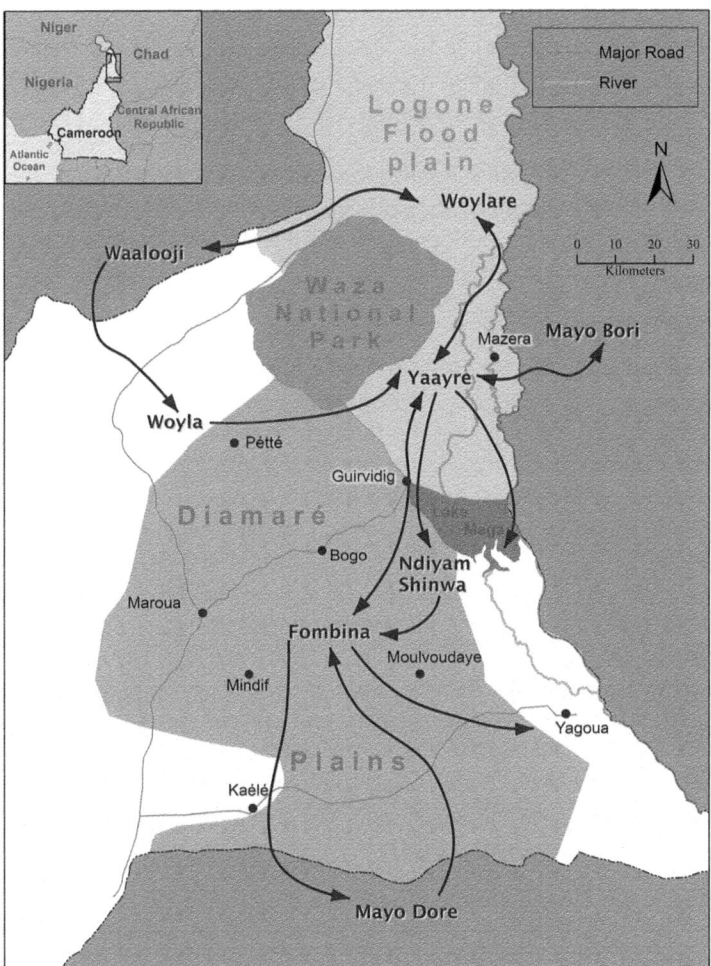

Fig. 1 Transhumance orbits in the Far North Region of Cameroon

Niger move with more than 200,000 cattle into the floodplain making it one of the most important dry season grazing lands in the Chad Basin (Seignobos 2000). Many remain there until the start of the rainy season in June, while others move south to the grazing lands that surround Lake Maga. Pastoralists find nutritious regrowth and surface water in the floodplain far into the dry season, when surrounding pastures have dried up. At the start of the rainy season, pastoralists return to the higher elevated dunes of the Diamaré or their respective countries.

The vegetation in the floodplain is relatively homogenous in terms of forage quantity and quality because of the extreme flatness of the area resulting in only limited variation in flooding depth and duration (Scholte 2007). There is a weak coupling between herbivores and vegetation as the predominantly perennial vegetation is controlled by flooding depth and duration and naturally protected against overgrazing because up to two-thirds of the biomass is stored underground. In addition aboveground biomass is generally inaccessible to livestock during the flooding for 6 months of the year (Scholte 2007).

Our study area is a 1000-km^2 section of the Logone Floodplain with Waza National Park in the west, the Logone River in the east, the irrigated rice fields of SEMRY in the south, and the village of Zina in the north. The study area overlaps with the pilot zone of the Waza Logone Project (1990–2003), which started reflooding of the pilot zone by opening old waterways in the dike along the Logone River in 1994 and 1996 (Scholte 2005).

As other African floodplains, such as the Inner Niger Delta (Mali), the Sudd (Sudan), and the Kafue Flats (Zambia), the Logone Floodplain is an important and complex social-ecological system in terms of biodiversity and livelihoods for local populations. The floodplain is used by multiple ethnic groups which make a living in different economic activities, including fishery (Kotoko, Musgum), agriculture (Musgum), and pastoralism (Arab, FulBe, Musgum). There are thus multiple common-pool resources, and the resulting management systems are complex (Haller 2010).

Here we focus on mobile pastoralists who are permanently on transhumance and use our study area in the Logone Floodplain at some point during the dry season. This category comprises approximately 1000 households of mobile pastoralists divided over approximately 130 camps that include Suwa Arabs and FulBe, subdivided in Jama'are, Mare, Alijam, Adanko, and Anagamba. These different FulBe groups are endogamous and have their own dialect, cattle breed, houses, and marriage system. The number of households and camps changes continually through the year and over the years as households leave one camp to join another and/or leave the study area altogether.

Case Study of Management of Open Access

Management of open access may not be as paradoxical as the literature on common property regimes suggests (McCay and Acheson 1987; Feeny et al. 1990; Ostrom 1990; Peters 1994; Lane 1998). Open access has been contrasted with common property regimes, which are managed by an identifiable community of interdependent users who can exclude outsiders and regulate use by members (McCay and Acheson 1987; Ostrom 1990). However, the first longitudinal study that we conducted of mobile pastoralists in the Logone Floodplain from 1993 to 1999 suggested that open access is managed (Scholte et al. 2006). The study focused on a 400-km^2 section of the Logone Floodplain that overlapped with the pilot zone of the Waza Logone Project, which started reflooding of the pilot zone by opening an old waterway in the embankment along the Logone River in 1994 and 1996 (Scholte 2005). This led to changes in vegetation and transhumance patterns of mobile pastoralists, which we documented in five different years between 1993 and 1999

(Scholte et al. 2006). Vegetation has shown a steady increase in cover of perennial grass species (from 41 to 75%), whereas no increase in invading plant species has been observed between 1993 and 2003 (Scholte 2005; Scholte et al. 2000). Grass productivity increased with the increasing aboveground biomass due to increased flooding as measured in 1994–1996 (Scholte 2007). Moreover, we found evidence that increase in grazing pressure matched increase in the available biomass in the floodplain.

Below we will describe how this self-organizing complex adaptive system works in which pastoralists redistribute themselves over the grazing resources within and outside the floodplain.

An Ethos of Open Access

Mobile pastoralists in the Logone Floodplain share a strong ethos of open access to common-pool grazing resources. They believe that every pastoralist has the same rights to use grazing lands, regardless of ethnicity, nationality, seniority, or socioeconomic status. Pastoralists emphatically argue that access is free and open for everyone; it does not matter whether pastoralists are coming from Cameroon or Nigeria, whether they are newcomers or old-timers, or whether they are FulBe or Arab. When asked about open access, pastoralists would say as a matter of fact, *na'i non, naa yimBe* "it's [about] cattle, not [about] people." For mobile pastoralists, keeping cattle is not only a way of making a living and a way of life, but one could argue that cattle are life because without them people cannot live as pastoralists. In this sense, to deny cattle access to grazing resources is to deny pastoralists life. This ethos of open access, which is shared among all mobile pastoralists in our study area, including absentee owners and their hired herders (Moritz et al. 2011), informs how pastoralists coordinate their movements and the use of common-pool grazing resources.

Customary Rights Over Campsites, Not Grazing Resources

When asked about their transhumance movements, pastoralists gave us the locations where they stayed, called *hoodaande* (pl. *koodaande*), which refers to the location of the tents and corrals, which depending on its size may occupy a circle with a diameter of about 250 to 400 m. The settlements, which we refer to as camps, consist of multiple tents that are either lined up south to north facing west toward the herds (e.g., FulBe Mare) or in a circle with the herds in the middle (e.g., Arabs). In the floodplain, camps are often located in depressions for easy access to water for humans and calves and protection from bush fires. Some *koodaande* are places where pastoralists stay for an extended period (sojourn), up to four months, while in other *koodaande* they stay for only a few days (transit). Different pastoralists may use the same *hoodaande* either for transit or sojourn.

However, *hoodaande* also refers to a larger area that incorporates multiple campsites. When taking GPS coordinates, we found that multiple camps give the same toponym for their *hoodaande*. Thus, a *hoodaande* can refer to a campsite but also an area with multiple campsites.

Pastoralists gain customary rights over campsites after two or three years of consecutive occupation in a particular season. Mobile pastoralists regularly return to the same site and put their houses in exactly the same location as previous years. After two or three years, people start referring to the campsite as *hoodaande wayne*, or the campsite of so-and-so, even if the campsite was earlier used by someone else for as long as 20 years. The customary rights only concern the locations of the tents and the corrals, but not the surrounding grazing resources or other potential campsites in the camp zone.

Pastoralists may retain customary rights for two or three years after they leave the campsite, when they become vacant and can be used by others. When pastoralists vacate a campsite, they do not so much retain the right to occupy the site, but the right to be asked for two of three years. Pastoralists can tell whether a site has been vacated or not, but they will also check with other pastoralists. Information about pastoralists' occupation of campsites is widely known and shared; everyone knows where everyone camps. In fact, the location of camps is usually the first topic of discussion among pastoralists after extended greetings.

Customary rights over campsites do not give pastoralists exclusive access over the common-pool grazing resources surrounding the campsite. Pastoralists only have customary rights over campsites, but not over camp zones. Moreover, the grazing radiuses of multiple campsites overlap (e.g., the herds in Lugge Banana share pastures with those from the camp zones of BaDDiwol, Kazre, Yadaka, and Cubuna) as the average grazing radius in the dry season is 4.5 km (Moritz et al. 2010). There is also no de facto regulation of access to common-pool grazing resources through controlled access to water as among the Turkana (McCabe 1990) or the Gabra (Robinson 2009). In the floodplain, most watering places are natural—rivers, ponds, depressions, and lakes—and located throughout the floodplain, while the artificial lakes dug by the Lake Chad Basin Commission are explicitly open for all pastoralists.

Pastoralists can set up camp wherever and whenever they want. Thus, access to camp zones is open, even when pastoralists have customary rights to campsites within these zones. No one is obliged to ask for permission from traditional or governmental authorities or other pastoralists to set up camp in the zones or near established campsites. This applies to all pastoralists, including newcomers from other groups or countries. Pastoralists may ask fellow pastoralists whether they can set up camp close by, but this request cannot be refused. Moreover, many pastoralists do not ask out of principle ("pastoralists never ask," explained one of our informants) or inform their neighbors about site decisions, not even when they set up camp next to another campsite. These rules are not limited to the floodplain; they also apply to the rainy season grazing areas in the Diamaré.

Some pastoralists expressed frustration to us that others set up camp so close to them, but no one argued that they have exclusive access or that it is "their site" and that others have to leave. If pastoralists are not content, their only option is to move. Sometimes conflicts arise when pastoralists try to chase away others by "accidentally" sending the herds through the other camp. But everyone knows, even the ones using these strategies, that they do not have the right and are violating the ethos of open access. We have come across very few conflicts among pastoralists over campsites, and in all conflicts the ethos of open access was reaffirmed as everyone discussed how someone violated the ethos. There is no formal system for punishment of violators, but the reputation of pastoralists denying open access to others is affected. In a sense, management of open access is not an oxymoron because there are clear rules about who has access to the common-pool grazing resources (all pastoralists) and who can be excluded (no one). The rules are reaffirmed in everyday practice every time pastoralists set up camps in new sites without asking. Moreover, these rules are meaningful to mobile pastoralists—without access to common-pool grazing resources, they cannot survive in this semiarid environment.

How Pastoralists Distribute Themselves Over Grazing Resources

Mobile pastoralists in the region use opportunistic grazing strategies that closely track resources, which are highly appropriate and effective ways to cope with the variable, unpredictable, and heterogeneous environments of Africa's drylands. Mobile pastoralists in the Far North Region are either moving or thinking about moving. They are continuously assessing the state of their grazing areas by monitoring the condition of their animals and those of others and will move to wherever they think their animals will do better.

The general transhumance pattern of mobile pastoralists in our study is as follows. In the rainy season, July–August, most mobile pastoralists camp in the Mindif-Moulvoudaye or the Pétté areas (Fig. 1). Within a week of the end of the rains in September–October, pastoralists move to the Logone Floodplain using existing transhumance routes. In the cold dry season, November–January, most mobile pastoralists are in the southern floodplain. They divide their herds and send the strongest animals on a separate transhumance (called *luci*) with young herders. In the hot dry season, February–May, most of the mobile pastoralists move either further north in the floodplain or south to the shores of Lake Maga. At the beginning of the rainy season, June, pastoralists leave the floodplain and follow the clouds and move wherever rains have fallen and fresh forage can be found.

There is considerable spatiotemporal variation in this transhumance pattern, due to the complex decision-making process in which multiple factors are considered simultaneously for each individual move, including proximity to markets, marriage arrangements with other camps, health of household members, and risk of attacks by cattle thieves. Nevertheless, there is considerable regularity in the transhumance patterns at population level, which is the result of the habitual movements of the herds in which animals develop *woowaande* (habitude) or preference for the pastures and campsites they visit habitually.

Pastoralists follow regular transhumance orbits in which they use established transhumance routes or corridors that connect their seasonal grazing areas. However, these transhumance orbits are subject to continuous change. Stenning has described how this happens through processes of migratory drift, "the gradual displacement of transhumance orbits," and migration, "the assumption of new transhumance orbits by a sudden and often lengthy movement" (1957, p. 59). Pastoralists adjust their orbits to the "normal" spatiotemporal variation in forage availability due to variation in rainfall patterns by changing the timing of their movements from one area to another, e.g., the rainy season area to the cold dry season area, or by moving to nearby campsites within one area. The result is a pattern of continuity and change, in which small changes from year to year cumulatively lead to significant changes in transhumance patterns over time. However, when confronted with major changes in forage availability like droughts or security threats, pastoralist may radically change their regular transhumance orbits. For example, many mobile pastoralists changed their transhumance orbits during the 1973–1974 droughts. Instead of an annual transhumance from Waalooji in Nigeria (rainy season) to the Yaayre (dry season), pastoralists moved between Fombina (rainy season) and the Yaayre (dry season) (Fig. 1). Similarly, the 1984–1985 drought sent some of these pastoralists further south to Chad, where they orbited between Fombina (rainy season) and Mayo Dore in Chad (dry season). While most returned to the Yaayre after the drought in 1986, others stayed in Chad. More recently, some of these pastoralists in Mayo Dore returned to Cameroon due to insecurity problems in Chad. Mobile pastoralists in the Chad Basin thus move back and forth within and between nations on overlapping transhumance orbits. Recently, in 2009–2010, a number of mobile pastoralists changed their transhumance orbits because of a deteriorating security situation in which they tried to avoid areas where criminal gangs kidnapped pastoralists' children for ransom (Moritz and Scholte 2011).

Stenning (1957) notes that FulBe pastoralists do not flee to areas they do not know. They have either been there before or they know people who are there now (see also Bassett and Turner 2007). We see a similar pattern in the Logone Floodplain. Through processes of migratory drift and migration, mobile pastoralists have created extensive networks of friends and family across the Chad Basin. Because pastoralists are relatively independent and autonomous, they do not migrate en masse; there are always some households or camps that remain behind. In addition, through marriages pastoralists create and maintain relations with groups on other transhumance orbits. Because of this extensive network, mobile pastoralists move with relative ease across borders within the Chad Basin. Pastoralists also redistribute themselves through changes in the social organization, for example, households frequently leave one camp to join another, or two camps may join in one site and separate in the next. The result is a pastoral population in flux and a continuous redistribution of pastoralists within and beyond the floodplain. To illustrate this point, most pastoralists who currently use the floodplain only came in the last 40 years. While pastoralists that used the floodplain prior to them, the FulBe Daneeji, have moved on to Chad and the Central African Republic.

No Regulation Through Taxation

There is ample evidence for open access among mobile pastoralists, but is it not possible that access to common-pool grazing resources is regulated through taxation by traditional and governmental authorities? We think that the payment of taxes does not regulate access to common-pool grazing resources. Pastoralists pay a transhumance tax, which is collected in each municipality that pastoralists camp in and ranges from about 10,000 FCFA ($20) to 12,000 FCFA ($24) per herd. On average pastoralists stay in three municipalities per year, resulting in 30,000 FCFA ($60) in transhumance tax, which seems high, and pastoralists complain about them. However, using conservative estimates of a herd of 50 cattle with an average value of 100,000 FCFA ($200) per animal, the transhumance tax amounts to 0.6% of their property value and only 3% of pastoralists' annual income from cattle sales. There is no indication that taxes regulate access, not even for poorer pastoralists.

Previously, we wrote that pastoralists announce their presence in the territory by paying a visit to the traditional authorities (Moritz et al. 2002). Now we know that pastoralists simply set up camp wherever they want because sooner rather than later the authorities will show up to collect the transhumance tax. Leaders of pastoral groups may visit the traditional authorities and pay tribute, but they do this to solidify their political position within their community, rather than to gain access to common-pool grazing resources for their followers. The leaders of pastoral groups we interviewed referred to the payments to traditional authorities as *ceede huDO* (literally money for grass) and *ceede sabur* (literally money for soap), which suggests that it is a small token gift rather than a tribute. More importantly, we found both in the 1990s and from 2008 to 2010 that no one is refused access, including a few pastoralists who explicitly refused to pay even a nominal amount to a chief they considered a crook. In sum, there is no evidence of regulation through taxation.

Moreover, the official national policy is that access to common-pool grazing resources is open to anyone, provided the animals are vaccinated and the transhumance tax is paid. When asked about the role of the authorities in regulating access, one pastoralist described it as follows: *Yamataa, kaDataa* "[we] don't ask, [and we are] not refused [access]."

Historical and Institutional Context

The system of open access to common-pool grazing resources is not a recent phenomenon in the Logone Floodplain. Until the beginning of the twentieth century, the floodplain was a site of endemic insecurity, which prevented FulBe pastoralists from using it (Seignobos and Jamin 2003). The nineteenth-century European travelers (Barth 1965, pp. 361–424) and those traveling in the beginning of the twentieth century described an area ravaged by war between pre-colonial polities of Kanuri and FulBe and Musgum and other ethnic groups (Bauer 2002, pp. 100–103). However, the colonial pacification in the 1920s opened up the area for pastoralists (Delclaux et al. 2010), and by the 1960s, pastoralists from all over the Diamaré went on transhumance to the study area (Mouchet 1960). Although there are no good descriptions of pastoral systems in the Logone Floodplain before the 1980s, the accounts of Mouchet (1960) and our informants suggest that there has been open access to common-pool grazing resources for a long time in the Logone Floodplain.

The notion of open access to common-pool grazing resources is also not limited to the Logone Floodplain; national laws and international agreements support it. It is a good example of nested institutions in which the management system of mobile pastoralists is supported by higher institutions (Ostrom 1990; Ostrom et al. 2002). Rangelands in the Logone Floodplain and the Far North Region are legally state property (Ordinance No. 74-1 of 1974). However, the law explicitly gives all pastoralists the right to use these common-pool resources, unless the state uses these grazing lands for other purposes such as wildlife conservation or agricultural development projects. National laws thus support pastoral mobility and the system of open access to grazing lands.

In addition, the Lake Chad Basin Commission has been supporting the system of open access to common-pool grazing resources since the 1960s, when it was created by the four countries bordering Lake Chad: Cameroon, Chad, Niger, and Nigeria. The aims of the commission are to regulate and control the use of water and other natural resources in the basin and to initiate, promote, and coordinate natural resource development projects and research. International agreements between Lake Chad Basin Commission member countries enable freedom of movement for pastoralists in the Chad Basin provided they have vaccinated their animals and paid the local and national taxes. This allows pastoralists from Chad, Niger, Nigeria, Cameroon, and more recently the Central African Republic and Sudan to travel freely within the Chad Basin if they can show their certificate of vaccination and tax receipts.

Discussion

Our case study raises two main questions: how representative is our case study of management of open access and what are its theoretical implications? First, how representative is this system of open access for other pastoralists in West and Central Africa? Is this system limited to the Chad Basin or to FulBe pastoralists only? We found indications that the system we describe for the Far North Region is common in other pastoral systems in West Africa, even when it is not labeled as such (Stenning 1957, p. 68; Frantz 1986; Horowitz 1986, p. 261; Swallow 1990) and it has also been described for pastoralists outside Africa (Glatzer 1992). It is also not limited to

FulBe pastoralists; Arab pastoralists, who originally came from Sudan and migrated westward to the Chad Basin in the last centuries, share the ethos of open access. However, not all pastoral systems in the Chad Basin or West Africa have open access, e.g., the Toubou and Arab in central Chad, who repeatedly clash over the ownership of wells and thereby access to grazing land.

Second, there are several theoretical implications of this case study. First, we are not only dealing with open access but also with an open system in which there are no social or natural boundaries, and this has implications for our understanding of pastoral systems and management of common-pool resources. Second, we think that the concept of the ideal free distribution, in which grazing pressure matches available resources, is useful to evaluate the effectiveness of this management system. Finally, our case study may serve as a model of a self-organizing management system of common-pool resources for other resource systems.

An Open System

FulBe pastoralists in the Far North Region say that they are like birds (*FulBe bana colli*); not tied to any place, they can go wherever they want and whenever they want. They have no territories, homelands, or home ranges, and they live interspersed with different groups of pastoralists and agriculturalists. The distribution of Fulfulde speakers in sub-Saharan Africa underscores the notion that their pastoral system is truly open system (Fig. 2). Originally from the Senegambia region, FulBe pastoralists have gradually moved eastward to Sudan and Ethiopia, northward into the Sahel, and southward into the subhumid zone.

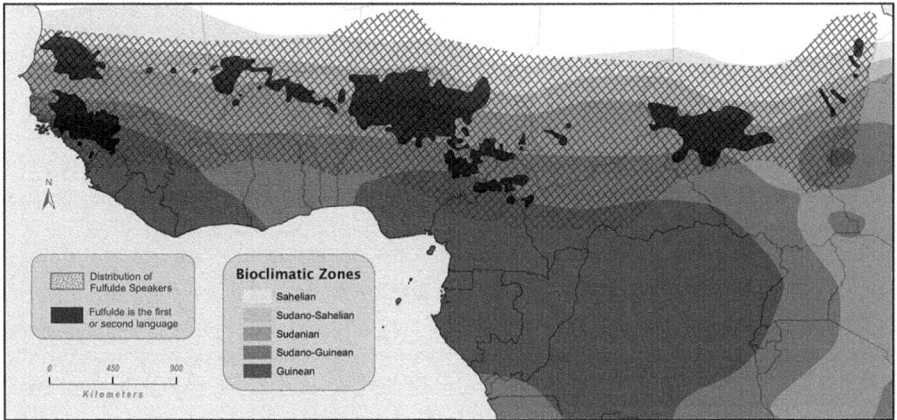

Fig. 2 Distribution of Fulfulde speakers in sub-Saharan Africa. Bioclimatic zones are derived from rainfall data from Nicholson et al. (1988), classifications from Bassett and Turner (2007), and the distribution of Fulfulde speakers from Boutrais (1994)

The continuous changing distribution of FulBe pastoralists across sub-Saharan Africa underscores that we are dealing with an open system. What seems stable and bounded at low spatiotemporal scales—the annual transhumance orbit—is highly dynamic and unbounded when the spatiotemporal scale is expanded. Stenning (1957) already explained how small changes in the annual transhumance—process called migratory drift—lead to considerable changes over time. However, we have tended to "box" mobile pastoralists in study areas and freeze their annual migrations in the ethnographic present. We have not made the conceptual leap to describe and understand mobile pastoral systems as open systems because our theoretical models assume that resources are bounded and limited. But these imagined boundaries disappear when pastoral systems are analyzed at larger spatiotemporal scales. When pastoral mobility is examined in a historical perspective at temporal scales of decades and centuries and at spatial scales beyond regions and nations, common-pool grazing resources are, for practical purposes, unbounded and unlimited.

The migrations of FulBe pastoralists over the last centuries show that there are no real boundaries. Pastoralists may sometimes be harassed at international borders, but this does not prevent them from crossing them. Political change often offered opportunities: the 19th FulBe Jihads and the colonial "pacification" opened up new grazing lands across West Africa, just as recent political turmoil and insecurity in Chad, the Central African Republic, and the Jos Plateau in Nigeria closed off grazing lands. There are also no apparent ecological boundaries that inhibit their expansion. FulBe pastoralists have moved north in the Sahel, entering grazing lands that were traditionally used by Tuareg, Tubu, and Arab pastoralists (Bonfiglioli 1988), and further south into subhumid zones by adapting their breeding strategies (Bassett and Turner 2007). FulBe pastoralists continue to move and exploit new ecological niches (Boutrais 1996).

Pastoralists in East Africa are also continuously on the move, and their territories have changed over time and continue to change despite being circumscribed by other pastoral groups (Turton 1991; Schlee 2010), but at smaller spatial scales and longer temporal scales than in West Africa, where pastoralists move across multiple countries into different ecological zones within decades (Boutrais 1996). There may be a number of different reasons for the differences between the two regions: geographic orientation, bioclimatic conditions, and a religion that transcends local groups. The east-west orientation of West Africa facilitates the eastward spread of FulBe pastoralists across the Sahelian and Sudano-Sahelian climatic zone as they could migrate over great distances within one bioclimatic zone. In East Africa, on the other hand, pastoralists are circumscribed by different climatic and ecological zones that were associated with tsetse flies and sleeping sickness. Bioclimatic conditions may also have contributed to a greater mobility of FulBe pastoralists in West Africa. Whereas West Africa is characterized by a monomodal rainfall pattern, the Greater Horn of Africa has a bimodal rainfall pattern and greater inter-annual variability in rainfall (Ellis and Galvin 1994). Consequently, West African pastoralists make longer transhumance movements to exploit the more predictable spatiotemporal rainfall patterns, whereas pastoralists in the Horn of Africa make much shorter nomadic movements to exploit less predictable spatiotemporal variability in rainfall patterns (Ellis and Galvin 1994). The practice of long-distance transhumance facilitates the migrations to new areas, as West African pastoralists have the habit of opportunistically seeking new grazing lands (Bassett and Turner 2007). Islam has further integrated West African pastoralists in a wider society that included villages, towns, and cities. The *umma*, or Muslim community, transcends the diversity of pastoral and non-pastoral populations and facilitated the pastoral migrations to new areas. Islamic jihads have also facilitated the spread of FulBe pastoralists and provided more security in areas that were previously inaccessible.

In addition, the pastoral system in the Far North Region is also an open system in the sense that there are no strong social boundaries. All who are committed to mobile pastoralism, in which the needs of animals are central, are members of the user group. And while there are distinct ethnic groups among pastoralists, these groups are not territorial, and the ethnic boundaries are permeable as people "enter" ethnic groups that they share transhumance routes with.

An Ideal Free Distribution of Mobile Pastoralists

The mechanisms of decision-making described here, as well as the finding that grazing pressure tracked productivity at the scale of the floodplain as a whole, are reminiscent of the predictions of negative density-dependent habitat selection models, such as the ideal free distribution (IFD) (Fretwell and Lucas 1969; Hamilton 2010). Negative density dependence results when the suitability of a habitat declines with increasing density of competitors on that patch. The dynamics of resources on the floodplain are characterized by accumulation of resources during the rainy and flooding season and gradual decline of these resources through desiccation and grazing in the dry season. This pattern conforms to that assumed in "depletion" models of the IFD (Sutherland 1996). Depletion models predict the spatiotemporal sequence and timing of patch exploitation, starting with the use of highest-quality patches early in the season and successively adding initially poorer patches as time goes on, and the quality of better patches declines through grazing (Sutherland 1996). The use of low-quality patches will also depend on overall density, with increasing use of low-quality patches when density is high (Mobaek et al. 2009). Thus, in depletion models, the population response to increasing consumer/resource ratio in any given patch is to increase the number of patches used.

Ideal free models do not necessarily alleviate the tragedy of the commons. Indeed, in depletion models, depletion may become severe over the whole landscape, as even very poor patches become occupied (Sutherland 1996). However, we argue that (1) because pastoralists live in an open system in which pastoralists can move into and out of the Logone Floodplain as well as within the floodplain, the number of available patches becomes very large at large spatial scales and (2) the spatiotemporal patterns of resource depletion and renewal, in which depleted patches are renewed and the spatial distribution of herders on the floodplain reset by the onset of the rainy season and flooding, full occupancy, and severe depletion of all patches in the limited time of the dry season, are unlikely. In other words, we expect that over a wide range of conditions, individuals can do better by moving rather than by increasing intensity of exploitation in a given patch.

We argue that the ideal free distribution, and, in particular, the depletion model, is a useful concept to describe the distribution of pastoralists in the floodplain. However, we do not argue that pastoralists will meet the quantitative predictions of any existing ideal free models. The pastoral system does not fit several of the assumptions of ideal free distribution models. In particular, travel times between habitats are non-negligible; cattle and herders are organized hierarchically into herds and camps, so that movement decisions of individual cattle and individual herders are not independent of those of other cattle and other herders; and regularity of transhumance routes limits the patches used by any single herder. Ideal free distribution models also assume perfect information of the relative quality of patches. While herders do not have perfect information, we assert that they are likely to have complete information, i.e., sufficient knowledge to predict with a certain probability the patch conditions, instead of perfect information, i.e., knowing the exact patch conditions (Kelly 1995, pp. 97–98). Results from spatial analyses of the distribution of grazing pressure and grazing resources show evidence of an ideal free distribution of mobile pastoralists in the Logone Floodplain (Moritz et al. 2014a, b).

The question is whether the ideal free distribution is the epiphenomenal consequence (Hunn 1982) of high mobility, low population density, and annual flooding, as Ruttan and Borgerhoff Mulder (1999, p. 634) suggest is the case in some East African pastoral systems, or whether there is management of common-pool resources in the floodplain. And if there is a management system, as we argue below, can we identify causal links that are responsible for the emergence of an ideal free distribution of mobile pastoralists in the floodplain? Simulations with an agent-based model show that individual pastoralists following simple movement of rules lead to the emergence of an ideal free distribution (Moritz et al. 2015).

Self-Organizing Management System

The openness of the pastoral management system in the Logone Floodplain does not mean that we cannot describe and analyze it using the theoretical framework of the commons. Since Ostrom (1990) published eight design principles for successful commons, more critical variables have been identified (Agrawal 2002). The challenge has been to develop general mechanisms that explain which sets of causal configurations of variables lead to successful management of common-pool resources (Poteete et al. 2010). Reviewing major comparative studies of the commons, Agrawal (2002) identified critical variables and proposed several causal mechanisms for successful commons. When we compare our case study of mobile pastoralists in the Logone Floodplain with Agrawal's list of critical variables (Fig. 3), there are two clear patterns. First, there is no good match in terms of the characteristics of the social and ecological systems, primarily because both systems

1. Resource system characteristics

a. <u>Small size</u>
b. <u>Well-defined boundaries</u>
c. Low levels of mobility
d. <u>Storage possible</u>
e. <u>Predictability</u>
2. Group characteristics
 	
    a. <u>Small size</u>
    b. <u>Clearly-defined boundaries</u>
    c. Shared norms
    d. <u>Social capital</u>
    e. <u>Leadership</u>
    f. <u>Interdependence</u>
    g. Heterogeneity of endowments/homogeneity in identity/interests
    h. Low levels of poverty
2. Relationship between resource system and group characteristics
 	
    a. Overlap in locations
    b. High dependency on resources
    c. Fairness in allocation
    d. Low level of user demand
    e. Gradual changes in demand
3. Institutional arrangements
 	
    a. Simple rules
    b. Locally devised rules
    c. Ease in enforcements
    d. Graduated sanctions
    e. Low-cost adjudication
    f. Accountability of monitors
4. Relationship between resource systems and institutional arrangements
 	
    1. Restrictions match resource
5. External environment
 	
    a. Technology
    b. New technologies
    c. Low articulation with markets
    d. Gradual change in articulation
    e. Central government
    f. Supportive external sanctions
    g. <u>External aid</u>
    h. Nested institutions

Fig. 3 Critical enabling conditions for the commons. We compared Agrawal's (2002) critical conditions for sustainability on the commons with management of open access in the Logone Floodplain and <u>underlined</u> those conditions that did not match

are not bounded. Second, there is a good match in terms of *relationships* between resource system, users, and governance system. In short, the social and ecological systems of mobile pastoralists in the Chad Basin are quite different from those that are normally associated with successful management of common-pool resources. However, the social and governance systems of mobile pastoralists are well adapted to the resource system in the Chad Basin.

However, the question remains what combination of variables is most critical for the management of open access in the Chad Basin. Following Agrawal's (2002) analytical approach, we have identified two causal links in which the first produces an ideal free type of distribution and the second results in sustainable exploitation of common-pool resources.

$$\text{Density – dependent distribution} = f(\text{spatiotemporal variation}$$
$$\text{of renewable common – pool resources, open access, freedom}$$
$$\text{of movement, complete information, independent decisions, habitude})$$

The first function describes how pastoralists distribute themselves in relation to common-pool grazing resources. We expect to find an ideal free type of distribution when mobile users with complete information, freedom and ability to move within and across nations, and independent decision-making capabilities have open access to depletable common-pool resources that are highly variable in space and time. Such a distribution will be resistant to strategies that overselect or overstay on certain patches, because the costs of overusing these patches fall most heavily on the individuals that overuse them (Hamilton 2010). However, it should be noted that it is not resistant to strategies that increase the rate of resource exploitation overall (see second function) nor is it resistant to increases in population where it is not an open system.

$$\text{Ecological sustainability}$$
$$= f\left(\text{subsistence economy, appropriate technology, low external investments}\right)$$

This second function describes how pastoralists exploit common-pool grazing resources in an open system described above. We expect ecological sustainability when it is primarily a subsistence system with appropriate technology and low external capital investments but also that external capital investment in large-scale, commercial ranching in same areas would likely result in a tragedy because of inappropriate technology, not because of open access.

Open Property Regime

We argue that open access is not just the epiphenomenal consequence of high mobility, low population density, or the absence of a private, state, or common property regime. For example, evolutionary models suggest that there is no reason to expect common property regimes when resources are unbounded and unlimited (Alvard 1998; Ruttan and Borgerhoff Mulder 1999) as is the case in the open system of mobile pastoralists in the Chad Basin that we have described here. However, we argue that this system of open access can be described as a property regime and not just as the absence of rules. Moritz (2016) has shown that there are other pastoral systems with similar open access to common-pool resources and proposed the concept of open property regimes to describe and explain these regimes. In pastoral systems where mobile pastoralists use common-pool grazing resources that are highly variable in space and time, an open property regime is appropriate because it is equitable, efficient, and sustainable. Moreover, open property regimes work as complex adaptive systems in which independent decision-making of highly mobile households results in an efficient distribution of the grazing pressure over available resources (Moritz et al. 2014a, b). Finally, open access does not have to lead to a tragedy of the commons, certainly not in mobile pastoral systems. On the contrary, there is evidence that the opposite, restricting open access and enforcing social and spatial boundaries, results in a tragedy of the commons because it limits pastoralists' mobility and flexibility.

The question is whether we can refer to this system as management. The ethos and practice of open access is a form of everyday management that regulate the use of common-pool resources in that there are two important outcomes: (1) the emergence of an ideal free-like distribution of mobile pastoralists and (2) the lack of major conflict among pastoralists. These outcomes require the everyday commitment of pastoralists to the ethos and practice of open access—it is not just the absence of rules. Rules are not only about exclusion but also about inclusion. Moreover, pastoralists themselves talk about open access not in terms of an absence of rules but in terms of rights for all. We envision the pastoral system in the Far North Region as a complex system in which one of the emergent properties is an ideal free distribution in which the distribution of mobile pastoralists matches that of the available common-pool grazing resources. Management, in this framework, is best understood as a self-organizing complex adaptive system in which management is the result of continuous interactions among individual pastoralists who are all following the rule of open access to common-pool grazing resources.

Moreover, the causal links that we identified as critical for the emergence of an ideal free distribution—open access, freedom of movement, networks across nations, complete information, and independent decision-making—are commitments to pastoral ways of being and the well-being of the herds (Goldschmidt 1971). The management of open access is not about the conservation of common-pool resources, it is about ensuring that pastoralists have the ability to move to wherever the resources are. Ultimately, it is about the sustainability of the pastoral system. Finally, mobile pastoralists themselves view grazing resources as a commons, albeit one for which there are no clear social or natural boundaries. They argue that nobody can be denied access to grass because it is essential for making a living; without grass they cannot continue their way of life, which is, just as open access, about cattle (*na'i non*).

Conclusion

Models and stories are effective ways to communicate research—the tragedy of the commons is a conceptual model as well as a story about pastoralists (McCay 2002). Ostrom (1990) has warned against the dangers of using models metaphorically for policy because they oversimplify the complexity of the management of common-pool resources. Nevertheless, scholars of common property systems have used the same hypothetical example of shepherds and the commons in theoretical arguments and game theoretical models to make the point that common-pool resources can be managed sustainably but that open access leads to a tragedy (Ostrom 1990; McCay 2002). We argue that the critics' rebuttal of the tragedy of the commons has unintentionally shaped how we think about pastoral management of common-pool resources. There is such a commitment to the pastoral commons that we see it even when pastoralists tell us that it is open access. The reluctance to describe a situation as open access is understandable because of its negative associations with tragedy of the commons. Hardin (1968) wrote that "freedom in a commons brings ruin to all," but in the Chad Basin where grazing resources are highly variable in space and time, it is critical that mobile pastoralists have freedom of movement and open access to common-pool resources. The conditions that we identified as being critical for this self-organizing management system of common-pool resources with open access—mobile users, shared information, freedom of movement, autonomous decision-making, and open access to depletable common-pool resources that are highly variable in space and time—may also be met and thus be relevant for other resource systems, including fisheries.

References

Agrawal, A. (2002). Common resources and institutional stability. In E. Ostrom, T. Dietz, N. Dolsak, P. C. Stern, S. Stonich, & E. U. Weber (Eds.), *The drama of the commons*. Washington, DC: National Academy Press.

Alvard, M. S. (1998). Evolutionary ecology and resource conservation. *Evolutionary Anthropology, 7*, 62–74.

Anderies, J. M., & Janssen, M. A. (2013). *Sustaining the commons*. Tempe: Center for the Study of Institutional Diversity.

Barth, H. (1965). *Travels and discoveries in North and Central Africa: Being a journal of an expedition undertaken under the auspices of H.B.M.'s government in the years 1849–1855* (Vols. I, II, and III). London: Frank Cass.

Bassett, T. J., & Turner, M. D. (2007). Sudden shift or migratory drift? Fulbe herd movements to the Sudano-Guinean region of West Africa. *Human Ecology, 35*(1), 33–49.

Bauer, F. (2002). *L'expédition allemande Niger-Bénoué - Lac Tchad (1902-1903)*. Paris: Karthala.

Behnke, R. H., & Scoones, I. (1993). Rethinking range ecology: Implications for rangeland management in Africa. In R. H. Behnke Jr., I. Scoones, & C. Kerven (Eds.), *Range ecology at disequilibrium: New models of natural variability and pastoral adaptation in African Savannas*. London: Overseas Development Institute.

Berkes, F. (2009). Revising the commons paradigm. *Journal of Natural Resources Policy Research, 1*(3), 261–264.

Bonfiglioli, A. M. (1988). Dudal: histoire de famille et histoire de troupeau chez un groupe de Wodaabe du Niger. In L. E. e. e. a. d. s. pastorales (Ed.), *Production pastorale et société*. Cambridge: Cambridge University Press & Éditions de la Maison des Sciences de l'Homme.

Boutrais, J. (1994). Pour une nouvelle cartographie des Peuls. *Cahiers d'etudes Africaines, 34*(1–3), 137–146.

Boutrais, J. (1996). *Hautes terres d'élevage au Cameroun. Vol. 1–3, Collection études et thèses*. Paris: ORSTOM Éditions.

Delclaux, F., Seignobos, C., Liénou, G., & Genthon, P. (2010). Water and people in the Yaéré floodplain (North Cameroon). In M. A. Álvarez (Ed.), *Floodplains: Physical geography, ecology and societal interactions*. Hauppauge, NY: Nova Publishers.

Dietz, T., Dolsak, N., Ostrom, E., & Stern, P. C. (2002). The drama of the commons. In E. Ostrom, T. Dietz, N. Dolsak, P. C. Stern, S. Stonich, & E. U. Weber (Eds.), *The drama of the commons*. Washington, DC: National Academy Press.

Ellis, J., & Galvin, K. A. (1994). Climate patterns and land-use practices in the dry zones of Africa. *BioScience, 44*(5), 340–349.

Ensminger, J., & Knight, J. (1997). Changing social norms: Common property, bridewealth and clan exogamy. *Current Anthropology, 18*(1), 1–24.

Feeny, D., Berkes, F., McCay, B. J., & Acheson, J. M. (1990). The tragedy of the commons: Twenty-two years later. *Human Ecology, 18*(1), 81–103.

Fernández-Giménez, M. E., & Le Febre, S. (2006). Mobility in pastoral systems: Dynamic flux or downward trend? *International Journal of Sustainable Development & World Ecology, 13*, 341–362.

Frantz, C. (1986). Fulani continuity and change under five flags. In M. Adamu & A. H. M. Kirk-Greene (Eds.), *Pastoralists of the West African Savanna*. Manchester: Manchester University Press.

Fratkin, E., Galvin, K. A., & Roth, E. A. (Eds.). (1994). *African pastoralist systems: An integrated approach*. Boulder, CO: Lynne Rienner Publishers.

Fretwell, S. D., & Lucas, J. H. J. (1969). On territorial behavior and other factors influencing habitat distribution in birds. *Acta Biotheoretica, 19*, 16–36.

Galaty, J. G. (1994). Rangeland tenure and pastoralism in Africa. In E. Fratkin, K. A. Galvin, & E. A. Roth (Eds.), *African pastoralists systems: An integrated approach*. Boulder, CO: Lynne Rienner Publishers.

Galvin, K. A. (2009). Transitions: Pastoralists living with change. *Annual Review of Anthropology, 38*, 185–198.

Glatzer, B. (1992). Pastoral territoriality in West Afghanistan: An organization of flexibility. In M. J. Casimir & A. Rao (Eds.), *Mobility and territoriality: Social and spatial boundaries among foragers, fishers, pastoralists, and peripatetics*. New York: Berg.

Goldschmidt, W. (1971). Independence as an element in pastoral social systems. *Anthropological Quarterly, 44*(3), 132–142.

Haller, T. (Ed.). (2010). *Disputing the floodplains: Institutional change and the politics of resource management in African Wetlands, African social studies series*. Leiden: Brill.

Hamilton, I. M. (2010). Foraging theory. In D. Westneat & C. Fox (Eds.), *Evolutionary behavioral ecology*. Oxford: Oxford University Press.

Hardin, G. (1968). The tragedy of the commons. *Science, 162*(3859), 1243–1248.

Homewood, K. (2008). *Ecology of African pastoralist societies*. Oxford: James Currey.

Horowitz, M. M. (1986). Ideology, policy, and praxis in pastoral livestock development. In M. M. Horowitz & T. M. Painter (Eds.), *Anthropology and rural development in West Africa*. Boulder, CO: Westview Press.

Hunn, E. S. (1982). Mobility as a factor limiting resource use in the Columbian Plateau of North America. In N. Williams & E. Hunn (Eds.), *Resource managers: North American and Australian Hunter-Gathers*. Boulder: Westview Press.

Kelly, R. L. (1995). *The foraging spectrum: Diversity in Hunter-Gatherer lifeways*. Washington, DC: Smithsonian Institution Press.

Lamprey, H. F. (1983). Pastoralism yesterday and today: The overgrazing problem. In F. Bourliere (Ed.), *Ecosystems of the world 13: Tropical savannas*. Amsterdam: Elsevier.
Lane, C. (Ed.). (1998). *Custodians of the commons: Pastoral land tenure in East and West Africa*. London: Earthscan.
McCabe, J. T. (1990). Turkana pastoralism: A case against the tragedy of the commons. *Human Ecology, 18*(1), 81–103.
McCay, B. J. (2002). Emergence of institutions for the commons: Contexts, situations and events. In E. Ostrom, T. Dietz, N. Dolsak, P. C. Stern, S. Stonich, & E. U. Weber (Eds.), *The drama of the commons*. Washington, DC: National Academy Press.
McCay, B. J., & Acheson, J. M. (1987). *The Question of the commons: The culture and ecology of communal resources, Arizona studies in human ecology*. Tucson, AZ: University of Arizona Press.
Mobaek, R., Mysterud, A., Egil Loe, L., Holand, Ø., & Austrheim, G. (2009). Density dependent and temporal variability in habitat selection by a large herbivore; an experimental approach. *Oikos, 118*(2), 209–218.
Moritz, M. (2016). Open property regimes. *International Journal of the Commons, 10*(2), 688–708.
Moritz, M., Hamilton, I. M., Chen, Y.-J., & Scholte, P. (2014a). Mobile pastoralists in the Logone Floodplain distribute themselves in an ideal free distribution. *Current Anthropology, 55*(1), 115–122.
Moritz, M., Hamilton, I. M., Scholte, P., & Chen, Y.-J. (2014b). Ideal free distributions of mobile pastoralists within multiple seasonal grazing areas. *Rangeland Ecology & Management, 67*(6), 641–649.
Moritz, M., Hamilton, I. M., Yoak, A., Scholte, P., Cronley, J., Maddock, P., et al. (2015). Simple movement rules result in ideal free distribution of mobile pastoralists. *Ecological Modelling, 305*(10), 54–63.
Moritz, M., Ritchey, K. K., & Kari, S. (2011). The social context of herding contracts in the Far North Region of Cameroon. *Journal of Modern African Studies, 49*(2), 263–285.
Moritz, M., & Scholte, P. (2011). Ethical predicaments: Advocating security for mobile pastoralists in weak states. *Anthropology Today, 27*(3), 12–17.
Moritz, M., Scholte, P., & Kari, S. (2002). The demise of the nomadic contract: Arrangements and rangelands under pressure in the Far North of Cameroon. *Nomadic Peoples, 6*(1), 124–143.
Moritz, M., Soma, E., Scholte, P., Juran, T., Taylor, L., Kari, S., et al. (2010). An integrated approach to modeling grazing pressure in pastoral systems: The case of the Logone Floodplain (Cameroon). *Human Ecology, 38*(6), 775–789.
Mouchet, J. (1960). *Enquête entomologique dans le Logone et Chari (13-25 mai 1960). I: Le Foyer de glossines du Logone et Chari. II: L'Anophélisme et les possibilités de lutte antipaludique. III: La Transhumance des "Foulbé" dans les "yaéré"*. Yaounde: IRCAM.
Mwangi, E., & Ostrom, E. (2009). Top-down solutions: Looking up from Africa's rangelands. *Environment, 51*(1), 35–44.
Niamir-Fuller, M. (1999a). Introduction. In M. Niamir-Fuller (Ed.), *Managing mobility in African rangelands: The legitimization of transhumance*. London: Intermediate Technology.
Niamir-Fuller, M. (1999b). Towards a synthesis of guidelines for legitimizing transhumance. In M. Niamir-Fuller (Ed.), *Managing mobility in African rangelands: The legitimization of transhumance*. London: Intermediate Technology.
Nicholson, S. E., Kim, J., & Hoopingarner, J. (1988). *Atlas of African rainfall and its interannual variability*. Tallahassee, FL: Department of Meteorology, The Florida State University.
Ostrom, E. (1990). *Governing the commons: The evolution of institutions for collective action*. Cambridge: Cambridge University Press.
Ostrom, E. (2007). A diagnostic approach for going beyond panaceas. *PNAS, 104*(39), 15181–15187.
Ostrom, E., Dietz, T., Dolsak, N., Stern, P. C., Stonich, S., & Weber, E. U. (2002). *The drama of the commons*. Washington, DC: National Academy Press.
Peters, P. E. (1994). *Dividing the commons: Politics, policy and culture in Botswana*. Charlottesville, VA: University Press Virginia.

Picardi, A. C., & Seifert, W. W. (1976). A tragedy of the commons in the Sahel. *Technology Review, 78*(6), 42–51.
Poteete, A. R., Janssen, M. A., & Ostrom, E. (2010). *Manuscript: Multiple methods in practice: Research on collective action and the commons*. Princeton, NJ: Princeton University Press.
Robinson, L. W. (2009). A complex-systems approach to Pastoral Commons. *Human Ecology, 37*(4), 441–451.
Ruttan, L. M., & Borgerhoff Mulder, M. (1999). Are East African pastoralists truly conservationists? *Current Anthropology, 40*(5), 621–652.
Schlee, G. (2010). Territorialising Ethnicity: The political ecology of pastoralism in northern Kenya and southern Ethiopia. In *Working paper*. Halle: Max Planck Institute for Social Anthropology.
Scholte, P. (2005). *Floodplain rehabilitation and the future of conservation and development: Adaptive management of success in Waza-Logone, Cameroon*. Leiden: Centre for Environmental Studies, Leiden University.
Scholte, P. (2007). Maximum flood depth characterises above-ground biomass in African shallowly flooded grasslands. *Journal of Tropical Ecology, 23*(1), 63–72.
Scholte, P., Kari, S., Moritz, M., & Prins, H. (2006). Pastoralist responses to floodplain rehabilitation in Northern Cameroon. *Human Ecology, 34*(1), 27–51.
Scholte, P., Kirda, P., Adam, S., & Kadiri, B. (2000). Floodplain rehabilitation in North Cameroon: Impact on vegetation dynamics. *Applied Vegetation Science, 3*, 33–42.
Seignobos, C. (2000). Élevage II: les transhumances. In C. Seignobos & O. Iyébi-Mandjek (Eds.), *Atlas de la province Extrême-Nord Cameroun*. Paris: IRD & MINREST.
Seignobos, C., & Jamin, F. (2003). *La case obus: historie et reconstitution*. Marseille: Patrimoime sans frontière.
Sinclair, A. R. E., & Fryxell, J. M. (1985). The Sahel of Africa: Ecology of a disaster. *Canadian Journal of Zoology, 63*, 987–994.
Stenning, D. J. (1957). Transhumance, migratory drift, migration; patterns of pastoral Fulani nomadism. *The Journal of the Royal Anthropological Institute of Great Britain and Ireland, 87*, 57–73.
Sutherland, W. J. (1996). *From individual behaviour to population ecology*. Oxford: Oxford University Press.
Swallow, B. M. (1990). *Strategies and Tenure in African livestock development, LTC paper #140*. Madison, WI: Land Tenure Center, University of Wisconsin.
Turner, M. D. (1999). The role of social networks, indefinite boundaries and political bargaining in maintaining the ecological and economic resiliency of the transhumance systems of Sudano-Sahelian West Africa. In M. Niamir-Fuller (Ed.), *Managing mobility in African rangelands*. London: IT Publications.
Turton, D. (1991). Movement, warfare and ethnicity in the lower Omo Valley. In J. G. Galaty & P. Bonte (Eds.), *Herders, warriors and traders: Pastoralism in Africa*. Boulder, CO: Westview Press.

Mollusc Harvesting in the Pre-European Contact Pacific Islands: Investigating Resilience and Sustainability

Frank R. Thomas

Introduction

Food production strategies emerged in the western half of the Pacific Island region at the end of the Pleistocene, after more than 30,000 years of human presence. Agricultural expansion and intensification eventually altered terrestrial environments on nearly every habitable island across the world's biggest ocean (Kirch and Hunt 1997). The impacts can be traced to the early stages of human settlement, leading in some cases to resource depression, extirpation, and extinction (Kirch 2009).

The influence of indigenous societies on marine resources on islands is not well documented (Morrison and Hunt 2007; Anderson 2008). Indeed, the influence of indigenous peoples on non-island marine resources is also understudied (Rick and Erlandson 2008). In the Pacific Islands, especially studying the role of indigenous and local knowledge pertaining to marine resource management remains a fruitful topic for research in light of suggestions that rapid dispersal across the southwest Pacific beginning about 3400 years ago could have been driven in part by the impact of early humans on nearshore and intertidal resources that could be efficiently harvested, such as flightless birds, colony-breeding birds, turtles, reef fish, and invertebrates, including molluscs (Kennett et al. 2006; Szabó and Amesbury 2011).

Changes observed in shell midden distribution (and other marine resources) have often been attributed to direct human impact (Shawcross 1975; Anderson 1979; Swadling 1986; Masse 1989; Harris and Weisler 2018a), although the influence of other processes are sometimes acknowledged (Spennemann 1987; Amesbury 2007; Morrison and Addison 2008; Morrison and Cochrane 2008; Campbell 2008; Aswani

---

F. R. Thomas (✉)
Pacific Studies, Oceania Centre for Arts, Culture and Pacific Studies, University of the South Pacific, Suva, Fiji
e-mail: thomas_fr@usp.ac.fj

and Allen 2009; Seeto et al. 2012; Ariana et al. 2017; Giovas 2018). Costal zones and islands present certain interpretative challenges in view of their susceptibility to natural changes linked to sea-level changes, tectonic events, erosion or sedimentation, and storms (Fitzpatrick 2007, 2012).

In examining the sustainability of mollusc extractive strategies, the absence of significant changes in the archaeological record may be indicative of non-mutually exclusive species attributes and environmental conditions, including species resilience, low human population densities, low impact technologies, efficient use of resources (e.g., through an understanding of environmental cues and fluctuations), and the application of intentional and unintentional management practices (Thomas 2014, 2015; Reeder-Myers et al. 2016).

Using primary data from Kiribati (Gilbert Islands), eastern Micronesia, this chapter reviews selected archaeological case studies from the Pacific Islands that could be explained by one or more of the abovementioned attributes and conditions. Relevant examples from other parts of the world are also presented.

Initial fieldwork in the Gilbert Islands was prompted by an interest in marine resource conservation in the Pacific, notably on atolls. Because of their small size, limited and at times fluctuating resources, and relative isolation, low coral islands are often depicted as marginal habitats for human settlement. While some communities did not endure (Anderson et al. 2000; Di Piazza and Pearthree 2001), a remarkable number of low coral islands (and other small islands) continued to support human populations for centuries, indicating a long history of resilience to environmental variability (Kirch and Yen 1982; Lilley 2008; Bridges and McClatchey 2009; McMillen et al. 2014; Lazrus 2015).

Despite their abundance on most atolls, marine resources were on occasion subjected to avoidance practices, which would have enabled stocks to recover (Akamichi 1986; Klee 1985; Merlin et al. 1997). It is against this background of anecdotal evidence for indigenous management and conservation (e.g., Zann 1985) that the present author sought to collect quantitative and qualitative data that could have explanatory value for understanding sustainable extractive strategies. The research was guided by optimal foraging theory (Stephens et al. 2007) and the testing of predictions from three models (patch choice, patch sampling, and risk) applied to mollusc gathering.

One of the shortcomings of research which portrays indigenous societies as conservationists stems from an imprecise definition of conservation that emphasizes effects rather than behavior (McDonald 1977; Wodzicki 1981; Taylor 1988). In the absence of an operational definition for conservation, it is often difficult to make sense of certain practices. Atoll societies are depicted as possessing intimate knowledge of their natural environment, resulting in the often untested assumption that people were consequently devising local strategies to live in balance with their environment.

Models derived from optimal foraging theory lead to some predictions about how organisms, including humans, should act under specific circumstances. It is predicted that they select food or prey types that maximize their short-term harvest rate. An increased availability of food is assumed to increase fertility and survivorship, and minimizing the amount of time spent foraging enables foragers to pursue other fitness-enhancing activities. Thus, natural selection would favor individuals that forage more efficiently. The optimal diet is usually determined by considering the amount of energy acquired to energy expended, as well as the time required to search and handle each prey type (handling includes time spent pursuing, capturing, harvesting, and processing a prey type into edible form).

When decisions are costly in terms of short-term harvest rate maximization, but increase the sustainability of the harvest, there is the possibility that conservation replaces optimal foraging as the strategic goal (Alvard 1993). While "genuine" conservation negates short-term efficiency, it may be compatible with long-term foraging strategies (De Boer and Prins 1989). Conservation for the sake of use ("resourcism" as defined by Oelschlaeger 1991, p. 286) should not be confused with other wilderness philosophies grounded in nonuse or moral principles (Ratcliffe 1976; Redford 1996; Sponsel 2012).

Methods

Study Area

The research draws on more than a decade of ethnographic and ethnoarchaeological observations and interviews, supplemented by archaeological and historical ecological data from Kiribati (Thomas 2009). Known since 1979 as the Republic of Kiribati, the 33 atoll and table reefs are spread over an area exceeding 3 million km^2 of ocean straddling the equator. The total land area, however, only slightly exceeds 800 km^2 (Fig. 1).

The very high ratio of reef to land area, typical of most atolls, provided early settlers and their descendants with an abundant source of protein as well as raw material (fish bone, coral, and shell) for the manufacture of tools and ornaments (Koch 1986). By contrast, the range of food crops that could sustain people on low coral islands was limited compared to what could be grown on the more fertile volcanic islands because of limited land, poor soils, and difficulty in securing fresh water. Nevertheless, coral island societies devised subsistence strategies that took full advantage of available resources, including introduced root and tree crops (Barrau 1965; Alkire 1978; Di Piazza and Pearthree 2004). Significantly, some coral islands appear to have been inhabited continuously for 2000 years or longer (Di Piazza 1999; Weisler 1999; Kayanne et al. 2011; Poteate et al. 2016; Levin et al. 2018).

Because of a lack of extensive data related to coral island paleoclimatology, together with a poor understanding of the extent of human-induced environmental impacts prior to Western contact, it remains unclear how people achieved sustainability (Allen 2006; Giovas 2006; Harris and Weisler 2018b). Insights gained from ethnographic and ethnoarchaeological observations, however, may help explain

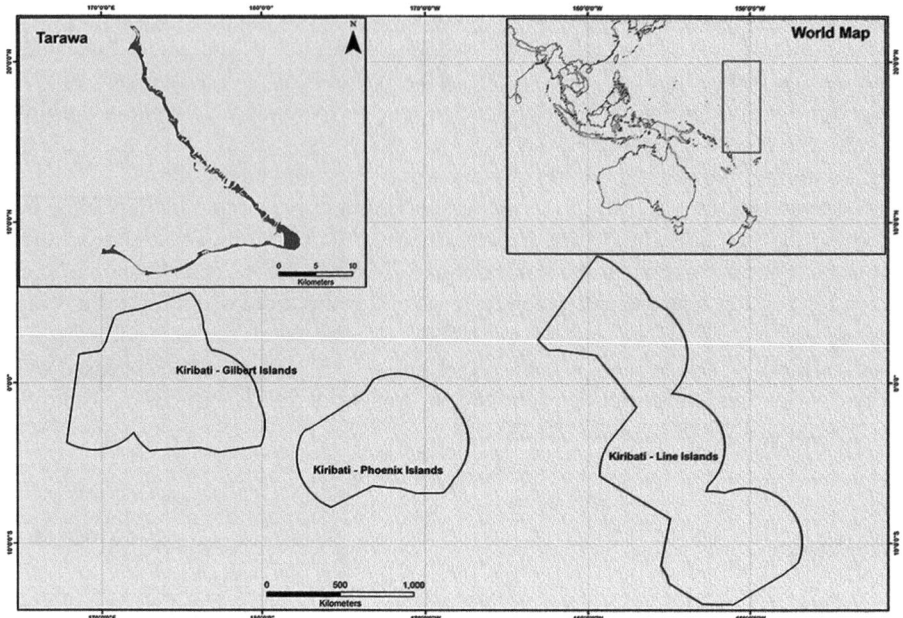

Fig. 1 Map of Kiribati (source: Pacific Community—SPC, modified by Deepak Bhartu)

some of the archaeological patterns found throughout Pacific Island shell middens, illustrating the sustained use of marine resources.

Data Collection and Observation

Data on mollusc gathering was collected from the atolls of Abaiang, Tarawa, Maiana, Abemama, and Tabiteuea between 1993 and 1998. Fieldwork resulted in 139.63 h. of direct observation (286.92 forager-hours) during 73 foraging trips. Semi-structured interviews with mollusc gatherers, representing 65 foraging trips, or approximately 88.5 h. of foraging effort (161 forager-hours), as well as an analysis of mollusc landings and associated questionnaires, courtesy of the Tarawa Lagoon Project (Abbott and Garcia 1995), representing about 191 h. of foraging time (257 forager-hours) during 83 foraging trips, provided additional quantitative and qualitative information. With data from published tables describing activity categories (Durnin and Passmore 1967; Norgan et al. 1974; Ulijaszek 1995), adjusted to this study, together with the energy content (kcal) of 24 mollusc prey types, the net energy gained per unit foraging time could be established for the observed samples (Thomas 2003, 2007). Data on prey resilience was compiled for 24 molluscs species (Thomas 1999, p. 180).

Results

Patch Choice

Three main patches in the intertidal to shallow subtidal regions of the lagoon are recognized: (1) nearshore, (2) sand flat, and (3) seagrass. The nearshore patch includes all features intersecting the shoreline, occasionally extending to within 100 m of shore where conglomerate tongues and/or gravelly sand spits occur. The sand flat is a wide, gently sloping expanse occupying most of the intertidal, but also comprises areas of mangrove. Seagrass beds are highly productive grounds for a variety of molluscs that are also important in fishing because of their high concentration of nutrients. A fourth patch, "offshore," is also recognized in the deeper section of the lagoon on South Tarawa where intensive harvesting of the cockle, *Anadara uropigimelana*, took place in the 1990s. On other atolls, intensive harvesting of the giant clam, *Tridacna maxima*, took place along the leeward reef platform (Fig. 2).

The ocean side of all atolls is less frequently exploited than the lagoon but includes three patch types: (1) nearshore, (2) reef flat, and (3) reef crest. The reef crest is similar to the lagoon side. The wide reef flat consists of a hard coralline surface interspersed by sandy pockets and some mangroves. The reef crest is seldom exploited compared to the other patches because of the limited time foragers can collect offshore during low spring tides and low overall returns.

Mollusc gathering is focused separately in the patches, each defined as "fine-grained environments" (MacArthur and Pianka 1966, p. 603), although on occasion

Fig. 2 *Tridacna maxima* harvesting (photo: F. Thomas)

foragers will visit and gather from more than one patch. Their locations are generally well known. Seagrass beds are the focus of the most intensive harvesting insofar as tide conditions permit (Paulay 2001). Observations of foraging behavior and interviews, together with examination of contemporary shell middens, suggest that overland travel usually takes place in the direction of the patches roughly facing human settlements, although once inside the patch, considerable movement may occur parallel to the shore.

Predictably, nearshore patches (on both lagoon and ocean sides) are significantly less productive than either seagrass or sand flats (seagrass vs. nearshore, two-tailed t-test, $t = 4.42$, $df = 9$, $p < 0.001$; sand flat vs. nearshore, $t = 3.44$, $df = 37$, $p = 001$). With the exception of one foraging trip, nearshore foraging took place only when the more productive patches were not easily accessible. The low overall returns from ocean reef flats in comparison to seagrass and sand flats are significant ($t = 3.14$, $df = 16$, $p = 0.006$; $t = 2.27$, $df = 34$, $p = 0.030$). Yet, reef flat foraging may demonstrate patch sampling and thus violate the assumption of constancy in patch quality.

The wide distribution of many mollusc prey types across extensive patches would probably not result in step function depletion (Kaplan and Hill 1992), where the energy gain per unit time remains constant until the last prey item is harvested, although for certain prey types that can be easily seen and distributed within relatively small patches, foragers may remain in a given patch until the energy gain drops to zero. For example, *T. maxima*, occurring on microatolls may provide a context for this foraging strategy. In most cases, however, foragers appear to leave patches when faced with diminishing returns.

The marginal value theorem addresses the issue of optimal time allocation to each patch (Charnov 1976). It assumes that foraging gradually depletes resources, resulting in a decline in the net return rate from each patch as a consequence of "exploitation depression." Heavy predation may also lead to "behavioral depression" (Charnov et al. 1976), when prey alter their behavior in ways that make them more difficult to be harvested. Diminishing returns can also result from changes in the foraging environment, without affecting patch productivity. In the context of mollusc gathering, changing tide levels may act as constraints on decisions either to continue searching in a high-ranking patch and face diminish returns, because of increasing difficulty in visually locating prey with the incoming tide, or to move to a less productive patch closer to shore.

A forager should leave a patch when the marginal capture rate (i.e., the instantaneous capture rate at the end of a foraging trip within that patch) drops to the average capture rate for the entire set of patches utilized (including travel time between patches). As the overall productivity of a habitat (set of patches) increases, less time should be spent in any one patch, whereas declining productivity should lead to an increase in optimal patch-stay times. Testing predictions from the marginal value theorem is made difficult by the need to collect detailed information on patterns of movement, time budgets, and return rates, none of which have been satisfactorily recorded in either this or other studies (Smith 1983; Kaplan and Hill 1992).

A correlate of the theorem referred to as the "differential time allocation" hypothesis (Smith 1991, p. 258) has been cited as a reasonable, albeit indirect test of the question of diminishing returns assumed in the theorem. According to this hypothesis, foragers ought to focus on the highest ranking patch while ignoring or dropping all others, given equal access. Because the most productive patch is expected to provide a higher gain than a lower ranking patch, then it should receive a greater allocation of foraging time. A switch to a lower ranking patch may be interpreted as a sign of decelerating gain in the high-ranking patch. Conditions similar to those described above were noted when foragers shifted their gathering activities from the low- to mid-intertidal sand flat to gather the bivalve, *Gafrarium pectinatum*, and then into the upper intertidal gravelly sands to search for the more widely dispersed bivalve, *Asaphis violascens*, when the incoming tide limited foragers' ability to locate prey in deeper, more productive areas.

As prey become less common as a result of predation, or as they become more cryptic in light of exploitative pressure, an efficient forager may decide that it no longer pays to stay in a patch and search for increasingly elusive prey. Provided that travel time to the next best patch is not too costly, a patch type can be temporarily abandoned. Depending on the biological attributes of prey within that patch and the time lapse between visits, prey types may be able to recover from intensive harvesting. Foragers are not paying short-term costs by leaving a patch because they can do better in another one. Alvard's (1993) distinction between conservation behavior per se from its effects ("epiphenomenal" conservation) is pertinent in this context in that conservation may incidentally follow optimal foraging decisions, as illustrated by patch switching.

Among all documented instances of patch switching (or movements within a patch perpendicular to the shoreline), there was little to support the suggestion that foragers were motivated by a desire to conserve resources. Rather, the motivation always appeared to be linked to diminishing returns and the need to move to other patches. When tide conditions changed, foragers either moved from low-ranked patches to high-ranked patches or vice versa. This behavior is consistent with short-term maximization.

Patch Sampling

Patch depletion and subsequent high spatiotemporal variation in prey recruitment often lead to situations where molluscs become unpredictable resources, with marked differences in clumping. The gastropod *Conomurex luhuanus* and the bivalve *G. pectinatum* exhibit some of the highest degrees of clumping (the former primarily through behavioral attributes; the latter by virtue of its density). However, while both could be defined as "patches," their specific distribution (epifaunal vs. infaunal) determines whether synchronous foraging by more than one forager will increase or reduce individual efficiency. For the highly conspicuous *C. luhuanus*, it does not pay for even a small party of two foragers to search a relatively restricted area. Depending on tide conditions, foragers may be separated from each other by several tens of meters. By contrast, the cryptic habits of dense *G. pectinatum* permit tighter clustering of individual foragers, sometimes on order of less than a meter, with little interference and competition. On the other hand, foragers are widely separated (often in excess of 100 m) while foraging on the ocean reef flat. This is consistent with the low density of high-ranked prey such as *Hippopus hippopus*. Unlike other infaunal prey, such as *G. pectinatum*, foragers rarely excavate more than one *A. violascens* in a single digging motion (which usually involves digging straight down into the hard, gravelly matrix compared to the shallower, scraping motions which characterize *G. pectinatum* harvesting in the sand flats).

Knowledge of patch quality based on environmental cues and the sharing of information with other foragers contrast with information *while* foraging (Stephens and Krebs 1986, p. 28). Models of information use (Stephens 2007) suggest that foragers do obtain information from conspecifics. Fluctuating resources require this kind of assessment strategy, but given the cost of sampling, under what circumstances would it be beneficial to sacrifice short-term return rates to acquire information for long-term gains?

Although yields may fluctuate from the dual impact of forager-dependent and forager-independent processes, to be of value, information about change should focus on those attributes of the environment that do not fluctuate too rapidly. For example, if large concentrations of mobile *C. luhuanus* are known to occur, such knowledge would provide little benefit in the long-term because the "patches" are likely to shift. However, the discovery of sedentary bivalves may be more valuable in planning future harvesting, bearing in mind competition from other foragers or marine organisms that feed on molluscs.

Together with rate of change, there should be large enough differences in return rates between patches or even between sections of patches to justify expanding effort in information acquisition. Patch depletion and the vagaries of successful prey recruitment (e.g., *A. uropigimelana* in the Bonriki-Temaiku seagrass area of South Tarawa) are important factors that determine the usefulness of an assessment strategy. The implication of a sampling strategy is the patch residence time, which differs from the marginal value theorem: foragers either stay longer or leave sooner than predicted by the theorem (Stephens and Krebs 1986, p. 91).

It is possible that the shift from the sand flat to seagrass at Bonriki-Temaiku began as a sampling strategy. Near Tebanga on Maiana, people focused almost exclusively on *G. pectinatum*. Foragers commonly limited their activities to the mid-intertidal, but in two observed cases, appeared to be sampling the low intertidal to assess the state of resources away from the shoreline. Interviews indicated that *A. uropigimelana* had once been abundant in the area, but then steadily declined, which resulted in foragers switching to *G. pectinatum*. Some foragers, however, had the opportunity to come into contact with high-ranked prey types while traveling to their small seaweed plots in the low intertidal. Reports on the status of molluscs occurring in the area filtered back to the community and encouraged people to search for *A. uropigimelana* in places they would normally bypass.

Another example of sampling strategy is illustrated by observations and interviews on the ocean reef flat. Foragers were monitoring giant clam distribution. Areas surveyed were carefully selected to avoid spending time in previously searched sections. Up to three months passed before a specific patch section was revisited, presumably to allow for the recovery of heavily depleted resources. However, "patch recovery time" (Bennett 1991) in one instance resulted in less than 20% of initial caloric intake derived from *H. hippopus*. It was suspected that other foraging groups had exploited some of the recovered biomass in the interim.

Natural selection specifies the conditions that may benefit from a sampling strategy, thus sacrificing short-term gains to acquire information for long-term gains, but unless *intent* to conserve can be established, patch sampling documented in this study cannot be considered a conservation strategy. While the distinction between intent and behavior should be kept, and predictions from foraging models are tested against behavior, the criterion of intent remains important in deciding whether a subsistence strategy is synonymous with genuine conservation or not (see Whitaker 2008 in the context of incipient aquaculture of intertidal resources). The third foraging model, risk, further examines the issue of intentional vs. unintentional management.

Risk

Risk is closely related to sampling (Winterhalder et al. 1999; Sosis 2002). Two strategies to reduce risk include resource sharing/reciprocal territorial access and hoarding/storage (Colson 1979; Smith and Boyd 1990). Both entail costs to the individual, but the costs for not employing them in appropriate contexts may be even higher.

Sharing and hoarding may be perceived as contrasting strategies to reduce risk, and the kinds of resources that are widely shared and those that are stored appear to be quite different. Because indigenous land tenure is still recognized, terrestrial production and food preservation belong to extended families. Most marine resources are no longer culturally regulated, which explains why a successful fisherman sometimes relinquishes part of his catch to distantly related kin or non-kin. Remnants of a more extensive marine tenure system, such as fish traps and "gardens" for the live storage of giant clams (Figs. 3 and 4), are at odds with the open-access policy governing lagoon and ocean habitats set up by the former British authorities. As a result, outer island councils have established bylaws in an attempt to control resource access (Thomas 2001). However, the effectiveness of these measures remains in doubt. Teuea (2018, p. 67) noted, recent efforts to conserve marine resources in Kiribati are "still largely driven by the government agenda and competence despite the projects being branded as community-based."

Sharing and hoarding need not be mutually exclusive. For example, some households might hoard pandanus paste or dried fish in times of abundance for possible sharing in times of scarcity. Risk aversion strategies are important in determining

Fig. 3 Fish trap (photo: F. Thomas)

Fig. 4 Giant clam "garden" (photo: F. Thomas)

whether intentional conservation or management has been selected for. Although sharing of certain marine resources does take place, in light of the open-access regime established during the colonial period, it is doubtful that sharing is meant to prevent overexploitation. Storage in the form of giant clam aquaculture, on the other hand, may indicate the application of both intentional and unintentional management practices, as discussed below.

Discussion

The ability of prey to withstand various levels of predation is a function of their biological (life history) and ecological characteristics. Some prey are more susceptible to overexploitation and extinction than others because of low reproductive rates and few natural predators, resulting in restricted mobility and the absence of effective defensive mechanisms and appropriate behavioral responses to intensified predation. Insular terrestrial fauna, such as flightless birds, are a case in point (Anderson 1989). Despite differences in recruitment between terrestrial and marine organisms, which would account for greater resilience of the latter to intensive predation (e.g., as a result of high fecundity or dispersal distances of pelagic larvae), overfishing and especially overharvesting of slow-moving invertebrates by selectively gathering the largest available molluscs can depress a resource's size range and average size. Overexploitation may lead to disruption in the entire ecosystem and to the loss of genetic diversity (McNeely et al. 1995, pp. 746–747). Extirpation, or local extinction, may also occur as evidenced by the giant clam, *T. gigas* (Munro 1989).

Catterall and Poiner (1987) have studied the life history and habitat information to assess resilience among some Australian intertidal molluscs. Species exhibited differences in their ability to withstand similar levels of predation by virtue of their size at maturity, intertidal burying, the presence of subtidal populations, benthic mobility, and the length of time for pelagic larvae to disperse before settling. The implications are that any apparent balance between prey and predator may be more closely related to a prey's biological and ecological properties which make it more difficult to deplete, rather than to the application of a conservation strategy (Poiner and Catterall 1988). The simultaneous harvest of natural mollusc predators may also lessen the overall impact of foraging strategies (McClanahan 1989, 1990). The notion that "folk management rules" (Acheson and Wilson 1996, p. 586; Anderson 1996, p. 174), including rules about fishing locations and techniques, are effective in conserving resources thus needs to be critically examined (Berkes et al. 2000; Gaymer et al. 2014; Aswani 2017).

To a large measure, prey resilience, together with flexible foraging strategies targeting a broad range of taxa, would account for the sustainable harvest for centuries of several molluscs species as illustrated by the analysis of shell middens in the Marshall Islands (Harris and Weisler 2018b), Kiribati (Thomas 2009, 2014), and other locales (e.g., Giovas 2016). Weisler (2001) presented evidence for the extirpation of the bullmouth helmet shell (*Cypraecassis rufa*) from Utrōk Atoll in the Marshalls. But the overall impression suggests little change in habitat selection, richness, evenness, or diversity. Moreover, the presence or absence of marine organisms in a particular habitat (and their subsequent representation in the archaeological record) appears to be partly determined by chaotic and unpredictable recruitment events that shape the structure of reef assemblages over time (Sale 1980; Paulay 2001; Thakar 2011).

Prey resilience is one attribute that may result in sustainability. But even highly resilient prey can become vulnerable if predation pressure increases because of harvest intensification linked to a growing predator population and/or the introduction of new extractive technologies. Patch switching can also lead to sustainable harvests, as noted above. While foragers following a diminishing returns curve are maximizing their short-term gains by moving across patches, prey are generally capable to recover.

Patch sampling may lead to deviations from short-term rate maximization assumed in the marginal value theorem. Because predictions from the latter model could not be properly tested, however, statements about patch sampling where foragers may either stay longer or leave sooner than predicted by the theorem remain inconclusive.

Storage is an effective risk reduction strategy, and by definition it involves delayed consumption. Although there are costs to storing foods (they may deteriorate rapidly or may be scavenged or stolen), the live storage of giant clams may be compared to other forms of animal husbandry (Alvard and Kuznar 2001). This practice has been reported from various Pacific Island communities, including Kiribati (MacLean 1978; Moir 1989b, pp. 494–497; Foster and Poggie 1993; Hviding 1993; Bliege Bird et al. 1995; Kinch 2003, 2008).

As noted above, there have been several instances of local extinction of the larger species of giant clams, notably *T. gigas* and *H. hippopus* in pre-European contact and historic times. Because of their long planktonic stage (allowing for wider dispersal but also resulting in high mortality rates), slow growth, low reproductive success of adults, and sporadic mass mortality in wild populations, giant clams are especially at risk (Penny and Willan 2014; Neo et al. 2015). Consequently, some island communities resorted to gathering live giant clams from deeper water and transplanting them to locations near the shoreline for later consumption. From Brooker Island in the Louisiade Archipelago of Papua New Guinea, Kinch (2008, p. 183) mentions that "Juvenile Tridacnidae are collected and placed in secret locations outside village houses or on the foreshore reefs where they can be harvested as needed." The initial gathering took place during calm weather. This was not directly observed in Kiribati nor could it be confirmed that gathering of giant clams for storage correlated with people's ability to satisfy their short-term energy needs by harvesting other higher-ranked mollusc or other resources, as assumed by optimal foraging theory. Return rates for *T. gigas* and *H. hippopus* are variable because of the wide range of sizes of individual prey items. Nevertheless, they may be regarded as high-ranking prey but still inferior to most other marine resources (Thomas 1999, p. 379). It may be that small prey items (<40 cm) may actually fall outside the optimal diet, so that transplanting them does not involve a short-term cost. Thus, giant clam "gardening" may be regarded as an example of both intentional and unintentional conservation.

The vulnerability of giant clams even to moderate levels of human predation would make them ideal candidates for testing hypotheses about the sustainable use of these resources through the presence of archaeological "gardens" indicated by the concentration of empty valves in shallow water, particularly since *T. gigas* is not naturally found in nearshore, shallow water environments prone to turbid conditions. In Kiribati, live tridacnids are sometimes placed inside fish traps (Thomas 1999, p. 382). Moir's (1989b, 1990) research on Takuu Atoll (a Polynesian "outlier" in Papua New Guinea) attempted to identify evidence of former "gardens." Her ethnohistorical investigations also led to the documentation of the former practice of "aging" *T. gigas* (after removal of the animal) in seawater prior to reduction for use as tool material. X-ray diffraction analysis and scanning electron microscopy confirmed that "aged" shell adzes were of superior workability and were also selected for ceremonial purposes.

Another dimension of marine "husbandry" involves species enhancement (see Ostraff 2003, pp. 142–143 for *limu* or marine algae in Tonga and fish ponds in Hawai'i Wyban 1992). As noted by Thomas (2015) in Kiribati and Williams (2016) in New Zealand, mollusc "gardens" incorporate aspects of habitat improvement and the creation of ecological niches that aim to increase resource availability productivity and in some cases reliability. This is complimented by "garden" allocation between extended families. From Abaiang Atoll, mollusc gatherers have been observed transplanting *A. uropigimelana* and *G. pectinatum*, alongside tridacnids (Fig. 5), in specially designated areas on the intertidal flat for future harvesting. These areas are sometimes demarcated by coral cobbles (Fig. 6).

From the Northwest Coast of North America (Lepofsky and Caldwell 2013; Groesbeck et al. 2014; Lepofsky et al. 2015), there is ethnographic and archaeologi-

Fig. 5 Gathering transplanted cockles alongside *Hippopus hippopus* (photo: F. Thomas)

Fig. 6 Giant clam "garden" demarcated by coral cobbles (photo: F. Thomas)

cal data supporting similar enhancement with selective clam harvests, the removal of shells and other debris, and the mechanical aeration of the sediment matrix. Mollusc conservation is inferred from 7000-year-old middens in coastal British Columbia near residential sites with the predominance of senile shells, as opposed to mature specimens, at long-term residential sites suggestive of less intensive harvest (Cannon and Burchell 2009).

As noted by Whitaker (2008), shell size reduction does not necessarily indicate declining foraging returns at a site if the currency being maximized is long-term productivity instead of immediate returns, with the removal of large individuals relieving competitive pressure allowing smaller individuals to move into patches and grow more rapidly. Conversely, significant size increases have been documented for *Gibberulus gibberulus* (Humped Conch) at Chelechol ra Orrak in Palau from ca. 3000 BP to present (Giovas et al. 2010) and *Nerita tessellata* (Tessellated Nerite) on Nevis in the West Indies (Giovas et al. 2013). In both cases several variables may be responsible, including foraging practices reducing intraspecific competition, environmental change, and anthropogenic practices (e.g., by removing the species' predators, resulting in increased longevity, with more individuals surviving longer to become larger before the onset of maturity). For Palau, increasing horticultural activities could also have played a role resulting in eutrophication which would have created or expanded habitats favored by this species.

The benefits of transporting unprocessed shells, even over great distances to keep them fresh for later consumption and trade or for other uses, have been widely documented (Buchanan 1988; Moir 1989a; Bliege Bird and Bird 1997). Conversely, shell middens may provide an incomplete picture of the range of species consumed

Fig. 7 Giant clam field processing (photo: F. Thomas)

in the past, with implications for questions about conservation and sustainability. Thomas' (2002) study of central-place foraging decisions (see also Bird 1997; Orians and Pearson 1979; Metcalfe and Barlow 1992) among Kiribati mollusc gatherers and the archaeological reflection of those decisions may also contribute to discussions on sustainability. If we can predict when it becomes efficient to field process prey types, then their underrepresentation in shell middens may be explained. By way of illustration, if there is a tendency to field process tridacnids, not intended to be placed in "gardens" (Fig. 7), their absence or low densities in archaeological deposits may not reflect avoidance or a conservation/management strategy. A number of ethnographic accounts document the processing and sometimes consumption of various mollusc species at the point of collection, with their shells discarded (Quilter and Stocker 1983; De Boer 2000; Deshpande-Mukherjee 2000), thus questioning the assumption that large molluscs are more profitable than smaller ones and always end up in middens in proportion to their encounter rate.

Conclusion

The archaeological record in the Pacific is rich with examples of stable long-term adaptations of humans to their environment, as well as significant ecological changes brought about even by small-scale, low-technology, indigenous societies prior to Western contact. Even the comparatively rich marine ecosystems have been altered by human harvesting of resources against the backdrop of changing environments (Nunn 2007; Rick et al. 2013). The interlinked topics of "sustainability" archaeology, historical ecology, and conservation biology (Dalzell 1998; Lyman and Cannon 2004; Hayashida 2005; Hardesty 2007; Rick and Lockwood 2012; Wolverton and Lyman 2012; Fitzpatrick and Erlandson 2018) highlight the many challenges faced by Pacific Island communities as they attempt to cope with changing environments, economies, and social values, which now more than ever pose a threat to sustainable livelihoods.

A focus on mollusc resources in the past, as well as in the present, has provided an integrated understanding of sustainability as a possible outcome, which can result from multiple factors (Keegan et al. 2008). While examples of negative human impacts have received considerable attention by archaeologists, the above review suggests that in several instances molluscs persisted. In each case, the archaeological record needs to incorporate a range of interpretative tools to explain prey resilience and overall stability (DiNapoli and Morrison 2016). Agent-based modelling applied to human-mollusc interactions (Morrison and Allen 2015, p. 9) may prove very useful in identifying "missing contextual information and new research questions." These include data about specific prey life-history traits, variation in management strategies and harvesting techniques or differences in collection and discard that structure the archaeological record.

Acknowledgments Many thanks to Ludomir Lozny for the invitation to contribute to this volume. Amrit Raj of the Faculty of Science, Technology and Environment, University of the South Pacific (USP), provided the map. Deepak Bhartu of USP's Centre for Flexible Learning assisted in modifying Fig. 1.

References

Abbott, R. R., & Garcia, J. (Eds.). (1995). *Management plan for Tarawa Lagoon, Republic of Kiribati: Volume III, management plan*. Santa Cruz, CA: BioSystems Analysis.

Acheson, J. M., & Wilson, J. A. (1996). Order out of chaos: The case of parametric fisheries management. *American Anthropologist, 98*, 579–594.

Akamichi, T. (1986). Conservation of the sea: Satawal, Micronesia. In A. Anderson (Ed.), *Traditional fishing in the Pacific: Ethnographical and archaeological papers from the 15th Pacific Science Congress* (pp. 15–33). Honolulu, HI: Pacific Anthropological Records No. 37, B. P. Bishop Museum.

Alkire, W. H. (1978). *Coral islanders*. Arlington Heights, IL: AHML.

Allen, M. S. (2006). New ideas about Late Holocene climate variability in the central Pacific. *Current Anthropology, 47*, 521–535.

Alvard, M. S. (1993). Testing the "ecologically noble savage" hypothesis: Interspecific prey choice by Piro hunters of Amazonian Peru. *Human Ecology, 21*, 355–387.

Alvard, M. S., & Kuznar, L. (2001). Deferred harvests: The transition from hunting to animal husbandry. *American Anthropologist, 103*, 295–311.

Amesbury, J. R. (2007). Mollusk collection and environmental change during the prehistoric period in the Mariana Islands. *Coral Reefs, 26*, 947–958.

Anderson, A. (1979). Prehistoric exploitation of marine resources at Black Rocks Point, Palliser Bay. In B. F. Leach & H. M. Leach (Eds.), *Prehistoric man in Palliser Bay* (pp. 49–65). Wellington: National Museum of New Zealand Bulletin No. 21.

Anderson, A. (1989). Mechanics of in the extinction of New Zealand moas. *Journal of Archaeological Science, 16*, 137–151.

Anderson, A. (2008). Short and sometimes sharp: Human impacts on marine resources in the archaeology and history of south Polynesia. In T. C. Rick & J. M. Erlandson (Eds.), *Human impacts on ancient marine ecosystems: A global perspective* (pp. 21–42). Berkeley, CA: University of California Press.

Anderson, A., Wallin, P., Martinsson-Wallin, H., Fankhauser, B., & Hope, G. (2000). Towards a first prehistory of Kiritimati (Christmas) Island, Republic of Kiribati. *Journal of the Polynesian Society, 109*, 273–293.

Anderson, E. N. (1996). *Ecologies of the heart: Emotion, belief, and the environment*. New York, NY: Oxford University Press.

Ariana, B., Lambrides, J., & Weisler, M. I. (2017). Late Holocene Marshall Islands archaeological tuna records provide proxy evidence for ENSO variability in the western and central Pacific Ocean. *Journal of Island and Coastal Archaeology*. https://doi.org/10.1080/15564894.2017.1 315350

Aswani, S. (2017). Customary management as TURFs: Social challenges and opportunities. *Bulletin of Marine Science, 93*, 3–12.

Aswani, S., & Allen, M. S. (2009). A Marquesan coral reef (French Polynesia) in historical context: An integrated socio-ecological approach. *Aquatic Conservation: Marine and Freshwater Ecosystems, 19*, 614–625.

Barrau, J. (1965). L'humide et le sec: An essay on ethnological adaptation to contrastive environments in the Indo-Pacific Area. *Journal of the Polynesian Society, 74*, 329–346.

Bennett, I. M. (1991). Barí loricarid collection and the value of information: An application of optimal foraging theory. *Human Ecology, 19*, 517–527.

Berkes, F., Colding, J., & Folke, C. (2000). Rediscovery of traditional ecological knowledge as adaptive management. *Ecological Applications, 10*, 1251–1262.

Bird, D. W. (1997). Behavioral ecology and the archaeological consequences of central place foraging among the Meriam. In C. M. Barton & G. A. Clark (Eds.), *Rediscovering Darwin: Evolutionary theory and archaeological explanation* (pp. 291–306). Arlington, VA: Archaeological Papers of the American Anthropological Association No. 7.

Bliege Bird, R. L., & Bird, D. W. (1997). Delayed reciprocity and tolerated theft: The behavioral ecology of food sharing strategies. *Current Anthropology, 38*, 49–78.

Bliege Bird, R. L., Bird, D. W., & Beaton, J. M. (1995). Children and traditional subsistence on Mer (Murray Island), Torres Strait. *Australian Aboriginal Studies, 1*, 2–17.

Bridges, K. W., & McClatchey, W. C. (2009). Living on the margin: Ethnoecological insights from Marshall Islanders at Rongelap Atoll. *Global Environmental Change, 19*, 140–146.

Buchanan, W. F. (1988). *Shellfish in prehistoric diet: Elands Bay, S. W. Cape Coast, South Africa*. Oxford: BAR International Series No. 455.

Campbell, G. (2008). Beyond means to meaning: Using distributions of shell shapes to reconstruct past collecting strategies. *Environmental Archaeology, 13*, 111–121.

Cannon, A., & Burchell, M. (2009). Clam growth-stage profiles as a measure of harvest intensity and resource management on the central coast of British Columbia. *Journal of Archaeological Science, 36*, 1050–1060.

Catterall, I., & Poiner, R. (1987). The potential impact of human gathering on shellfish populations with reference to some NE Australian intertidal flats. *Oikos, 50*, 114–122.

Charnov, E. L. (1976). Optimal foraging: The marginal value theorem. *Theoretical Population Biology, 9*, 129–136.

Charnov, E. L., Orians, G. H., & Hyatt, K. (1976). Ecological implications of resource depression. *American Naturalist, 110*, 247–259.

Colson, E. (1979). In good years and in bad: Food strategies of self-reliant societies. *Journal of Anthropological Research, 35*, 18–29.

Dalzell, P. (1998). The role of archaeological and cultural-historical records in long-range coastal fisheries resources management strategies and policies in the Pacific Islands. *Ocean & Coastal Management, 40*, 237–252.

De Boer, W. F. (2000). *Between the tides: The impact of human exploitation on an intertidal ecosystem, Mozambique*. Veenendaal: Universal Press.

De Boer, W. F., & Prins, H. H. T. (1989). Decisions of cattle herdsmen in Burkina Faso and optimal foraging models. *Human Ecology, 17*, 445–463.

Deshpande-Mukherjee, A. (2000). An ethnographic account of contemporary shellfish gathering on the Konkan Coast, Maharashtra. *Man and Environment, 25*(2), 79–92.

Di Piazza, A. (1999). Te bakoa. Two old earth ovens from Nikunau Island (Republic of Kiribati). *Archaeology in Oceania, 34*, 40–42.

Di Piazza, A., & Pearthree, E. (2001). An island for gardens, an island for birds and voyaging: A settlement pattern for Kiritimati and Tabuaeran, two "mystery islands". *Journal of the Polynesian Society, 110*, 149–170.

Di Piazza, A., & Pearthree, E. (2004). *Sailing routes of old Polynesia: The prehistoric discovery, settlement and abandonment of the Phoenix Islands*. Honolulu, HI: Bishop Museum Press.

DiNapoli, R. J., & Morrison, A. E. (2016). Human behavioral ecology and Pacific archaeology. *Archaeology in Oceania*. https://doi.org/10.1002/arco.5124

Durnin, J. V. G. A., & Passmore, R. (1967). *Energy, work and leisure*. London: Heinemann.

Fitzpatrick, S., & M. (2012). On the shoals of giants: Natural catastrophes and the overall destruction of the Caribbean's archaeological record. *Journal of Coastal Conservation, 16*, 173–186.

Fitzpatrick, S. M. (2007). Archaeology's contribution to island studies. *Island Studies Journal, 2*, 77–100.

Fitzpatrick, S. M., & Erlandson, J. M. (2018). Island archaeology, model systems, the Anthropocene, and how the past informs the future. *Journal of Island and Coastal Archaeology, 13*, 283–299.

Foster, K. B., & Poggie Jr., J. J. (1993). Customary marine Tenure and mariculture management in outlying communities of Pohnpie [sic] State, Federated States of Micronesia. *Ocean & Coastal Management, 20*, 1–22.

Gaymer, C. F., Stadel, A. V., Ban, N. C., Cárcamo, P. F., Ierna Jr., J., & Lieberknecht, L. M. (2014). Merging top-down and bottom-up approaches in marine protected areas planning: Experiences from around the globe. *Aquatic Conservation: Marine and Freshwater Ecosystems, 24*, 128–144.

Giovas, C. M. (2006). No pig atoll: Island biogeography and the extirpation of a Polynesian domesticate. *Asian Perspectives, 45*, 69–95.

Giovas, C. M. (2016). Though she be but little: Resource resilience, Amerindian foraging, and long-term adaptive strategies in the Grenadines, West Indies. *Journal of Island and Coastal Archaeology*. https://doi.org/10.1080/15564894.2016.1193572

Giovas, C. M. (2018). Pre-Columbian Amerindian lifeways at the Sabazan Site, Carriacou, West Indies. *Journal of Island and Coastal Archaeology, 13*, 161–190.

Giovas, C. M., Clark, M., Fitzpatrick, S. M., & Stone, J. (2013). Intensifying collection and size increase of the tessellated nerite snail (*Nerita tessellata*) at the Coconut Walk Site, Northern Lesser Antilles, AD 890-1440. *Journal of Archaeological Science*. https://doi.org/10.1066/j.jas.2013.05.008

Giovas, C. M., Fitzpatrick, S. M., Clark, M., & Abed, M. (2010). Evidence for size increase in an exploited mollusc: Humped conch (*Strombus gibberulus*) at Chelechol ra Orrak, Palau from ca. 3000-0 BP. *Journal of Archaeological Science*. https://doi.org/10.1016/j.jas.2010.06.013

Groesbeck, A. S., Rowell, K., Lepofsky, D., & Salomon, A. K. (2014). Ancient clam gardens increased shellfish production: Adaptive strategies from the past can inform food security today. *PLOS One*. https://doi.org/10.1371/journal.pone.0091235

Hardesty, D. (2007). Perspectives on global-change archaeology. *American Anthropologist, 109*, 1–7.

Harris, M., & Weisler, M. (2018a). Prehistoric human impacts to marine mollusks and intertidal ecosystems in the Pacific Islands. *Journal of Island and Coastal Archaeology, 13*, 235–255.

Harris, M., & Weisler, M. (2018b). Two millennia of mollusc foraging on Ebon Atoll, Marshall Islands: Sustained marine resource use on a Pacific atoll. *Archaeology in Oceania, 53*, 41–57.

Hayashida, F. M. (2005). Archaeology, ecological history, and conservation. *Annual Review of Anthropology, 34*, 43–65.

Hviding, E. (1993). *The rural context of Giant Clam mariculture in Solomon Islands: An anthropological study*. Manila: ICLAR Technical Report No. 39.

Kaplan, H., & Hill, K. (1992). The evolutionary ecology of food acquisition. In E. A. Smith & B. Winterhalder (Eds.), *Evolutionary ecology and human behavior* (pp. 167–201). New York: Aldine de Gruyter.

Kayanne, H., Yasukochi, T., Yamaguchi, T., Yamano, H., & Yoneda, M. (2011). Rapid settlement of Majuro Atoll, central Pacific, following its emergence at 2000 years CalBP. *Geophysical Research Letters, 38*(L20405). https://doi.org/10.1029/2011GL049163

Keegan, W. F., Fitzpatric, S. M., Sealey, K. S., LeFebvre, M. J., & Sinell, P. T. (2008). The role of small islands in marine subsistence strategies: Case studies from the Caribbean. *Human Ecology, 36*, 635–654.

Kennett, D., Anderson, A., & Winterhalder, B. (2006). The ideal free distribution, food production, and the colonization of Oceania. In D. Kennett & B. Winterhalder (Eds.), *Behavioral ecology and the transition to agriculture* (pp. 265–288). Berkeley, CA: University of California Press.

Kinch, J. (2003). Marine mollusc use among the women of Brooker Island, Louisiade Archipelago, Papua New Guinea. *SPC Women and Fisheries Information Bulletin, 13*, 5–14.

Kinch, J. (2008). From prehistoric to present: Giant clam (Tridacnidae) use in Papua New Guinea. In I. A. Antczak & R. Cipriani (Eds.), *Early human impact on megamolluscs* (pp. 179–188). Oxford: BAR International Series No. 1865.

Kirch, P. V. (2009). Human impacts, pre-European. In R. G. Gillespie & D. A. Clague (Eds.), *Encyclopedia of islands* (pp. 414–418). Berkeley, CA: University of California Press.

Kirch, P. V., & Hunt, T. L. (Eds.). (1997). *Historical ecology in the Pacific Islands: Prehistoric environmental and landscape change*. New Haven, CT: Yale University Press.

Kirch, P. V., & Yen, D. E. (1982). *Tikopia: The prehistory and ecology of a Polynesian Outlier*. Honolulu, HI: Bishop Museum Press.

Klee, G. A. (1985). Traditional marine resource management in the Pacific. In J. A. McNeeley & D. Pitt (Eds.), *Culture and conservation: The human dimension in environmental planning* (pp. 193–202). London: Croom Helm.

Koch, G. (1986). *The material culture of Kiribati*. Suva: Institute of Pacific Studies, University of the South Pacific.

Lazrus, H. (2015). Risk perception and climate adaptation in Tuvalu: A combined cultural theory and traditional knowledge approach. *Human Organization, 74*, 52–61.

Lepofsky, D., & Caldwell, M. (2013). Indigenous marine resource management on the northwest coast of North America. *Ecological Processes*. https://doi.org/10.1186/2192-1709-2-12

Lepofsky, D., Smith, N. F., Cardinal, N., Harper, J., Morris, M., (Elroy White), G., et al. (2015). Ancient shellfish mariculture on the northwest coast of North America. *American Antiquity, 80*, 236–259.

Levin, M. J., Seikel, K., & Miles, A. (2018). *Subsistence and settlement on Pingelap Atoll: Results from the 2017 field season* (Technical Report). Retrieved November 11, 2018, from http://www.researcgate.net/publication/324507113

Lilley, I. (2008). Apocalypse now (and avoid the rush): Human dimensions of climate change in the Indo-Pacific. *Archaeology in Oceania, 43*, 35–40.

Lyman, R. L., & Cannon, K. P. (Eds.). (2004). *Zooarchaeology and conservation biology*. Salt City, UT: University of Utah Press.

MacArthur, R. H., & Pianka, E. A. (1966). On optimal use of a patchy environment. *American Naturalist, 100*, 603–609.

Maclean, J. L. (1978). The clam gardens of Manus. *Harvest, 4*, 160–163.

Masse, W. B. (1989). *The archaeology and ecology of fishing in the Belau Islands, Micronesia*. Doctoral Dissertation, Department of Anthropology, Southern Illinois University at Carbondale, Carbondale, IL. Available from ProQuest Dissertations and Theses database (UMI No. 9117421).

McClanahan, T. R. (1989). Kenyan coral reef-associated gastropod fauna: A comparison between protected and unprotected reefs. *Marine Ecology Progress Series, 53*, 11–20.

McClanahan, T. R. (1990). Kenyan coral reef-associated gastropod assemblages: Distribution and diversity patterns. *Coral Reefs, 9*, 63–74.

McDonald, D. R. (1977). Food taboos: A primitive environmental protection agency (South America). *Anthropos, 72*, 734–748.

McMillen, H. L., Ticktin, T., Friedlander, A., Jupiter, S. D., Thaman, R., Campbell, J., et al. (2014). Small islands, valuable insights: Systems of customary resource use and resilience to climate change in the Pacific. *Ecology and Society, 194*, 44. Retrieved November 11, 2018, from. https://doi.org/10.5751/ES-06937-190444

McNeely, J. A., Gadgil, M., Levèque, C., Padoch, C., & Redford, K. (1995). Human influences on biodiversity. In V. H. Heywood & R. T. Watson (Eds.), *Global biodiversity assessment* (pp. 715–821). Cambridge: Cambridge University Press.

Merlin, M., Capellle, A., Keene, T., Juvik, J., & Maragos, J. (1997). *Keinikkan im meḷan Aelōn̄ Kein: Plants and environments of the Marshall Islands*. Honolulu, HI: East-West Center.

Metcalfe, D., & Barlow, K. R. (1992). A model for exploring the optimal trade-off between field processing and transport. *American Anthropologist, 94*, 340–356.

Moir, B. G. (1989a). A review of tridacnid ecology and some possible implications for archaeological research. *Asian Perspectives, 27*, 95–121.

Moir, B. G. (1989b). *Mariculture and material culture on Takuu Atoll: Indigenous cultivation of Tridacna gigas (Mollusca: Bivalvia) and its implications for pre-European technology, resource management, and social relations on a Polynesian Outlier*. Doctoral Dissertation, Department of Anthropology, University of Hawaii, Honolulu, HI. Available from ProQuest Dissertations and Theses database (UMI No. 8926393).

Moir, B. G. (1990). Comparative studies of "fresh" and "aged" *Tridacna gigas* shell: Preliminary investigations of a reported technique for pretreatment of tool material. *Journal of Archaeological Science, 17*, 329–345.

Morrison, A. E., & Addison, D. J. (2008). Assessing the role of climate change and human predation on marine resources at the Fatu-ma-Futi Site, Tutuila Island, American Samoa: An agent based model. *Archaeology in Oceania, 43*, 22–34.

Morrison, A. E., & Allen, M. S. (2015). Agent-based modelling, molluscan population dynamics, and archaeomalacology. *Quaternary International.* https://doi.org/10.1016/j.quaint.2015.09.004

Morrison, A. E., & Cochrane, E. E. (2008). Investigating shellfish deposition and landscape history at the Natia Beach Site, Fiji. *Journal of Archaeological Science, 35*, 2387–2399.

Morrison, A. E., & Hunt, T. L. (2007). Human impacts on the nearshore environment: An archaeological case study from Kaua'i, Hawaiian Islands. *Pacific Science, 61*, 325–345.

Munro, J. L. (1989). Fisheries for giant clams (Tridacnidae: Bivalvia) and prospects for stock enhancement. In J. F. Caddy (Ed.), *Marine invertebrate fisheries: Their assessment and management* (pp. 541–558). New York: John Willey & Sons.

Neo, M. L., Eckman, W., Vincentuan, K., Teo, S. L.-M., & Todd, P. A. (2015). The ecological significance of giant clams in coral ecosystems. *Biological Conservation, 181*, 111–123.

Norgan, N. G., Ferro-Luzzi, A., & Durnin, J. V. G. A. (1974). The energy and nutrient intake and the energy expenditure of 204 New Guinean adults. *Philosophical Transactions of the Royal Society of London, Series B, 268*, 309–348.

Nunn, P. D. (2007). *Climate, environment and society in the Pacific during the last millennium*. Amsterdam: Elsevier.

Oelschlaeger, M. (1991). *The idea of wilderness: From prehistory to the age of ecology*. New Haven, CT: Yale University Press.

Orians, G. H., & Pearson, N. E. (1979). On the theory of central place foraging. In D. J. Horn, G. R. Stairs, & R. D. Mitchell (Eds.), *Analysis of ecological systems* (pp. 155–177). Columbus, OH: Ohio State University Press.

Ostraff, M. (2003). *Contemporary uses of limu (marine algae) in the Vava'u Group, Kingdom of Tonga: An ethnobotanical study*. Doctoral Dissertation, School of Environmental Studies and Department of Geography, University of Victoria, Victoria, BC, Canada. Available from ProQuest Dissertation and Theses database (UMI No. NQ90965).

Paulay, G. (2001). Benthic ecology and biota of Tarawa Lagoon: Influence of equatorial upwelling, circulation, and human harvest. *Atoll Research Bulletin, 487*, 1–41.

Penny, S. S., & Willan, R. (2014). Description of a new species of giant clam (Bivalvia: Tridacnidae) from Ningaloo Reef, Western Australia. *Molluscan Research, 34*, 201–211.

Poiner, I. R., & Catterall, C. P. (1988). The effects of traditional gathering on populations of the marine gastropod *Strombus luhuanus* linne [sic] 1758, in southern Papua New Guinea. *Oecologia, 76*, 191–199.

Poteate, A. S., Fitzpatrick, S. M., Ayres, W. S., & Thompson, A. (2016). First radiocarbon chronology for Mwoakilloa (Mokil) Atoll, Eastern Caroline Islands, Micronesia. *Radiocarbon, 58*, 169–178.

Quilter, J., & Stocker, T. (1983). Subsistence economies and the origin of Andean complex societies. *American Anthropologist, 85*, 545–562.

Ratcliffe, D. A. (1976). Thoughts towards a philosophy of nature conservation. *Biological Conservation, 9*, 45–53.

Redford, K. H. (1996). Getting to conservation. In K. H. Redford & J. A. Mansour (Eds.), *Traditional peoples and biodiversity conservation in large tropical landscapes* (pp. 251–265). Arlington, VA: Nature Conservancy.

Reeder-Myers, L., Rick, T., Lowery, D., Wah, J., & Henkes, G. (2016). Human ecology and coastal foraging at Fishing Bay, Maryland, USA. *Journal of Ethnobiology, 36*, 595–616.

Rick, T. C., & Erlandson, J. M. (Eds.). (2008). *Human impacts on ancient marine ecosystems: A global perspective*. Berkeley, CA: University of California Press.

Rick, T. C., Kirch, P. V., Erlandson, J. M., & Fitzpatrick, S. M. (2013). Archaeology, deep history, and the human transformation of island ecosystems. *Anthropocene, 4*, 33–45.

Rick, T. C., & Lockwood, R. (2012). Integrating paleobiology, archaeology, and history to inform biological conservation. *Conservation Biology, 27*, 45–54.

Sale, P. F. (1980). Assemblages of fish on patch reefs – predictable or unpredictable? *Environmental Biology of Fishes, 5*, 243–249.

Seeto, J., Nunn, P., & Sanjana, S. (2012). Human-mediated prehistoric marine extinction in the tropical Pacific? Understanding the presence of *Hippopus hippopus* (Linn. 1758) in ancient shell middens on the Rove Peninsula, southwest Viti Levu Island, Fiji. *Geoarchaeology, 27*, 2–17.

Shawcross, W. (1975). Some studies of the influences on prehistoric human predation on marine animal population dynamics. In R. W. Casteel & G. I. Quimby (Eds.), *Maritime adaptations of the Pacific* (pp. 39–66). The Hague: Mouton.

Smith, E. A. (1983). Anthropological application of optimal foraging theory: A critical review. *Current Anthropology, 24*, 625–651.

Smith, E. A. (1991). *Inujjuamiut foraging strategies: Evolutionary ecology of an Arctic hunting economy*. New York: Aldine de Gruyter.

Smith, E. A., & Boyd, R. (1990). Risk and reciprocity: Hunter-gatherer socioecology and the problem of collective action. In E. Cashdan (Ed.), *Risk and uncertainty in tribal and peasant economies* (pp. 167–191). Boulder, CO: Westview Press.

Sosis, R. (2002). Patch choice decisions among Ifaluk fishers. *American Anthropologist, 104*, 583–598.

Spennemann, D. H. R. (1987). Availability of shellfish resources on prehistoric Tongatapu, Tonga: Effects of human predation and changing environment. *Archaeology in Oceania, 22*, 81–96.

Sponsel, L. E. (2012). *Spiritual ecology: A quiet revolution*. Santa Barbara, CA: Praeger.

Stephens, D. W. (2007). Models of information use. In D. W. Stephens, J. S. Brown, & R. C. Ydenberg (Eds.), *Foraging behavior and ecology* (pp. 31–58). Chicago, IL: University of Chicago Press.

Stephens, D. W., Brown, J. S., & Ydenberg, R. C. (Eds.). (2007). *Foraging: Behavior and ecology*. Chicago, IL: University of Chicago Press.

Stephens, D. W., & Krebs, J. R. (1986). *Foraging theory*. Princeton, NJ: Princeton University Press.

Swadling, P. (1986). Lapita shellfishing: Evidence from sites in the Reef/Santa Cruz Group, southeast Solomons. In A. Anderson (Ed.), *Traditional fishing in the Pacific: Ethnographical and archaeological papers from the 15th Pacific Science Congress* (pp. 137–148). Honolulu, HI: Pacific Anthropological records No. 37, B. P. Bishop Museum.

Szabó, K., & Amesbury, J. R. (2011). Molluscs in a world of islands: The use of shellfish as a food resource in the tropical Asia-Pacific region. *Quaternary International, 239*, 8–18.

Taylor, K. L. (1988). Deforestation and Indians in Brazilian Amazonia. In E. O. Wilson (Ed.), *Biodiversity* (pp. 138–144). Washington, DC: National Academy Press.

Teuea, T. (2018). *Drivers and motivations for community-based marine conservation in North Tarawa, Kiribati*. Master's Thesis, School of Geography, Earth Science and Environment, Faculty of Science and Technology, University of the South Pacific, Suva, Fiji. Retrieved November 12, 2018, from http://digilib.library.usp.ac.fj/gsdl/collect/usplibr1/index/assoc/HASH10bb.dir/doc.pdf.

Thakar, H. B. (2011). Intensification of shellfish exploitation: Evidence of species-specific deviation from traditional expectations. *Journal of Archaeological Science, 38*, 2596–2605.

Thomas, F. R. (1999). *Optimal foraging and conservation: The anthropology of mollusk gathering strategies in the Gilbert Islands Group, Kiribati*. Doctoral Dissertation, Department of Anthropology, University of Hawai'i, Honolulu, HI. Available from ProQuest Dissertations and Theses database (UMI No. 9940631).

Thomas, F. R. (2001). Remodeling marine tenure on the atolls: A case Study from western Kiribati, Micronesia. *Human Ecology, 29*, 399–422.

Thomas, F. R. (2002). An evaluation of central-place foraging among mollusk gatherers in western Kiribati, Micronesia: Linking behavioral ecology with ethnoarchaeology. *World Archaeology, 34*, 182–208.

Thomas, F. R. (2003). Shellfish gathering in Kiribati, Micronesia: Nutritional, microbiological, and toxicological aspects. *Ecology of Food and Nutrition, 42*, 91–127.

Thomas, F. R. (2007). The behavioral ecology of shellfish gathering in western Kiribati, Micronesia 1: Prey choice. *Human Ecology, 35*, 179–194.

Thomas, F. R. (2009). Historical ecology in Kiribati: Linking past with present. *Pacific Science, 63*, 567–600.

Thomas, F. R. (2014). Shellfish gathering and conservation on low coral islands: Kiribati perspectives. *Journal of Island and Coastal Archaeology, 9*, 203–218.

Thomas, F. R. (2015). Marginal islands and sustainability: 2,000 years of human settlement in eastern Micronesia. *Economic- and Ecohistory, 11*, 64–74.

Ulijaszek, S. J. (1995). *Human energetics in biological anthropology*. Cambridge: Cambridge University Press.

Weisler, M. I. (1999). The antiquity of aroid pit agriculture and significance of buried A horizons on Pacific atolls. *Geoarchaeology, 14*, 621–654.

Weisler, M. I. (2001). Life on the edge: Prehistoric settlement and economy on Utrōk Atoll, northern Marshall Islands. *Archaeology on Oceania, 36*, 109–133.

Whitaker, A. R. (2008). Incipient aquaculture in prehistoric California? Long-term productivity and sustainability vs. immediate returns for the harvest of marine invertebrates. *Journal of Archaeological Science, 25*, 1114–1123.

Williams, J. (2016). Seafood "gardens". *Journal of the Polynesian Society, 124*, 433–444.

Winterhalder, B., Lu, F., & Tucker, B. (1999). Risk-sensitive adaptive tactics: Models and evidence from subsistence studies in biology and anthropology. *Journal of Archaeological Research, 7,* 301–348.

Wodzicki, K. (1981). Some nature conservation problems in the South Pacific. *Biological Conservation, 21,* 5–18.

Wolverton, S., & Lyman, L. (Eds.). (2012). *Conservation biology and applied zooarchaeology.* Tucson, AZ: University of Arizona Press.

Wyban, C. A. (1992). *Tide and current: Fishponds of Hawai'i.* Honolulu, HI: University of Hawai'i Press.

Zann, L. P. (1985). Traditional management and conservation of fisheries in Kiribati and Tuvalu atolls. In K. R. Ruddle & R. E. Johannes (Eds.), *The traditional knowledge and management of coastal systems in Asia and the Pacific* (pp. 53–77). Jakarta: UNESCO/Regional Office for Science and Technology for Southeast Asia.

Environment and Landscapes of Latin America's Past

Vernon L. Scarborough, Christian Isendahl, and Samantha Fladd

What is the role of archaeology in assessing the human ecological future of the planet? Can examining the engineered landscape of the past, perhaps especially in the New World prior to Western *entradas*, generate insights that map out alternative pathways toward modeling our futures globally? What can be gleaned from past understandings of and interactions with the material world? The eclectic field of investigation and practice currently emerging at the intersection of historical ecology, relational ontology, and applied archaeology demonstrates the capacity of the historical and anthropological sciences to detail long-term human-environmental processes. In particular, past case studies of both different and analogous approaches to the world can help contextualize and inform on present conditions, providing models for human-environment interactions that can speak to issues of adaptation and sustainability (see also Isendahl and Stump 2019).

Although the practical applications of historical and anthropological data have gained attention in recent years, alternatives to the accepted present are not new. Central and South America have long provided the geographical and biophysical stimulation for the emergence of a new way of evaluating coupled human-nature dynamics for burgeoning modern Western sciences. Early explorers noted the less technologically altered environments of the New World compared to the rural and urban landscapes of Europe that formed their frames of reference; two centuries after Old World colonization, European researchers were still able to arrive at their ecological insights as a consequence of the massive scale and complexity of environmental

---

V. L. Scarborough (✉)
University of Cincinnati, Cincinnati, OH, USA
e-mail: scarbovl@ucmail.uc.edu

C. Isendahl
University of Gothenburg, Gothenburg, Sweden

S. Fladd
Crow Canyon Archaeological Center, Cortez, CO, USA

interactions in place, ecosystems that were not yet so marred and altered by the furious, technology-driven exploitation of industrializing western Europe. Nevertheless, these and subsequent explorers were unaware of the complexities and scale of human-environmental interactions in the pre-Columbian past, and their notes and published observations fed the colonial myth of the New World as a pristine wilderness: a stereotypic myth that archaeological and historical ecological research has since firmly laid to rest (Denevan 1992, 2001; Krech 2000; Balée 2013).

At the turn of the nineteenth century, Alexander von Humboldt opened Western minds to an alternative ontological view of interconnectedness in the sciences and the humanities (Wulf 2015) that implicitly underpinned pre-Columbian worldviews and epistemologies. Humboldt's South American insights stimulated Darwin's work and his ultimate explanation for the origins of species (1859), though the latter strongly emphasized the Hobbesian "crimson of tooth and claw" theme developed further in what has later become known as social Darwinism (cf. Darwin 1871). Haeckel's mid-century notion of "oecologie" (ecology) is a direct extension of Humboldt's fusing of non-Western epistemologies and ontologies to an establishment of Western understandings emphasizing the interdependence of all biophysical things (see Wulf 2015, pp. 352–371). Much of the ecological orientation championed by Humboldt and his disciples continues to clash with capitalism, resource overexploitation and advanced technologies, and the masking of the intrinsic trade-offs of technological development for environment resources by way of deeply imbedded neoliberal market philosophies emphasizing constant economic growth. We are at a turning point in our history with 2018 the hottest year yet. But let's examine how the world was ecologically positioned on the eve of the greatest colonization transformation of the Holocene, the Americas before and after 1492 (Denevan 1992, 2001; Doolittle 2001; Whitmore and Turner 2001; Mann 2005, 2011; Crosby 2009), and whether or not such an assessment might inform our possible futures.

Technology, Labor, and Worldviews

How different was the engineered landscape in the western hemisphere from the eastern on the eve of European conquest? Quite (Denevan 2001; Doolittle 2001; Whitmore and Turner 2001). Europe was on a *technotasking* trajectory from the outset of their notion of civilization (Scarborough 2003; Scarborough and Burnside 2010); i.e., it was associated with a societal complexity identified with technological breakthroughs and a rigid socioeconomic and sociopolitical hierarchy. Although not capitalism as we know it, the guild system was well established in feudal Europe by the medieval period and the trajectory for exploiting the natural world deeply rooted in ideology. The Biblical Old Testament argued and argues that "man" needs to "replenish the earth, and subdue it: and have dominion over the fish of the sea, and over the fowl of the air, and over every living thing that moves upon the earth" (Genesis 1:28).

Of principal concern in the western hemisphere was the role of *labortasking*, i.e., the cooperative aggregation of skilled labor pools often organized heterarchically

(Crumley 1995; Scarborough 2003; Scarborough and Burnside 2010). In assessing the influence of labor, it is important to emphasize the reduced presence of disease vectors or their microbial loads for New World populations (McMichael et al. 1999). The relative rarity of domesticated animals and the crossover diseases that frequently swept through Old World populations suggest that native New World diseases were less virulent in impact prior to the introduction of European diseases, especially smallpox epidemics. Because of the long history of domesticated animals in close proximity to humans, many of the zoonotic diseases of the Old World were less devastatingly exposed to populations over time than they were when rapidly introduced to newly encountered indigenous peoples (Borah and Cook 1964; Dobyns 1966, 1983; McNeill 1977). In the pre-Columbian past, New World population numbers appear to have been extremely elevated when compared with early archaic states—primary states without previous urban developments—of the Old World based on lower disease loads and technologies that were not yet driven by huge investments in warfare (Scarborough 2005), though warmongering was clearly a major element of all societies (see Arendt 1970; Flannery and Marcus 2012).

Without combative technological advances precipitated by the wheel (from chariots to gears for the catapult), domesticated animals (from horsemen and the stirrup to Hannibal's elephant drivers), or metal tools (from the bronze slashing sword to cannonballs projected with gunpowder), which developed in the Old World, death and destruction were significantly reduced in the pre-Columbian Americas. When coupled with lessened communicative disease, human population expanded fast. Although census data for the Early Dynastic Period of Sumer in 2700 BCE compared to the Tzacualli Period of the Valley of Mexico in 100 CE—two primary states—is somewhat conjecture, the largest urban center of the former, Uruk, had a projected population of 50,000 (Redman 1978, p. 264; Adams 1981, p. 85), while Teotihuacan, the first city of the latter, was at least twice its size at a comparable level of social complexity (Millon 1973) *but* without the significant suite of technologies (Scarborough 2000, 2005). Of telling merit, the rise of civilization or true social complexity occurred two to three times faster following the domestication of most plants in the New World as opposed to the Old—Southwest Asia—yet another index of population growth and labor organization (Scarborough 2000). What all this identifies is an entirely different set of worldviews and institutions guiding processes toward increasing social complexity (Beddoe et al. 2009).

The pre-Western occupation of the New World represents an aberrant way of organizing a landscape and ecology when compared with the European colonization model [do recall that Childe (1950) had difficulties in accommodating the Maya as an ancient example of statecraft]. Researchers have long acknowledged that cultures possess different beliefs and worldviews, although recent discussions take this argument further to question whether different groups actually inhabit the same world at all (e.g., Alberti et al. 2011; Harris and Robb 2012; Fowler and Harris 2015; Thomas 2015; Fowler 2016). Leaving aside philosophical debates over material realities (sensu Fowles in Alberti et al. 2011), the significance of relations between humans and things, including the environmental setting, should not be overlooked. Thousands of years of personal and material relationships shaped societies before the New and Old Worlds came into sudden, direct contact half a millennium ago. Working from an understanding that ontological perspectives fundamentally shape perceptions of and interactions with material culture, conceptions of the environment were highly distinct. We suggest the European need to tame our ecological dominion was not a driving force in the western hemisphere where characteristics largely reserved for humans in the Old World were shared with the natural world, for example, "…trees from which one begs forgiveness before felling them and which are honored once felled" (López Austin 1980, p. 346; Descola 2005, pp. 212–213). New World technologies were fashioned from clay, wood, and stone and built with the power of immediate human toil.

Recent archaeological and anthropological research demonstrates the extensiveness of landscape modification in Amazonia (e.g., Roosevelt 1994; Balée 1998, 2013; Heckenberger 2005; Balée and Erickson 2006; Neves 2006; Woods et al. 2009; Schaan 2012; Rostain 2013; Erickson 2019; Watling et al. 2017), a diverse and dynamic culture area that only a couple of decades ago was considered a backwater of social development greatly overshadowed by the sophistication of groups occupying the Andes (e.g., Meggers 1996). Amazonia serves as an ideal case through which to introduce the diametrically opposed set of institutions organizing much of the juxtaposition between the New and Old Worlds. First, the imposition of a Western model of socioeconomic and sociopolitical organization on most indigenous societies, in which semitropical environments are viewed as unfit for social complexity with their heavy rates of biological "turnover" (Meggers 1996), demonstrates a clear lack of contextual understanding. These models assume technological breakthroughs are necessary for societies to move beyond "primitive" lifeways (Scarborough and Burnside 2010). Second, early urban centralization characterized by elaborate stone, brick, and earthen monuments—towering pyramids, ziggurats, palaces, and the like—surrounded by household and industry densities of massive scales is viewed as prerequisite for true social complexity. Although such centers of urban development do occur in the New World—with Teotihuacan and Chan Chan as perfect examples of intuitive and textbook definitions of a "city" based on formal traits such as density and scale—they do not fit the expected pattern of urban landscape order within an Old World frame of reference (Scarborough and Valdez 2009, 2014).

The abundance of labor in the pre-Columbian New World provided less impetus for "technological breakthroughs"; and without these, the institutional relationships made by New World populations within their biophysical world were conceptualized differently. Tenochtitlan was the largest city built in the New World prior to Spanish arrival; and though densely occupied, it was an invention of an "alternative" engineering interplay of land, water, and society—the "dream" to an Old World invader (del Castillo 1963, pp. 214–215) (Fig. 1). The Aztec integration of landlocked islands, marshlands, and shallow lakes into a city's infrastructure and social fabric in concert with saline diluting springs and blue-green *Spirulina* algae consumption was a world away from the technological drive to drain wetlands and harvest monocropped grains common in Europe and much of West, Central, and East Asia.

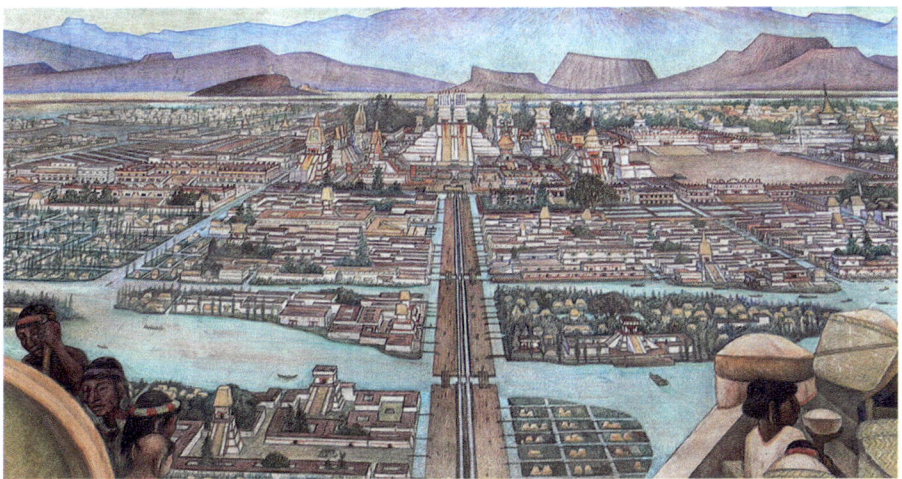

Fig. 1 Tenochtitlan by Diego Rivera (1945)

Although royalty and conquest were clearly part and parcel of New World civilizations, what drove institutional order was community alliance (see cf. Kohler et al. 2017; Feinman and Carballo 2018) that involved considerable intrigue and military action, as was recorded by early Spanish accounts of the Aztec and Inka (Rowe 1946; Hassig 1988). Given the size of pre-Columbian populations and their close relationship with the generational life cycles of nature, the anathema of life sacrifice—especially that of humans in densely occupied regions of Mesoamerica or highland and coastal Peru—became an organizing principle of these evolving secondary and tertiary states. While impossible for our own societal institutions to fathom today, these blood sacrifices reveal a relationship with the natural order quite different from our own (see Pennock 2012). They introduce an aberrant mindset on the world stage that evolved as an ideology embracing natural earthly and solar rhythms, which metastasized into the role of public displays of heart extraction and bodily dismemberments. The Aztec took these corporeal worshipful acts to disastrous levels, but many groups in the New World were prone to similar bodily practices (Carrasco 1999).

From our vantage, the inconceivable institution of human sacrifice, sometimes elevated to nearly an industrial level that has been purported for the Aztec (Durán 1994[1588?]), was a consequence of the alignment of two factors. The first was the reverence in the New World for humanity's interdependence with all natural cycles, and the second was the elevated number of people in those resource-abundant regions of the New World and the role of work without draft animals, the wheel, or metal tools (see Kohler et al. 2017). Although these two forces could converge in any number of ways—the excesses of the Aztec, for instance—they were always fundamental underpinnings of society. Given these two vectors, how were varied environments managed and created throughout the New World, and how can these arrangements inform on future ecological decisions?

Forests

In the Old World European context, forests could be frightening places teaming with wild things and housing malevolent spirits and ancestral ghosts. *Grimms' Fairy Tales* devote a great deal of time to "black forests" and capture the frightful tree-lain curtain concealing anything from hidden mischief to the truly evil. Cleared tofts, crofts, or agricultural homesteads allowed the visibility and security of planting monocropped grains—wheat, barley, oats, and rye—and some pasturage for stock and necessitated the removal of trees in wooded zones. Before coal (and even before domestic animal dung), trees were an obvious fuel for warmth, cooking, and the firing of ceramics or metals, so deforestation accomplished many ends. The mythology of dark activities harbored by a forest further justified their clear-cutting and the accelerating emphasis on the sharpened and enduring edge of iron and subsequent steel-producing technologies. Technology drove rapid environmental change of the Eurasia landmass beginning with the first cities and large-scale agriculture (Redman 1999; Ruddiman 2005). Domesticated animals in concert with the evolving set of tools used to sow and harvest grains—perhaps especially the animal-drawn ard and plow but, much before that, the wheel, the early use of metals, and even the sail for navigation—all contributed to severe and rapid alteration of the landscape. The creation of a heavily modified, human-made environment defined perceptions and a basic template of what was appropriate for a colonized New World, a worldview drawing from a clear indifference toward the natural world.

The ethos toward the environment associated with indigenous New World populations might be inferred by the complex imagery found in pre-Columbian iconography and related artistry. Among the most telling Mesoamerican imagery recorded ethnographically and revealed through epigraphic decipherment concerns the concepts of *way* and *nagual*; the former denotes the co-essence between a person and a biophysical phenomenon in ancient Maya contexts (Freidel et al. 1993; Houston and Stuart 1989), while the latter refers to a social role transforming a person into an animal in the ethnohistorical and contemporary record of Nahuatl speakers (Houston and Stuart 1989; Descola 2005, pp. 212–216; Sandstrom 2019). Not dissimilar imagery is apparent at Andean and coastal plain *huaca* monuments of South America (Moseley 1992), and the Amazon Basin peoples continue to celebrate the animated spiritual world of plant and animal as an indivisible part of the human societal condition (Viveiros de Castro 2004; Descola 2005). Unlike shamanism with its global manifestations associated with more mobile populations, urbanized and highly sedentary groups were invested in these worldviews. Personhood in such settings was not bounded within the human body, instead extending to and through the material world (e.g., Alberti et al. 2011; Harris and Robb 2012; Fowler and Harris 2015; Fowler 2016). The heavily forested environmental setting housed both the local population and their nonhuman companions within a complex cultural landscape.

Vast tracks of tropical to semitropical forest were densely occupied in Central and South America. The ancient Maya built one of the great primary civilizations on their karst understory, and we are now finding an elevated level of landscape engineering within the great Amazonian river drainages, the latter altered by a routine of soil chemistry and microbial manipulation (*terra preta*) unknown to the West (Lehmann et al. 2003; Glaser and Woods 2004; Woods et al. 2009). Forests were surely cut but in a manner that frequently and deliberately cultivated economically beneficial species by differentially culling less useful ones (Balée 2013; Ford and Nigh 2015). Carneiro (1979) demonstrates the high-energy expenditures involved in felling tropical rainforest tree species with lithic technology, but the lack of metal tools was hardly a constraining factor. Instead, productive arboricultural harvesting strategies and agroforestry systems necessitated that broad swathes of timber were not taken out. Prior to colonialism, technological advances such as those associated with metal were not required given the existence of a very different ecological sensibility and an associated large labor force throughout the Americas.

Numerous cultivars were conserved, managed, or domesticated by hybridizing with related and neighboring subspecies. "Kitchen gardens" or gardening zones in proximity to an extended household were places where composted refuse was deposited to increase soil fertility but also created the potential for genetic crossovers as when a rare and useful mutation could provide viable food, fiber, fuel and housing materials (Killion 1992; Balée and Erickson 2006; Balée 2013; Ford and Nigh 2015). Forest density as well as plant, animal, and soil microbial composition varied radically from area to area and region to region, but ecological relationships with the "skin of the earth" were not dissimilar in that people worked with the indigenous species to harvest a myriad of botanicals. The process of domesticating a landscape was accretional in nature; over generations the occupied environs were transformed to subtle degrees to allow for the growth of more human consumables for the increasing populations. The marvelously complex interplay between plants, animals, and people in blended and hybridized contexts found in various iconographies captures the same generational processes playing out in their evolving biophysical ecology.

Tropical forests of the pre-Columbian New World were less likely to be modified in the manner apparent in the Old World (portions of Africa, South Asia, and Southeast Asia were clearly a different case; Scarborough 2003; Scarborough and Lucero 2011). Forests were changed by humans, but not to the degree imposed by Europeans. The literature now associated with Central and South America and particularly in greater Amazonia shifts the ontological paradigm as it demonstrates how entire societies were able to view their humanity as but an extension of and developed in tandem with the biophysical world (Alberti et al. 2011; Harris and Robb 2012; Fowler and Harris 2015; Fowler 2016). This is not to suggest that overexploitation was entirely an unlikely occurrence; surely the notion of an "ecological Indian" (see Krech 2000) is likely only a bit more of an appropriate moniker than an ecological Spaniard of the sixteenth century. The difference between what is now Latin America and Europe rests in their social relations and frames their past means of production as well as differing conceptual understandings of the material world. Technologies have ruled the West and forced a buffering from the biophysical environment, but this was not the social or institutional pathway for the New World (Fig. 2).

Fig. 2 Tropical forest deforestation: before and after

Hills

Where the terrain was hilly or mountainous, another labor-intensive landscape investment was frequently made by way of extensive terracing, particularly—but not exclusively—in the Andes (Donkin 1979; Farrington 1985; Denevan 2001). Although a very early adaptation employed by farming communities globally, terracing was not advanced significantly through technological breakthroughs as it was a labor-dependent construction effort. In some non-mountainous forested zones—such as the Maya Lowlands or Amazonia where slope angularity was modest and tree cover and roots reduced erosion as identified at Tikal, Guatemala (Lentz et al. 2015)—terracing was less apparent, but in other such environments, agricultural terracing was both intensive and extensive with complementary and highly developed road systems [see Caracol, Belize (Chase and Chase 2014)]. In semiarid settings where water scarcity prevailed year-round, terracing was frequently widespread and associated with sometimes complex canalization or channelizing (Moseley 1992; Scarborough 2003; Minnis et al. 2006). Along these lines, Peruvian terracing, the most elaborate by far, was also initiated early (Donkin 1979). The Inka and their forbearers were notably associated with extensive road networks (Hyslop 1984); but at the far northwestern end of Mesoamerica in the US Southwest, the arid ancestral Puebloans at Chaco Canyon also constructed well-defined road networks (Vivian 1990).

Wetlands

Wetlands were also incrementally altered and likely expanded to accommodate spiking populations in the context of less complex technological advancements. These naturally moist and organically rich settings were managed by digging extensive canal networks allowing the ordered and seasonally drained control of water levels for irrigating adjacent, elevated, and "mucked" agricultural plots or raised fields sometimes covering several square kilometers (Denevan 2001; Whitmore and Turner 2001; Scarborough 2006, 2007; Erickson 2006, 2019) (Fig. 3).

These infrastructural changes cultivated tremendous food production systems stimulating environmental expansion of wetlands into adjacent low-lying grassland savanna, the latter much less productive until the late introduction of grass-grazing cattle and the Spanish and Portuguese views of ecological conquest. Grassland settings that could be inundated in the context of ditched and raised field system were altered (Denevan 2001; Erickson 2019), as neither the singularity of monocropped grains nor animal husbandry proved attractive enough for pre-Columbian populations to develop. Vast agricultural fields were also avenues for the movement of goods and services between communities by way of the navigational advantage of shallow draft canoes plying interconnected canals and regional river systems. In such environments, the advantages of wheeled carts and the beasts of burden to pull

Fig. 3 Raised fields

them would at best have been minimal, which helps to explain the lack of such technologies, especially in vast lowland settings like Amazonia or the Maya Lowlands.

Human communities in these environments were as interdependent as the natural biophysical rhythms of their engineered landscapes. Elsewhere, Scarborough and Valdez (2009, 2014) have suggested that an alternate economy organized these places with "resource-specialized communities" developing in which all communities could draw from the redundancy of many resources; for instance, through time and networking, communities might well initiate the production of one or two kinds of refined resources like particular ceramics or specialized stone tool types that were exchanged for a variety of tobacco. The ethnographic view of a closed corporate community inspired by a model of isolation and insularity is a condition of colonization and depopulation following the conquest by Europeans (Wolf 1957). A particular example of a well-defined and sizable community through pre-Columbian time is the site of Colha in northern Belize—the Maya Lowlands—with its industrial scale production and processing of chert tools (Shafer and Hester 1983) and its exchange network throughout the greater region. Thus, the economic movement of resources gave concrete form to an extensive network of individuals and communities that spanned the landscape (e.g., Helms 1998; Lucero 2003, 2006). Generally speaking, we envision a widespread and subtler exchange of natural and refined resources knitting together a region materially and socially, reflective of the same biophysical processes that affected the interplay between plants, animals, and humans in every other context. These worldview tenets were significantly less prone to major ecological disruptions associated with the land- and water-altering technologies of the colonizing West (Scarborough and Burnside 2010).

"Pathways of Memory and Power" (Abercrombie 1998)

Movement throughout multiple regions of the New World was crucial for fostering distant relationships, accessing nonlocal resources, and maintaining social and symbolic ties to important landscape features (e.g., Bender 1993; Brady and Ashmore 1999; Van de Guchte 1999). Landscapes are constructed with the local population and become imbued with memory and history (e.g., Gow 1990; Schwartz 1990; Ashmore and Knapp 1999). Sacred places populated this animated landscape, creating a ritualized network through which people, ancestors, and materials moved (e.g., Nielsen 2008). Although the degree of formalization varied, elaborate systems traversing the landscape were evident in many societies. For instance, the Puebloan road network emanating from Chaco Canyon is often interpreted as largely symbolic in nature, linking communities to important landscape features, although several also connect smaller communities to one another (e.g., Vivian 1997a, b; Kantner 2003; Friedman et al. 2017).

Of special merit is the suite of studies now apparent from South America, from the Andean coastal plain to portions of the Amazon Basin. The complex investment in the "Nazca Lines" and geoglyphs to the recently identified ditched alignments of lowland Bolivia and Brazil arguably introduced an inscribed memory to the built environment at a monumental scale and without formal economic underpinnings (Reinhard 1996). In the case of Inka Peru, ethnohistory indicates a social memory manifest in the *ceque* system, perhaps most apparently radiating out of the capital city of Cuzco and defining pathways tied to coordinates of space and time in the context of ritual and myth (Zuidema 1964; Abercrombie 1998) (Fig. 4).

Abercrombie (1998) by way of Zuidema (1989) further makes the case for the quipu as a mnemonic device perhaps replicating social memory pathways of the *ceque* system landscape itself. While speculative and without clear ethnohistorical support, the road systems documented and emanating from Chaco Canyon by the eleventh century may reflect the same kind of spatial syntax with the historied landscape as is well-articulated for the Inka (Fig. 5). Although frequently difficult to meaningfully interpret from the archaeological record, the engineered landscapes of the New World could be highly animated and drawn from spiritual and sacred experience, further entwining cultural and natural worlds.

A Maya Case Study

The complex sociopolitical and ideological Maya of the southern Yucatán Peninsula in today's southern Mexico, northern Guatemala, and Belize capture a composite example of many of the landscape alteration threads noted above. During the Late

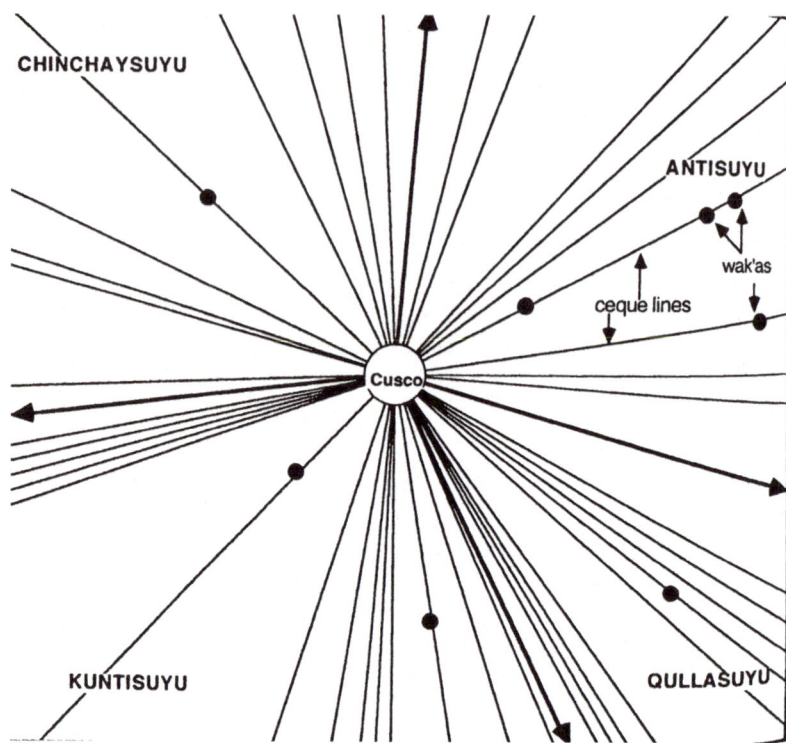

Fig. 4 *Ceque* lines radiating out from the center of Cusco (Abercrombie 1998, Fig. 5.4)

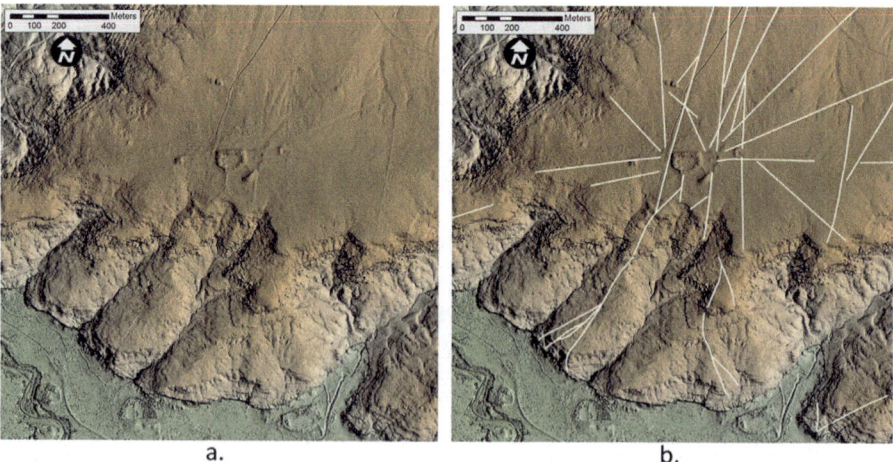

Fig. 5 Chaco road segments converging at the great house of Pueblo Alto: (**a**) hillshaded lidar image and (**b**) marked road segments on lidar image. (Friedman et al. 2017, Fig. 11)

Preclassic period (400 BCE–100 CE), advanced sedentists gravitated toward the large, seasonally wet *bajos* or internally draining swamps that cover over 40% of the Maya Lowlands today. Because of the extended availability of water during the four-five months of annual seasonal drought and the abundance of organic resources in proximity, these low-lying settings were zones of high resource return for limited labor investment—a passive resource extraction system (Tainter et al. 2018)—given they had not been significantly harvested by earlier populations. With the introduction of several cultivars, among them domesticated varieties of maize, bean, and squash, these settings were converted into "concave microwatersheds" that were engineered to direct precipitation and natural runoff from the immediate sloping surrounds into flanking and low-lying bajo-margin localities (Fig. 6). Late Preclassic urban settlement centers were frequently positioned in these settings to capture potable water as well as accommodate cropping needs, sometimes in the context of drained or raised field systems. Forests were likely culled to accommodate food, fiber, fuel, and building needs but in the context of a stone-based technology with clearly limited cutting power relative to a technotasking economy. Nevertheless, with time the maintenance of these built environments was made more expensive with increasing populations accelerating hilly flank erosion, at least in part due to slash-and-burn agricultural activities and related resource exploitation and extractions. Coupled with a suggested extended drought near the end of the Late Preclassic period that likely dried some soil-securing vegetation and precipitated increased slope erosion (Dunning et al. 2014; Wahl et al. 2014), the concave basins that had been an easily altered and harvested environment began to infill with eroding sediment changing the groundwater flow and prematurely burying some planting surfaces as well as potential dwellings.

Under these conditions and into the florescence of the subsequent Classic period (200–800 CE), the Lowland Maya relocated their largest centers—like Tikal—to

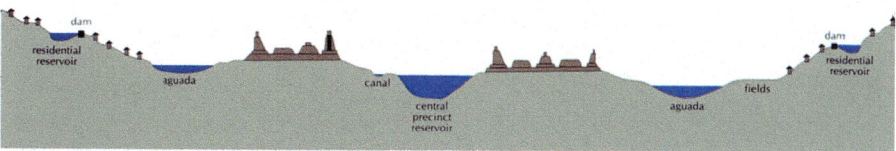

Fig. 6 Concave and convex microwatersheds

the summits of those adjacent hills and ridges that formerly flanked the concave microwatersheds (Figs. 6 and 7). Under these new settlement conditions, the topography was literally inverted to accommodate a much more controlling catchment of the water resource and, by extension, the engineered landscape. A convex microwatershed was constructed which resulted in the frequently towering pyramids, acropolises and related architecture that the popular press most associates with Maya civilization. To build these monuments, quarrying entailed sometimes deep depressions in proximity to these erections that were subsequently converted to elevated reservoirs. Because these centers were imperviously paved to accommodate the traffic received across courtyards and sometimes huge plazas, they shed the seasonal rainfall. These plastered surfaces were designed to move run off by way of canting the flow of water into the frequently sizable reservoirs, literally transporting water from elite to commoner domains. The symbolic significance of commoners receiving water from the ruling class reiterates the intertwinement of people with the local ecology, while aligning powerful groups more closely with the natural world (Brady and Ashmore 1999; Lucero 2006). In turn, the reservoirs were positioned in a cascading manner from the summits of the central administrative centers with their pyramids and ballcourts to the low-lying *bajos*. Our best evidence for terracing in the Maya area appears in the Early Classic when the transition from the concave to the convex microwatershed land-use adaptation occurs (Dunning et al. 2014). Although terracing was in place to accommodate mid-slope building space as well as agricultural ends, they were highly effective in curbing erosional concerns—the latter effectively affecting and relocating some Maya centers. These

Fig. 7 Tikal, Guatemala: a convex microwatershed or "water mountain"

changes also altered perceptions of the hills themselves, emphasizing the interworking of human labor and natural features (see also Van de Guchte 1999 for a discussion of Inca terracing.)

During the Late Classic period, the costs associated with complex landscape alterations increased tremendously and the ease of harvesting a living from a naturally passive ecosystem that used the stored abundance of millennial ecosystem energy (Scarborough 2018) had been significantly consumed. The Classic period had organizationally "metabolized" the Late Preclassic setting and introduced a highly evolved labortasking environment that required a high level of social complexity to maintain; the energy return on investment had disappeared and now required costly governing structures (Isendahl et al. 2014).

The collapse or great fragmentation of the Maya around the late ninth century CE was somewhat rehearsed at the end of the Late Preclassic period with the abandonment of the concave microwatershed land-use adaptation. Again, a major drought impinged on the socioenvironmental setting (Kennett et al. 2012), and population overshoot in concert with the conspicuous consumption of the elite and organizational parameters stressed the population centers. Nevertheless, a clever set of landscape and advanced sociocultural adaptations had allowed the Maya to increase their societal complexity. This investment in a new kingship order and flamboyant displays of power was energy resource costly however, and it was likely that the embedded set of governing and institutional flaws ultimately led to systemic regional collapse (see Jackson 2013). The environment was accretionally "metabolized" to a point of criticality and the arrival of an extended period of drought catalyzed in a perfect storm (Scarborough 2018).

Discussion and Conclusion

Following the Fertile Crescent's emphasis of literally living on top of one another or the classic tell city, towns and subsequent cities in the Old World tended toward nucleation (Scarborough 2018). Once a community removed the forest and drained the swamp, neighbors could gravitate toward one another in closer and closer proximity: a technotasking mode accommodating economies of scale but one accenting the separation between people and the biophysical world (Scarborough and Isendahl 2019). The focus of labortasking and an alternate worldview emphasizing continuity between people and the material/natural world of the Americas favored an altogether different social arrangement that did not blend well with the imported European model. The role of the colonial embrace is especially apparent in the Tarascan region of west Mexico where, as Christopher Fisher et al. (2003) point out, raised fields and highly constructed slope terracing were abandoned for Western adaptations to agricultural production. Wetlands were not viewed as viable spaces for agriculture, let alone settlement, and they were rapidly drained when possible. The grand spaces of Tenochtitlan were also considered a liability by way of the lakes that surrounded the city when the Spanish arrived, though Bernal Diaz del

Castillio—as noted above—states that the city was like a "dream" given the parched and arid landscapes of his Andalusian home.

It is true that romanticizing indigenous peoples is never a good idea, and we have pretty good information to suggest that the Maya, for instance, may well have overharvested their forests and environmental resources in part because of growing populations late in their Classic Period florescence (600–850 CE) (Lentz et al. 2015). Nevertheless, large tracks of the Maya Lowlands do not seem to have suffered severe denudation, and at least some migration of peoples into less densely occupied areas like Belize in the sixth to eighth centuries may well have accommodated the growth in more centralized regions like today's northeastern Petén, Guatemala (Scarborough et al. 2003), where really sizable cities like Tikal were located as well as nearby Calakmul (actually in far southern Campeche state, Mexico).

Today the global world fetishizes technology and views it as a series of more and greater innovations frequently designed to distance ourselves from the perils of nature, aka fundamental ecological principles (Commoner 1971). Although often widely understood as the path toward a more sustainable future, technological innovation in our modern world is not driven a priori by altruistic goals or commitment to the public good. At centers of institutional information and knowledge—universities, think tanks, corporate research, and development divisions—technological breakthroughs frame asymmetrical economic exchange systems that keep the few affluent at the expense of the many (Hornborg 2001). Technological innovation today is dependent on resource extraction and monetary return associated with established economic trajectories of nation-states, multinational agreements, and globally operating corporate identities. The West has historically built much of its economy and sociopolitical identity on resource capital obtained from cheap labor costs frequently located elsewhere. Ecological overexploitation from rare earths to more abundant coal or oil to growing demand for domesticated animal protein is a function of each and every technological breakthrough. What really is the benefit to overall human well-being in the availability of cell phones, related communications, and the unchecked flow of misinformation or the consumption of massive amounts of flesh, methane production, and significant agribusiness alterations to the environment, if the cost is global warming and the concentration of the world's monetary wealth with eight individuals responsible for half of humanity's GDP capital (Oxfam 2017)? Technology is at the stage in human development for which it has much to be answerable; it demands more energy—labor and processed resources—to advance and more institutional organization to globalize (Tainter and Allen 2019).

In closing, it is suggested here that Alexander von Humboldt tapped into a worldview that already preceded his arrival to the New World. As a keen observer, skilled scientist and quick study, he rapidly connected his European training and respect for the natural world into an understanding of the interdependency of humanity and the biophysical world; in fact, his revelations clearly articulated the overexploitation of natural resources as accented by the one-way dependency of a colonizing European society on the treatment of the planet. Those lessons appear to have been well known to the labortasking New World cultures as determined by their lack of focus on technological aids in harvesting and altering their engineered environments, and their initial review by Humboldt may well have introduced our modern view of "ecology." Although we are unlikely to return to a "low-tech" set of adaptations anytime soon, a more measured assessment of the unintended consequences of our environmentally exploitative actions could be implemented (Scarborough and Isendahl 2019). By using archaeological analogies or cases of difference, perhaps we can work toward useful ecological ends drawing on the manner by which past societies utilized our blue-green planetary resources.

Acknowledgments Scarborough wishes to thank the Pre-Columbian Studies Division at Dumbarton Oaks (DO) in Washington, DC, for providing the forum for developing this piece. At the invitation of DO and the Museo del Oro (Bogota), an abbreviate presentation of this material was given by Scarborough in Bogota, Colombia, on March 22, 2018.

References

Abercrombie, T. A. (1998). *Pathways of memory and power*. Madison, WI: University of Wisconsin Press.
Adams, R. M. C. (1981). *Heartland of cities*. Chicago, IL: University of Chicago Press.
Alberti, B., Fowles, S., Holbraad, M., Marshall, Y., & Witmore, C. (2011). "Worlds otherwise" archaeology, anthropology, and ontological difference. *Current Anthropology, 52*(6), 896–912.
Arendt, H. (1970). *On violence*. New York: Harcourt Brace.
Ashmore, W., & Knapp, A. B. (Eds.). (1999). *Archaeologies of landscape: Contemporary perspectives*. Malden, MA: Blackwell Publishers.
Balée, W. (Ed.). (1998). *Advances in historical ecology*. New York: Columbia University Press.
Balée, W. (2013). *Cultural forests of the Amazon: A historical ecology of people and their landscapes*. Tuscaloosa, AL: University of Alabama Press.
Balée, W., & Erickson, C. L. (Eds.). (2006). *Time and complexity in historical ecology: Studies in the neotropical lowlands*. New York: Columbia University Press.
Beddoe, R., Costanza, R., Farley, J., Garza, E., Kent, J., Kubiszewski, I., et al. (2009). Overcoming systemic roadblocks to sustainability: The evolutionary redesign of worldviews, institutions, and technologies. *Proceedings of the National Academy of Sciences, 106*(8), 2483–2489.
Bender, B. (1993). *Landscape: Politics and perspectives*. Oxford: Berg.
Borah, W. W., & Cook, S. F. (1964). *The aboriginal populations of Central Mexico on the eve of Spanish conquest*. Berkeley, CA: University of California Press.
Brady, J. E., & Ashmore, W. (1999). Mountains, caves, water: Ideational landscapes of the ancient Maya. In W. Ashmore & A. Bernard Knapp (Eds.), *Archaeologies of landscape: Contemporary perspectives* (pp. 124–145). Malden, MA: Blackwell Publishers.
Carneiro, R. L. (1979). Tree felling with the stone axe: An experiment carried out among the yanomamö indians of southern Venezuela. In C. Kramer (Ed.), *Ethnoarchaeology: Implications for archaeology* (pp. 21–58). New York: Columbia University Press.
Carrasco, D. (1999). *City of sacrifice: The Aztec empire and the role of violence in civilization*. Boston: Beacon Press.
Chase, D. Z., & Chase, A. F. (2014). Path dependency in the rise and denouement of a classic Maya City: The case study of Caracol, Belize. In A. F. Chase & V. L. Scarborough (Eds.), *The resilience and vulnerability of ancient landscapes: Transforming Maya archaeology through IHOPE* (Archaeological Papers of the American Anthropological Association, No. 24) (pp. 142–154). Hoboken, NJ: Wiley.
Childe, V. G. (1950). The urban revolution. *Town Planning Review, 21*, 3–17.

Commoner, B. (1971). *The closing circle: Nature, man and technology*. New York: Alfred A. Knopf.
Crosby, A. W. (2009). *Ecological imperialism: The biological expansion of Europe, 900–1900*. New York: Cambridge University Press.
Crumley, C. L. (1995). Heterarchy and the analysis of complex societies. *Archaeological Papers of the American Anthropological Association, 7*(1), 1–5.
Darwin, C. (1859). *The origins of species by means of natural selection, or the preservation of favored races in the struggle for life*. London: John Murray.
Darwin, C. (1871). *The descent of man, and selection in relation to sex* (Vol. 2). London: John Murray.
del Castillo, D. B. (1963). *The conquest of New Spain* (J. M. Cohen, Trans.). New York: Penguin.
Denevan, W. M. (1992). The pristine myth: The landscape of the Americas in 1942. *Annals of the Association of American Geographers, 82*(3), 369–385.
Denevan, W. M. (2001). *Cultivated landscapes of native Amazonia and the Andes*. New York: Oxford University Press.
Descola, P. (2005). *Beyond nature and culture*. Chicago, IL: University of Chicago Press.
Dobyns, H. F. (1966). Estimating aboriginal American populations: An appraisal of techniques with a new hemispheric estimate. *Current Anthropology, 7*, 395–416.
Dobyns, H. F. (1983). *Their number become thinned: Native American population dynamics in eastern North America*. Knoxville, TN: University of Tennessee Press.
Donkin, R. A. (1979). Agricultural terracing in the aboriginal New World. In *Viking fund publications in anthropology 56*. Tucson, AZ: Published for the Wenner-Gren Foundation for Anthropological Research by the University of Arizona Press.
Doolittle, W. E. (2001). *Cultivated landscapes of native North America*. New York: Oxford University Press.
Dunning, N., Wahl, D., Beach, T., Jones, J., Luzzadder-Beach, S., & McCormick, C. (2014). The end of the beginning: Drought, environmental change and the preclassic to classic transition in the east-Central Yucatan peninsula. In G. Iannone (Ed.), *The great Maya droughts in cultural context* (pp. 107–129). Boulder, CO: University of Colorado Press.
Durán, F. D. (1994[1588?]) *The history of the indies of New Spain* (D. Heyden, Trans.). Norman: University of Oklahoma Press.
Erickson, C. L. (2006). The domesticated landscapes of the Bolivian Amazon. In W. Balee & C. L. Erickson (Eds.), *Time and complexity in historical ecology* (pp. 235–278). New York: Columbia University Press.
Erickson, C. L. (2019). Pre-Columbian water Management in Lowland South America. In V. L. Scarborough (Ed.), *Water and humanity: Historical overview*. Paris: UNESCO.
Farrington, I. (Ed.). (1985). *Prehistoric intensive agriculture in the tropics* (British Archaeological Series, International Series, no. 232). Oxford: BAR.
Feinman, G. M., & Carballo, D. M. (2018). Collaborative and competitive strategies in the variability and resiliency of large-scale societies in Mesoamerica. *Economic Anthropology, 5*, 7–19.
Fisher, C. T., Pollard, H. P., Israde-Alcantara, I., Garduno-Monroy, V. H., & Banerjee, S. K. (2003). A reexamination of human-induced environmental change within the Lake Patzcuaro Basin, Michoacan, Mexico. *Proceedings of the National Academy of Sciences, 100*(8), 4957–4962.
Flannery, K., & Marcus, J. (2012). *The creation of inequality*. Cambridge: Harvard Press.
Ford, A., & Nigh, R. (2015). *The Maya forest garden: Eight millennia of sustainable cultivation of the tropical woodlands*. Walnut Creek, CA: Left Coast Press.
Fowler, C. (2016). Relational personhood revisited. *Cambridge Archaeological Journal, 26*(3), 397–412.
Fowler, C., & Harris, O. J. T. (2015). Enduring relations: Exploring a paradox of new materialism. *Journal of Material Culture, 20*(2), 127–148.
Freidel, D., Schele, L., & Parker, J. (1993). *Maya cosmos: Three thousand years on the shaman's path*. New York: William Morrow.

Friedman, R. A., Sofaer, A., & Weiner, R. S. (2017). Remote sensing of Chaco roads revisited. *Advances in Archaeological Practice, 5*(4), 365–381.

Glaser, B., & Woods, W. I. (Eds.). (2004). *Explorations in Amazonian dark earths*. Berlin: Springer.

Gow, P. (1990). Land, people, and paper in Western Amazonia. In E. Hirsch & M. O'Hanlon (Eds.), *The anthropology of landscape: Perspectives on place and space* (pp. 43–62). Oxford: Clarendon Press.

Harris, O. J. T., & Robb, J. (2012). Multiple ontologies and the problem of the body in history. *American Anthropologist, 114*(4), 668–679.

Hassig, R. (1988). *Aztec warfare: Imperial expansion and political control*. Norman, OK: University of Oklahoma Press.

Heckenberger, M. J. (2005). *The ecology of power: Culture, place, and personhood in the southern Amazon, a.D. 1000–2000*. New York: Routledge.

Helms, M. (1998). *Access to origins: Affines, ancestors, and aristocrats*. Austin, TX: University of Texas Press.

Hornborg, A. (2001). *The power of the machine: Global inequalities of economy, technology, and environment*. Walnut Creek, CA: Altamira Press.

Houston, S., & Stuart, D. (1989). The way glyph: Evidence for "co-essences" among the classic Maya. In *Research reports on ancient Maya writing 30*. Washington, DC: Center for Maya Research.

Hyslop, J. (1984). *The Inka road system*. New York: Academic Press.

Isendahl, C., Dunning, N. P., & Sabloff, J. A. (2014). Growth and decline in classic Maya Puuc political economies. In A. F. Chase & V. L. Scarborough (Eds.), *The resilience and vulnerability of ancient landscapes: Transforming Maya archaeology through IHOPE* (Archaeological Papers of the American Anthropological Association, No. 24) (pp. 43–55). Hoboken, NJ: Wiley.

Isendahl, C., & Stump, D. (2019). Conclusion: Anthropocentric historical ecology, applied archaeology, and the future of a useable past. In C. Isendahl & D. Stump (Eds.), *The Oxford handbook of historical ecology and applied archaeology* (pp. 581–597). Oxford: Oxford University Press.

Jackson, S. E. (2013). *Politics of the Maya court: Hierarchy and change in the late classic period*. Norman: University of Oklahoma Press.

Kantner, J. (2003). Rethinking Chaco as a system. *Kiva, 69*(2), 207–227.

Kennett, D. J., Breitenbach, S. F. M., Aquino, V. V., Asmersom, Y., Awe, J., Baldini, J. U. L., et al. (2012). Development and disintegration of Maya political systems in response to climate change. *Science, 338*, 788–791.

Killion, T. W. (1992). *Gardens of prehistory: The archaeology of settlement agriculture in greater Mesoamerica*. Tuscaloosa, AL: University of Alabama Press.

Kohler, T. A., Smith, M. E., Bogaard, A., Feinman, G. M., Peterson, C. E., Betzenhauser, A., et al. (2017). Greater post-neolithic wealth disparities in Eurasia than in North America and Mesoamerica. *Nature, 551*(7682), 619.

Krech III, S. (2000). *The ecological Indian: Myth and history*. New York: W.W. Norton and Company.

Lehmann, J., Kern, D. C., Glaser, B., & Woods, W. I. (Eds.). (2003). *Amazonian dark earths: Origin, properties, management*. Dordrecht: Kluwer.

Lentz, D. L., Dunning, N. P., & Scarborough, V. L. (Eds.). (2015). *Tikal: Paleoecology of an ancient Maya city*. New York: Cambridge University Press.

López Austin, A. (1980). *The human body and ideology: Concepts of the ancient Nahuas*. Salt Lake City, UT: University of Utah Press.

Lucero, L. (2003). The politics of ritual: The emergence of classic Maya rulers. *Current Anthropology, 44*, 523–558.

Lucero, L. (2006). *Water and ritual: The rise and fall of classic Maya rulers*. Austin, TX: University of Texas Press.

Mann, C. C. (2005). *1491: New revelations of the Americas before Columbus*. New York: Vintage.

Mann, C. C. (2011). *1493: Uncovering the new world Columbus created*. New York: Knopf.

McMichael, A. J., Bolin, B., Costanza, R., Daily, G. C., Folke, C., Lindahl-Kiesslig, K., et al. (1999). Globalization and the sustainability of human health: An ecological perspective. *Bioscience, 49*(3), 205–210.

McNeill, W. H. (1977). *Plagues and peoples.* New York: Anchor.

Meggers, B. J. (1996). *Amazonia: Man and culture in a counterfeit paradise* (Rev. ed.). Washington, DC: Smithsonian Institution Press.

Millon, R. (1973). Urbanization at Teotihuacan, Mexico. In *The Teotihuacan map, part 1* (Vol. 1). Austin, TX: University of Texas Press.

Minnis, P. E., Whalen, M. E., & Emerson Howell, R. (2006). Fields of power: Upland agriculture in the Prehispanic Casas Grandes polity, Chihuahua, Mexico. *American Antiquity, 71,* 707–722.

Moseley, M. E. (1992). *The Incas and their ancestors.* London: Thames and Hudson.

Neves, E. (2006). *Arqueologia de Amazonia.* Rio de Janeiro: Jorge Zahar.

Nielsen, A. E. (2008). The materiality of ancestors: *Chullpas* and social memory in the late prehispanic history of the South Andes. In B. J. Mills & W. H. Walker (Eds.), *Memory work: Archaeologies of material practices* (pp. 207–232). Santa Fe: School for Advanced Research Press.

Oxfam. (2017). https://www.oxfam.org/en/pressroom/pressreleases/2017-01-16/just-8-men-own-same-wealth-half-world

Pennock, C. D. (2012). Mass murder or religious homicide? Rethinking human sacrifice and interpersonal violence in Aztec society. *Historical Social Research, 37*(3), 276–302.

Redman, C. L. (1978). *The rise of civilization.* San Francisco: W.H. Freeman.

Redman, C. L. (1999). *Human impact on the ancient environments.* Tucson, AZ: University of Arizona Press.

Reinhard, J. (1996). *The Nazca lines: A new perspective on their origin and meaning* (6th ed.). Lima: Editorial Los Pinos.

Roosevelt, A. C. (Ed.). (1994). *Amazonian Indians from prehistory to the present: Anthropological perspectives.* Tucson, AZ: University of Arizona Press.

Rostain, S. (2013). *Islands in the rainforest: Landscape management in pre-Columbian Amazonia.* Walnut Creek, CA: Left Coast Press.

Rowe, J. H. (1946). *Inca culture at the time of the conquest.* Washington D.C: US Government Printing Office.

Ruddiman, W. F. (2005). *Plows, plagues, and petroleum: How humans took control of climate.* Princeton, NJ: Princeton University Press.

Sandstrom, A. R. (2019). Water and the sacred in Mesoamerica. In V. L. Scarborough (Ed.), *Water and humanity: Historical overview.* Paris: UNESCO.

Scarborough, V. L. (2000). Resilience, resource use, and socioeconomic organization: A Mesoamerican pathway. In G. Bawden & R. Reycraft (Eds.), *Natural disaster and the archaeology of human response* (pp. 195–212). Albuquerque: Maxwell Museum of Anthropology and the University of New Mexico Press.

Scarborough, V. L. (2003). *The flow of power: Ancient water systems and landscapes.* Santa Fe: School of American Research Press.

Scarborough, V. L. (2005). Landscapes of power. In V. L. Scarborough (Ed.), *A catalyst for ideas: Anthropological archaeology and the legacy of Douglas W. Schwartz* (pp. 209–228). Santa Fe: School of American Research Press.

Scarborough, V. L. (2006). An overview of Mesoamerican water systems. In L. J. Lucero & B. L. Fash (Eds.), *Precolumbian water management: Ideology, ritual and power* (pp. 223–236). Tucson, AZ: University of Arizona Press.

Scarborough, V. L. (2007). Colonizing a landscape: Water and wetlands in ancient Mesoamerica. In V. L. Scarborough & J. Clark (Eds.), *The political economy of ancient Mesoamerica: Transformations during the formative and classic periods* (pp. 163–174). Albuquerque: University of New Mexico Press.

Scarborough, V. L. (2018). A framework for facing the past. In E. Holt (Ed.), *Water and power in past societies*. Albany, NY: Suny Press.

Scarborough, V. L., & Burnside, W. R. (2010). Complexity and sustainability: Perspectives from the ancient Maya and the modern Balinese. *American Antiquity, 75*(2), 327–363.

Scarborough, V. L., & Isendahl, C. (2019). Crosscultural archaeology and the role of the seasonally wet tropics in informing the present. In S. Rost (Ed.), *Irrigation and early states: New directions*. Chicago, IL: Oriental Institute, University of Chicago Press.

Scarborough, V. L., & Lucero, L. (2011). The non-hierarchical development of complexity in the semitropics: Water and cooperation. *Water History, 2*(2), 185–205.

Scarborough, V. L., & Valdez Jr., F. (2009). An alternative order: The dualistic economies of the ancient Maya. *Latin American Antiquity, 20*(1), 207–227.

Scarborough, V. L., & Valdez Jr., F. (2014). The alternative economy: Resilience in the face of complexity from the eastern lowlands. In A. F. Chase & V. L. Scarborough (Eds.), *The resilience and vulnerability of ancient landscapes: Transforming Maya archaeology through IHOPE* (Archaeological papers of the American Anthropological Association, no. 24) (pp. 124–141). Hoboken, NJ: Wiley.

Scarborough, V. L., Valdez Jr., F., & Nicholas, D. (Eds.). (2003). *Heterarchy, political economy, and the ancient Maya: The three Rivers region of east-Central Yucatán peninsula*. Tucson, AZ: University of Arizona Press.

Schaan, D. P. (2012). *Sacred geographies of ancient Amazonia: Historical ecology of social complexity*. Walnut Creek, CA: Left Coast Press.

Schwartz, N. B. (1990). *Forest society: A social history of Peten, Guatemala*. Philadelphia: University of Pennsylvania Press.

Shafer, H. J., & Hester, T. R. (1983). Ancient Maya Chert workshops in northern Belize, Central America. *American Antiquity, 48*, 519–543.

Tainter, J. A., & Allen, T. F. H. (2019). Energy gain and the evolution of organization. In C. Isendahl & D. Stump (Eds.), *The Oxford handbook of historical ecology and applied archaeology* (pp. 558–577). Oxford: Oxford University Press.

Tainter, J. A., Scarborough, V. L., & Allen, T. F. H. (2018). Resource gain and complexity: Water past and future. In F. Sulas & I. Pikirayi (Eds.), *Water and society: Resilience, decline, and revival from ancient times to the present*. London: Routledge.

Thomas, J. (2015). The future of archaeological theory. *Antiquity, 89*, 1287–1296.

Van de Guchte, M. (1999). The Inca cognition of landscape: Archaeology, ethnohistory, and the aesthetic of alterity. In W. Ashmore & A. Bernard Knapp (Eds.), *Archaeologies of landscape: Contemporary perspectives* (pp. 149–168). Malden, MA: Blackwell Publishers.

Viveiros de Castro, E. B. (2004). Exchanging perspectives: The transformation of objects into subjects in Amerindian ontologies. *Common Knowledge, 10*(3), 463–484.

Vivian, R. G. (1990). *The Chacoan prehistory of the San Juan basin*. New York: Academic Press.

Vivian, R. G. (1997a). Chacoan roads: Function. *Kiva, 63*, 35–68.

Vivian, R. G. (1997b). Chacoan roads: Morphology. *Kiva, 63*, 7–34.

Wahl, D., Byrne, R., & Anderson, L. (2014). An 8700 year paleoclimate reconstruction from the southern Maya lowlands. *Quaternary Science Reviews, 103*, 19–25.

Watling, J., Iriarte, J., Mayle, F. E., Schaan, D., Pessenda, L. C. R., Loader, N. J., et al. (2017). Impact of pre-Columbian "geoglyph" builders on Amazonian forests. *Proceedings of the National Academy of Sciences, 114*(8), 1868–1873.

Whitmore, T. M., & Turner II, B. L. (2001). *Cultivated landscapes of middle america in the eve of the conquest*. New York: Oxford University Press.

Wolf, E. R. (1957). Closed corporate peasant communities in Mesoamerica and Central Java. *Southwestern Journal of Anthropology, 13*(1), 1–18.

Woods, W. I., Teixeira, W. G., Lehmann, J., Steiner, C., WinklerPrins, A., & Rebellato, L. (Eds.). (2009). *Amazonian dark earths: Wim Sombroek's vision*. Berlin: Springer.

Wulf, A. (2015). *The invention of nature: Alexander von Humboldt's new world.* New York: Vintage.
Zuidema, R. T. (1964). *The ceque system of Cuzco: The social organization of the capital of the Inca.* Leiden: E.S. Brill.
Zuidema, R. T. (1989). A quipu calendar from Ica, Peru, with a comparison to the ceque calendar from Cuzco. In A. F. Aveni (Ed.), *World archeoastronomy* (pp. 341–351). Cambridge: Cambridge University Press.

The Scale, Governance, and Sustainability of Central Places in Pre-Hispanic Mesoamerica

Gary M. Feinman and David M. Carballo

Cooperation and competition have long been recognized as fundamental characteristics of the human career (Mead 1937). For generations, anthropologists have had serious interest in evaluating how variability in this axis of behavior relates to the emergence, durability, and diversity of large-scale societies (Fuentes 2004; Carballo et al. 2014). Still, as Trigger (2003, p. 3) observed, researchers continue to work for an appropriate balance between general and specific factors (or processes and history) in developing frameworks for understanding cultural and behavioral variability viewed in deep, temporal perspective through the archaeological record. We address these issues through a comparative analysis of pre-Hispanic Mesoamerican urban centers that focally examines differences in the ways that they were governed and how organizational variation relates to their size and longevity. In this way, we focus on both the social mechanisms (Hedström and Swedberg 1996) that likely impacted long-term sustainability as well as the outcomes of deep historical process (Grant 2004, p. 24).

Framing Urbanism in Pre-Hispanic Mesoamerica

Pre-Hispanic Mesoamerica has long been recognized as a cultural region where early cities and large-scale polities arose autochthonously (e.g., Steward 1949; Adams 1966). Given the impediments to communication and resource extraction relative to ancient Eurasia (e.g., the lack of beasts of burden and wheeled transport

G. M. Feinman (✉)
Integrative Research Center, Field Museum of Natural History, Chicago, IL, USA
e-mail: gfeinman@fieldmuseum.org

D. M. Carballo
Department of Anthropology, Boston University, Boston, MA, USA

and the markedly limited and relatively late use of metal implements), the significant size and durability of pre-Hispanic Mesoamerican urban centers have raised special interest (Wright 1989, p. 99). How were these preindustrial cooperative arrangements organized? Were they durable, and if so, what accounts for their comparative sustainability across time? Large-scale cooperative arrangements are rare in the natural world (Melis and Semmann 2010; Carballo 2013; Sterelny 2013; Carballo and Feinman 2016), and humans are the only species that sustains them among individuals who are not necessarily close kin. Thus, the socioeconomic processes and mechanisms that underpin such human aggregations, the relative degrees of cooperation and coercion involved, and how such interpersonal relations and different forms of governance impact the scale and durability of such formations are key issues for understanding pre-Hispanic Mesoamerica that also potentially have broader temporal and geographic implications (Acemoglu and Robinson 2012; Middleton 2012).

The study of pre-Hispanic Mesoamerica underwent a significant shift in emphasis during the mid-twentieth century (Wolf 1994, pp. 3–4) as research foci gravitated from temples and tombs to the study of regional settlement patterns, urban layouts, domestic economies, and agrarian production. In parallel, Eric Wolf and other intellectual giants of anthropology (Armillas 1951; Palerm and Wolf 1957; Sanders and Price 1968; Wolf 1976) ushered in new theoretical perspectives that not only gave greater prominence to economic matters but asked questions such as how pre-Hispanic Mesoamerican cities were ruled and what sustained those who governed. Frankly, the analyses that we undertake here would not have been possible before the multiple generations of investigations that began more than seven decades ago as well as the conceptual frames that inspired and guided them (Palerm 2017).

With explicitly comparative interests, Wolf and colleagues (Palerm and Wolf 1957; Sanders and Price 1968) understandably drew heavily on the models and conceptual frames that were predominant in much of anthropology at that time in their efforts to understand pre-Hispanic Mesoamerican polities (Feinman and Nicholas 2012; Wolf 1994). Inspired by elements of Marxist thought, these cultural evolutionary theoretical perspectives were heavily grounded in extant interpretations of the development of urban societies in Eurasia (Childe 1942; Polanyi et al. 1957; Wittfogel 1957; Marx 1971). The frames stressed despotic rule, generally funded by command economies in which production and distribution were presumed centered on the ruler. Coercive forms of rule were taken as a given, a perspective that did not challenge the prior (and other) dominant theoretical approach at that time, culture history, which tends to afford great importance to the actions of the elite (see Trigger 1989; Carballo et al. 2014). Likewise, this vision of pre-Hispanic Mesoamerican rule found seeming support from the one historical case where documents relevant to the fiscal foundations of power were available, the Aztec empire, which appeared at the time to have been financed through coercively derived tribute (Barlow 1949).

Yet the same empirical investigations that were inspired by early cultural evolutionary frames subsequently have led to serious doubts regarding the presumed key tenets of those conceptual perspectives; in particular there is little empirical support for the notion that despotic rulers centrally controlled pre-Hispanic Mesoamerican economic production or distribution (Offner 1981a, b; Baker 1998; Feinman and Nicholas 2012). In fact, most production for exchange was carried out domestically (Feinman 1999; Hirth 2009), and markets were important across Mesoamerica long before the Aztec empire (Feinman and Garraty 2010; Garraty and Stark 2010; Kowalewski 2012; Hirth and Pillsbury 2013). Even the financing of that empire was dependent principally on taxes, in both labor and goods, while tribute was secondary and very much intertwined with markets and other mechanisms of distribution (Berdan 1977, 1985; Smith 2015). Therefore, if most aspects of pre-Hispanic Mesoamerican economies were not centrally controlled, was governance universally coercive as proposed? What would non- or less-coercive sociopolitical systems look like, and how much variance in governance was there? How closely is diversity in political organization, urban size, and the duration of specific cities linked to regional cultural traditions, in accord with culture historical expectations (Gillespie 1993), or do other frames exist that could help account for variability along these axes?

Until recently, the major frameworks (e.g., cultural evolution and culture history) that have considered the diversity and dynamics of pre-Hispanic Mesoamerican urban centers and their political hinterlands have focused almost exclusively at the scale of societies, often treating societies as if they were organisms with a holistic, stage-like life cycle (see Butzer 2012). Throughout history no predictable formula or timetable for the life cycle and ultimate collapse of societies has ever been advanced, and it is simply not demonstrable with empirical data (Turchin 2003, p. 26). Although diachronic analysis repeatedly has illustrated that the power of particular places and specific dynasties and regional populations have ebbed and flowed over time, the precise timing of these oscillations is neither externally preset nor regular, and instead, it relates to the dynamic relations between people and the challenges they face. As Boettiger and Hastings (2013, p. 158) state more generally, "no 'one-size-fits-all' property has been found that signals the imminent collapse of a complex system."

Collectivity in Premodern Urban Societies

The examination of urban collapse and transformation requires multiscalar approaches that probe the "black boxes" of human social dynamics and organization, which in a basic sense entails the consideration of the shifting relations between followers and leaders (Blanton 2010, 2012). At the same time, these approaches must take into account networks and relations that extend beyond regions and political boundaries (e.g., Wolf 1982). No longer can we restrict considerations of individual agency solely to small elite subsets of populations (see Nassaney and Sassaman 1995, pp. xxi–xxii). Although power must be seriously considered, leadership is always dyadic and implies a consideration of the objectives of followers as well as those on top (Ahlquist and Levi 2011, p. 5). This relational aspect of leadership is a particular consideration for ancient cities and states, where the frictions of population and governance at a distance placed real constraints on the degrees of control, the maintenance of boundaries, and a reliance on force and power alone (Smith 2005). Instead, following broader social science literature on collective action (Levi 1988; Adger 2003; Blanton 2010; Blanton and Fargher 2008, 2011, 2016; Carballo 2016), we frame our consideration of past large-scale societies using a comparative perspective, one that recognizes institutional variation and the resultant responses to challenges and perturbations.

Decades ago in an effort to compare pre-Hispanic Mesoamerican civilizations diachronically, the senior author and colleagues (Blanton et al. 1996; Feinman 1995, 2001) advanced a conceptual frame that considered variability along an axis of political strategy within hierarchical societies termed "corporate" and "network." Newer work has more explicitly connected this frame with collective-action theory in order to consider a broader spectrum of individual and group interests undergirding variability in social organization and to connect archaeological concerns with a broader literature in the social and behavioral sciences (Blanton and Fargher 2008, 2011, 2016; Feinman 2010; Fargher et al. 2011; Carballo et al. 2014; Carballo and Feinman 2016; Feinman and Nicholas 2016a). In outlining characteristics, such as the uses of urban space (Castells 1978, pp. 15–21; Blanton and Fargher 2011; Carballo 2016; Wade 2017), indicative of what we consider more or less collective forms of organization in past large-scale societies (Table 1), we understand that all variables are gradated spectra with differing levels of visibility in the archaeological record. Some of the less collective formations are consistent with patron-client or highly autocratic systems known historically and ethnographically, though we recognize these are not a social "type" and vary through time and culture area (Crumley 1987). Less collective formations generally have a single or small number of principals or despots, who are able to highly concentrate or monopolize power with very

Table 1 Axes of collectivity for premodern complex societies

More collective	Less collective
Internal revenues: Regularized taxation, a focus on staple finance and regional goods	External revenues: Long-distance trade, importance of portable wealth, spoils of war, control of spot resources
More communally owned or managed land	Less communally owned or managed land
Fewer disparities of wealth in life and death	Greater disparities of wealth in life and death
Greater potential for shared power	Greater potential for individualized power
Political ideology emphasizes abstract principles of offices and strength of the polity, cosmology, and fertility	Political ideology emphasizes lineal descent systems for succession and legitimation, divine kingship, and royal patron deities
Not centered on palaces	Centrality of palaces
Monumental architecture fosters access (e.g., open plazas, wide access ways, community temples)	Monumental architecture fosters exclusivity (e.g., elite tombs and memorials, dynastic temples)
Greater expenditures on public goods	Smaller expenditures on public goods

limited checks, although their specific titles and associated structures may vary (Blanton and Fargher 2016, pp. 115–158).

Following the work of Levi (1988) and Blanton and Fargher (2008), we emphasize that a key factor determining variability in the organization of large-scale societies is the form of political financing and whether revenues are largely internal (more communal resources) or external (less communal), as this directly impacts the levels of accountability that leaders face from commoners and the likelihood that governance and power will tend toward being either shared/distributed or individualized (e.g., D'Altroy and Earle 1985; Moore 2004; Broms 2015; Blanton and Fargher 2016, pp. 106–114). In addition to greater accountability for governing authorities, higher levels of internal financing and communal resources often correlate with higher dissemination of public goods and bureaucratization of civic offices, together creating systems that may grow larger and have greater sustainability in the face of societal perturbations.

More collective formations require investments both to exact internal resource and to provision public goods and services. In contrast, more autocratic or despotic formations rely on coercion, a means of social control that over deep time is both expensive and provides incentives to slack, resist, or out-migrate (Levi 1988; Smith 2005). Autocratic rulers tend to wield power transactionally through interpersonal relations and networks. As a result, infrastructural investments and bureaucracies generally tend to be underdeveloped, especially when economic production and distribution are not centrally controlled.

More collectively organized governance should be associated with greater investment in public goods that benefit the local populace. Infrastructural investments such as wide and coherently networked streets and roads (Blanton and Fargher 2011, pp. 509–512), marketplaces, public meeting spots (plazas), and defensive features should all be fostered and more heavily supported when governance is collective. Significant allotments in these realms tend to leave archaeological traces. With collective forms of governance, greater investments in provisioning in the face of disasters would be expected, although material remnants of such practices may be hard to decipher without documents. These relationships between forms of governance and the allocation of space for public aggregations and expressions of subaltern voice are not restricted to the past, as Klinenberg (2018) underscores in discussing forms of social infrastructure and its variability in contemporary cities and neighborhoods.

Based on these relational social mechanisms and past findings, we suspect that more collective formations should be larger than less collective or more autocratic formations (Dubreuil 2010; Feinman 2013; Carballo et al. 2014, p.114; Blanton and Fargher 2016, p. 40, 264). The cases we present from pre-Hispanic Mesoamerica support this relationship, which stands in contrast to long-held presumptions that cooperation is most evident in small groups and that group size should be inversely related to sustainability (e.g., Olson 1965, p. 36).

Governance in Pre-Hispanic Mesoamerican Central Places

As a means of evaluating the frameworks and hypotheses that we have proposed, we coded data from 26 pre-Hispanic Mesoamerican cities and proto-urban centers whose classification as cities is debated by regional specialists. The important criterion for the latter, which all date to the Formative period Olmec horizon, is that they were the prominent political centers within their respective regions (Fig. 1). We began by identifying in the literature for pre-Hispanic Mesoamerica large settlements/regional centers with solid estimates of population and longevity of occupation. For the first, we relied on publications with population estimates based on systematic site mapping, regional survey, or other empirically based assessment. For the second, our ideal was to record the years at which the estimated population was at 50% or above its proposed maximum. This proved to be possible in only a few instances, and we more often had to default to reported apogee of settlement populations. Our interest in community longevity or duration also precluded us from including many well-documented Postclassic cities in this aspect of the analysis as the histories of these localities were truncated by Spanish conquest, colonialism, and associated vectors of disease. Centers were then coded for criteria along a spectrum of collectivity in which a score of one signified the most collective and zero signified the least, with half-point scores awarded for intermediate cases (Table 2); the collectivity score for each center sums the values for political economy, governance, and architecture and ranges from 0 to 3. Because of the aforementioned truncation due to Spanish invasion as well as a few instances where we lacked suitable demographic estimates, each of the 26 cases was not included in every analysis. Although we recognize that this is a preliminary investigation into an issue with many potential confounding variables, we think that the findings are sufficiently significant to report as we anticipate further research and refinement.

Table 3 lists all the cities and urban centers in the study, including the values applied for population, apogee, and collectivity. Sources listed in the final column are primarily for population and apogee, whereas our collectivity scoring drew on our understanding of a much larger literature on these sites (see Carballo 2016, p. 120). We present the coding of each value so that our colleagues who study ancient Mesoamerica can evaluate our distillation of this literature. For population figures, which can range widely by author, we endeavored to select conservative estimates that had an empirical basis.

We emphasize that our coding does not ascribe single cultures or regional traditions to one side of the spectrum or the other and that, indeed, variability is discernible both diachronically and synchronically within cultural areas (Fig. 2a). For instance, less collective formations are more characteristic of the Preclassic Gulf Coast, Classic Maya, and Postclassic highlands in the Mixteca-Puebla (or Eastern Nahua) interaction sphere (Pohl 2003). These societies tended to be palace-centric and focused on prestige economies and individualized leadership—the best examples are certain Classic period Maya cities at which governance was organized following an institution of divine kingship (the *k'uhul ajaw*). More collective

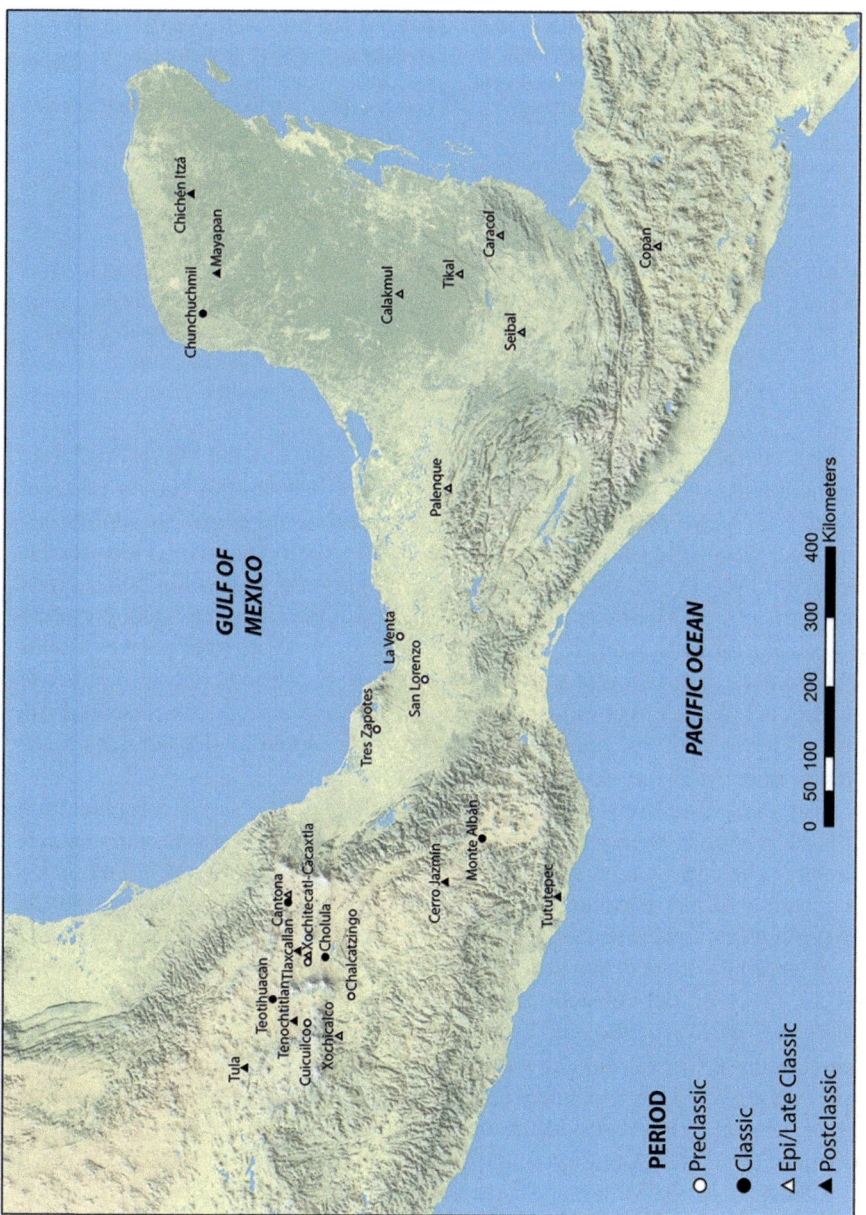

Fig. 1 Mesoamerica with sites used in the analysis

Table 2 Axes of collectivity coded for Mesoamerican cases

Variable/collectivity score	1—More collective	0—Less collective
Political economy	Internal financing with greater focus on staple goods and market exchange; more muted socioeconomic differentiation	External financing with greater focus on prestige goods derived from long-distance exchange or control of spot resources; palace-centric production; more heightened socioeconomic differentiation
Governance	"Faceless" rulership; low mortuary differentiation; secular and bureaucratized political offices	Highly conspicuous rulers in burials and iconography; individualized rulers; divine kingship
Architecture	Emphasis on communal architecture over palaces, including temples, plazas, access ways; art emphasizing public goods	Emphasis on palaces so that their elaboration and centrality match or exceed more communal architecture; art emphasizing exclusive access

formations characterized the Preclassic highlands, much of the Maya Preclassic, Classic highland states such as Monte Albán and Teotihuacan, Postclassic Tula, and the Postclassic Maya polities of explicitly shared rule (*multepal*). Variability also was apparent within the Classic Maya world, with northern Yucatecan cities such as Chunchuchmil scoring firmly in the collective category and Caracol in Belize coded only slightly less so. The more collective societies in the sample tended to emphasize the social infrastructure of public space and monuments over palaces, suprahousehold infrastructural projects such as terrace or irrigation networks, household and market economies over palace and prestige economies, and more shared rule with no evidence of divine kingship (a later example would be the Aztec name for paramount ruler: *huey tlatoani*, or "great speaker").

In other words, we consider the degree of collectivity to have been potentially rather fluid over time, even within specific regions, with collaborative and competitive strategies having been pursued simultaneously in all societies and in flux during the occupation of any particular city (Feinman 2018). The Classic Maya city of Copán provides an illustrative example, thanks to the availability of both epigraphic and architectural evidence. We scored Copán in the aggregate at the less collective end of the spectrum but consider that it fluctuated over time. Following the major political crisis when its thirteenth king was captured and killed by a rival city, the fourteenth king of Copán initiated a collaborative strategy of more consensual aristocratic rule centered on a council house to get the dynasty back on its footing, before the fifteenth king reversed this strategy and dedicated the longest preserved pre-Hispanic text in the Americas to the glory of the dynasty (Fash 2002; Fash et al. 1992). Likewise, in the Valley of Oaxaca, a transition from more collective to less collective governance with increasing focus on the palace is documented for the end of the Classic period and into the Postclassic period (Feinman and Nicholas 2016b). There is not a simple highland-lowland dichotomy; lowland centers such as Tres

Table 3 Mesoamerican cities and urban centers used in analysis

Site	Period	Apogee	Maximum population	Political economy	Leaders	Architecture	Collectivity score	Sources
Cacaxtla	Epiclassic/Late Classic	250	15,000	0.5	0.5	0	1	Serra Puche and Lazcano (2008, 2011)
Calakmul	Epiclassic/Late Classic	400	50,000	0	0	0.5	0.5	Folan et al. (2008), Turner (1990)
Cantona	Classic-Epiclassic	650	60,000	1	1	0.5	2.5	García Cook (2003)
Caracol	Epiclassic/Late Classic	250	100,000	0.5	0.5	1	2	Chase and Chase (2017, 2009)
Cerro Jazmín	Postclassic	400	17,000	0	0	0.5	0.5	Pérez et al. (2011)
Chalcatzingo	Preclassic	500	1000	0.5	0.5	1	2	Grove (1987)
Chichén Itzá	Postclassic	350	24,500	0.5	0.5	1	2	Cobos (2003), Hassig (1992)
Cholula	Classic-Epiclassic	750	–	1	1	1	3	Plunket and Uruñuela (2005), Uruñuela et al. (2009)
Chunchuchmil	Classic	300	38,500	0.5	1	1	2.5	Dahlin (2009), Magnoni et al. (2012)
Copán	Epiclassic/Late Classic	250	10,000	0	0	0	0	Fash (2008), Webster (2008)
Cuicuilco	Preclassic	700	20,000	1	1	1	3	Pastrana and Ramírez (2012), Plunket and Uruñuela (2012)
La Venta	Preclassic	300	3000	0	0	0	0	Rust (1992, 2008)
Mayapan	Postclassic	300	16,000	0.5	1	1	2.5	Peraza Lope et al. (2006)
Monte Albán	Classic	1100	25,000	1	0.5	1	2.5	Blanton (1978)
Palenque	Epiclassic/Late Classic	300	7500	0	0	0	0	Barnhart (2008)
San Lorenzo	Preclassic	300	8000	0	0	0	0	Arieta Baizabal (2013), Coe and Diehl (1981), Cyphers (2012)

(continued)

Table 3 (continued)

Site	Period	Apogee	Maximum population	Political economy	Leaders	Architecture	Collectivity score	Sources
Seibal	Epiclassic/Late Classic	200	7500	0	0	0	0	Tourtellot (1990)
Tenochtitlan	Postclassic	–	212,500	1	0.5	0.5	2	Calnek (2003), Smith (2008)
Teotihuacan	Classic	600	100,000	1	1	1	3	Cowgill (2008)
Tikal	Epiclassic/Late Classic	400	55,000	0	0	0.5	0.5	Culbert et al. (1990), Haviland (2008)
Tlaxcallan	Postclassic	–	35,000	1	1	1	3	Fargher et al. (2011)
Tres Zapotes	Preclassic	600	3000	1	1	0.5	2.5	Pool (2010), Pool and Loughlin (2015, 2016)
Tula	Postclassic	300	50,000	1	1	0.5	2.5	Healan (2012), Mastache and Cobean (2003)
Tututepec	Postclassic	–	16,000	0.5	0	0	0.5	Joyce et al. (2004), Levine (2017)
Xochicalco	Epiclassic/Late Classic	250	12,000	1	0.5	1	2.5	Hirth (2003)
Xochitecatl	Preclassic	700	–	1	1	1	3	Serra Puche (2012), Serra Puche and Lazcano (2011)

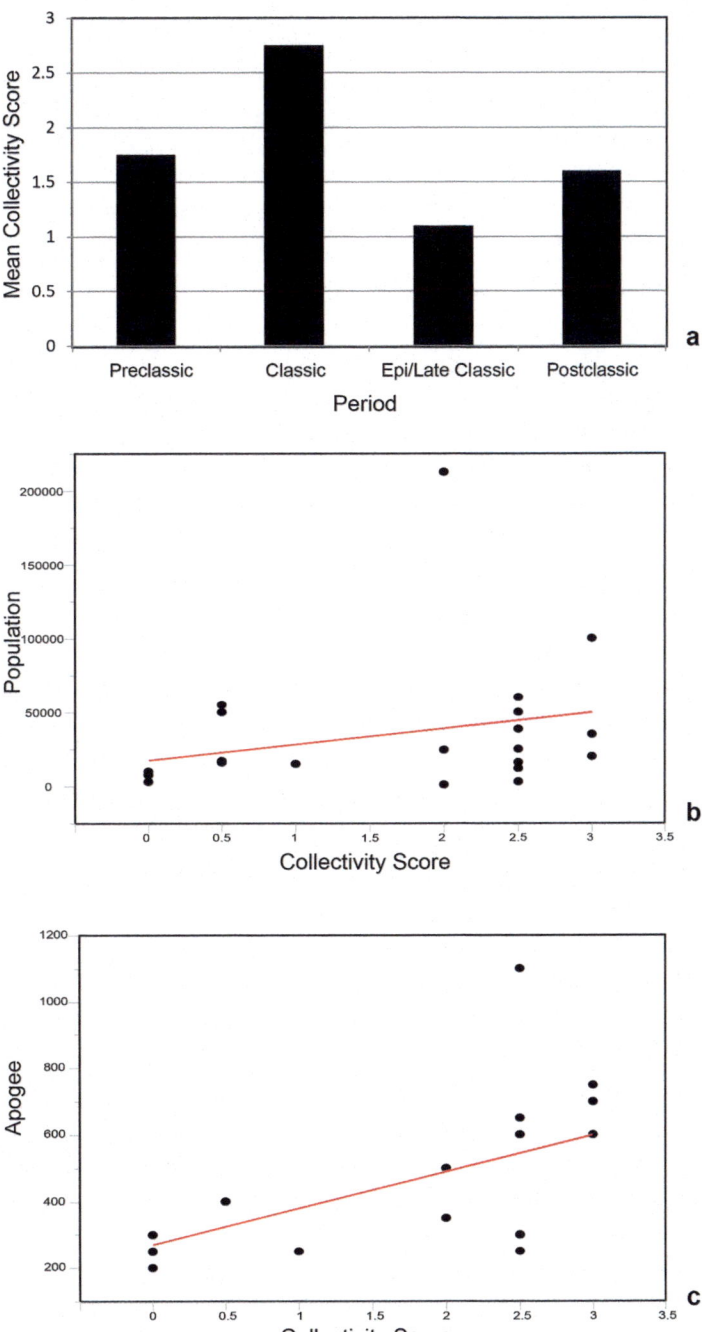

Fig. 2 Results of analyses. (**a**) Mean collectivity scores for sites grouped by chronological period. Periods are roughly as follows: Preclassic, 1200 BC–AD 100; Classic, AD 100–600; Epiclassic/Late Classic, AD 600–900; Postclassic, AD 900–1500. (**b**) Weak positive correlation between collectivity and population ($r = 0.28$, $p = 0.95$). (**c**) Moderate to strong positive correlation between collectivity and apogee ($r = 0.59$, $p = 0.95$).

Zapotes and Mayapan have relatively high scores for collectivity, while highland centers such as Cacaxtla and Cerro Jazmín do not. These examples underscore historical variability for each particular environmental context, city, or regional history. We necessarily gloss over a discussion of this variation here to evaluate broader trends that are visible when we consider degrees of collectivity in an aggregate sense.

Results and Discussion

With the above caveats in mind, we have discovered patterns that align with models that contrast the properties of more as opposed to less collective formations (Blanton and Fargher 2008, 2016; Acemoglu and Robinson 2012). The three key attributes that we coded tend to co-occur, so that most (21 of 26) cases cluster at one or the other end of the continuum (either 0–0.5 or 2.5–3). Collectively oriented cities in pre-Hispanic Mesoamerica had longer apogees and larger maximal populations that support the proposed relationship between size/growth and collectivity (see Carballo et al. 2014, p. 114). Cities in the sample with collectivity scores of 2 or higher had a mean population of 49,821 (median = 30,000) and a mean apogee of 525 years (median = 550); those with collectivity scores of 1 or lower had a mean population of 18,900 (median = 12,500) and a mean apogee of 311 years (median = 300). Cumulatively, more collective urban centers in Mesoamerica were more than twice as large in population and endured 55–60% longer than the less collectively organized settlements in the sample.

Correlations are positive when both population (Fig. 2b) and apogee (Fig. 2c) are plotted against the collectivity score—again indicating that collective settlements were larger and more durable—but the correlation between collective formations and durability is stronger. Of the 23 cases with population data, there is a weak positive correlation ($r = 0.28$, $p = 0.95$) with collectivity score; of the 22 cases with apogee data, there is a moderate to strong positive correlation ($r = 0.59$, $p = 0.95$) with the collectivity score. We note, however, that variance is high, and not all collective settlements were large or long-lived. Thus, the nature of the specific challenges and perturbations faced in particular contexts would seem to be relevant. The results also indicate that the largest collective cases may have been somewhat less stable than midsized ones, perhaps due to oversized political ambitions and rapid expansionism, which potentially could outstrip extant social contracts and institutions. Another consideration is that the early centers in Mesoamerica tended to be more collective in organization compared to the later examples (Fig. 2a; Table 3). El Mirador, an early lowland Maya city that was not included in our sample due to an absence of explicit demographic estimates, also would fit this pattern. The cyclical pulses of urbanization and state formation observable between the El Mirador and Calakmul regions (Marcus 2012) further demonstrate the fluidity in collectivity that could operate in a single sphere of cultural interaction.

Although we recognize that these historical shifts within cities, polities, and regions are important, we suspect that the broader pattern we have detected underscores that more collective cases from Mesoamerica exhibited generally greater sustainability to the sorts of perturbations that pre-Hispanic peoples in this part of the world faced most often, namely, periodicities in production related to adequate land and water for agriculture (i.e., droughts, inundations, soil erosion) and cultural factors (i.e., warfare, shifting exchange networks). These findings dovetail a related cross-cultural analysis (Peregrine 2017) of cases from across the pre-Hispanic Americas in which societies with greater political participation tended to be more durable. Anthropologists and ecologists (e.g., Wilken 1987; Eakin 2006) have documented variability in resource management strategies that could be applicable to the more in-depth evaluation of this hypothesis using cases from the archaeological record where agricultural regimes, paleoclimatic reconstructions, and other possible perturbations are well documented. Examples might involve the construction and maintenance of small-scale hydraulic works, residential and agricultural terracing, communal systems of land tenure, intensive household multicrafting, and commoner participation in exchange networks and markets (Carballo 2016, pp. 22–36). Currently, however, archaeological cases from Mesoamerica with fine-grained data that speak to these diverse strategies of resource management are the exception rather than the rule.

Our comparative analysis of pre-Hispanic Mesoamerican urban centers provides an empirical first step in supporting the proposition that the governance of these settlements varied and more than half were not despotically ruled. It opens a new line of inquiry that we think requires further study: the sociopolitical ramifications of there being none of the major military or transportation bottlenecks in Mesoamerica that historians of early Eurasian (and other) societies identify as important mechanisms in driving social change (Turchin 2003; Morris 2010; Earle 2011; Boix 2015). As Mesoamerican technological evolution unfolded, there was no centralizing impact from the monopolization of bronze weaponry through control of scarce tin deposits nor "democratizing" or "decentralizing" effects of the adoption of more widely available iron. Likewise, in Mesoamerica there was never a stark inequality in military and transportation technologies that developed in Eurasia with the chariot, serious naval capabilities, or fortified palace keeps. In Mesoamerica, military might came through the control of large infantries using weapons made primarily from widely available stone—all of which underpin generally more balanced political relations as compared to Eurasian contexts. Of course, in all areas of the world, depending on the specific ways that power and governance were financed and distributed, humans have coalesced in both more and less collectively organized political formations (Blanton and Fargher 2008, 2016).

A further finding was that the cities in the sample that had more collective forms of governance and resource management were somewhat larger and more durable than the less collective systems whose political financing was derived primarily from trade, war booty, or the control of spot resources along with individualized rulership based on supernatural sanctioning. The latter form of organization likely placed less collective systems at greater risk when long-distance alliances vacillated and exchange networks changed or during other ecological and cultural perturbations. Although relative environmental risk may be an important variable in the propensity for collective governance and social institutions (e.g., more precocious leadership systems may have developed in less risky environments), it is clear that risk cannot explain all the variability, because we see the historical fluctuation between more and less collective systems in the same environment and even synchronic variability within subregions of Mesoamerica. For these reasons we emphasize the role of institutions, as framed by a broad cross-disciplinary theory of collective action, as a basis to generate more robust comparative models for communal-resource management and cultural sustainability.

Acknowledgments We thank Ludomir Lozny and Thomas McGovern for their editorial leadership, which has culminated with the publication of this chapter. Christopher Pool, Peter Peregrine, Linda Nicholas, Daniel Finkelstein, and Michael E. Smith provided highly constructive comments to help us improve the manuscript. Pool also generously provided unpublished data. All misrepresentations of the cases in the study remain our own. An earlier version of this manuscript was presented in a 2013 session at the American Anthropological Association meeting.

References

Acemoglu, D., & Robinson, J. A. (2012). *Why nations fail*. New York: Crown.
Adams, R. M. C. (1966). *The evolution of urban society*. Chicago: Aldine.
Adger, W. N. (2003). Social capital, collective action, and adaptation in climate change. *Economic Geography, 79*, 387–404.
Ahlquist, J. L., & Levi, M. (2011). Leadership: What it means, what it does, and what we want to know about it. *Annual Review of Political Science, 14*, 1–24.
Arieta Baizabal, V. (2013). *Densidad poblacional olmeca y sus implicaciones en el sitio arqueológico de San Lorenzo, Veracruz*. PhD dissertation, Universidad Nacional Autónoma de México, Mexico City.
Armillas, P. (1951). Tecnología, formaciones socio-económicas, y religión en Mesoamérica. In S. Tax (Ed.), *The civilizations of ancient America, twenty-ninth international congress of Americanists* (pp. 19–30). Chicago: University of Chicago Press.
Baker, J. L. (1998). The state and wetland agriculture in Mesoamerica. *Culture & Agriculture, 20*, 78–86.
Barlow, R. H. (1949). *The extent of the empire of the Culhua Mexica*. Ibero-Americana 28. Berkeley, CA: University of California Press.
Barnhart, E. L. (2008). Palenque: Urban city of the ancient Maya. In A. G. Mastache, R. H. Cobean, Á. García Cook, & K. G. Hirth (Eds.), *Urbanism in Mesoamerica* (Vol. 2, pp. 165–195). Mexico City: Instituto Nacional de Antropología e Historia.
Berdan, F. F. (1977). Distributive mechanisms in the Aztec economy. In R. H. Halperin & J. Dow (Eds.), *Peasant livelihood: Studies in economic anthropology and cultural ecology* (pp. 91–101). New York: St. Martin's Press.
Berdan, F. F. (1985). Markets in the economy of ancient Mexico. In S. Plattner (Ed.), *Markets and marketing* (pp. 339–367). Lanham, MD: University Press of America.
Blanton, R. E. (1978). *Monte Albán: Settlement patterns at the ancient Zapotec capital*. New York: Academic Press.
Blanton, R. E. (2010). Collective action and adaptive socioecological cycles in premodern states. *Cross-Cultural Research, 44*, 41–59.
Blanton, R. E. (2012). Cities and urbanism in prehispanic Mesoamerica. In D. L. Nichols & C. A. Pool (Eds.), *The Oxford handbook of Mesoamerican archaeology* (pp. 708–725). Oxford: Oxford University Press.

Blanton, R., & Fargher, L. (2008). *Collective action in the formation of pre-modern states.* New York: Springer.

Blanton, R., & Fargher, L. (2011). The collective logic of pre-modern cities. *World Archaeology, 43*, 505–522.

Blanton, R. E., & Fargher, L. F. (2016). *How humans cooperate: Confronting the challenges of collective action.* Boulder, CO: University Press of Colorado.

Blanton, R. E., Feinman, G. M., Kowalewski, S. A., & Peregrine, P. N. (1996). A dual-processual theory for the evolution of Mesoamerican civilization. *Current Anthropology, 37*, 1–14.

Boettiger, C., & Hastings, A. (2013). From patterns to predictions. *Nature, 493*, 157–158.

Boix, C. (2015). *Political order and inequality: Their foundations and their consequences for human welfare.* New York: Cambridge University Press.

Broms, R. (2015). Putting up or shutting up: On the individual-level relationship between tax-paying and political interest in a developmental context. *Journal of Development Studies, 51*, 93–109.

Butzer, K. W. (2012). Collapse, environment, and society. *Proceedings of the National Academy of Sciences USA, 109*, 3632–3639.

Calnek, E. (2003). Tenochtitlan-Tlatelolco: The natural history of a city. In W. T. Sanders, A. G. Mastache, & R. H. Cobean (Eds.), *Urbanism in Mesoamerica* (Vol. 1, pp. 149–202). Mexico City: Instituto Nacional de Antropología e Historia.

Carballo, D. M. (Ed.). (2013). *Cooperation and collective action: Archaeological perspectives.* Boulder, CO: University Press of Colorado.

Carballo, D. M. (2016). *Urbanization and religion in ancient central Mexico.* New York: Oxford University Press.

Carballo, D. M., & Feinman, G. M. (2016). Cooperation, collective action, and the archaeology of large-scale societies. *Evolutionary Anthropology, 25*, 288–296.

Carballo, D. M., Roscoe, P., & Feinman, G. M. (2014). Cooperation and collective action in the cultural evolution of complex societies. *Journal of Archaeological Method and Theory, 21*, 98–133.

Castells, M. (1978). *City, class and power.* London: Macmillan.

Chase, A. F., & Chase, D. Z. (2009). Symbolic egalitarianism and homogenized distributions in the archaeological record at Caracol, Belize: Method, theory, and complexity. *Research Reports in Belizean Archaeology, 6*, 15–24.

Chase, D. Z., & Chase, A. F. (2017). Caracol, Belize, and changing perceptions of Ancient Maya society. *Journal of Archaeological Research, 25*, 185–249.

Childe, V. G. (1942). *What happened in history.* Harmondsworth: Penguin.

Cobos, R. (2003). Ancient community form and social complexity at Chichen Itza, Yucatan. In A. G. Mastache, W. T. Sanders, & R. H. Cobean (Eds.), *Urbanism in Mesoamerica.* (Vol. 1, pp. 451–472). Mexico City: Instituto Nacional de Antropología e Historia.

Coe, M. D., & Diehl, R. A. (1981). *In the land of the Olmec.* Vol. 1 of *The archaeology of San Lorenzo Tenochtitlán.* Austin, TX: University of Texas Press.

Cowgill, G. L. (2008). An update on Teotihuacan. *Antiquity, 82*, 962–975.

Crumley, C. L. (1987). Celtic settlement before the conquest: The dialectics of landscape and power. In C. L. Crumley & W. H. Marquardt (Eds.), *Regional dynamics: Burgundian landscapes in historical perspective* (pp. 403–429). New York: Academic Press.

Culbert, T. P., Kosakowsky, L. J., Fry, R. E., & Haviland, W. A. (1990). The population of Tikal, Guatemala. In T. Patrick Culbert & D. S. Rice (Eds.), *Precolumbian population history in the Maya Lowlands* (pp. 103–122). Albuquerque, NM: University of New Mexico Press.

Cyphers, A. (2012). *Las bellas teorías y los terribles hechos: Controversias sobre los olmecas del Preclásico Inferior.* Mexico City: Instituto de Investigaciones Antropológicas, Universidad Nacional Autónoma de México.

D'Altroy, T. N., & Earle, T. K. (1985). Staple finance, wealth finance, and storage in the Inka economy. *Current Anthropology, 26*, 187–206.

Dahlin, B. H. (2009). Ahead of its time? The remarkable Early Classic Maya economy of Chunchuchmil. *Journal of Social Archaeology, 9*, 341–367.

Dubreuil, B. (2010). *Human evolution and the origins of hierarchies: The state of nature*. New York: Norton.

Eakin, H. (2006). *Weathering risk in rural Mexico: Climatic, institutional, and economic change*. Tucson, AZ: University of Arizona Press.

Earle, T. (2011). Chiefs, chieftaincies, chiefdoms, and chiefly confederacies: Power in the evolution of political systems. *Social Evolution & History, 10*, 27–54.

Fargher, L. F., Heredia Espinoza, V. Y., & Blanton, R. E. (2011). Alternative pathways to power in Late Postclassic highland Mesoamerica. *Journal of Anthropological Archaeology, 30*, 306–326.

Fash, B., Fash, W., Lane, S., Larios, R., Schele, L., Stomper, J., & Stuart, D. (1992). Investigations of a classic Maya Council house in Copán, Honduras. *Journal of Field Archaeology, 19*, 419–442.

Fash, W. L. (2002). Religion and human agency in ancient Maya history: Tales from the hieroglyphic stairway. *Cambridge Archaeological Journal, 12*, 5–19.

Fash, W. L. (2008). Ideology and exchange in the evolution of a pluri-ethnic city on the eastern frontier of Mesoamerica. In A. G. Mastache, R. H. Cobean, Á. García Cook, & K. G. Hirth (Eds.), *Urbanism in Mesoamerica* (Vol. 2, pp. 197–226). Mexico City: Instituto Nacional de Antropología e Historia.

Feinman, G. M. (1995). The emergence of inequality: A focus on strategies and processes. In T. D. Price & G. M. Feinman (Eds.), *Foundations of social inequality* (pp. 255–279). New York: Plenum Press.

Feinman, G. M. (1999). Rethinking our assumptions: Economic specialization at the household scale in ancient Ejutla, Oaxaca, Mexico. In J. M. Skibo & G. M. Feinman (Eds.), *Pottery and people: A dynamic interaction* (pp. 81–98). Salt Lake City, UT: University of Utah Press.

Feinman, G. M. (2001). Mesoamerican political complexity: The corporate–network dimension. In J. Haas (Ed.), *From leaders to rulers* (pp. 151–175). New York: Kluwer/Plenum Press.

Feinman, G. M. (2010). A dual-processual perspective on the power and inequality in the contemporary United States: Framing political economy for the present and the past. In T. D. Price & G. M. Feinman (Eds.), *Pathways to power: New perspectives on the emergence of social inequality* (pp. 255–288). New York: Springer.

Feinman, G. M. (2013). The emergence of social complexity: Why more than population size matters. In D. M. Carballo (Ed.), *Cooperation and collective action: Archaeological perspectives* (pp. 35–56). Boulder, CO: University Press of Colorado.

Feinman, G. M. (2018). The governance and leadership of prehispanic Mesoamerican polities: New perspectives and comparative implications. *Cliodynamics: The Journal of Quantitative History and Cultural Evolution, 9*(2), 1–39. https://escholarship.org/uc/irows_cliodynamics

Feinman, G. M., & Garraty, C. P. (2010). Preindustrial markets and marketing: Archaeological perspectives. *Annual Review of Anthropology, 39*, 331–344.

Feinman, G. M., & Nicholas, L. M. (2012). The late prehispanic economy of the valley of Oaxaca, Mexico: Weaving threads from data, theory, and subsequent history. *Research in Economic Anthropology, 32*, 225–258.

Feinman, G. M., & Nicholas, L. M. (2016a). Framing the rise and variability of past complex societies. In L. F. Fargher & V. Y. Heredia Espinoza (Eds.), *Alternative pathways to complexity* (pp. 271–289). Boulder, CO: University Press of Colorado.

Feinman, G. M., & Nicholas, L. M. (2016b). After Monte Albán in the Central Valleys of Oaxaca: A reassessment. In R. K. Faulseit (Ed.), *Beyond collapse: Archaeological perspectives on resilience, revitalization, and transformations in complex societies* (pp. 43–69). Carbondale, IL: Southern Illinois University Press.

Folan, W. J., Fletcher, L. A., Hau, J. M., Moreles L., A., Domínguez C., M., González H., R., et al. (2008). Calakmul, Campeche, Mexico: Patterns representative of its urban capital and regional state. In A. G. Mastache, R. H. Cobean, Á. García Cook, & K. G. Hirth (Eds.), *Urbanism in Mesoamerica* (Vol. 2, pp. 285–347). Mexico City: Instituto Nacional de Antropología e Historia.

Fuentes, A. (2004). It's not all sex and violence: Integrated anthropology and the role of cooperation and social complexity in human evolution. *American Anthropologist, 106*, 710–718.

García Cook, Á. (2003). Cantona: The city. In A. G. Mastache, W. T. Sanders, & R. H. Cobean (Eds.), *Urbanism in Mesoamerica* (Vol. 1, pp. 311–343). Mexico City: Instituto Nacional de Antropología e Historia.

Garraty, C. P., & Stark, B. L. (Eds.). (2010). *Archaeological approaches to market exchange in ancient societies*. Boulder, CO: University Press of Colorado.

Gillespie, S. D. (1993). Power, pathways, and appropriations in Mesoamerican art. In D. S. Whitten & N. E. Whitten Jr. (Eds.), *Imagery and creativity: Ethnoaesthetics and art worlds in the Americas* (pp. 67–107). Tucson, AZ: University of Arizona Press.

Grant, J. (2004). Sustainable urbanism in historical perspective. In A. Sorensen, P. J. Marcutullio, & J. Grant (Eds.), *Towards sustainable cities: East Asian, North American, and European perspectives on managing urban regions* (pp. 24–37). Burlington, VT: Ashgate.

Grove, D. C. (Ed.). (1987). *Ancient Chalcatzingo*. Austin, TX: University of Texas Press.

Hassig, R. (1992). *War and society in ancient Mesoamerica*. Berkeley, CA: University of California Press.

Haviland, W. A. (2008). Tikal, Guatemala: A Maya way to urbanism. In A. G. Mastache, R. H. Cobean, Á. García Cook, & K. G. Hirth (Eds.), *Urbanism in Mesoamerica* (Vol. 2, pp. 259–283). Mexico City: Instituto Nacional de Antropología e Historia.

Healan, D. M. (2012). The archaeology of Tula, Hidalgo, Mexico. *Journal of Archaeological Research, 20*, 53–115.

Hedström, P., & Swedberg, R. (1996). Social mechanisms. *Acta Sociologica, 39*, 281–308.

Hirth, K. G. (2003). *Ancient urbanism at Xochicalco: The evolution and organization of a pre-Hispanic society*. Salt Lake City, UT: University of Utah Press.

Hirth, K. G. (Ed.). (2009). *Housework: Craft production and domestic economy in ancient Mesoamerica*. Archeological Papers 19. Washington, DC: American Anthropological Association.

Hirth, K. G., & Pillsbury, J. (Eds.). (2013). *Merchants, markets, and exchange in the pre-Columbian world*. Washington, DC: Dumbarton Oaks Research Library and Collection.

Joyce, A. A., Workinger, A. G., Hamann, B., Kroefges, P., Oland, M., & King, S. M. (2004). Lord 8 Deer 'Jaguar Claw' and the land of the sky: The archaeology and history of Tututepec. *Latin American Antiquity, 15*, 273–297.

Klinenberg, E. (2018). *Palaces for the people*. New York: Crown.

Kowalewski, S. A. (2012). A theory of the ancient Mesoamerican economy. *Research in Economic Anthropology, 32*, 187–224.

Levi, M. (1988). *Of rule and revenue*. Berkeley, CA: University of California Press.

Levine, M. N. (2017). Tututepec: A Mixtec imperial capital in southern Oaxaca. In D. L. Nichols & E. Rodríguez-Alegría (Eds.), *The Oxford handbook of the Aztecs* (pp. 509–521). New York: Oxford University Press.

Magnoni, A., Ardren, T., Hutson, S. R., & Dahlin, B. H. (2012). Living in the city: Settlement patterns and the urban experience at Classic period Chunchucmil, Yucatan, Mexico. *Ancient Mesoamerica, 23*, 313–343.

Marcus, J. (2012). Maya political cycling and the story of the Kaan polity. In G. E. Braswell (Ed.), *The ancient Maya of Mexico: Interpreting the past of the northern Maya Lowlands* (pp. 88–114). Sheffield: Equinox Publishing.

Marx, K. (1971). *A contribution to the critique of political economy*. London: Lawrence and Wishart.

Mastache, A. G., & Cobean, R. H. (2003). Urbanism at Tula. In A. G. Mastache, W. T. Sanders, & R. H. Cobean (Eds.), *Urbanism in Mesoamerica* (Vol. 1, pp. 217–255). Mexico City: Instituto Nacional de Antropología e Historia.

Mead, M. (Ed.). (1937). *Cooperation and competition among primitive peoples.* New York: McGraw-Hill Book Company.

Melis, A. P., & Semmann, D. (2010). How is human cooperation different? *Philosophical Transactions of the Royal Society B, 365,* 2663–2674.

Middleton, G. (2012). Nothing lasts forever: Environmental discourses on the collapse of past societies. *Journal of Archaeological Research, 20,* 257–307.

Moore, M. (2004). Revenues, state formation, and the quality of governance in developing countries. *International Political Science Review, 25,* 297–319.

Morris, I. (2010). *Why the west rules—For now: The patterns of history, and what they reveal about the future.* New York: Picador.

Nassaney, M. S., & Sassaman, K. E. (1995). Introduction: Understanding native American interactions. In M. S. Nassaney & K. E. Sassaman (Eds.), *Native American interactions: Multiscalar analyses and interpretations in the Eastern Woodlands* (pp. xix–xxxviii). Knoxville, TN: University of Tennessee Press.

Offner, J. (1981a). On the inapplicability of 'oriental despotism' and the Asiatic mode of production to the Aztecs of Texcoco. *American Antiquity, 46,* 43–61.

Offner, J. (1981b). On Carrasco's use of "first principles." *American Antiquity, 46,* 69–74.

Olson, M. (1965). *The logic of collective action: Public goods and the theory of groups.* Cambridge, MA: Harvard University Press.

Palerm, Á., & Wolf, E. R. (1957). Ecological potential and cultural development in Mesoamerica. *Pan American Union Social Science Monograph, 3,* 1–37.

Palerm, J. V. (2017). The greatest generation: Apropos of Sidney Mintz. *American Ethnologist, 44,* 414–424.

Pastrana, A., & Ramírez, F. (2012). *Reinterpretando Cuicuilco.* Paper presented at the 77th Annual Meeting of the Society of American Archaeology, Memphis.

Peraza Lope, C., Masson, M. A., Hare, T. S., & Delgado Kú, P. C. (2006). The chronology of Mayapan: New radiocarbon evidence. *Ancient Mesoamerica, 17,* 153–175.

Peregrine, P. N. (2017). Political participation and long-term resilience in pre-Columbian societies. *Disaster Prevention and Management: An International Journal, 26,* 314–329.

Pérez, V., Anderson, K. C., & Neff, M. K. (2011). The Cerro Jazmín archaeological project: Investigating prehispanic urbanism and its environmental impact in the Mixteca Alta, Oaxaca. Mexico. *Journal of Field Archaeology, 36,* 83–99.

Plunket, P., & Uruñuela, G. (2005). Recent research in Puebla prehistory. *Journal of Archaeological Research, 13,* 89–127.

Plunket, P., & Uruñuela, G. (2012). Where east meets west: The Formative in Mexico's Central Highlands. *Journal of Archaeological Research, 20,* 1–51.

Pohl, J. M. D. (2003). Creation stories, hero cults, and alliance building: Confederacies of central and southern Mexico. In M. E. Smith & F. F. Berdan (Eds.), *The Postclassic Mesoamerican world* (pp. 61–66). Salt Lake City, UT: University of Utah Press.

Polanyi, K., Arensberg, C., & Pearson, H. (Eds.). (1957). *Trade and market in early empires.* Glencoe, IL: Free Press.

Pool, C. A. (2010). Stone monuments and earthen mounds: Polity and placemaking at Tres Zapotes, Veracruz, Mexico. In J. E. Clark, J. Guernsey, & B. Arroyo (Eds.), *The place of stone monuments: Context, use, and meaning in Mesoamerica's Preclassic transition* (pp. 97–126). Washington, DC: Dumbarton Oaks Research Library and Collection.

Pool, C. A., & Loughlin, M. L. (2015). *Early urbanization in the Formative Gulf Lowlands, Mexico.* Paper presented at the Early Mesoamerican Urbanism Conference, Antigua, Guatemala.

Pool, C. A., & Loughlin, M. L. (2016). Tres Zapotes: The evolution of a resilient polity in the Olmec heartland of Mexico. In R. K. Faulseit (Ed.), *Beyond collapse: Archaeological perspectives on resilience, revitalization, and transformation in complex societies* (pp. 287–312). Carbondale, IL: Southern Illinois University Press.

Rust, W. F. (1992). New ceremonial and settlement evidence at La Venta, and its relation to Preclassic Maya cultures. In E. C. Danien & R. J. Sharer (Eds.), *New theories on the ancient*

Maya (pp. 123–129). University Museum Monograph 77. Philadelphia, PA: University Museum, University of Pennsylvania.
Rust, W. F. (2008). *A settlement survey of La Venta, Tabasco, Mexico*. PhD dissertation, University of Pennsylvania, Philadelphia, PA.
Sanders, W. T., & Price, B. J. (1968). *Mesoamerica: The evolution of a civilization*. New York: Random House.
Serra Puche, C. M. (2012). *Xochitécatl* (2nd ed.). Tlaxcala, Mexico: Instituto de la Cultura.
Serra Puche, C. M., & Lazcano, J. C. (2008). Urban configuration at Cacaxtla-Xochitecatl. In A. G. Mastache, R. H. Cobean, Á. García Cook, & K. G. Hirth (Eds.), *Urbanism in Mesoamerica* (Vol. 2, pp. 133–164). Mexico City: Instituto Nacional de Antropología.
Serra Puche, C. M., & Lazcano, J. C. (2011). *Vida cotidiana, Xochitécatl-Cacaxtla: Días, años, milenios*. Mexico City: Instituto de Investigaciones Antropológicas, Universidad Nacional Autónoma de México.
Smith, M. E. (2008). *Aztec city-state capitals*. Gainesville, FL: University Press of Florida.
Smith, M. E. (2015). The Aztec empire. In A. Monson & W. Scheidel (Eds.), *Fiscal regimes and the political economy of premodern states* (pp. 71–114). New York: Cambridge University Press.
Smith, M. L. (2005). Networks, territories, and the cartography of ancient states. *Annals of the Association of American Geographers, 95*, 832–849.
Sterelny, K. (2013). Cooperation in a complex world: The role of proximate factors in ultimate explanations. *Biological Theory, 7*, 358–367.
Steward, J. H. (1949). Cultural causality and law: A trial formulation of the development of early civilizations. *American Anthropologist, 51*, 1–27.
Tourtellot, G. (1990). Population estimates for Preclassic and Classic Seibal, Peten. In T. P. Culbert & D. S. Rice (Eds.), *Precolumbian population history in the Maya Lowlands* (pp. 83–102). Albuquerque, NM: University of New Mexico Press.
Trigger, B. G. (1989). *A history of archaeological thought*. New York: Cambridge University Press.
Trigger, B. G. (2003). *Understanding early civilizations*. New York: Cambridge University Press.
Turchin, P. (2003). *Historical dynamics: Why states rise and fall*. Princeton, NJ: Princeton University Press.
Turner II, B. L. (1990). Population reconstruction for the central Maya Lowlands: 1000 B.C. to A.D. 1500. In T. P. Culbert & D. S. Rice (Eds.), *Precolumbian population history in the Maya Lowlands* (pp. 301–324). Albuquerque, NM: University of New Mexico Press.
Uruñuela, G., Plunket, P., & Robles, A. (2009). Cholula: Art and architecture of an archetypal city. In W. L. Fash & L. López Luján (Eds.), *The art of urbanism: How Mesoamerican kingdoms represented themselves in architecture and imagery* (pp. 135–171). Washington, DC: Dumbarton Oaks Research Library and Collection.
Wade, L. (2017). Unearthing democracy's roots. *Science, 355*, 1114–1118.
Webster, D. (2008). The regional setting of the 8th century Copán polity: Implications for Maya urbanism. In A. G. Mastache, R. H. Cobean, Á. García Cook, & K. G. Hirth (Eds.), *Urbanism in Mesoamerica* (Vol. 2, pp. 227–258). Mexico City: Instituto Nacional de Antropología e Historia.
Wilken, G. C. (1987). *Good farmers: Traditional agricultural resource management in Mexico and Central America*. Berkeley, CA: University of California Press.
Wittfogel, K. (1957). *Oriental despotism*. New Haven, CT: Yale University Press.
Wolf, E. R. (Ed.). (1976). *The Valley of Mexico: Studies in pre-Hispanic ecology and society*. Albuquerque, NM: University of New Mexico Press.
Wolf, E. R. (1982). *Europe and the people without history*. Berkeley, CA: University of California Press.
Wolf, E. R. (1994). Explaining Mesoamerica. *Social Anthropology, 2*, 1–17.
Wright, H. T. (1989). Rise of civilizations: Mesopotamia to Mesoamerica. *Archaeology, 42*(1), 46–48, 96–100.

The Native California Commons: Ethnographic and Archaeological Perspectives on Land Control, Resource Use, and Management

Terry L. Jones and Brian F. Codding

California is a culturally distinctive region of the New World where the hunting and gathering lifeway persisted for 13,500 years with no reliance on domesticated foods until after historic contact. Exceptions were the widespread cultivation of tobacco and some experimentation with Southwestern crops around the southeastern edges of the modern state (Kroeber 1925). A case has been made rightfully that the absence of agriculture was perhaps less significant than generally assumed (Bean and Lawton 1976) since the acorn-reliant economies that distinguish Native California provided a base for large, sedentary communities with lineal kinship organization, and some political structures more typical of farming-based societies. Still, the relationship between these hunting, fishing, and collecting adaptations to the environment was different from that of indigenous agriculturalists inasmuch as the staple food sources were acquired through resource extraction rather than cultivation. In most cases, these resources clearly fit the definition of a commons, or rather, common-pool resources: those that provide a finite quantity of food over some period so that each individual's use limits the amount available to others (Ostrom 2002; Ostrom et al. 1994). This then opens resources to the tragedy of the commons: the rational decision is for each individual to maximize their own gain, but with everyone reaching that conclusion, the commons itself becomes harvested unsustainably to everyone's loss (Hardin 1968).

California provides a particularly important example of hunter-gatherer use of the commons because it has two fairly robust sources of information on resource acquisition, land control, and ecology: the ethnographic record and a heavily

---

T. L. Jones (✉)
Department of Social Sciences, California Polytechnic State University, San Luis Obispo, CA, USA
e-mail: tljones@calpoly.edu

B. F. Codding
Department of Anthropology, University of Utah, Salt Lake City, UT, USA

investigated archaeological past (Moratto 1984; Jones and Klar 2007). The ethnographic record provides a synchronic account of the basic resources used by native peoples, associated technologies, and the sociopolitical structures that organized exploitation. Ethnographic interpretations in recent decades have tended to emphasize elements of management and stewardship of the commons (e.g., Shipek 1989, 1993; Blackburn and Anderson 1993; Anderson 2005; Lightfoot and Parrish 2009) by indigenous cultures. The deep diachronic perspective of archaeology provides a test for interpretations of these elements, corroborating some cases of long-standing, culturally mediated, sustainable use of resources (e.g., salmon in the Northwest), but in others, it illuminates the cumulative impacts from self-interested, short-term decision-making, consistent with a tragedy of the commons (e.g., the flightless duck). The majority of ecological cases, however, show resource exploitation strategies that were non-conservation oriented but nonetheless had minimal or at best equivocal effects on vitality and longevity of faunal populations.

Ethnographic California

The most widely accepted estimate for California's indigenous population at the time of the establishment of the first Spanish Mission in 1769 is 340,000 (Baumhoff 1963) and possibly more. California was also marked by a significant degree of cultural diversity—reflected by a complex linguistic mosaic—and relatively small-scale political organization. The speakers of no fewer than 78 distinct languages, representing 10 linguistic families (Golla 2011) (Fig. 1), resided in sedentary and semisedentary villages organized into 400–500 micro-tribes or "tribelets," each with populations between 200 and 600 individuals. The sociopolitical structure and resource base of these small organizations varied across the state (Milliken 2010).

History of Research

The first accounts of Native Californians were written by Spanish and English seafarers between the sixteenth and nineteenth centuries who recorded only the most cursory information on coastal societies with whom they had very brief encounters. Beginning in 1769 with the start of Spanish colonization, written accounts by mission padres included more detailed information on population numbers and, in some cases, village names and locations. The Russians who built an outpost at Fort Ross in northern California (1812–1842) recorded observations of Native people as well. These accounts were followed by harsher, more racist descriptions from the American era after 1846 (Heizer and Almquist 1971) especially during the Gold Rush when Native Californians were trying to survive what were essentially attempts at genocide (Castillo 1978; Norton 1979; Lindsay 2012).

The formal record of Native Californian culture only began to be collected systematically in 1901 when Alfred Kroeber initiated salvage ethnography after

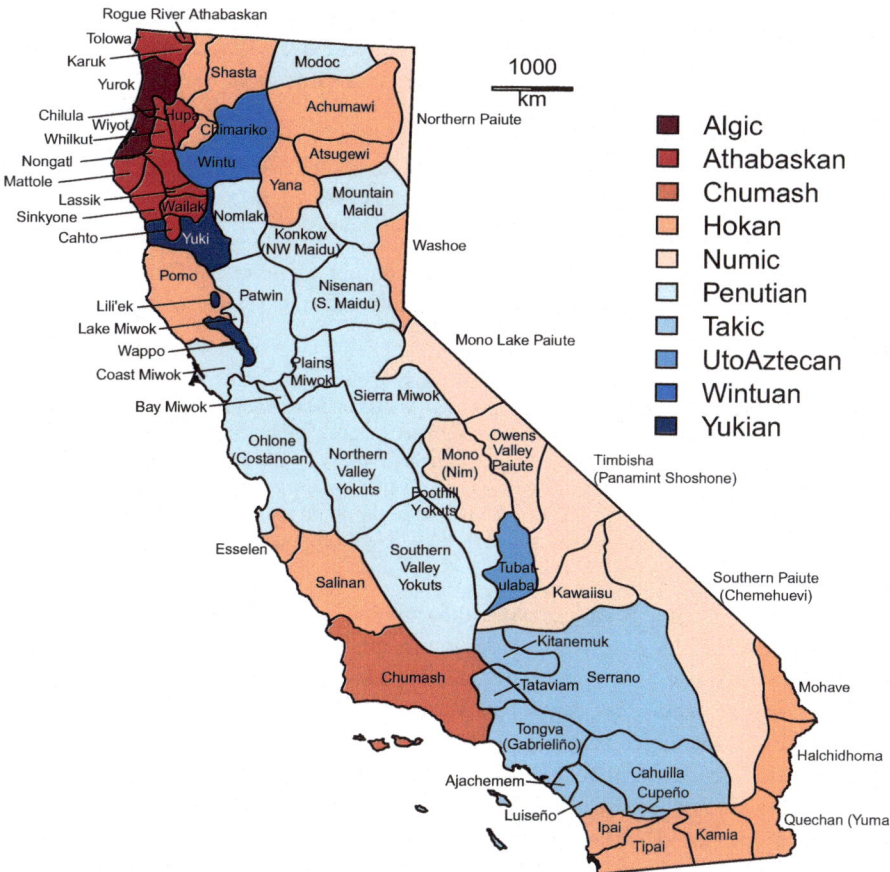

Fig. 1 Language territories of indigenous California

indigenous populations had suffered 130 years of cultural disruption, population decline, acculturation, and settlement reshuffling. The salvage ethnography effort culminated in a major summarizing publication by Heizer (1978) (also Jorgensen 1980) after which time anthropological research became more politically conscious. The salvage ethnographers tended to simply list the floral and faunal species exploited by Native people along with the technologies used to capture and collect them. Ethnographies from the 1970s onward, however, began to emphasize cultural knowledge about the distribution and edibility of species along with notions of environmental stewardship and ecological balance as part of broader attempts to advocate for California Indians (see Margolin 1978). The new generation of ethnographers also began to provide much more detail on the resources exploited by Native peoples (e.g., Bean 1972, 1978) and associated them with a bounteous precontact California that has suffered significantly following the arrival of Euro-Americans (e.g., Shipek 1978, p. 610). In the last two decades, these efforts have advanced the idea that indigenous Californians actively managed the California landscape to increase its productivity (Shipek 1989; Anderson 1993, 2005; Lightfoot and

Parrish 2009), particularly through controlled burning (Levy 1978; Stewart 2002; Lightfoot and Lopez 2013). From this perspective, Native Californians were not merely the beneficiaries of a rich environment but architects of it.

The Hunting and Gathering Resource Base

Since at least 1925 it has been recognized that hunter-gatherers in California had at their disposable a rich and almost unthinkably diverse resource base. Kroeber described it thusly:

> The food resources of California were bountiful in their variety rather than in their overwhelming abundance...If one supply failed, there were hundreds of others to fall back upon. If a drought withered the corn shoots, if the buffalo unaccountably shifted, or if the salmon failed to run, the very existence of people in other regions was shaken to its foundations. But the manifold distribution of available food in California and the working out of corresponding means of reclaiming them prevented a failure of the acorn crop from producing similar effects. It might produce short rations and racking hunger, but scarcely starvation. (Kroeber 1925, p. 524)

The number of resources available to California Indians was indeed staggering with hundreds of edible plants, terrestrial mammals, marine mammals, birds, and insects. Mead (2014) lists over 1300 species of plants used by Native Californians for food, medicine, shelter, and other purposes. Variation in the spatial and seasonal availability of these resources was a key factor in the control and exploitation of the commons. Kroeber's point that there were untold options available to indigenous people in the face of localized shortages is not an insignificant one, but there were nonetheless perhaps 20–30 resources upon which Native California was dependent. Many of these have been carefully evaluated in recent decades in terms of their distribution and potential food value vis-à-vis caloric yields versus processing costs (e.g., Bettinger et al. 1997).

Acorns

Acorns were the defining resource of Native California; their key traits and the manner in which they were exploited have been studied extensively (e.g., Bean and Saubel 1961; Baumhoff 1963; Gifford 1971; Basgall 1987; Bettinger and Wohlgemuth 2006; Lightfoot and Parrish 2009; Wohlgemuth 2004, 2010; Bettinger 2015). Eight main species of oaks were exploited, and vegetation dominated by one or more of these species was present throughout the state generally between near sea level and intermediate elevations. However, distribution of oaks was not uniform, with groves of the most productive species distributed patchily. Acorns contain high amounts of tannic acid; nuts were rendered into a nontoxic, highly nutritious food by grinding them with mortar and pestle and leaching the tannins out with water (Bettinger and Wohlgemuth 2006). Converting them to a useful food thus required discovery of a means to rid them of the tannic acid and willingness to devote a significant amount of labor to process them. Basgall (1987) was the first to highlight the labor-intensive character of the acorn resource, while Bettinger (2015) has more recently emphasized the need to store acorns—much like that agricultural crops. Acorns were available only in the fall when in some parts of California they occurred in massive quantities. Bettinger (2015) further emphasizes that the acorn is a "back-loaded" with significant storage and processing costs *after* harvest. Acorns were stored in large, highly visible granaries within villages, providing a reliable food source through the winter and spring. These stores were valuable commodities worthy of both theft and protection (Bettinger 2015).

Other Plant Foods

While acorns were the primary staple, a multitude of other plant foods was also relied upon, many of which provided higher caloric returns. These include nontoxic nuts such as from pines (Whelan et al. 2013) and native walnuts, small-seeded annuals and grasses like chia and native barley, and terrestrial roots such as brodiaea and blue dicks (Bettinger and Wohlgemuth 2006; Gill 2013, 2015, 2016). While nuts became available in the fall in California, small seeds tend to ripen in the spring, and terrestrial roots were a late winter-early summer resource. In arid Southern California, agave, screwbeans, and pinyon pine nuts were of equal importance to acorns; screwbeans and pinyon nuts were stored in large quantities in specialized granaries (Bettinger and Wohlgemuth 2006). Much like acorns, these plant resources were distributed throughout most of Southeastern California.

Terrestrial Mammals

Varied topography and a diverse vegetation mosaic provided Native California with a wide array of animal resources (Heizer 1978; Hildebrandt and Carpenter 2006). Much like acorns, deer were a common prey throughout the state and were prominent in dietary profiles in many areas especially Central California. They were pursued by ambush and stalking with bow and arrow and deer-head mask decoys (Baumhoff 1978). Cottontail and jack rabbits were also exploited statewide but were more abundant in the oak and chaparral habitat of Central California. Tule elk were the largest game animal in Central California and were available in large numbers in some areas. Roosevelt elk were important in the northwest and bighorn sheep and pronghorn in the southeast. The larger herbivores aggregate in herds of various sizes, the precontact seasonal movements of which have been so disrupted in historic times that their patterns are no longer clear. However, in the elevationally diverse areas, such as the Sierra Nevada (Fig. 2), black-tailed deer moved into the higher elevations in the summer, retreating downward in the fall. Almost certainly, such seasonal migrations brought herds of large herbivores into contact with multiple communities of Native people.

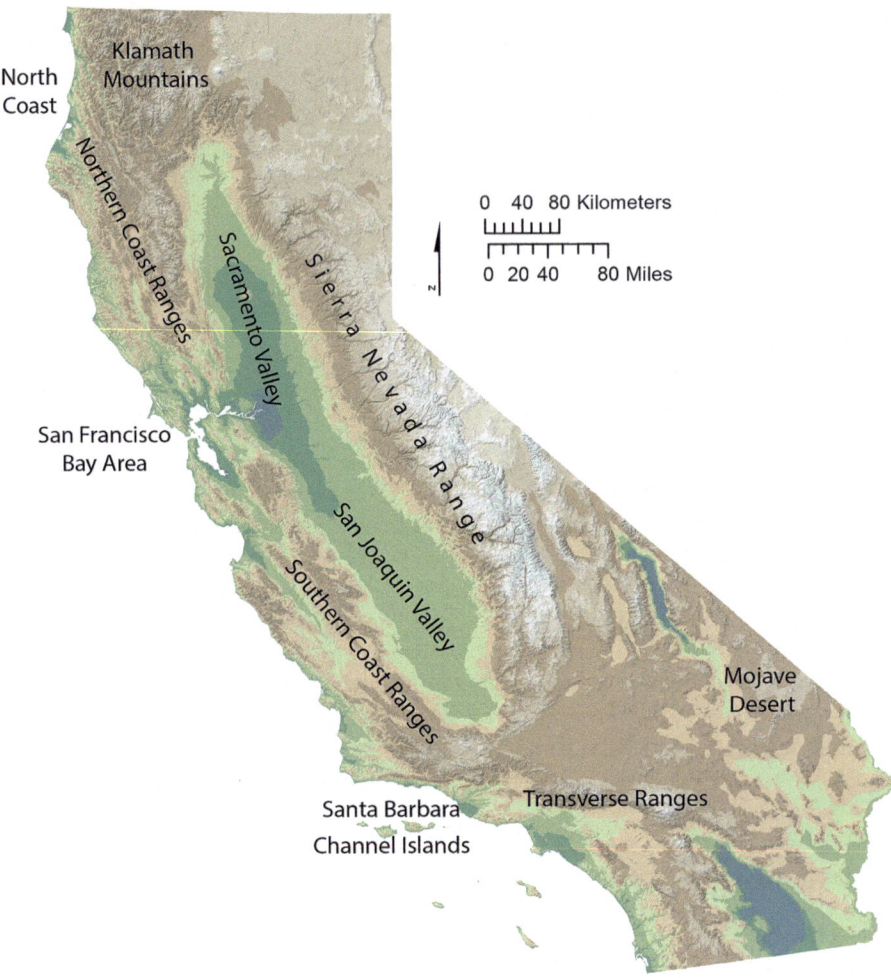

Fig. 2 Major geographic provinces and features of California

Marine Mammals

Marine mammals important to Native Californians include two types: large migratory species such as northern and southern fur seals, California sea lions, Steller sea lions, and northern elephant seals and smaller, more elusive residents that did not migrate such as harbor seals and sea otters (Hildebrandt and Jones 1992). The archaeological record suggests that elephant seals, highly visible today, were minimally present prehistorically (Rick et al. 2012), while northern fur seals were more common (Gifford-Gonzalez et al. 2005). These animals were hunted for their meat and blubber but also perhaps more importantly for their furs. Otter pelts were especially important as prestige and trade items (see, e.g., Gamble 2008). In Northwestern

California fairly specialized maritime technologies including ocean going dugout canoes and harpoons were used to exploit seals and sea lions in offshore contexts. The distances covered by the migratory breeders were substantial with species like fur seals and California sea lions moving between the Aleutian and Channel Islands. Such movements meant that these animal populations were accessible to hundreds of Native communities along the west coast of North America.

Anadromous Fish

Salmon was the defining food for northwestern groups like the Yurok and Karuk although these California groups distinguished themselves from the fishing societies to the north by combining the anadromous fishery with exploitation of acorns. Anadromous fish split their lives between the sea and rivers where they spawn. They were exploited by indigenous people along the rivers where they were extremely prolific. Larger rivers like the Klamath and Sacramento provided abundant fish along hundreds of miles during the spawning season (Baumhoff 1963, 1978; Hamilton et al. 2005). In contrast to acorns, salmon are a front-loaded resource that required abundant sophisticated equipment in the form of weirs, dip nets, and harpoons to exploit (Kroeber and Barrett 1960; Bettinger 2015; Tushingham and Christiansen 2015). These technologies were used in various combinations by large numbers of communities along the rivers who harvested salmon during the brief seasonal spawning window and dried and stored it in substantial quantities for later consumption.

Marine Fish

A tremendous quantity and diversity of marine fish was available to shoreline communities along the west coast of California. The list of species exploited is lengthy. For Southern California it was summarized by Salls (1988); for the central coast by Gobalet and Jones (1995) and Gobalet et al. (2004), and for the north by Tushingham and Christiansen (2015). The ethnographic record for the exploitation of this resource is not robust, but in most cases fishing seems to have been shore-based, using hook and line and nets. Tule balsas and/or dugouts were also used to access nearshore schooling species such as herring and sardines (Breschini and Haversat 1994). Estuaries like San Francisco Bay, Morro Bay, and Agua Hedionda were spawning areas for many species, providing a constant influx of large numbers of fish. An exception to these trends was the northern and southern Channel Islands where Chumash and Gabrielino speakers employed more sophisticated sewn-plank canoes to occasionally access pelagic species (Bernard 2004; Arnold and Bernard 2005; Gamble 2008). The islands were also the only places where marine fish was a dietary staple, supplemented not by acorns (which are minimal or nonexistent on the islands) but other insular vegetal resources (Gill 2013).

Waterfowl

In 1833, George Yount, an early American hunter and trapper, recorded the following upon encountering San Francisco Bay:

> The wild geese, & every species of water fowl darkened the surface of every bay, & frith, & upon the land, in flocks of millions, they wandered in quest of insects, & cropping the wild oats which grew there in richest abundance. When disturbed, they arose to fly, the sound of their wings was like that of distant thunder. (Camp and Yount 1923, p. 52)

California provides key stopovers along the Pacific Flyway, which is a north-south route used by birds migrating between Alaska and South America. Prime habitats for these resting places were the wetlands of the Central Valley and coastal estuaries. Waterfowl were often taken in bulk by stretching nets across flyways in tule wetlands (Levy 1978, p. 404; Olmsted and Stewart 1978, p. 228). Eggs were also harvested (Olmsted and Stewart 1978, p. 226).

Littoral Resources

Shellfish were an extremely abundant but spatially restricted resource gathered from the intertidal zone along the length of California. In estuaries like San Francisco Bay, the dominant species were clams, cockles, and oysters, the exploitation of which between ca 5000 and 200 cal BP resulted in the Bay's famous shell mounds, almost all of which are today gone or drastically altered. On the open rocky coast which dominates most of the California shoreline, mussels, abalone, limpets, gumboot chiton, and turban snails were collected. The latter, small, labor-intensive snails, are extremely abundant on the southern islands where they dominate many middens (Raab and Yatsco 1992). Abalones in the Monterey Bay area were collected, dried, and stored (Dietz and Jackson 1981). Shellfish were transported inland as food as far as 30–40 km (Hildebrandt and Levulett (1997)). Shells of clams in the north, and the purple olive in Central and Southern California, provided the material for shell bead money that, along with abalone shell ornaments, were traded widely throughout western North America (Bennyhoff and Hughes 1987; Hughes and Milliken 2007).

Controls on Resource Acquisition and the Commons

By far the single most important factor that effected the manner in which the California resource base was exploited was the existence of small, highly autonomous polities that Kroeber (1962) famously dubbed "tribelets." While the exact structure of these communities varied across the state (Milliken 2010; Bettinger 2015)—some had no formal leadership structure (e.g., the Yurok [Kroeber 19,325]), while others featured chiefdom-like hierarchies (e.g., Chumash [Arnold 1992; Gamble 2008])—they all were characterized by well-defined territories that provided resource access only to community members. Kroeber stated:

> ...all the Indians of California belonged to definite groups. These groups were characterized by a sense of cohesion: each formed a unit. People belonged to one or another. There was never doubt as to which group an individual was a member of...each group was autonomous or self-governing, in native opinion...each group claimed,. and was admitted by others, to own and use a certain territory. (Kroeber 1962, p. 29)

The population of these groups ranged from 100 to 600 people, with a total of perhaps 500–600 tribelets within Native California. Sizes ranged from 100 to 500 square miles (Kroeber 1962, p. 37). Tribelet boundaries were well known, marked, and defended (McCorkle 1978, p. 697). Intergroup violence was often precipitated by real or alleged use of resources held by another group. At a minimum, tribelet territories insured access to certain resources for group members so that intra-tribelet territory was a commons of sorts for group members only. However, within tribelets, individual families sometimes laid claim to specific trees or groves that were marked for exclusive use. Food, especially acorns, was a private, owned commodity (Bettinger 2015). Resource ownership by individuals and families was especially developed among the Yurok of Northwestern California (Kroeber 1925). Bettinger (2015) has referred to the tribelet arrangement as "orderly anarchy." The situation provided no basis for large-scale cooperative efforts of the type needed to coordinate conservation and/or management of species that ranged beyond the limits of individual territories.

Well-delineated, bounded tribelets insured access to specific sets of resources for localized groups. For example, most tribelet territories included patches of oaks, and other vegetable resources, but only some had access to resources with more restricted distribution such as salmon, marine shellfish, and fish. A case has been made that chiefly systems of redistribution acted to even out imbalances between habitats and resources (King 1976; Anderson 2005, p. 247) and that shell money functioned to assist that process (Chagnon 1970). Goods such as salt, acorns, fish, beads, and obsidian also flowed between communities in systems of long-distance conveyance (Davis 1961; Hughes and Milliken 2007). Groups could trespass on lands held by others, but not without consequence as summarized in this account by Pilling (1950) of Yokuts, or Tulares, residents of the Central Valley, making a pilgrimage to the coast at Monterey: "The Tulares came once a year and bathed in Monterey Bay and scraped their skin. They stayed about two weeks. They fought with the Carmel Indians when they came. The Tulares took back mussels and abalones" (Pilling 1950, p. 440).

Cases have been made for various activities within tribelets that enhanced resource productivity. Foremost among these is controlled burning, the positive effects of which were initially brought to the fore by Lewis (1973) who argued that Native use of fire increased the diversity and productivity of California landscapes. The robust game populations and expansive, productive oak forests and grasslands of precontact California were seen according to this new perspective as the results of thousands of years of skillful management by Native people. In reference to Lewis's work, Bean and Lawton wrote:

> Lewis has demonstrated that fire was a major factor in a system of aboriginal environmental relationships and functioned in a number of ways to increase both animal and plant resources in California...Burning the woodlands grassbelt, particularly in areas near villages, would

have concentrated game in specific locations for ready accessibility in hunting, since browse in burned-over areas would have been richer. Thus we suggest burning may have constituted a form of game management or incipient herding. (Bean and Lawton 1976, p. 39)

The likely positive effects of controlled burning have subsequently been discussed by Anderson (2005), Cuthrell et al. (2012), Lightfoot and Parrish (2009), Lightfoot and Lopez (2013), Stewart (2002), and Timbrook et al. 1982 (among others). There can be little doubt that intentionally lit fires increased the productivity of some habitats, particularly grasslands, by removing dead material and recycling nutrients (Anderson 2005, p. 265) resulting in increased seed yields. Anderson (2005, p. 264) further suggests that fire was combined with intentional sowing of some seeds, essentially as an early form of cultivation. Peri and Patterson (1993) made a case that Pomo weavers also enhanced the productivity of patches of plants useful for basketry by loosening the ground around their roots and removing weeds and rocks (also arguing for a form of "cultivation") (Peri and Patterson 1993, p. 175). We can assume that such activities tended to occur at locations owned or controlled by individuals or families within tribelets. Lightfoot and Parrish (2009) and Heizer and Elsasser (1980) emphasize the likelihood that the effects of controlled burning would have been greatest closest to villages. Ethnographic accounts further suggest that Native Californians had at least 70 different reasons for burning (Kay 1995; Lewis 1973).

Lightfoot et al. (2013) propose alternate scenarios for controlled burning programs in Native California. On the one hand, they suggest that fires were set to promote intermediate-return subsistence goals, specifically to enhance foraging efficiency and hunting success. Under this scenario, fires would be lit by individuals with little coordination among members of the broader community. An alternative that these authors favor is that anthropogenic burns were integrated within community-level resource management practices intentionally designed to enhance diversity, productivity, and predictability. They further surmise that anthropogenic burning practices that were scrupulously managed by community collectives are associated with increasing territorialism, greater defense of resource patches, secure storage facilities, and restricted access of goods to people outside the collective (Lightfoot et al. 2013, p. 387). These traits match characterizations of California tribelets very closely.

While some of the territory held within tribelets can be considered at least partially a commons for group members, a definition more consistent with the modern concept of the commons focuses on birds, fish, marine, and terrestrial mammals that migrated through California and were accessible/pursued by, in some cases, hundreds of unrelated, autonomous communities. These were shared resources akin to those discussed by Hardin (1968) in reference to contemporary tragedies of the commons. In Native California there is at least one well-documented case of effective and highly coordinated exploitation of such a commons resource: salmon. The largest rivers in the northwest had two seasonal salmon runs, one in the spring and the other in the fall. Construction of fish dams along the rivers was strictly controlled by rituals that limited the number of days that any given community could use their dam. This restriction ensured that some fish continued further upriver to spawn or to be captured by similarly time-restricted fish dams built by other communities. Accounts of the fish taken at any given dam indicate substantial numbers, but equally large were the numbers of fish that passed through each community before and after dams were constructed. While there was certainly much bickering among groups, this system of ritually restricted catches allowed for a great number of communities to exploit the salmon resource sustainably up and down the major rivers of northern California (Swezey and Heizer 1977).

The degree to which there was comparable intergroup coordination and/or localized restraint in the exploitation of other migrating or otherwise widely available and shared resources like seals, deer, waterfowl, and marine fish is not especially clear from most ethnographic sources. Anderson (2005, p. 247) emphasizes the degree to which killed animals such as deer and sea lions were shared among group members but also acknowledges that hunting territories were owned by specific individuals and that sharing was in part payment for authorized or unauthorized use of a particular tract. More importantly, while sharing and chiefly intragroup redistribution were effective means of making best use of variable food resources, such mechanisms do not speak to the possible cumulative effects of localized exploitation on the overall, larger populations of migrating animals. Evidence for such effects or the lack thereof are more in the domain of archaeology which over the last 20–30 years has accumulated substantial archaeofaunal information on the relative intensity of human exploitation of commons resources, and, more importantly, long-term, cumulative effects.

Diachronic Perspectives on Use of the Commons

Interest in the possible cumulative effects of prehistoric exploitation of native fauna and flora can be traced back to the 1960s in California and beyond when Hardin (1968) argued that the disappearance of Pleistocene megafauna was perhaps the ultimate example of a prehistoric tragedy of the commons, suggesting that overhunting by humans over a 1000-year span was the cause for the disappearance of 37 genera of mostly large animals. Also referred to as the blitzkrieg hypothesis, Martin's idea was that skilled hunters from Asia entered the Americas via Beringia and encountered populations of large, naive animals that were then systematically hunted out of existence. Outside of California, the overkill hypothesis is supported by a small number of sites with the remains of extinct mammoths such as Blackwater Draw in New Mexico, as well as sites that show Pleistocene exploitation of herds of extinct buffalo. There are no data from within California that support overkill, and 50 years of excavations have yielded little or no additional compelling evidence from within the state or beyond. Some still cling to the notion that "people took control of" of the North American ecology as soon as they arrived, killing off megafauna and initiating burning (Nowacki et al. 2012), but most archaeologists today recognize the many shortcomings and weak empirical support for the hypothesis (Meltzer 2015), including the fact that the majority of animals that went extinct have never been recovered from archaeological context. Most archaeologists argue that primary causality must lie in environmental factors relating to climate (Meltzer 2015). A contested yet parsimonious hypothesis posits an extraterrestrial impact ca. 12,900 cal BP as an explanation for the relatively sudden disappearance of many, many animals (Firestone et al. 2007; Kennett et al. 2008; Wittke et al. 2013).

While the overkill hypothesis is at best highly unlikely, it does bring to the fore questions about the process of the human infill of California, beginning ca.13,500 cal BP from origins in northeastern Asia, and what the actual relationships were between the incoming populations and the massive, diverse, highly productive California environment. For the initial colonists, all of the state would have initially been a commons, but by ethnographic times, hundreds of firmly entrenched tribelets divided the state into tightly controlled resource territories. The question of when the ethnographic pattern emerged is one of several interrelated issues for which archaeology provides at least some perspective. The other two issues illuminated by archaeology are the histories of animal and plant exploitation.

Antiquity of Tribelets

In general, the sequence of human colonization of California follows predictions of ideal free distribution models, with the highest productivity areas settled earliest (Codding and Jones 2013). Nearly all of California, including daunting environments like Death Valley, was settled early in the Holocene. Exceptions were the White Mountains of Eastern California and parts of the Northwest Coast which saw little human exploitation until 3000–2000 cal BP. It seems that once these more challenging settings were annexed, the stage was set for the emergence of territoriality (Codding and Jones 2013). The general consensus among Californians is that tribelet territorialism and Chumash chiefdoms developed very late in prehistory. Bettinger (2015) argued that tribelets evolved relatively suddenly ca. 1000 cal BP, supporting similar assessments by Fredrickson (1974, p. 49) Chartkoff and Chartkoff (1984, p. 242). Most estimates for the evolution of Chumash chiefdoms date it only slightly earlier ca. 1500–1000 cal BP (Arnold 1992; Kennett 2005). Prevailing explanations for the emergence of these organizational systems vary; Bettinger (2015) attributes tribelets to the appearance of the bow and arrow, consequent changes in hunting practices, and intensive focus on stored acorns. In the Santa Barbara Channel, prevailing models emphasize the emergence of powerful leaders who organized craft specialization (including bead and canoe production) and increased intergroup trade. Most scholars ultimately attribute the shift toward greater cultural complexity in the Santa Barbara area to paleoenvironmental flux, specifically drought during the Medieval Climatic Anomaly (Arnold 1992; Stine 1994; Raab and Larson 1997; Jones et al. 1999; Kennett and Kennett 2000) although this is not accepted by all (see Gamble 2005). In both central and southern California, shifts in political organization ca. 1000 cal BP were accompanied by increased interpersonal violence (Lambert 1994; Kennett and Kennett 2000; Schwitalla et al. 2014).

There is modest evidence to suggest that prior to the emergence of tribelets, there was more interregional interaction in Native California. Long-distance conveyance of beads seems to have reached its highest levels during the Middle Period (ca. 2600–1000 cal BP). After 1000 cal BP, there seems to have been greater exchange of beads and obsidian over shorter distances (Jackson and Ericson 1994). In the Santa Barbara area, sublethal cranial violence showed an all-time peak also during the Middle Period (Walker 1989). This differs from the lethal projectile violence that peaked during the Late Period in Central California. Codding et al. (2018) have suggested that territoriality was most strongly expressed in areas where the resources base required greater amounts of large-scale cooperative behavior and that the larger the group, the greater amount of intergroup violence. Kay (1994) suggested that warring communities are beneficial to animal populations because no-man zones between competing communities provide potential safe havens for herds. The degree to which such phenomena could have seriously mitigated impacts to animal populations is at best unclear.

Exploitation of Migratory Animals

While Pleistocene overkill can be rejected, California archaeologists in the last few decades have accumulated significant information on patterns of Holocene animal exploitation, including cases for human impact on the most desirable, generally larger, species, depressing their populations so that smaller, more elusive, lower-ranked species were pursued as alternatives. These models argue that the Native California population was so high by at least the late Holocene that overreliance on deer, elk, and sea lions inevitably led to depression of the game populations. Among the first such models to be put forward was an explicit case for a prehistoric tragedy of the commons among marine mammals by Hildebrandt and Jones (1992) who argued that when congregated in rookeries, seals and sea lions represent highly attractive resources vulnerable to overpredation. Using archaeofaunal data from sites along the Oregon and California coasts, they pointed to many cases where the remains of terrestrially breeding species (northern fur seals, Guadalupe fur seals, California sea lions, and Steller's sea lions) decreased through time at the expense of smaller, more elusive, aquatic breeders (sea otters and harbor seals). These trends were argued to represent overexploitation of highly ranked taxa, and their replacement by lower-ranked species pursued with sophisticated watercraft and maritime weaponry. Initially supported with modest zooarchaeological evidence, this model has been researched and debated exhaustively in subsequent decades (e.g., Etnier 2002; Hildebrandt and Jones 2002; Lyman 2003; Gifford-Gonzalez et al. 2005; Gifford-Gonzalez and Sunseri 2009; Whitaker and Hildebrandt 2011; Gifford-Gonzalez 2011; Jones et al. 2011), and in most cases, the original patterns have not been confirmed. Lyman (2003) acknowledged the likelihood that meta-populations (essentially the entire species or the commons as we define it here) would almost certainly have been depressed by widespread overhunting—but that not all local exploitation was necessarily non-sustainable or impactful. Re-examination of data from the Northwest Coast, by Whitaker and Hildebrandt 2011, for example, found no clear evidence for overhunting, but no evidence for conscious conservation either. They favor an interpretation that sea lion hunting was more a form of prestige hunting than subsistence driven and that what may appear to represent conscious conservation of a commons resource was in this instance more a case of epiphenomenal sustainable hunting with small numbers of hunters exploiting a resource so substantial that they had no significant effect on it one way or the other. Lyman (2003) suggests that exploitation of subadult male seal and sea lions is the most sustainable form of hunting, because of their expendability with respect to breeding. Etnier (2002) found this age-sex class well-represented at the Ozette site on the coast of Washington. However, Gifford-Gonzalez and Sunseri (2009) report assemblages dominated by females and young from an apparent mainland fur seal rookery in Central California. This represents a clear case on efficient, but nonconservation-oriented, hunting. Porcasi et al. (2000) reported a similar preference for female sea lions and fur seals on San Clemente Island. Gifford-Gonzalez (2011) reports that the northern fur seal population in Central California waned late in prehistory but rejects overhunting as the cause, attributing the decline instead to complex climatic factors rather than human overexploitation. Jones et al. (2011) made the exact same case on the central coast where an exhaustive zooarchaeological review of pinnipeds and otters revealed a pattern opposite to what had originally been posed by Hildebrandt and Jones: sea otters were the most heavily exploited marine mammal early, followed later by sea lions. Moreover, DNA analysis showed a clear preference for the easily captured female otters. Despite such a nonconservation-oriented approach, sea otters became more abundant in the record over time. This pattern was also interpreted as epiphenomenal nonconservation.

More recently, a case has been made for large-scale coordinated hunting of sea otters off the coast of southern California by Braje (2016). The Northern Channel Islands have long been known to contain sites with dense concentrations of unusually large red abalone shells. Radiocarbon results has shown that these "red abalone middens" date between ca. 8250 and 5250 cal BP (Glassow 2015). In the present-day ecological structure of nearshore waters, red abalone sizes and populations are kept in check by sea otters who are voracious feeders on them and other subtidal mollusks. Braje (2016) surmises that the presence of red abalone middens marks a period when otter populations were low, further suggesting that Native hunters intentionally engaged in a large-scale coordinated effort to reduce otter populations in order to encourage abalone growth. However, this proposal is conjectural.

Significant debate has also taken place around the possible depression of deer populations in Central California. Broughton (1994a, 1999) argued that overhunting of deer and elk in the San Francisco Bay area led to declining yields and a forced focus thereafter on the more elusive sea otters. Based on these findings, Broughton made an explicit statement about management of the commons in Native California:

> Insofar as my analyses have shown that Native American foragers had profound impacts on the fish, mammal, and bird species of the San Francisco Bay area, they call into question the widely held belief that native peoples maintained a harmonious

> relationship with the animal populations with whom they shared the land.... Perceived harmony is almost surely a function of limited technologies and low population densities.... There is no compelling reason to think that Native Americans will provide better stewardship of threatened habitats than any other peoples. (Broughton 1999, p. 72)

Subsequent research by Whitaker's (2009), however, raised serious doubts about depression of deer populations in the San Francisco Bay area. He showed that deer would have been able to readily maintain their numbers in the face of Native exploitation—without any program of active conservation or management. Elk, however, may be a different story. More recently, Broughton et al. (2013) provided preliminary support for the depression of tule elk through the analysis of ancient DNA, which suggest a genetic bottleneck prior to historic contact. Recent work by Fisher (2018) illustrates a rather clear case of anthropogenic resource depression, and rebound, in the northern Sierra Nevada foothills, where detailed faunal analyses of a fine-grained record reveal a long-term decline in the proportion of artiodactyls exploited, followed by a rebound in their numbers coincident with the Euro-American-caused decline in American Indian populations.

A proposal has also been made that migratory waterfowl were suppressed in precontact California. In the San Francisco Bay area, larger-bodied geese declined in favor of ducks and marine birds between 2700 and 700 years ago (Broughton 2004). Broughton (2004, p. 1) further contends that the historical observations of enormous flocks of geese and ducks in California were the product of catastrophic decline in human populations during the protohistoric period (A.D. 1540–1769), but he fails to explain why or how bird populations were not depressed earlier in the Bay Area since human occupation there dates back to at least 9000 cal BP (Milliken et al. 2007). Jones and Codding (2018), however, show a significant decline in remains of seabirds along the Pecho Coast of Central California between ca. 10,000 and 2550 cal BP which they attribute to overexploitation of nesting colonies on the remote open coast and offshore rocks. Contributing to the Pecho sequence was the extinction of the flightless duck which is the only clear, empirically supported case of a prehistoric tragedy of the commons in California, if not all of North America. Radiocarbon dates from central and southern California show that the vulnerable flightless bird was rendered extinct ca. 2800 cal BP following 8000 years of exploitation (Jones et al. 2008). It is suspected that Native hunters pursued the birds at offshore nesting colonies using watercraft to harvest both adults and eggs. The importance of the flightless duck cannot be overstated inasmuch as it is a clear case of the cumulative effects, of efficient, self-interested, and seemingly unconstrained hunting bringing about the ultimate tragedy: extinction.

The archaeology and prehistory of fish along the California coast, however, contrasts with the flightless duck. Broughton (1994b, 1997) made early cases for overexploitation of fish in the Sacramento River and San Francisco Bay, but these were flawed by methodological and sample-size issues. Broughton et al. (2015) made a slightly improved argument for overexploitation of sturgeon, but more compelling studies by Stevenson and Butler (2015) and Campbell and Butler (2010) show long-term stability in salmon fishing in Northwestern California. The archaeofaunal record from this region provides support for the effectiveness of ritually mediated management of the salmon resource along the river as described by Swezey and Heizer (1977). With respect to marine fishes, Jones et al. (2016) compared modern fishery yields with the archaeological record and concluded that there was no evidence for human impact (positive or negative) on the nearshore ocean fishery prehistorically. Modern yields are staggering in their volume relative to the precontact human population, making it obvious that Native fishers could not have affected this resource and that it provided a reliable staple that was exploited heavily during times of reduced terrestrial productivity (Jones et al. 2017).

Shellfish

Shellfish were a spatially restricted resource within tribelet territories, accessed by group members. With such restricted access, some tribelets may have been completely excluded from accessing preferred shellfish (Whitaker and Byrd 2014). While there has long been suspicion that shellfish were vulnerable to overexploitation (e.g., Botkin 1980; Salls 1992), confirmation of this was slow in coming. Jones (1996) found evidence for diminution in California sea mussels over time on the Big Sur coast, but these findings were subsequently found to be methodologically flawed. Since then, multiple studies on the southern California Islands have found evidence for diminution over time in abalone (Braje et al. 2007; Erlandson et al. 2008; Rick 2011) due to increasingly frequent harvests. Thakar et al. (2017) suggested that factors other than harvesting intensity could explain the decrease in shell size over time, but the original explanation still seems most parsimonious. Humans likely effected the mean size of individuals in shellfish beds over time, but they did not extirpate species or cause species replacements despite arguments to the contrary (e.g., Raab and Yatsko 1992). A further case advanced by Whitaker (2008) that stripping of large patches of mussel beds in Northwestern California equated to incipient aquaculture (in that it encouraged rapid recolonization and growth of new mussels) is likely better explained as epiphenomenal to optimal harvesting decisions. Modern-day commercial aquaculture shows that a more selective harvesting strategy for mussels fosters the highest sustainable yields (Yamada and Peters 1988).

Plant Exploitation and Controlled Burning

While the ethnographic record makes it abundantly clear that Native people collected a wide range of plant foods including significant quantities of acorns, and that they regularly burned the landscape, the prehistory of these activities and their possible large-scale cumulative effects have been nearly impossible to discern. That controlled burning increases diversity and productivity of the land and reduces the chance of catastrophic wild fire have been reasonably well established for decades (see Minnich 1983). Further, most scholars (e.g., Lightfoot and Parrish 2009) agree that cumulative effects of Native burning would have been greatest near villages. The archaeological challenges involved in determining when, how, and with what level of intensity burning was conducted, however, have proven considerable.

Statewide diachronic patterns of plant exploitation are only recently being defined. Important are studies by Wohlgemuth (2010), Gill (2013), and Reddy and Erlandson (2012). Preservation issues make it hard to generalize about the early Holocene (ca. 10,000–500 cal BP), but findings from the Cross Creek site in Central California yielded evidence for exploitation of small grass and forb seeds and yucca (Fitzgerald 2000), which seems almost certainly to reflect climatic conditions warmer and drier than present. In contrast, on the Channel Islands, brodiaea bulbs and other geophytes seem to have dominated the plant component of the diet throughout the Holocene (Gill 2016; Gill and Hoppa 2016). Acorns became part of the diet by at least mid-Holocene (Wohlgemuth 2010) reflecting a combination of climatic amelioration and/or population growth (Codding and Jones 2016). Following initial adoption of the acorn, there is regional variability in relative intensity of use over time (Wohlgemuth 2010), but most areas seem to show highest use late, ca 700–200 cal BP. Bettinger (2015) explicitly links peak acorn exploitation with the emergence of tribelets during the Late Prehistoric Period.

Studies attempting to trace the prehistory of burning have been confounded by an inability to distinguish natural from anthropogenic fires (Codding and Bird 2013; Cowart and Byrne 2013, pp. 348–349) and climatically induced diachronic variation from anthropogenic variation. In an intensive multidisciplinary investigation of controlled burning in Central California, Lightfoot et al. (2013) discovered evidence for increased frequency of landscape fires ca. 1000 cal BP but acknowledged that this date also coincides with the onset of warmer, drier climate during the Medieval Climatic Anomaly and that climate change could have been equally responsible for the increase in fires (Swetnam 1993). Furthermore, Lightfoot et al. (2013) were unable to determine in any meaningful way the organizational structure surrounding burning or whether it was conducted by individuals whose goals were largely short-term or part of a large-scale communal management programs within tribelets. Like many previous scholars (Lewis 1973; Stewart 2002; Anderson 2005), they argue for masterful management of the landscape, but cannot identify its signature archaeologically.

The inability to distinguish climatically induced vegetation change from anthropogenic change has plagued many other estimates for the date when burning was initiated. While it stands to reason that the earliest human colonists could have used fire to help settle California, as suggested by Nowacki et al. (2012), charcoal is also evident in the paleoenvironmental record before humans arrived. Wiegel (1993) suggested that an increase in charcoal in stratified deposits in Northwestern California ca. 5000 years ago marks the initiation of burning and the establishment of grassy meadows in the heavily forested mountains, but this date corresponds with the peak of early-mid Holocene warming. Importantly, a study of the paleo-charcoal record by Mensing et al. (1999) showed clear evidence for occasional, major conflagrations in pre-European California which suggests that controlled burning did not give Native people full control of the landscape. The degree to which the widespread reliance upon acorns during ethnographic times was the end-product of a long-term management program focused on controlled burning remains somewhat equivocal.

Summary and Discussion

California provides an excellent proving ground for conceptualizations of the effects of hunter-gatherers on commons resources. Ethnographic California was marked by a profusion of small, autonomous polities (tribelets) within which access to resources were tightly controlled. Tribelet territories were known and protected. Incursions were punished. Acorns collected and stored within these communities were the key subsistence resource. Ethnographic accounts and limited archaeological findings suggest that acorns and other plant resources within tribelets benefitted from regular controlled burning. It has been argued that the intra-tribelet communities collectively managed resources within their territories (Anderson 2005; Lightfoot and Parrish 2009; Lightfoot et al. 2013), but the archaeological record provides no definitive support or refutation of these ideas. Shellfish exploitation within these communities, however, shows impacts from overly frequent harvesting—but this was far from a tragedy of the commons.

The real test for treatment of the commons by California hunter-gatherers, however, comes in the form of their exploitation of larger, mostly migratory animals, including anadromous fish (salmon), deer, seals, sea lions, and waterfowl that were shared and accessed by, in some cases, hundreds of separate, independent communities. Here the diachronic record reveals three distinct long-term patterns. First, there is evidence for cases where human harvest seems to have had no significant effects even in the face of pursuit strategies that were decidedly nonconservation-oriented. Marine fish, sea lions on the northwest coast, and sea otters all seem to have been exploited without impact to populations, representing what we characterize as epiphenomenal conservation. Second, there is the case of the salmon fishery in Northwestern California where ethnographically documented, ritually mediated exploitation effectively allowed for a sustainable fishery that is documented archaeologically (Campbell and Butler 2010; Stevenson and Butler 2015). Finally, however, there is the case of the flightless duck which was hunted to extinction over an 8000-year period because of its vulnerability and apparent lack of restraint by hunters and egg collectors. This was indeed the same type of tragedy that befell flightless birds elsewhere in the Pacific after the arrival humans (Steadman 1995), but the process played out much more slowly in California.

The California anthropological record also shows decided overzealousness among researchers eager to portray Native Californians alternately as masterful stewards of the commons or thoughtless over hunters. Perhaps not surprisingly, the California archaeological record clearly illuminates two ends of the spectrum in terms of human behavior. In this regard, California hunter-gatherers are perhaps best characterized as no different from other modern humans in their overall treatment of the commons.

References

Anderson, M. (2005). *Tending the wild*. Berkeley, CA: University of California Press.
Anderson, M. K. (1993). Native Californians as ancient and contemporary cultivators. In T. C. Blackburn & M. K. Anderson (Eds.), *Before the wilderness: Environmental management by native Californians* (pp. 151–174). Menlo Park, CA: Ballena Press.
Arnold, J. E. (1992). Complex hunter-gatherer-fishers of prehistoric California: Chiefs, specialists, and maritime adaptations of the Channel Islands. *American Antiquity, 57*, 60–84.
Arnold, J. E., & Bernard, J. (2005). Negotiating the coasts: Status and the evolution of boat technology in California. *World Archaeology, 37*, 109–131.
Basgall, M. E. (1987). Resource intensification among hunter-gatherers: Acorn economies in prehistoric California. *Research in Economic Anthropology, 9*(198), 21–52.
Baumhoff, M. A. (1978). Environmental background. In R. F. Heizer (Ed.), *California* (pp. 16–24). Vol. 8 of Handbook of North American Indians, edited by William C. Sturtevant. Washington, DC: Smithsonian Institution.
Baumhoff, M. A. (1963). Ecological determinants of aboriginal California populations. *University of California Publications in American Archaeology and Ethnology, 49*(2), 155–336.
Bean, L. J. (1978). Cahuilla. In R. F. Heizer (Ed.), *California* (pp. 575–587). Vol. 8 of Handbook of North American Indians, edited by William C. Sturtevant. Washington, DC: Smithsonian Institution.
Bean, L. J., & Saubel, K. S. (1961). *Cahuilla ethnobotanical notes: The aboriginal uses of oak* (Archaeological Survey Annual Report 1960–1961, pp. 237–245). University of California, Los Angeles.
Bean, L. J. (1972). *Mukat's people: The Cahuilla Indians of southern California*. Berkeley, CA: University of California Press.
Bean, L. J., & Lawton, H. (1976). Some explanations for the rise of cultural complexity in native California with comments on proto-agriculture and agriculture. In L. J. Bean & H. Lawton (Eds.), *Native Californians: A theoretical retrospective* (pp. 19–48). Menlo Park, CA: Ballena Press.
Bennyhoff, J. A., and R. E. Hughes. (1987). "Shell Bead and Ornament Exchange Networks Between California and the Western Great Basin." Anthropological Papers of the American Museum of Natural History 64(2).
Bernard, J. (2004). Status and the swordfish: The origins of large-species fishing among the Chumash. In J. Arnold (Ed.), *Foundations of Chumash complexity* (pp. 25–51). Los Angeles: Cotsen Institute of Archaeology, University of California, Los Angeles.
Bettinger, R. L., & Wohlgemuth, E. (2006). California plants. In D. Stanford, B. D. Smith, D. H. Ubelaker, & E. J. E. Szathmáry (Eds.), *Environment, origins, and population* (pp. 274–283). Vol. 3 of Handbook of North American Indians, edited by Douglas H. Ubelaker. Washington, DC: Smithsonian Institution.
Bettinger, R. L. (2015). *Orderly anarchy: Sociopolitical evolution in aboriginal California*. Oakland, CA: University of California Press.
Bettinger, R. L., Malhi, R., & McCarthy, H. (1997). Central place models of acorn and mussel processing. *Journal of Archaeological Science, 24*(10), 887–899.
Blackburn, T. C., & Anderson, M. K. (Eds.). (1993). *Before the wilderness: Environmental management by native Californians*. Menlo Park, CA: Ballena Press.
Botkin, S. (1980). Effects of human exploitation on shellfish populations at Malibu Creek, California. In T. K. Earle & A. L. Christianson (Eds.), *Modeling change in prehistoric subsistence economies* (pp. 121–139). New York: Academic Press.
Braje, T. J. (2016). *Shellfish for the celestial empire: The rise and fall of commercial abalone fishing in California*. Salt Lake City, UT: University of Utah Press.
Braje, T. J., Kennett, D. J., Erlandson, J. M., & Culleton, B. J. (2007). Human impacts on nearshore shellfish taxa: A 7000 year record from Santa Rosa Island, California. *American Antiquity, 72*(4), 735–736.

Breschini, G. S., and T. Haversat. (1994). "Rumsen seasonality and population dynamics." In L. J. Bean (Ed.), *The Ohlone past and present: Native Americans of the San Francisco Bay region* (193–202.) Menlo Park, CA: Ballena Press.

Broughton, J. M. (1999). *Resource depression and intensification during the late Holocene, San Francisco Bay: Evidence from the Emeryville Shellmound vertebrate fauna.* Berkeley, CA: University of California Anthropological Records 32.

Broughton, J. M. (2004). Prehistoric human impact on California birds: Evidence from the Emeryville Shellmound avifauna. *Ornithological Monographs, 56*, 1–90.

Broughton, J. M. (1994a). Declines in mammalian foraging efficiency during the late Holocene, San Francisco Bay. *Journal of Anthropological Archaeology, 13*, 371–401.

Broughton, J. M. (1994b). Late holocene resource intensification in the Sacramento River Valley, California: The vertebrate evidence. *Journal of Archaeological Science, 21*, 501–514.

Broughton, J. M. (1997). Widening diet breadth, declining foraging efficiency, and prehistoric harvest pressure: Ichthyofaunal evidence from the Emeryville Shellmound, California. *Antiquity, 71*(274), 845–862.

Broughton, J. M., Kelly Beck, R., Coltrain, J. B., O'Rourke, D. H., & Rogers, A. R. (2013). A late Holocene population bottleneck in California tule elk *(Cervus elaphus nannodes)*: Provisional support from ancient DNA. *Journal of Archaeological Method and Theory, 20*, 495–524.

Broughton, J. M., Martin, E. P., McEneaney, B., Wake, T., & Simons, D. D. (2015). Late Holocene anthropogenic depression of sturgeon in San Francisco Bay, California. *Journal of California and Great Basin Anthropology, 35*(1), 3–27.

Camp, C. L., & Yount, G. C. (1923). The chronicles of George C. Yount: California pioneer of 1826. *California Historical Society Quarterly, 2*(1), 3–66.

Campbell, S. K., & Butler, V. L. (2010). Archaeological evidence for resilience of Pacific northwest salmon populations and the socioecological system over the last ~7,500 years. *Ecology and Society, 15*(1), 17.

Castillo, E. D. (1978). The impact of Euro-American exploration and settlement. In R. F. Heizer (Ed.), *California* (pp. 99–127). Vol. 8 of Handbook of North American Indians, edited by William G. Sturtevant. Washington, DC: Smithsonian Institution.

Chagnon, N. A. (1970). *Ecological and adaptive aspects of California shell money* (Archaeological Survey Rep. 12, pp. 1–25). University of California, Los Angeles.

Chartkoff, J. L., & Chartkoff, K. K. (1984). *The archaeology of California.* Stanford, CA: Stanford University Press.

Codding, B. F., Parker, A. K., & Jones, T. L. (2018). Territorial behavior among Western North American foragers: Allee effects influence within group cooperation and between group conflict. *Quaternary International.* In press.

Codding, B. F., & Bird, D. (2013). A global perspective on traditional burning in California. *California Archaeology, 5*(2), 199–208.

Codding, B. F., & Jones, T. L. (2013). Environmental productivity predicts colonization, migration, and demographic patterns in prehistoric California. *Proceedings of the National Academy of Science, 110*(36), 14569–14573.

Codding, B. F., & Jones, T. L. (2016). External impacts on internal dynamics: Effects of paleoclimatic and demographic variability on acorn exploitation along the Central California coast. In D. Contreras (Ed.), *The archaeology of human-environment interactions* (pp. 195–210). Oxford: Routledge.

Cowart, A., & Byrne, R. (2013). A paleolimnological record of late Holocene vegetation change from the central California coast. *California Archaeology, 5*(2), 334–349.

Cuthrell, R. Q., Striplen, C., Hylkema, M., & Lightfoot, K. G. (2012). A land of fire: Anthropogenic burning on the central coast of California. In T. L. Jones & J. E. Perry (Eds.), *Contemporary issues in California archaeology* (pp. 153–174). Walnut Creek, CA: Left Coast Press.

Davis, J. T. (1961). *Trade routes and economic exchange among the Indians of California* (Archaeological Survey Rep. 54). Berkeley, CA: University of California.

Dietz, S. A., & Jackson, T. L. (1981). *Report of archaeological excavations at nineteen archaeological sites for the stage 1 Pacific Grove-Monterey consolidation project of the regional sew-*

erage system. Archaeological Consulting and Research Services, Santa Cruz. Copies available from Northwest Archaeological Information Center, Department of Anthropology. Rohnert Park, CA: Sonoma State University.

Erlandson, J. M., Rick, T. C., Todd, J., Braje, A. S., & Vellanoweth, R. L. (2008). Human impacts on ancient shellfish: A 10,000 year record from San Miguel Island, California. *Journal of Archaeological Science, 35*(8), 2144–2152.

Etnier, M. A. (2002). *The effects of human hunting on northern fur seal (Callorhinus ursinus) migration and breeding distributions in the late Holocene*. Ph.D. dissertation, University of Washington.

Firestone, R. B., West, A., Kennett, J. P., Becker, L., Bunch, T. E., Revay, Z. S., et al. (2007). Evidence for an extraterrestrial impact 12,900 years ago that contributed to the megafaunal extinctions and Younger Dryas cooling. *Proceedings of the National Academy of Science, 104*(41), 16016–16021.

Fisher, J. L. (2018). Protohistoric artiodactyl rebound and resource deintensification in northern California. *Journal of Archaeological Science Reports, 19*, 420–429.

Fitzgerald, R. T. (2000). *Cross creek: An early Holocene/Millingstone site*. California State Water Project, San Luis Obispo County Archaeological Society Coastal Branch Series Paper no. 12.

Fredrickson, D. A. (1974). Cultural diversity in early central California: A view from the North Coast Ranges. *Journal of California Anthropology, 1*(1), 41–54.

Gamble, L. H. (2008). *The Chumash world at European contact: Power, trade, and feasting among complex hunter-gatherers*. Berkeley, CA: University of California Press.

Gamble, L. H. (2005). Culture and climate: Reconsidering the effect of palaeoclimatic variability among Southern California hunter-gatherer societies. *World Archaeology, 37*(1), 92–108.

Gifford, E. W. (1971). California balanophagy. In R. F. Heizer & M. A. Whipple (Eds.), *The California Indians: A source book* (pp. 301–305). Berkeley, CA: University of California Press.

Gifford-Gonzalez, D. (2011). Monterey Bay fur seals: Distribution, dates, and ecological implications. In T. J. Braje & T. C. Rick (Eds.), *Human impacts on seals, sea lions, and sea otters: Integrating archaeology and ecology in the Northeast Pacific* (pp. 221–242). Berkeley, CA: University of California Press.

Gifford-Gonzalez, D., Newsome, S. D., Koch, P. L., Guilderson, T. P., Snodgrass, J. J., & Burton, R. K. (2005). Archaeofaunal insights on pinniped-human interactions in the northeastern Pacific. In G. G. Monks (Ed.), *The exploitation and cultural importance of sea mammals* (pp. 19–38). New York: Oxbow Books.

Gifford-Gonzalez, D., & Sunseri, C. K. (2009). An earlier extirpation of fur seals in the Monterey bay region: Recent findings and social implications. *Proceedings of the Society for California Archaeology, 21*, 89–102.

Gill, K. M. (2015). *Ancient plant use and the importance of geophytes among the Island Chumash of Santa Cruz Island, California*. Ph.D. dissertation, University of California, Santa Barbara, CA.

Gill, K. M. (2013). Paleobotanical investigations on the channel islands: Current directions and theoretical considerations. In C. S. Jazwa & J. E. Perry (Eds.), *California's channel islands: The archaeology of human-environment interactions* (pp. 113–136). Salt Lake City, UT: University of Utah Press.

Gill, K. M. (2016). 10,000 years of geophyte use among the island Chumash of the northern Channel Islands. *Fremontia, 44*(3), 34–38.

Gill, K. M., & Hoppa, K. M. (2016). Evidence for an island Chumash geophyte-based subsistence economy on the northern Channel Islands. *Journal of California and Great Basin Anthropology, 36*(1), 51–71.

Glassow, M. A. (2015). Chronology of red abalone middens on Santa Cruz island, California, and evidence for subsistence and settlement change. *American Antiquity, 80*(4), 745–759.

Gobalet, K. W., & Jones, T. L. (1995). Prehistoric native American fisheries of the Central California coast. *Transactions of the American Fisheries Society, 124*(6), 813–823.

Gobalet, K. W., Schulz, P. D., Wake, T. A., & Siefkin, N. (2004). Archaeological perspectives on native American fisheries of California with emphasis on steelhead and salmon. *Transactions of the American Fisheries Society, 133*(4), 801–833.

Golla, V. (2011). *California Indian languages*. Berkeley, CA: University of California Press.
Hamilton, J. B., Curtis, G. L., Snedaker, S. M., & White, D. K. (2005). Distribution of anadromous fishes in the upper Klamath River watershed prior to hydropower dams—A synthesis of the historical evidence. *Fisheries, 30*(4), 10–20.
Hardin, G. (1968). The tragedy of the commons. *Science, 162*(3859), 1243–1248.
Heizer, R. F. (Ed.). (1978). *Handbook of North American Indians* (Vol. 8, California). Washington, DC: Smithsonian Institution.
Heizer, R. F., & Almquist, A. J. (1971). *The other Californians*. Berkeley, CA: University of California Press.
Heizer, R. F., & Elsasser, A. B. (1980). *The natural world of the California Indians*. Berkeley, CA: University of California Press.
Hildebrandt, W. R., & Carpenter, K. (2006). California animals. In D. Stanford, B. D. Smith, D. H. Ubelaker, & E. J. E. Szathmáry (Eds.), *Environment, origins, and population. Vol. 3 of handbook of North American Indians* (pp. 284–291). Washington D.C.: Smithsonian Institution.
Hildebrandt, W. R., & Jones, T. L. (2002). Depletion of prehistoric pinniped populations along the California and Oregon coasts: Were humans the cause? In C. E. Kay & R. T. Simmons (Eds.), *Wilderness and political ecology: Aboriginal influences and the original state of nature* (pp. 72–110). Salt Lake City: University of Utah Press.
Hildebrandt, W. R., & Levulett, V. A. (1997). Middle Holocene adaptations on the northern California coast: Terrestrial resource productivity and its influence on the use of marine foods. In J. M. Erlandson & M. A. Glassow (Eds.), *Archaeology of the California coast during the middle Holocene* (pp. 143–150). Los Angeles: Cotsen Institute of Archaeology, University of California.
Hildebrandt, W. R., & Jones, T. L. (1992). Evolution of marine mammal hunting: A view from the California and Oregon coasts. *Journal of Anthropological Archaeology, 11*(4), 360–401.
Hughes, R. E., & Milliken, R. T. (2007). Prehistoric material conveyance. In T. L. Jones & K. A. Klar (Eds.), *California prehistory: colonization, culture, and complexity* (pp. 259–271). New York, NY: Altimira Press.
Jackson, T. L., & Ericson, J. E. (1994). Prehistoric exchange systems in California. In T. G. Baugh & J. E. Ericson (Eds.), *Prehistoric exchange systems in North America* (pp. 385–415). New York, NY: Plenum Press.
Jones, T. L., Brown, G., Raab, L. M., McVickar, J., Spaulding, G., Kennett, D. J., et al. (1999). Environmental imperatives reconsidered: Demographic crises in western North America during the medieval climatic anomaly. *Current Anthropology, 40*(2), 137–156.
Jones, T. L., & Codding, B. F. (2018). *Foragers on America's western edge: The archaeology of California's Pecho coast*. Salt Lake City: University of Utah Press.
Jones, T. L. (1996). Mortars, pestles, and division of labor in prehistoric California: A view from big Sur. *American Antiquity, 61*(2), 243–264.
Jones, T. L., Culleton, B. J., Larson, S., Mellinger, S., & Porcasi, J. F. (2011). Toward a prehistory of the southern sea otter (*Enhydra lutris nereis*). In T. Rick & T. Braje (Eds.), *Humans and marine ecosystems: Archaeology and historical ecology of northeastern pacific seals, sea lions, and sea otters* (pp. 243–272). Berkeley, CA: University of California Press.
Jones, T. L., Jones, D. A., Hadick, K., Gobalet, K. W., Porcasi, J., & Hildebrandt, W. R. (2017). The Morro Bay Fauna: Evidence for a medieval droughts refugium on the Central California coast. *American Antiquity, 82*(2), 203–222.
Jones, T. L., & Klar, K. A. (Eds.). (2007). *California prehistory: Colonization, culture, and complexity*. New York: AltaMira Press.
Jones, T. L., Porcasi, J. F., Erlandson, J. M., Dallas Jr., H., Wake, T. A., & Schwaderer, R. (2008). The protracted holocene extinction of California's flightless sea duck (*Chendytes lawi*) and its implications for the Pleistocene overkill hypothesis. *Proceedings of the National Academy of Science, 105*(11), 4105–4108.
Jones, T. L., Terry, L., Gobalet, K. W., & Codding, B. F. (2016). The archaeology of fish and fishing on the central coast of California: The case for an under-exploited resource. *Journal of Anthropological Archaeology, 41*(2016), 88–108.

Jorgensen, J. G. (1980). *Western Indians: Comparative environments, languages, and cultures of 172 Western American Indian tribes.* San Francisco: WH Freeman.
Kay, C. E. (1994). Aboriginal overkill. *Human Nature, 5*(4), 359–398.
Kay, C. (1995). Technical commentary: Aboriginal overkill and native burning: Implications for modern ecosystem management. *Western Journal of Applied Forestry, 10*(4), 121–126.
Kennett, D. J. (2005). *The island Chumash; Behavioral ecology of a maritime society.* Berkeley, CA: University of California Press.
Kennett, D. J., Kennett, J. P., West, G. J., Erlandson, J. M., Johnson, J. R., Hendy, I. L., et al. (2008). Wildfire and abrupt ecosystem disruption on California's northern Channel Islands at the Allerød-Younger Dryas boundary (13.0-12.9 ka). *Quaternary Science Review, 27*(27–28), 2528–2543.
Kennett, D. J., & Kennett, J. P. (2000). Competitive and cooperative responses to climate instability in coastal southern California. *American Antiquity, 65*(2), 379–395.
King, C. (1976). Chumash intervillage economic exchange. In L. J. Bean & T. C. Blackburn (Eds.), *Native Californians: A theoretical retrospective* (pp. 289–318). Ramona, CA: Ballena Press.
Kroeber, A. L. (1925). *Handbook of the Indians of California* (Bureau of American Ethnology Bull. 78). Washington, DC: Smithsonian Institution.
Kroeber, A. L. (1962). The nature of land-holding groups in aboriginal California. In D. H. Hymes & R. F. Heizer (Eds.), *Two papers on the aboriginal ethnography of California* (Vol. 56, pp. 19–58). Berkeley, CA: California Archaeological Survey Reports.
Kroeber, A. L., & Barrett, S. A. (1960). Fishing among the Indians of northwestern California. *University of California Anthropological Records, 21*(1), 1–210.
Lambert, P. M. (1994). *War and peace on the western front: A study of violent conflict and its correlates in prehistoric hunter-gatherer societies of coastal Southern California.* Ph.D. dissertation, Department of Anthropology, University of California, Santa Barbara, CA.
Levy, R. (1978). Eastern Miwok. In R. F. Heizer (Ed.), *California* (pp. 398–413). Vol. 8 of Handbook of North American Indians, edited by William C. Sturtevant. Washington DC: Smithsonian Institution.
Lewis, H. (1973). *Patterns of Indian burning in California: Ecology and ethnohistory.* Ramona, CA: Ballena Press.
Lightfoot, K. G., Cuthrell, R. Q., Boone, C. M., Byrne, R., Chavez, A. B., Collins, L., et al. (2013). Anthropogenic burning on the Central California coast in late Holocene and early historical times: Findings, implications, and future directions. *California Archaeology, 5*(2), 368–388.
Lightfoot, K. G., & Lopez, V. (2013). The study of indigenous landscape management practices in California: An introduction. *California Archaeology, 5*(2), 1–12.
Lightfoot, K. G., & Parrish, O. (2009). *California Indians and their environment.* Berkeley, CA: University of California Press.
Lindsay, B. C. (2012). *Murder state: California's native American genocide, 1846–1873.* Lincoln, NE: University of Nebraska Press.
Lyman, R. L. (2003). Pinniped behavior, foraging theory, and the depression of metapopulations and nondepression of a local population on the southern northwest coast of North America. *Journal of Anthropological Archaeology, 22*(2003), 376–388.
Margolin, M. (1978). *The Ohlone way.* Berkeley, CA: Hey Day Books.
McCorkle, T. (1978). Intergroup Conflict. In R. F. Heizer (Ed.), *California. Handbook of the North American Indians* (Vol. 8, pp. 694–700). Washington, D.C.: Smithsonian Institution.
Mead, G. R. (2014). *The ethnobotany of the California Indians.* La Grande, OR: E-Cats Worlds.
Meltzer, D. (2015). Pleistocene overkill and north American mammalian extinctions. In D. Brenneis & K. B. Strier (Eds.), *Annual review of anthropology* (pp. 33–53). Palo Alto, CA: Annual Reviews.
Mensing, S. A., Michaelsen, J., & Byrne, R. (1999). A 560-year record of Santa Ana fires reconstructed from charcoal deposited in the Santa Barbara Basin, California. *Quaternary Research, 51*(3), 295–305.
Milliken, R. T. (2010). *Contact-period community distribution model: A dynamic digital atlas and wiki encyclopedia* (Vol. 1: Introduction, Report prepared for California Department of

Transportation, District 6, Environmental Branch, Fresno). Davis: Far Western Anthropological Research Group, Inc.

Milliken, R. T., Fitzgerald, R. T., Hylkema, M. G., Origer, T., Groza, R., Wiberg, R., et al. (2007). Punctuated culture change in the San Francisco Bay area. In T. L. Jones & K. A. Klar (Eds.), *California prehistory: colonization, culture, and complexity* (pp. 99–124). New York, NY: Altimira Press.

Minnich, R. A. (1983). Fire mosaics in southern California and northern Baja California. *Science, 219*(4590), 1287–1294.

Moratto, M. J. (1984). *California archaeology*. Orlando, FL: Academic Press.

Norton, J. (1979). *Genocide in northwestern California*. San Francisco: Indian Historian Press.

Nowacki, G. J., MacClerry, D. W., & Lake, F. K. (2012). Native Americans, ecosystem development, and historical range of variation. In J. A. Wiens, G. D. Hayward, H. D. Stafford, & C. M. Giffen (Eds.), *Historical environmental variation in conservation and natural resource management* (pp. 76–91). Hoboken, NJ: Wiley-Blackwell.

Olmsted, D. L., & Stewart, O. (1978). Achumawi. In R. F. Heizer (Ed.), *California* (pp. 225–235). Vol. 8 of Handbook of North American Indians, edited by William C. Sturtevant. Washington DC: Smithsonian Institution.

Ostrom, E. (2002). Common-pool resources and institutions: Toward a revised theory. *Handbook of Agricultural Economics, 2*, 1315–1339.

Ostrom, E., Gardner, R., & Walker, J. (1994). *Rules, games, and common-pool resources*. Ann Arbor, MI: University of Michigan Press.

Peri, D. W., & Patterson, S. M. (1993). The basket is in the roots, that's where it begins. In T. C. Blackburn & K. Anderson (Eds.), *Before the wilderness: Environmental management by native Californians* (pp. 175–195). Menlo Park, CA: Ballena Press.

Pilling, A. R. (1950). The archaeological implications of an annual coastal visit for certain Yokuts groups. *American Anthropologist, 52*(3), 438–440.

Porcasi, J. F., Jones, T. L., & Mark Raab, L. (2000). Trans-Holocene marine mammal exploitation on San Clemente Island, California: A tragedy of the commons revisited. *Journal of Anthropological Archaeology, 19*(2000), 200–220.

Raab, L. M., & Larson, D. O. (1997). Medieval climatic anomaly and punctuated cultural evolution in coastal southern California. *American Antiquity, 62*(2), 319–336.

Raab, L. M., & Yatsko, A. (1992). Ancient maritime adaptations of the California bight: A perspective from San Clemente Island. In T. L. Jones (Ed.), *Essays on the maritime prehistory of California* (pp. 173–194). Davis: University of California, Center for Archaeological Research, Publication 10.

Reddy, S. N., & Erlandson, J. M. (2012). Macrobotanical food remains from a trans-Holocene sequence at daisy cave (CA-SMI-261), San Miguel Island, California. *Journal of Archaeological Science, 39*(1), 33–40.

Rick, T. C. (2011). Weathering the storm: Coastal subsistence and ecological resilience on late Holocene Santa Rosa Island, California. *Quaternary International, 239*(1–2), 135–146.

Rick, T. C., DeLong, R. L., Erlandson, J. M., Braje, T. J., Jones, T. L., Arnold, J. E., et al. (2012). Where were the northern elephant seals? Holocene archaeology and biogeography of *Mirounga angustirostris*. *The Holocene, 21*(7), 1159–1166.

Salls, R. A. (1988). *Prehistoric fisheries of the California bight*. Ph.D. dissertation, Archaeology Program, University of California, Los Angeles.

Salls, R. A. (1992). Prehistoric subsistence change on California's channel islands: Environmental or cultural? In T. L. Jones (Ed.), *Essays on the prehistory of maritime California* (pp. 157–172). Davis, CA: Center for Archaeological Research at Davis Publication 10. University of California.

Schwitalla, A. W., Jones, T. L., Pilloud, M. A., Codding, B. F., & Wiberg, R. S. (2014). Violence among foragers: The bioarchaeological record from central California. *Journal of Anthropological Archaeology, 33*(2014), 66–83.

Shipek, F. C. (1978). History of southern California mission Indians. In R. F. Heizer (Ed.), *California* (pp. 610–618). Vol. 8 of Handbook of North American Indians, edited by William G. Sturtevant. Washington, DC: Smithsonian Institution.

Shipek, F. C. (1989). An example of intensive plant husbandry: The Kumeyaay of southern California. In D. R. Harris & G. C. Hillman (Eds.), *The evolution of plant exploitation: Foraging and farming* (pp. 379–388). Boston: Unwin Hyman.

Shipek, F. C. (1993). Kumeyaay plant husbandry: Fire, water, and erosion management. In T. C. Blackburn & M. K. Anderson (Eds.), *Before the wilderness: Environmental management by native Californians* (pp. 379–388). Menlo Park, CA: Ballena Press.

Steadman, D. W. (1995). Prehistoric extinctions of Pacific island birds: Biodiversity meets zooarchaeology. *Science, 267*(5201), 1123–1131.

Stevenson, A. E., & Butler, V. (2015). The Holocene history of fish and fisheries of the upper Klamath basin, Oregon. *Journal of California and Great Basin Anthropology, 35*(2), 169–188.

Stewart, O. C. (2002). *Forgotten fires: Native Americans and the transient wilderness*. Norman, OK: University of Oklahoma Press.

Stine, S. (1994). Extreme and persistent drought in California and Patagonia during mediaeval time. *Nature, 369*, 546–549.

Swetnam, T. W. (1993). Fire history and climate change in giant sequoia groves. *Science, 262*(5135), 885–889.

Swezey, S. L., & Heizer, R. F. (1977). Ritual management of salmonid fish resources in California. *Journal of California and Great Basin Anthropology, 4*(1), 6–29.

Thakar, H. B., Glassow, M. A., & Blanchette, C. (2017). Reconsidering evidence of human impacts: Implications of within-site variation of growth rates in *Mytilus californianus* along tidal gradients. *Quaternary International, 427*(Part A), 151–159.

Timbrook, J., Johnson, J. R., & Earle, D. D. (1982). Vegetation burning by the Chumash. *Journal of California and Great Basin Anthropology, 4*(2), 163–186.

Tushingham, S., & Christiansen, C. (2015). Native American fisheries of the northwestern California and southwestern Oregon coast: A synthesis of fish bone data and implications for late Holocene storage and socio-economic organization. *Journal of California and Great Basin Anthropology, 35*(2), 189–216.

Walker, P. L. (1989). Cranial injuries as evidence of violence in prehistoric Southern California. *American Journal of Physical Anthropology, 80*(3), 313–323.

Whelan, C. S., Whitaker, A. R., Rosenthal, J. S., & Wohlgemuth, E. (2013). Hunter-gatherer storage, settlement, and the opportunity costs of women's foraging. *American Antiquity, 78*(4), 662–678.

Whitaker, A. R. (2008). Incipient aquaculture in prehistoric California?: Long-term productivity and sustainability vs. immediate returns for the harvest of marine invertebrates. *Journal of Archaeological Science, 35*(4), 1114–1123.

Whitaker, A. R. (2009). Are deer really susceptible to resource depression? Modeling deer (*Odocoileus hemionus*) populations under human predation. *California Archaeology, 1*(1), 93–108.

Whitaker, A. R., & Byrd, B. F. (2014). Social circumscription, territoriality, and the late Holocene intensification of small-bodied shellfish along the California coast. *The Journal of Island and Coastal Archaeology, 9*(2), 150–168.

Whitaker, A. R., & Hildebrandt, W. R. (2011). Why were northern fur Seals spared in northern California? A cultural and archaeological explanation. In T. Rick & T. Braje (Eds.), *Human and marine ecosystems: Archaeology and historical ecology of northeastern Pacific seals, sea lions, and sea otters* (pp. 197–219). Berkeley, CA: University of California Press.

Wiegel, L. E. (1993). Prehistoric burning in northwestern California. In G. White, P. Mikkelsen, W. R. Hildebrandt, & M. E. Basgall (Eds.), *There grows a green tree: Papers in honor of David a. Fredrickson* (pp. 213–216). Davis, CA: Center for Archaeological Research at Davis, University of California.

Wittke, J. H., Weaver, J. C., Bunch, T. E., Kennett, J. P., Kennett, D. J., Moore, A. M., et al. (2013). Evidence for deposition of 10 million tonnes of impact spherules across four continents 12,800 y ago. *Proceedings of the National Academy of Sciences, 110*(23), E2088–E2097.

Wohlgemuth, E. (2004). *The course of plant food intensification in native central California.* Ph.D. dissertation, University of California, Davis.

Wohlgemuth, E. (2010). Plant resource structure and the prehistory of plant use in Central Alta California. *California Archaeology, 2*(1), 57–76.

Yamada, S. B., & Peters, E. E. (1988). Harvest management and the growth and condition of submarket size mussels, *Mytilus californianus. Aquaculture, 74*(3–4), 293–299.

Identifying Common Pool Resources in the Archaeological Record: A Case Study of Water Commons from the North American Southwest

Michael J. Aiuvalasit

Introduction

Elinor Ostrom (2005, p. 79) defined common pool resources (CPRs) as natural or human-made resources of a size or with inherent characteristics that makes it costly, but not impossible to exclude from use by potential beneficiaries. Rules, norms, and institutions develop around CPRs to maintain equity and to keep "free riders" from over-exploiting shared resources. Therefore, studies of natural resources managed as commons offer an ideal opportunity to examine relationships between the environment and society. Ostrom (1990, 2005) and other interdisciplinary economists, political scientists, and anthropologists have developed a body of theory to study common pool resources and the social institutions designed by communities to govern them. Water, a resource which in arid ecosystem requires infrastructure to deliver to users, is particularly amenable to managing as a CPR (Ostrom 1993). Researchers have studied attributes of long-lived water systems, such as the *subak* rice-paddy system in Bali (e.g., Lansing and Kremer 1993) or the *huerta* irrigation system in Valencia, Spain (e.g., Ostrom 1990), to demonstrate how sustainable self-organized water resource arrangements can be in maintaining resource production and forming enduring social institutions (Ostrom 1993).

Researchers who study CPRs largely focus on extant, directly observable systems. For example, when Ostrom (2000) discussed the "evolution of social norms," it was in reference to evolutionary theory and collective action applied to the understanding how rules and institutions develop and not archaeology. Archaeological research that explicitly addresses the organization of CPRs is limited. There are three reasons for such lacuna. First, CPR theory is a relatively recent body of work. Although the questions driving CPR research are inherently interdisciplinary,

M. J. Aiuvalasit (✉)
Southern Methodist University, Dallas, TX, USA
e-mail: maiuvalasit@mail.smu.edu

archaeologists are neither listed as authors in the formative research into commons at what is now called the *Ostrom Workshop*; nor have any archaeologists published in the *International Journal of the Commons*. Historians, who examine written records regarding laws and practices surrounding institutions and resources, find themselves in a similar situation. *The International Journal of the Commons* only recently published a volume on historical analyses of CPRs (e.g., Laborda-Pemán and de Moor 2016). Second, the primary focus of archaeologists on material culture makes identifying rules, norms, and individual decision-making surrounding resource management particularly challenging. Archaeologists can use their datasets to make inferences about norms and institutions in the past, but cannot make direct observations of these behaviors (Nelson et al. 2010). Finally, archaeologists have developed their own body of theory about resource management and the rise of social complexity. These studies are rooted in political and evolutionary ecology and focus mostly on the emergence of leadership and political hierarchies, rather than how cooperative decision-making sustains long-term resource management (e.g., Scarborough 2003; Blanton and Fargher 2008).

Archaeologists acknowledge the prospects for using CPR theory (e.g., Carballo 2013; Blanton and Fargher 2016), and interdisciplinary researchers do occasionally turn to archaeology for long-term data sets (Anderies 2006; Lansing et al. 2009). Yet, there are only a few archaeological case studies linking material culture in the archaeological record to research questions regarding CPRs. Lindholm et al. (2013) identified archaeological commons in pre-industrial boreal forests of Northern Sweden by associating ethnohistorical records of forest use to archaeological site distributions. Archaeologists used site distributions and material evidence for seasonal or focused resource extraction in the greater North American Southwest and California to infer common land tenure regimes (e.g., Kohler 1992; Eerkens 1999; Bayman and Sullivan 2008). Blanton and Fargher (2016) and Lozny (2010) have synthesized regional-scale archaeological records using Ostrom's design principles, a set of attributes commonly found in robust CPR arrangements, to reinterpret existing archaeological datasets using collective action theory. Still, archaeological data offer great potential to develop research designs and data collection strategies to study CPR arrangements of the past.

In this chapter, I present one such archaeological case study by examining how the long-term sustainability of communities relates to differences in the emergence of CPR water management strategies. I used geoarchaeological methods to develop chronologies of water storage features, called reservoirs, at Ancestral Pueblo villages in the Jemez Mountains of New Mexico. By combining ethnographic analogy, collective action theory, and supporting archaeological evidence, I argue that these archaeological features served as CPR for domestic use of water. Through direct radiometric dating of these water features, I develop independent chronologies of infrastructure histories, which I then compare with the existing archaeological models of village population histories and hydroclimate records of water availability. My approach allows for a better understanding of how water management practices influenced cultural trajectories, particularly in relationship to exogenous environmental shocks, such as drought, and must be considered with other archaeological evidence to model the emergence of collective action strategies for resource management. I conclude by theorizing how the results of this archaeological study contribute to understanding of the relationships between emergent public institutions and community sustainability, as well as tradeoffs in CPRs.

Ancestral Pueblo Water CPRs in the Jemez Mountains of New Mexico

When archaeologists look to the North American Southwest for case studies of the relationships between water and indigenous communities, they turn to the extensive irrigation networks of the Hohokam in Central Arizona (e.g., Purdue and Berger 2015) or the current debates regarding the extent of water management at Chaco Canyon on the Colorado Plateau of New Mexico (Wills 2017; Scarborough et al. 2018)—not the Jemez Mountains.

The Jemez Mountains are in North-Central New Mexico and consist of the collapsed caldera and resurgent domes of the Valles Caldera in the Southern Rocky Mountains (Fig. 1).

A series of high elevation plateaus (5200–8000 ft) form a skirt ringing the caldera. These plateaus, particularly the Jemez Plateau on the southern margin and the Pajarito Plateau along the southeastern margin, are optimally situated along

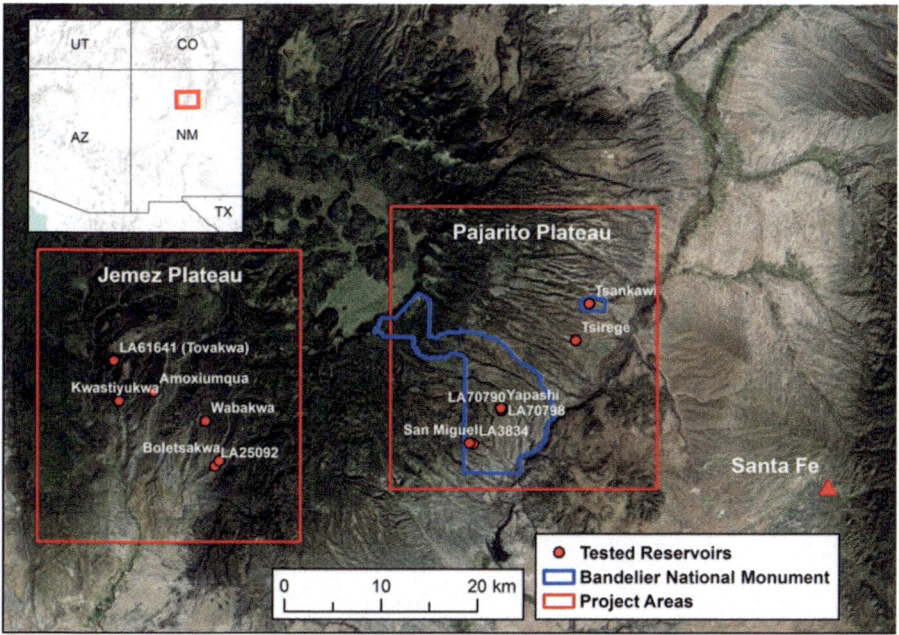

Fig. 1 Overview of study areas and archaeological sites with tested water reservoir features

elevation and precipitation gradients that agricultural modelers recently identified as being some ideal locations for dryland maize farming (Bocinsky and Kohler 2014). Water management is not a prerequisite for growing crops in these regions. Beginning in the late developmental period (AD 1050–1200), Ancestral Pueblo agriculturalists began to settle and farm the mesa-tops of both plateaus (Orcutt 1999; Kulisheck 2005; Ortman 2016). These early settlements were small hamlets, likely of multiple or extended families. Due in part to an influx of migrants from other regions (Ortman 2012), populations grew at the end of the Coalition period (AD 1200–1350), and communities coalesced into villages during the Classic period (AD 1350–1600). The largest of these prehistoric villages, Kwastiyukwa on the Jemez Plateau, was estimated to be a community of over 1,400 people (Liebmann et al. 2016). Regional population estimates reflect divergent cultural histories between the Jemez and Pajarito Plateaus (Fig. 2).

The Pajarito Plateau, which saw a rapid rise in population, was largely depopulated by AD 1450, except for villages in a few well-watered locations such as Frijoles Canyon (Ortman 2016). Tree-ring-based paleoprecipitation records show that the decline of regional population on the Pajarito Plateau in the fifteenth century correlates with more frequent droughts (Touchan et al. 2011). This falls at the beginning of global models of the Little Ice Age (Grove 2004); however, expressions of this phenomenon in the North American Southwest are mixed (Hall 2018). Archaeologists hypothesize that droughts played a factor in pushing people off the Pajarito Plateau toward the well-watered lowlands of the Rio Grande Valley (Kohler et al. 2004). Both archaeological evidence (Duwe 2011) and the oral traditions of

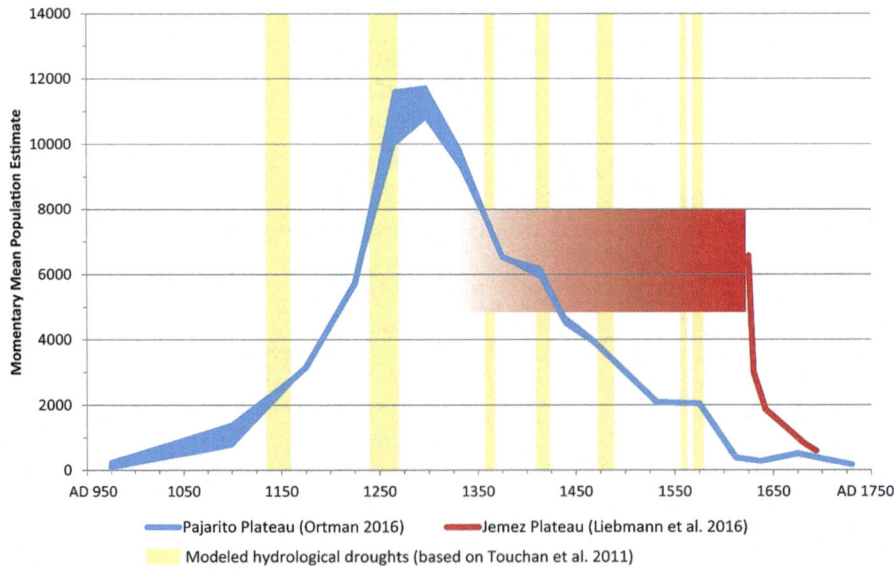

Fig. 2 Regional momentary mean population estimates and modeled periods of hydrological droughts

modern-day *Keres-* and *Tewa*-speaking communities, who retain direct association with their Ancestral mesa-top villages, support these affiliations and histories (Levine and Merlan 1997). By contrast, mesa-top settlements on the Jemez Plateau by the Ancestral *Towa* speaking Jemez endured until Spanish removal in the sixteenth and seventeenth centuries (Sando 1982; Liebmann et al. 2016). The Jemez Plateau region shares similar physical settings, dryland farming strategies, and culture histories to the Pajarito, yet the attributes contributing to the endurance of the Jemez people are unconsidered. Based on the shared physical contexts, potential for agricultural production, and adaptive strategies, it is not unreasonable to hypothesize that decisions surrounding resource management may have factored into the long-term sustainability of mesa-top communities.

While the mesa-tops are ideal locations for rain-fed dryland agriculture, the highly permeable tuff bedrock that makes up these mesas limits the amount of surface water available for domestic uses. Surface water is usually only found in narrow bottoms of deeply cut canyons, often far below agricultural surfaces. Many of these streams, particularly on the Pajarito Plateau, sustain only seasonal or intermittent flows during snowmelt runoffs and monsoonal rainfalls in the summer and early fall (Purtymun 1995; Allen 2004). Seasonal dry periods are periodically exacerbated by regional droughts as well (Bowen 1996). Such hydrological conditions presented a dilemma for Ancestral Pueblo peoples. The mesa-tops were an ideal context for dryland farming, but sources of water for domestic use, such as drinking, cooking, and mortar mixing, were limited. Therefore, communities of mesa-top agriculturalists, who farmed these lands for nearly a thousand years, had to adapt to a context with inherent tradeoffs between reliable agricultural production and limited options for nearby reliable domestic water sources.

Ancestral Pueblo communities across both the Jemez and Pajarito Plateaus constructed small water catchment basins at some of their largest villages (Fig. 1). These archaeological features, called reservoirs, consist of horseshoe-shaped earthen and stone berms to form the impoundment, with storage basins excavated down to bedrock that subsequently infilled with sediments during and after their use (Fig. 3).

They were built on mesa-tops to impound surface runoff from rainfall in low-order catchments before water spilled into canyon-bottom drainages. They are found almost exclusively in direct association with villages, rather than near agricultural features such as canals or terraces. Although archaeologists have long recorded these basins and berms as water storage features (Elliott 1982; Crown 1987), their utilitarian function is debated (Snead 2006). None of the reservoir features in the Jemez Mountains have been systematically tested to determine when and how they were used in relationship to the culture histories of indigenous populations.

I thus argue, following the logic presented by others who discussed archaeological proxies for collective action (for instance, Kohler et al. 2012), that these features served as common pool water resources for mesa-top Ancestral Pueblo communities. Ethnological and ethnohistorical records of Pueblo reservoirs used at mesa-top communities at Acoma and Hopi, as well as the descendant *Tewa* community of

Fig. 3 Reservoir feature at the site of Amoxiumqua

Ohkay Owingeh in the nineteenth and twentieth centuries, show that the construction and maintenance of reservoirs was coordinated at the community level. Rules and norms guided the construction (Whiteley 1988), water extraction (Beaglehole 1937; Sekaquaptewa 1969), routine maintenance (Ortiz 1969), and protection of water quality (Paytiamo 1932; Nabhan 1982) of these features. Property relationships surrounding water could be highly contingent upon the nature of the resource. For example, while access arrangements around springs or small bedrock catchments changed depending upon availability and demand (e.g., Beaglehole 1937, p. 13; Sekaquaptewa 1969, p. 21), yet the records of reservoir use, albeit limited in number, reflect practices driven by communal management.

The contexts of reservoir features at mesa-top sites in the Jemez Mountains also suggest that they were CPRs. They are typically within 100 meters of village centers and without any physical barriers to limit access. This would make it hard to exclude community members from using water from these features. Berms forming the impoundment for the basins range in height from 0.2 to 1.7 m above the basins. Basins were excavated 0.36–1.44 m down to bedrock, and basin diameters span from 12 to 36 m^2 (Table 1).

These water storage basins are small when compared to others in the ancient world (Scarborough 2003); but due to their size and structure, they would require communal-level coordination of labor to build. Based on my hydrological calculations of surface runoff, I estimated the volumes of water that could be stored in these basins from typical yearly high-runoff rainfall events. Using a 10 L a day per-person water requirement (Gleick 2000), the volume of water generated by these runoff

Table 1 Reservoir measurements and modeled water supply

Site	Max. population estimate	Reservoir measurements					Modeled water budget	
		Sed. thickness (m)	Berm height above basin (m)	Max basin diameter (m)	Max storage volume (m³)	Catchment area (m²)	Runoff estimates (m³)[a]	Water days estimate[b]
Amoxiumqua (LA481)	717	0.50	1.73	36.0	1261.03	7205	150.57	21
Boletsakwa (LA136)	413	1.00	0.31	15.5	132.90	2160	45.43	11
Boletsakwa-2 (LA25092)		1.44	1.30	25.0	717.35	6253	78.47	19
Kwastiyukwa (LA482)	1444	0.60	0.85	21.0	318.87	1120	28.88	2
Tovakwa (LA61641)	1240	0.72	1.20	33.0	729.85	100,566	731.6[c]	59
Wabakwa (LA478)	297	0.68	0.45	30.0	307.88	1108	23.76	8
Haatse/San Miguel (LA370)	100	0.64	0.40	14.0	64.80	2318	45	45
Haatse/San Miguel LA3834		0.36	0.30	12.0	41.47	494	6[c]	6
Tsankawi-1 (LA211)	300	0.40	0.75	22.5	189.67	3535	69	23
Tsankawi-2 (LA211)		0.40	0.50	20.0	150.80	2406	27[c]	9
Tsankawi-3 (LA211)		0.46	0.35	15.0	95.43	6242	96	32
Tsirege (LA170)	600	1.07	0.20	30.0	399.00	37,075	402[c]	67

(continued)

Table 1 (continued)

Site	Max. population estimate	Reservoir measurements					Modeled water budget	
		Sed. thickness (m)	Berm height above basin (m)	Max basin diameter (m)	Max storage volume (m³)	Catchment area (m²)	Runoff estimates (m³)[a]	Water days estimate[b]
Yapashi (LA250)	350	0.78	1.23	25.0	526.22	8834	171.5	49
Yapashi (LA70790)		0.55	0.20	22.5	176.71	5646	17.5[c]	5
Yapashi (LA70798)		0.40	0.07	18.0	70.87	1587	66.5[c]	19

[a]Runoff estimates are based on 1-year maximum rainfall event (3.68 cm on Jemez Plateau, 3.51 cm on Pajarito Plateau) and high-runoff coefficient number (CN = 93) reflective of compacted surfaces of catchment areas in village settings

[b]Estimate of water days is based on runoff estimate and a budget of 10 L of water for each village occupant

[c]A runoff coefficient number of 87 (typical of Class C soil in this region) was selected when catchment areas were outside of the site footprint

events, and population estimates, I modeled the number of days that a community's maximum population could meet their water needs using water from their reservoir(s). My estimates show that these features supplied water seasonally and could not meet all of a community's water needs. When the reservoirs did not hold water, villagers would face high costs to acquire their domestic water from natural sources (see Owens 1892; Sekaquaptewa 1969). Therefore, each dip of a jar into the reservoir to collect water brought members of the community one step closer to the inevitable long walk to a natural water source, which would further incentivize the establishment of community-wide rules of use and conservation practices.

Results of Chronological Investigations of Ancestral Pueblo CPR Reservoirs

Determining when these features were constructed and how long they were used is critical for understanding the degree to which CPR water management factored into the long-term sustainability of Ancestral Pueblo communities. Geoarchaeological studies of reservoirs in the North American Southwest, such as those by Murrell (2006), MacWilliams et al. (2009), and Benson et al. (2014), demonstrate that integrating sedimentary records with paleoecological and hydrological analyses is effective for modeling the use-life histories of reservoirs. Direct radiometric dating of the reservoir features, rather than relying on the analysis of the palimpsest of artifacts that over hundreds of years accumulated in and around reservoirs at these villages, presents an opportunity to reconstruct the use-life histories of these features with an independent chronological line of evidence (e.g., Aiuvalasit et al. 2010; Huckleberry et al. 2016). This approach has proven to generate new insights into relationships between water management practices and local sociopolitical histories (Neely et al. 2015).

I established chronologies of reservoirs as part of geoarchaeological investigations of 15 features at nine Ancestral Pueblo villages across both regions. As opposed to more invasive excavations, I cored representative sections of reservoir basins, berms, and control samples from the catchment areas to collect sediments and soils reflective of feature use (Fig. 4).

I presented detailed results of multi-proxy analyses of water storage potential and paleoecological indices of water quality these reservoirs elsewhere (Aiuvalasit 2017). Here, I focus exclusively on their chronology. Chronologies come from accelerated mass spectrometry (AMS) radiocarbon dating of charcoal from three contexts within each reservoir. Dated charcoal from natural soils buried below earthen reservoir berms (i.e., *paleosols*) provided estimates of *terminus post quem* dates to constrain the construction date of the reservoir, as these buried surfaces could only date to before the reservoirs were built. When no paleosols were present below berm fill, I sampled charcoal from the berm construction fill. Berm fill provides an approximate date for berm construction and use. I then analyzed multiple

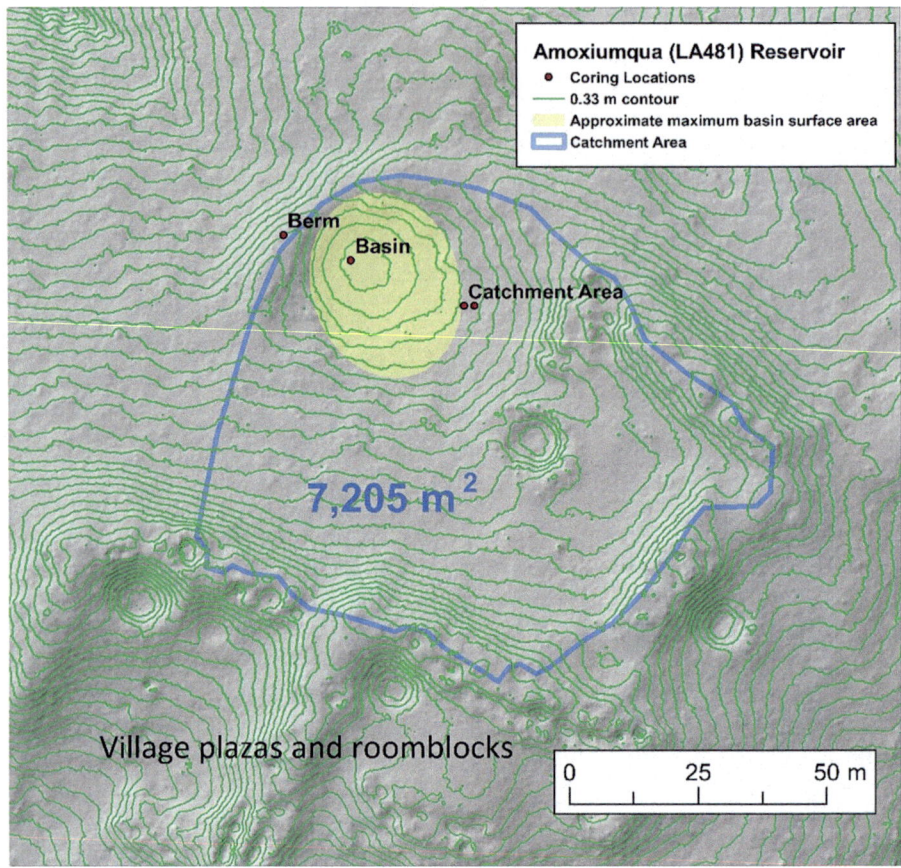

Fig. 4 Testing locations and labeled segments of the Amoxiumqua reservoir

samples from the stratified, water-laid sediments infilling the reservoir basins. In all sampling contexts, I selected macrobotanically identifiable short-lived charred plant tissues for dating, such as pine needles, bark scales, and grass cuticles. Dating short-lived plant tissues reduced the possibility of inadvertently dating old wood, which is frequently preserved in arid settings (Schiffer 1986), as well as the in-built ages of wood tissues (Gavin 2001) in a setting where trees can be hundreds of years old. This approach more precisely targets the sedimentation and construction events than dating bulk soils or wood charcoal. Sixty-one short-lived charred plant tissues were analyzed from key stratigraphic contexts by the W. M. Keck Carbon Cycle Accelerator Mass Spectrometry Laboratory at UC Irvine (Table 2).

The results of AMS analyses were calibrated to calendar years using Intcal13 (Reimer et al. 2013) in OxCAL 4.2 (Ramsey and Lee 2013). Modern radiocarbon measurements were calibrated to calendar years using the CALIBomb software (Reimer et al. 2004). Using the BCAL software package with stratigraphic contexts as priors (Buck et al. 1999), I modeled probability distributions using Bayesian

Table 2 Results of radiocarbon dating

KECK lab #	Sample ID	Context and depth below surface (cm)	Material dated	^{14}C age (BP)	2-σ calibrated dates (OxCal 4.2)
Amoxiumqua [LA 481] (n = 6)					
161,827	AMO 2.310	Basin (19)	Woody twig	265 ± 20	1526–1557, 1631–1667, 1784–1796
172,749	AMO2.3 13	Basin (25)	Needle bundle and seed frags	475 ± 15	1420–1446
161,826	AMO 2.216	Basin (31)	Needle	545 ± 35	1310–1360, 1386–1438
165,051	AMO 2.125	Basin (41)	Angio leaf tissue	600 ± 25	1299–1370, 1380–1407
170,990	AMO 3.211	Berm (21)	Needle and twig xylem	685 ± 15	1276–1300, 1368–1382
165,068	AMO 3.152	Berm (115)	Angio leaf and axis	935 ± 25	1031–1157
Boletsakwa [LA 136] (n = 7)					
172,750	BOL 2.408	Basin (14–16)	Charred angio xylem fragments	175 ± 15	1667–1684, 1734–1784, 1796–1807, 1929-modern
165,050	BOL 2.421	Basin (40–42)	Charred needle bundle base	485 ± 15	1417–1444
172,751	BOL 2.434	Basin (62–68)	Charred angio xylem fragments	865 ± 20	1056–1076, 1153–1222
161,823	BOL 2.441	Basin (80–82)	Charred woody twig	780 ± 25	1218–1277
161,822	BOL 2.444	Basin (86–88)	Charred forb axes	780 ± 30	1210–1281
165,048	BOL 3.110A	Berm (18–20)	Charred xylem and stem	425 ± 20	1433–1483
165,049	BOL 3.110B	Berm (18–20)	Charred xylem (exterior ring?)	335 ± 15	1486–1636
Boletsakwa-2 [LA 25092] (n = 3)					
170,991	BOL2 2.129	Basin (56–58)	Charred bark scale fragment	315 ± 20	1493–1602, 1615–1645
168,921	BOL2 2.165–166	Basin (128–132)	Charred angio wood xylem	485 ± 35	1331–1338, 1397–1461
165,052	BOL2 3.129–132	Berm (57–65)	Charred needle fragment	720 ± 25	1256–1299, 1371–1379
Kwastiyukwa [LA 482] (n = 5)					
165,053	KWA 2.109	Basin (16–18)	Charred wood xylem	280 ± 15	1523–1559, 1631–1658

(continued)

Table 2 (continued)

KECK lab #	Sample ID	Context and depth below surface (cm)	Material dated	^{14}C age (BP)	2-σ calibrated dates (OxCal 4.2)
172,753	KWA 2.319	Basin (33–39)	Aggregated charred cuticle, needle bundle, microchar of xylem, and cuticle	490 ± 15	1415–1442
165,054	KWA 2.227	Basin (52–54)	Charred wood xylem fragments	575 ± 15	1316–1355, 1388–1412
165,057	KWA 2.232	Basin (62–65)	Charred wood xylem	890 ± 15	1048–1086, 1123–1138, 1149–1210
165,058	KWA 3.130	Berm (62–64)	Charred wood xylem fragments	920 ± 15	1040–1110, 1116–1161
Haatse/San Miguel [LA370] (n = 4)					
170,999	SMG 2.107	Basin (10–14)	Aggregated charred bark scale and base of leaf bundle	Modern	–
172,757	SMG 2.108	Basin (10–16)	Aggregated charred cuticle, angio bark scales, and xylem	475 ± 15	1420–1446
172,758	SMG 2.231	Basin (60–64)	Aggregated microchar of angio twig and wood xylem	615 ± 15	1297–1330, 1338–1398
172,759	SMG 3.109	Berm (12–18)	Aggregated charred cuticle and angio xylem	740 ± 25	1225–1233, 1243–1290
Haatse/San Miguel [LA3834] (n = 3)					
172,754	LA 3834_2.208	Basin (10–16)	Aggregated charred cuticle and xylem fragments	470 ± 20	1418–1450
170,993	LA 3834 2.218	Basin (34–36)	Aggregated charred cuticle and angio xylem	585 ± 20	1306–1364, 1385–1411
172,755	LA 3834_3.105	Berm (4–10)	Aggregated microchar of cuticle and xylem frags	1115 ± 45	777–793, 802–846, 856–1017
Tovakwa [LA 61641] (n = 5)					
165,060	TOV 2.509–510	Basin (16–20)	Charred needle	790 ± 30	1190–1279
161,824	TOV 2.121	Basin (40–42)	Charred needle	Modern	–
161,825	TOV 2.128	Basin (54–56)	Charred needle	Modern	–

(continued)

Table 2 (continued)

KECK lab #	Sample ID	Context and depth below surface (cm)	Material dated	^{14}C age (BP)	2-σ calibrated dates (OxCal 4.2)
168,922	TOV 2.331–332	Basin (60–64)	Aggregated wood xylem	805 ± 25	1189–1271
165,059	TOV 3.150	Berm (110–112)	Charred needle	1100 ± 20	892–990
Tsankawi [LA 211] (n = 11)					
172,760	TK1_2.207	Basin (8–14)	Aggregated microchar of cuticle and needle frags	495 ± 15	1413–1440
171,000	TK1_2.221	Basin (36–42)	Aggregated charred cuticles, bark scales, and pine needle fragment	470 ± 15	1422–1448
172,763	TK1_3.412	Berm (19–25)	Aggregated microchar of cuticle, needle frag, cambium, bark scale	650 ± 15	1285–1316, 1355–1390
172,764	TK2_2.405	Basin (6–10)	Aggregated charred angio wood xylem	535 ± 15	1330–1340, 1396–1431
172,765	TK2_2.412	Basin (24–26)	Aggregated charred angio wood xylem	485 ± 20	1414–1445
171,003	TK2_2.319	Basin (34–38)	Aggregated charred bark scales, cuticle fragments, and xylem/bark scale	930 ± 15	1039–1155
171,004	TK2_3.310	Basin (18–24)	Aggregated charred twig xylem, cuticle, and seed fragments	675 ± 15	1278–1305, 1365–1385
171,005	TK3_2.410	Basin (18–20)	Aggregated charred pine needle frag, cuticle, and leaf bundle fragment	580 ± 15	1313–1358, 1387–1410
171,006	TK3_2.316	Basin (34–36)	Aggregated charred seed and needle fragments	550 ± 15	1324–1345, 1392–1423
171,007	TK3_3.209	Berm (16–18)	Charred bark scale fragment	335 ± 20	1481–1639
172,766	TK3_3.217	Berm (28–34)	Aggregated microchar of angio wood xylem and cuticle	425 ± 15	1436–1472
Tsirege [LA 170] (n = 4)					
171,008	TSR 2.117	Basin (30–34)	Aggregated charred xylem	535 ± 15	1330–1340, 1396–1431

(continued)

Table 2 (continued)

KECK lab #	Sample ID	Context and depth below surface (cm)	Material dated	^{14}C age (BP)	2-σ calibrated dates (OxCal 4.2)
171,009	TSR 2.140	Basin (74–80)	Aggregated charred cuticle, twig xylem, poss. Needle bundle	455 ± 15	1427–1451
171,010	TSR 2.251	Basin (96–102)	Aggregated charred cuticle, stem, possible needle bundle fragment	545 ± 15	1325–1345, 1393–1426
171,011	TSR 3.139	Berm (76–80)	Aggregated charred seed and cuticle	600 ± 15	1304–1365, 1383–1403
Wabakwa [LA 478] (n = 2)					
172,767	WAB 2.309	Basin (16–18)	Aggregated charred needle and cuticle fragments	Modern	–
172,768	WAB 2.318	Basin (34–36)	Charred bark scale-twig fragment	795 ± 15	1219–1265
Yapashi [LA 250] (n = 5)					
172,769	YAP 2.408	Basin (10–16)	Aggregated microchar of charred cuticle and angio wood xylem fragments	510 ± 15	1409–1436
171,012	YAP 2.118	Basin (30–36)	Aggregated wood xylem, cuticles, and possible bark scale	590 ± 20	1304–1365, 1384–1409
171,013	YAP 2.137	Basin (68–74)	Aggregated wood xylem, cuticle, and possible needle bundle fragment	585 ± 15	1310–1360, 1386–1409
172,770	YAP 3.311	Berm (20–22)	Charred angio xylem	540 ± 15	1328–1342, 1395–1428
172,771	YAP 3.327	Berm (52–54)	Charred angio twig xylem	665 ± 15	1281–1308, 1361–1387
Yapashi [LA70790] (n = 3)					
170,994	LA70790_2.118	Basin (32–36)	Aggregated charred needle fragment, bark scales, and cuticle	685 ± 15	1276–1300, 1368–1382
170,995	LA70790_2.128	Basin (50–56)	Aggregated charred bark scales, cuticle, twig xylem fragments	770 ± 25	1220–1280

(continued)

Table 2 (continued)

KECK lab #	Sample ID	Context and depth below surface (cm)	Material dated	^{14}C age (BP)	2-σ calibrated dates (OxCal 4.2)
172,756	LA70790_3.306	Basin (8–12)	Aggregated microchar of leaf cuticle and angio wood xylem fragments	630 ± 15	1293–1322, 1348–1393
Yapashi [LA70798] (n = 3)					
170,996	LA70798_2.114	Basin (22–28)	Aggregated charred cuticle, fine twig xylem, and poss. Leaf bundle fragments	650 ± 30	1280–1326, 1343–1395
170,997	LA70798_2.121	Basin (36–42)	Aggregated charred cuticle, seeds, and poss. Cambium fragment	605 ± 15	1301–1368, 1381–1401
170,998	LA70798_3.309	Berm (18–20)	Charred xylem	865 ± 20	1056–1076, 1153–1222

calibrations. Feature use-life histories are estimated as the inclusive range of AMS date probability distributions of samples from sedimentation within the basin. In a few cases, I extended the age ranges of feature beyond the basin sediment dates to include dates from the berm construction sequence, but they are always no older than dates from the paleosols. Inherent uncertainties in radiometric dating and sedimentation rates, as represented in the probability distributions of the calibrated samples, limit chronological resolution of feature use to decadal- or century-scale correlations with cultural and drought chronologies.

I compared the chronologies of feature use-life histories to occupation histories at the Ancestral Pueblo villages associated with the reservoirs and tree-ring-based drought periodicities (Fig. 5).

I defined drought periodicities within the dendroclimatological record local to the Jemez Mountains (Touchan et al. 2011) using a standard deviation approach to isolate protracted dry periods (Ingram 2010). Chronologies of village occupation histories and population estimates on the Pajarito Plateau are based on Ortman's (2016) analysis apportioning Ancestral Pueblo village population densities by applying ethnohistorically derived models of village settlement densities to site-specific room counts and ceramic-based chronologies. Site-specific estimates are summed for all of the sites in the region to generate momentary mean population estimates for both regions (Fig. 2) and site-specific population histories (Fig. 6).

In case of the Jemez Plateau, complacent stylistic changes in ceramic styles limits the chronological resolution when estimating village occupation histories. Diachronic estimates of Jemez population histories at individual sites are based on ethnohistorical records of Pueblo village population densities similar to Ortman's

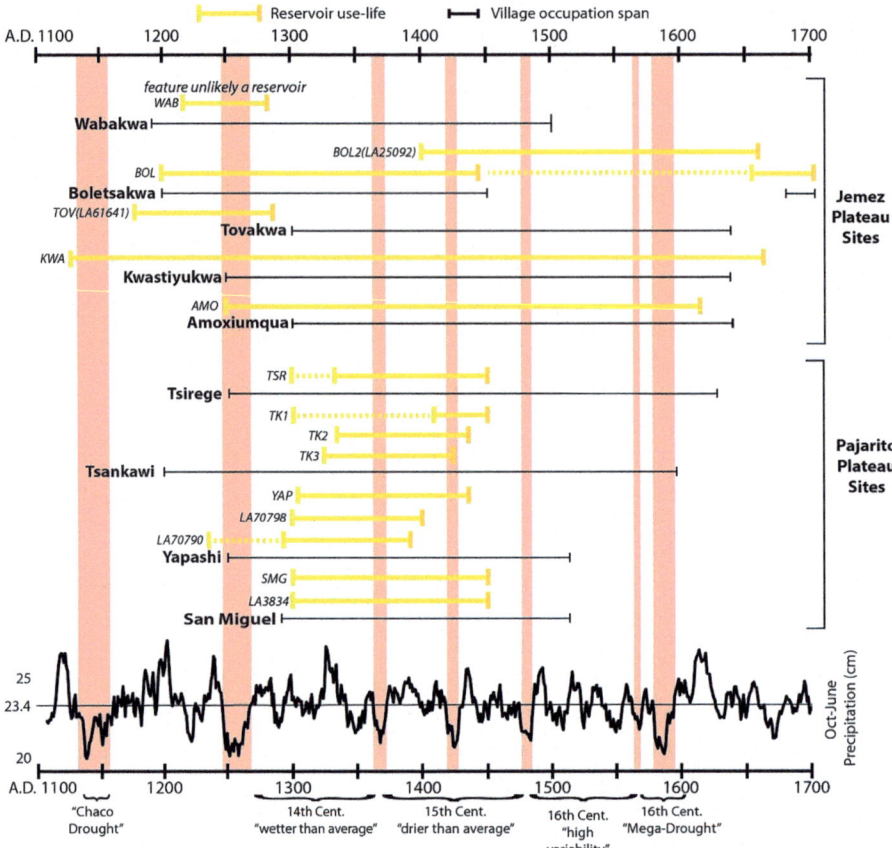

Paleoprecipitation model with 9-yr moving averages from Touchan et al. 2011. Modeled hydrological droughts are highlighted. Occupation chronologies based on Orcutt 1999, Ortman 2012, and Ortman 2016.

Fig. 5 Reservoir use-life histories, village occupation spans, and paleoprecipitation model for all tested features (AD 1100–1700)

approach, but instead correlate population estimates to rubble mound volumes (Liebmann et al. 2016). Diachronic population estimates for the Jemez Plateau are limited to broad ranges until the times of historical records by the Spanish.

Jemez Plateau

On the Jemez Plateau, each of the reservoirs had its own unique use-history relative to its village's occupation sequence (Fig. 5). For example, it is not likely that the features at Wabakwa and Tovakwa functioned as reservoirs during the life of their villages. The reservoir at Wabakwa is a very small feature with an unusual

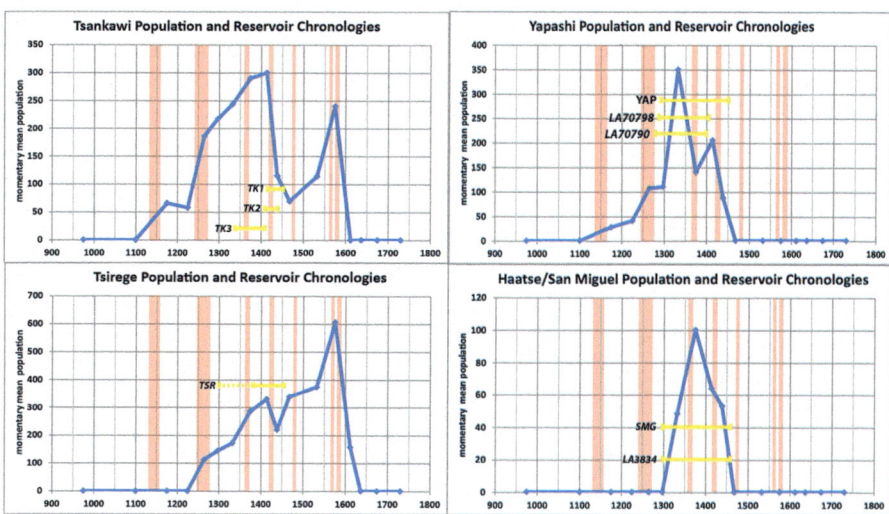

Fig. 6 Momentary mean population estimates of the four village sites on the Pajarito with tested reservoir features (Ortman 2016)

elongated J-shaped berm, rather than a U-shaped earthen berm typical to all of the other reservoirs. Its catchment area is very small and its basin filled with gravelly sediments unlike any of the other reservoirs. It is located near historical erosion control features and immediately downslope of a historic two-track road. There was little charcoal suitable for dating from the basin sediments of the Wabakwa feature. One charcoal sample dated to the thirteenth century, while another produced a modern date (Table 2). This feature was probably not a reservoir, and instead may have been an infilled borrow pit or possibly an early historic erosion control feature. Lacking a reservoir may have introduced vulnerabilities to water scarcity at Wabakwa, as this community is far from perennial water sources. It also happens to be the only site I tested on the Jemez Plateau that was not occupied into historic time periods, meaning that water scarcity cannot be ruled out as a driver of the earlier depopulation of Wabakwa. By contrast, the large 30 m diameter reservoir at Tovakwa produced a use-life history spanning the late eleventh and twelfth centuries—which pre-dates the occupation sequence at Tovakwa. The berm is breached, and the very large catchment area upslope of the feature would produce surface runoff that would overwhelm the storage potential of its basin. The feature is located 600 m away from the village site, and there is a natural, albeit intermittent, water source closer to Tovakwa than its reservoir.

As at Tovakwa, the construction of the reservoir at Kwastiyukwa also preceded the initial occupation date of its village. The four radiocarbon dates from the 60 cm thick basin sediments of fine-grained silts and clays accumulated gradually throughout the entire span of the village occupation. Its 21 m diameter basin and nearly 1 m high berm could have accommodated an appreciable quantity of water; however, its small, low-gradient catchment area of only 1120 m^2 could not generate much runoff.

Kwastiyukwa has the highest modeled population of any mesa-top village in the Jemez Mountains (Liebmann et al. 2016), yet its small reservoir could only provide a tiny fraction of the water needed by the community when it reached its peak population of over 1,400 people. The early use histories of Tovakwa and Kwastiyukwa confirm previously unidentified utilization of mesa-tops in the Jemez Mountains, where presumably small groups coordinated the construction of water storage features. Archaeological investigations by Ford (2013) at Jemez Cave, a stratified multicomponent cave in the region with archaeological deposits that date to the developmental period identified a mixed subsistence regime utilizing lowland horticulture in the canyon bottoms and upland hunting and gathering during this early period. *Maize* pollen recovered in a core from the buried paleosol below the reservoir berm at the Jemez site of Amoxiumqua (Aiuvalasit and Kiahtipes 2017) indicates that Ancestral Pueblo farmers were cultivating mesa-tops during this time. Tovakwa and Kwastiyukwa may reflect the emergence of collective action strategies to collect surface water—whether to attract game, domestic water, or for agricultural water (e.g., Anderson and Potter 2015).

The chronologies of the reservoirs at Amoxiumqua and Boletsakwa closely align with village occupation histories. Due to their sizes, both of these features could provide appreciable amounts of domestic water during the occupations of Ancestral Pueblo villages. The reservoir at Amoxiumqua has a large basin (36 m diameter) and berm (1.7 m high), and the basin is proportional to store potential runoff volumes generated by its 7,205 m^2 catchment area. The four radiocarbon dates from basin sediments indicate that it was constructed at or immediately before village formation around AD 1300 and that it was used throughout the long village occupation history. Geoarchaeological evidence of basin truncations suggests clean-out events, reflecting coordinated maintenance of this feature (Aiuvalasit 2017; Aiuvalasit and Kiahtipes 2017). Boletsakwa has two features, one immediately near the village (BOL1) and another (BOL2 or LA 25092) approximately 650 m away on the same mesa-top surface. A thick accumulation sequence in the Boletsakwa BOL1 reservoir, coupled with a berm likely reconstructed in the fifteenth century, suggests that it was used beginning in the late twelfth or early thirteenth centuries, remodeled in the fifteenth century, and reused during the reoccupation of the site during and after the Pueblo Revolt era (1680–1692) (Liebmann 2012). The second reservoir feature near Boletsakwa is much larger, and its use history spanned a portion of the village's history with little evidence for occupation. Its distance from the site of Boletsakwa, and location on a part of the mesa with numerous small 1–2 room fieldhouses and agricultural features, suggests it may have served as a source for agricultural water as well as domestic water when the village was later reoccupied.

In sum, use histories of reservoirs and site chronologies on the Jemez Plateau reflect village-specific solutions to water management problems, with neither correlations in use with periods of droughts nor regional synchronicity in construction. Collective action solutions to water scarcity were undertaken early in cultural sequences. It cannot be ruled out that these features and emerging institutions for water management may have signaled the success of collective action approaches to solving resource stress in these new environments. Water infrastructure then may have served as loci for the local emergence of institutional arrangements and communities on the mesa-tops of the Jemez Plateau. In the cases of Kwastiyukwa, Amoxiumqua, and Boletsakwa, these features were maintained throughout the village occupation histories—even if they did not always provide appreciable quantities of water for growing communities. This suggests the endurance of collective action strategies around water, through what certainly would be shifting forms of social organization as populations grew and village dynamics became increasingly complex over hundreds of years of occupation.

Pajarito Plateau

I tested nine reservoirs associated with four large Ancestral Pueblo villages on the Pajarito Plateau. All of the features were constructed around or after AD 1300 (Fig. 5). Their construction fell within the longest drought-free period after the major drought that occurred at the end of the thirteenth century. Except for reservoirs at the site of San Miguel and possibly one of the three reservoirs at Yapashi (site LA70790), all of the features were constructed after villages were established. None of Pajarito reservoirs were repurposed features from the Coalition period, even though small catchment basins dating to the Coalition period are reported at small agricultural sites in the region (Gauthier personal communication). Instead of being catalysts for the emergence of village life like on the Jemez Plateau, it appears reservoirs reflect community-wide coordination to manage water after communities had already formed. Temporal overlap of reservoir construction suggests that ideas and practices for water management spread rapidly across the region concomitant with community coalescence. Similar water features are recorded in other regions of the Southwest, including in the Four Corners region that date to the twelfth and thirteenth centuries (e.g., Wilshusen et al. 1997). The late thirteenth-century migrants to the Pajarito Plateau are hypothesized to have come from this region, potentially catalyzing new approaches to community-making in the greater Northern Rio Grande region (Ortman 2012), based in part on legacies of prior successes, and failures, of sociopolitical organization (Glowacki 2015).

The effort to construct and potentially maintain multiple reservoirs at villages on the Pajarito Plateau suggests a different form of coordination for resource management than on the Jemez Plateau. Villages with single reservoir features are more common on the Jemez Plateau, while only the site of Tsirege on the Pajarito Plateau had one reservoir. All of the other sites I tested had multiple features. Pajarito Plateau reservoirs, especially at the sites with multiple features were typically smaller, with basins averaging just <20 m in diameter and berms averaging only 0.4 m high. The combined volume of water stored in these features could provide appreciable quantities of water for these communities (see Table 1); however, constructing multiple features would require greater coordination of labor and make their maintenance more critical in order to meet community's demands.

By the early to middle 1400s, none of the reservoirs I tested on the Pajarito Plateau were in use. This time period overlaps with increasingly frequent hydrological droughts and rapid decline in the regional population. Droughts in the early 1400s would reduce the number of runoff generating events that would fill the reservoirs. Geomorphological studies on the Central Pajarito Plateau found a mantling of eolian sands on mesa-top surfaces dates to this time period (Drakos and Reneau 2007), which could have accelerated basin infilling with easily transported sediment in basin runoff. The interior walls of these small basins were frequently rock-lined, which was potentially a strategy to mitigate the impact of high-magnitude runoff events on the integrity of the berms. It was not uncommon to find basins nearly completely infilled with sediment. The most effective strategy to efficiently store water in these basins would have been routine maintenance. However, I found neither stratigraphic nor sedimentological evidence for unconformities or truncations that would reflect clean-out events. Instead, after potentially up to 100–150 years of using reservoirs, communities on the Pajarito Plateau chose to not maintain their water storage features as declining populations saw fewer and fewer years with basin-filling rainfall events.

While reservoir features on the Pajarito Plateau were largely constructed during peak regional populations, these features were not always built or used during peak village populations. The villages of Tsirege and Tsankawi continued to be occupied after AD 1450 (Fig. 6). Even though regional populations declined during this time, both villages experienced late population increases. The Ancestral Pueblo population at Tsirege peaks in the late sixteenth century. By that point, its reservoir, which is breached, had not likely been used in over 100 years. Tsankawi saw a late population rebound as well, although both villages were depopulated by the early seventeenth century. In both cases, the nearest perennial water source—alluvial wetlands in Pajarito Canyon near Tsirege and Basalt Spring near Tsankawi—could provide close (<1 h one-way walk) domestic water for these villages (Aiuvalasit 2017). This wasn't the case for Yapashi and San Miguel, where the decline of village populations correlates to the fifteenth-century droughts and the end of reservoirs. Neither San Miguel nor Yapashi are near perennial water; therefore, it cannot be ruled out that water scarcity may have been a factor in the depopulation of these communities.

Decisions surrounding water management made in the early Classic had long-lasting consequences for Ancestral *Tewa* and *Keres* communities. Populations became increasingly aggregated into a few communities, yet overall the regional populations fell, leaving only few communities, all centered near permanent water sources. While some communities continued to be successful until the early seventeenth century, the decline in regional population suggests that individuals, households, and potentially larger social units were leaving the mesa-tops. Movement of Ancestral Pueblos off the Plateau likely contributed to the rise in regional populations seen during the fourteenth and fifteenth centuries in the Chama Valley of the adjacent Northern Rio Grande region (Ortman 2016). Duwe and Anschuetz (2013) see these movements as a fundamental response to resource insecurity in the region.

Oral traditions indicate that Ancestral *Tewa* and *Keres* moved off of the mesa-tops and into aggregated pueblo communities along the Northern Rio Grande and its tributaries (Levine and Merlan 1997). Water storage features are reported at some large aggregated Ancestral Pueblo sites in the Northern Rio Grande (Snead 2006). One feature, and the attendant social institutions for its communal management, was documented at the Pueblo community of Ohkay Owingeh, where it continued to be used into the twentieth century (Ortiz 1969). The transfer of social institutions for water management from mesa-top contexts to valley bottoms, potentially reoriented around irrigation, has been hypothesized (Dozier 1970, p. 153). These observations raise a key point: while collective action approaches to water management practices enhanced fragilities to water scarcity on the Pajarito, the social institutions that formed in these contexts likely endured in the growing and increasingly aggregated Ancestral Pueblo settlements in the Northern Rio Grande.

Discussion and Conclusions: Archaeological Insights into the Commons

This comparative case study of long-term water management as a commons demonstrates how archaeological data can provide insights to the study of CPR systems. First, this study shows how the timing of the emergence of institutions to manage resources as commons can greatly influence the longevity of communities. Resilient resource management systems—i.e., systems that can withstand shocks and still maintain function—are often a product of the coevolution of management regimes and social institutions (e.g., Ostrom 1990; Lansing et al. 2009). CPRs or other resource arrangements which are adopted, particularly during periods of resource scarcity, or imposed by "top-down" management, often fail (Saunders 2014). These observations are echoed by hazards researchers, who find that resilient communities typically have robust management strategies preceding a shock, such as a drought, while vulnerable communities that respond ad hoc usually do not (Wilhite and Buchanan-Smith 2005).

By determining when and how Ancestral Pueblo communities organized water management systems between two adjacent regions, I was able to present a comparative examples where climate and hydrological factors were far more similar than they would be in an inter-regional comparison. Water management systems of the Jemez Plateau developed seemingly in situ with the incipient settlement of aggregated communities on mesa-tops. Water management, and the institutional arrangements associated with it, appears to have been entrained early in the culture histories of communities far from water on the mesas of the Jemez Plateau. These communities endured through periodic droughts and the presumed reworking of social arrangements as communities grew ever larger through time. In some cases, reservoirs were used and maintained even after communities grew to a size where these legacy infrastructures could provide only a small fraction of the overall water needs of a community. By contrast, reservoirs on the Pajarito Plateau were adopted after communities had already started forming, likely due to water demands driven by rapid aggregation, by institutions for resource management brought into the region by migrants adapting to both new physical and social contexts. This infrastructure may have worked during the quiescent climate regimes in the fourteenth century, but by the fifteenth century, frequent droughts made the multiple small reservoir features constructed at villages on the Pajarito Plateau far less effective than the larger features on the Jemez Plateau.

The second lesson of CPR research demonstrated in this study is that robust strategies for managing one type of resource often generate fragilities in other resource arrangements (Anderies et al. 2007). Communities are always tasked with addressing multiple resource needs, which often involve tradeoffs when strategies enacted for managing one resource class are suboptimal for another. Across the Jemez Mountains, successful dryland agriculture on mesa-tops produced fragilities in securing access to domestic water. Hydrological conditions made communities situated in contexts ideal for agriculture vulnerable to water scarcity and high water acquisition costs. Technological solutions, in the form of constructing reservoirs close to villages, served to reduce these vulnerabilities, but increasing demand over time due to rising populations, shocks to the hydrological system in the form of droughts, and shifts in regional economies all can expose fragilities within collective action approaches to water management. While sharing within a community and trade can mediate food scarcity, and Kohler et al. (2004) provide evidence for this on the Pajarito, solving challenges associated with meeting domestic water needs is always more immediate and constrained by technological, hydrological, and social limits attendant to local conditions. Archaeologists can provide long-term perspectives on these tradeoffs (Hegmon 2017), especially if we focus on identifying clear proxies in the archaeological record for decision-making surrounding resource management. In so doing, archaeological research has the potential to articulate the dynamics of sustainable solutions to resource management dilemmas at the nexus of food, water, and energy (sensu Liu et al. 2018), to provide lessons for issues so pressing for modern-day communities across the planet.

Acknowledgment This work was made possible through coordination, and permitting with three federal agencies (National Park Service, Department of Energy, and US Forest Service), as well as in consultation with descendant Pueblo communities. Funding for data collection was provided by the Institute for the Study of Earth and Man at SMU, the William P. Clements Center for Southwest Studies Interdisciplinary Research Grant at SMU, and a Geological Society of America Grant Graduate Student Research Grant. Funding for analyses was provided by the National Science Foundation Doctoral Dissertation Research Improvement Award #1445083 and support from a National Science Foundation Dynamics of Coupled Natural and Human Systems (CNH) Award #1114898.

References

Aiuvalasit, M. J. (2017). *Common goods in uncommon times: Water, droughts, and the sustainability of ancestral pueblo communities in the Jemez Mountains, New Mexico, AD 1100–1700*. Dissertation, Southern Methodist University, Dallas, Texas.

Aiuvalasit, M. J., & Kiahtipes, C. (2017). Assessing the potential for pollen preservation from ancestral Pueblo water reservoir features, Jemez Mountains, New Mexico. *Newsletter of the New Mexico Archaeological Council, 1*, 2–9.

Aiuvalasit, M. J., Neely, J. A., & Bateman, M. D. (2010). New radiometric dating of water management features at the prehistoric Purrón Dam Complex, Tehuacán Valley, Puebla, México. *Journal of Archaeological Science, 37*(6), 1207–1213.

Allen, C. D. (2004). Ecological patterns and environmental change in the in the Bandelier landscape. In T. A. Kohler (Ed.), *Archaeology of Bandelier National Monument: Village formation on the Pajarito plateau, New Mexico* (Vol. 12, pp. 19–68). Albuquerque, NM: University of New Mexico.

Anderies, J. M. (2006). Robustness, institutions, and large-scale change in social-ecological systems: The Hohokam of the Phoenix Basin. *Journal of Institutional Economics, 2*(02), 133–155.

Anderies, J. M., Rodriguez, A. A., Janssen, M. A., & Cifdaloz, O. (2007). Panaceas, uncertainty, and the robust control framework in sustainability science. *Proceedings of the National Academy of Sciences, 104*(39), 15194–15199.

Anderson, K. C., & Potter, J. M. (2015). Chronostratigraphic and paleoenvironmental evidence for marsh habitats during the Early Pueblo I (AD 700–900) occupation of Ridges Basin, southwest Colorado, USA. *Geoarchaeology, 30*(2), 100–119.

Bayman, J. M., & Sullivan, A. P. (2008). Property, identity, and macroeconomy in the prehispanic southwest. *American Anthropologist, 110*(1), 6–20.

Beaglehole, E. (1937). *Notes on Hopi economic life* (Vol. 15). New Haven, CT: Yale University Publications in Anthropology.

Benson, L. V., Griffin, E. R., Stein, J. R., Friedman, R. A., & Andrae, S. W. (2014). Mummy Lake: An unroofed ceremonial structure within a large-scale ritual landscape. *Journal of Archaeological Science, 44*, 164–179.

Blanton, R., & Fargher, L. (2008). *Collective action in the formation of pre-modern states*. New York, NY: Springer.

Blanton, R. E., & Fargher, L. F. (2016). *How humans cooperate: Confronting the challenges of collective action*. Boulder, CO: University Press of Colorado.

Bocinsky, R. K., & Kohler, T. A. (2014). A 2,000-year reconstruction of the rain-fed maize agricultural niche in the US southwest. *Nature Communications, 5*, 1–12.

Bowen, B. M. (1996). Rainfall and climate variation over a sloping New Mexico plateau during the North American monsoon. *Journal of Climate, 9*(12), 3432–3442.

Buck, C. E., Christen, J. A., & James, G. N. (1999). Towards BCal: An on-line bayesian radiocarbon calibration facility. *Mémoires de la Société préhistorique française, 26*, 113–117.

Carballo, D. M. (2013). Labor collectives and group cooperation in pre-Hispanic Central Mexico. In D. M. Carballo (Ed.), *Cooperation and collective action: Archaeological perspectives* (pp. 243–274). Boulder, CO: University Press of Colorado.

Crown, P. L. (1987). Water storage in the prehistoric southwest. *Kiva, 52*(3), 209–228.

Dozier, E. P. (1970). *The Pueblo Indians of North America*. Prospect Heights, Ill: Waveland Press.

Drakos, P. G., & Reneau, S. L. (2007). Episodic eolian events and preservation of mesa top archaeological sites on the Pajarito Plateau, New Mexico. In B. S. Kues, S. A. Kelley, & V. W. Lueth (Eds.) (pp. 121–130). Albuquerque, NM.

Duwe, S. G. (2011). *The prehispanic tewa world: Space, time, and becoming in the Pueblo southwest*. Tucson, AZ: The University of Arizona.

Duwe, S. G., & Anschuetz, K. F. (2013). Ecological Uncertainly and Organizational Flexibility on the Prehistoric Tewa Landscape: Notes from the Northern Frontier. In B. J. Vierra (Ed.),

From Mountaintop to Valley Bottom Understanding Past Land Use in the Northern Rio Grande Valley, New Mexico (pp. 95–112). Salt Lake City, Utah: University of Utah Press.

Eerkens, J. W. (1999). Common pool resources, buffer zones, and jointly owned territories: Hunter-gatherer land and resource tenure in Fort Irwin, Southeastern California. *Human Ecology, 27*(2), 297–318.

Elliott, M. L. (1982). *Large Pueblo sites near Jemez Springs, New Mexico (Cultural Resources Report 1)*. Santa Fe, NM: Santa Fe National Forest.

Ford, R. I. (2013). The Cultural Ecology of Jemez Cave. In B. J. Vierra (Ed.), From Mountaintop to Valley Bottom Understanding Past Land Use in the Northern Rio Grande Valley, New Mexico (pp. 69–80). Salt Lake City, Utah: University of Utah Press.

Gavin, D. G. (2001). Estimation of inbuilt age in radiocarbon ages of soil charcoal for fire history studies. *Radiocarbon, 43*(1), 27–44.

Gleick, P. H. (2000). *The world's water 2000–2001: The biennial report on freshwater resources*. Washington, D.C.: Island.

Glowacki, D. M. (2015). *Living and leaving: A social history of regional depopulation in thirteenth-century Mesa Verde*. Tucson, AZ: University of Arizona Press.

Grove, J. M. (2004). *Little ice ages: Ancient and modern*. New York, NY: Taylor & Francis.

Hall, S. A. (2018). Paleoenvironments of the American Southwest. In B. J. Vierra (Ed.), The Archaic Southwest: Foragers in an Arid Land (pp. 16–28): University of Utah Press.

Hegmon, M. (Ed.). (2017). *The give and take of sustainability: Archaeological and anthropological perspectives on tradeoffs*. Cambridge, UK: Cambridge University Press.

Huckleberry, G., Ferguson, T. J., Rittenour, T., Banet, C., & Mahan, S. (2016). Identification and dating of indigenous water storage reservoirs along the Rio San José at Laguna Pueblo, western New Mexico, USA. *Journal of Arid Environments, 127*, 171–186.

Ingram, S. E. (2010). *Human vulnerability to climatic dry periods in the prehistoric U.S. southwest*. Tempe, AZ: Arizona State University.

Kohler, T. A. (1992). Field houses, villages, and the tragedy of the commons in the early northern Anasazi Southwest. *American Antiquity, 57*(4), 617–635.

Kohler, T. A., Cockburn, D., Hooper, P. L., Bocinsky, R. K., & Kobti, Z. (2012). The coevolution of group size and leadership: An agent-based public goods model for prehispanic Pueblo societies. *Advances in Complex Systems, 15*(01n02), 1150007.

Kohler, T. A., Herr, S., & Root, M. J. (2004). The rise and fall of towns on the pajarito (A.D. 1375-1600). In T. A. Kohler (Ed.), *Archaeology of Bandelier National Monument: Village formation on the Pajarito plateau, New Mexico* (Vol. 12, pp. 215–264). Albuquerque, NM: University of New Mexico.

Kulisheck, J. (2005). *The archaeology of Pueblo population change on the Jemez plateau A.D. 1200 to 1700: The effects of Spanish contact and conquest*. Dallas, TX: Southern Methodist University.

Laborda-Pemán, M., & de Moor, T. (2016). History and the commons: A necessary conversation. *International Journal of the Commons, 10*(2), 517. https://doi.org/10.18352/ijc.769

Lansing, J. S., Cox, M. P., Downey, S. S., Janssen, M. A., & Schoenfelder, J. W. (2009). A robust budding model of Balinese water temple networks. *World Archaeology, 41*(1), 112–133.

Lansing, J. S., & Kremer, J. N. (1993). Emergent properties of Balinese water temple networks: Coadaptation on a rugged fitness landscape. *American Anthropologist, 95*(1), 97–114.

Levine, F., & Merlan, T. (1997). *Bandelier national monument ethnographic literature search and consultation*. Unpublished report prepared for Bandelier National Monument.

Liebmann, M. (2012). *Revolt: An archaeological history of Pueblo resistance and revitalization in 17th century New Mexico*. Tucson, AZ: University of Arizona Press.

Liebmann, M. J., Farella, J., Roos, C. I., Stack, A., Martini, S., & Swetnam, T. W. (2016). Native American depopulation, reforestation, and fire regimes in the Southwest United States, 1492-1900 CE. *Proceedings of the National Academy of Sciences of the United States of America, 113*(6), E696–E704.

Lindholm, K.-J., Sandström, E., & Ekman, A.-K. (2013). The archaeology of the commons. *Journal of Archaeology and Ancient History, 10*, 3–49.

Liu, J., Hull, V., Godfray, H., Charles, J., Tilman, D., Gleick, P., et al. (2018). Nexus approaches to global sustainable development. *Nature Sustainability, 1*(9), 466.

Lozny, L. R. (2010). Cooperate or compete? Is collective action a viable way to develop sustainable political regimes? *Social Evolution & History, 9*(2), 173–205.

MacWilliams, A. C., Kuehn, D. D., Murrell, M. L., & Leckman, P. O. (2009). FB 9122 Reservoir. In A. C. MacWilliams, B. Vierra, & K. Schmidt (Eds.), *Archaeological mitigation at FB 17 (LA 91017) and FB 9122 (LA 30116) on the Dona Ana Range, Fort Bliss, Dona Ana County, New Mexico* (pp. 155–212). El Paso, TX: Statistical Research.

Murrell, M. L. (2006). *An investigation of prehistoric water management in the Chupadera Arroyo Basin, Central New Mexico*. Las Cruses, NM: New Mexico State University.

Nabhan, G. P. (1982). Papago Indian desert agriculture and water control. In C. F. Hutchinson (Ed.), *Application of remote sensing in evaluating floodwater farming on the Papago Indian reservation: Completion report* (pp. 41–80). Tucson, AZ: University of Arizona.

Neely, J. A., Aiuvalasit, M. J., & Clause, V. A. (2015). New light on the prehistoric Purrón Dam Complex: Small corporate group collaboration in the Tehuacán Valley, Puebla, México. *Journal of Field Archaeology, 40*(3), 347–364.

Nelson, M. C., Kintigh, K., Abbott, D. R., & Anderies, J. M. (2010). The cross-scale interplay between social and biophysical context and the vulnerability of irrigation-dependent societies: Archaeology's long-term perspective. *Ecology and Society, 15*(3), 31.

Orcutt, J. D. (1999). Chronology. In R. P. Powers & J. D. Orcutt (Eds.), *The Bandelier archeological survey* (Intermontain cultural resources management program, professional paper) (Vol. 57, pp. 85–116). Santa Fe, NM: National Park Service, Department of the Interior.

Ortiz, A. (1969). *The Tewa world: Space, time, being, and becoming in a Pueblo society*. Chicago, IL: University of Chicago Press.

Ortman, S. G. (2012). *Winds from the North: Tewa origins and historical anthropology*. Salt Lake City, Utah: University of Utah Press.

Ortman, S. G. (2016). Uniform probability density analysis and population history in the northern Rio Grande. *Journal of Archaeological Method and Theory, 23*(1), 95–126.

Ostrom, E. (1990). *Governing the commons: The evolution of institutions for collective action*. Cambridge, UK: Cambridge University Press.

Ostrom, E. (1993). Design principles in long-enduring irrigation institutions. *Water Resources Research, 29*(7), 1907–1912.

Ostrom, E. (2000). Collective action and the evolution of social norms. *Journal of Economic Perspectives, 14*(3), 137–158.

Ostrom, E. (2005). *Understanding institutional diversity*. Princeton, NJ: Princeton University Press.

Paytiamo, J. (1932). *Flaming Arrow's people*. New York, NY: Duffield and Green.

Purdue, L. E., & Berger, J.-F. (2015). An integrated socio-environmental approach to the study of ancient water systems: The case of prehistoric Hohokam irrigation systems in semi-arid Central Arizona, USA. *Journal of Archaeological Science, 53*, 586–603.

Purtymun, W. D. (1995). *Geologic and hydrologic records of observation wells, test holes, test wells, supply wells, springs, and surface water stations in the Los Alamos area (LA-12883-MS)*. Los Alamos, NM: Los Alamos National Laboratory.

Ramsey, C. B., & Lee, S. (2013). Recent and planned developments of the program OxCal. *Radiocarbon, 55*(2–3), 720–730.

Reimer, P. J., Bard, E., Bayliss, A., Beck, J. W., Blackwell, P. G., Ramsey, C. B., et al. (2013). IntCal13 and Marine13 radiocarbon age calibration curves 0–50,000 years cal BP. *Radiocarbon, 55*(4), 1869–1887.

Reimer, P. J., Brown, T. A., & Reimer, R. W. (2004). Discussion: Reporting and calibration of post-bomb 14C data. *Radiocarbon, 46*(3), 1299–1304.

Sando, J. S. (1982). *Nee Hemish, a history of Jemez Pueblo* (1st ed.). Albuquerque, NM: University of New Mexico Press.

Saunders, F. P. (2014). The promise of common pool resource theory and the reality of commons projects. *International Journal of the Commons, 8*(2), 636–656.

Scarborough, V. L. (2003). *The flow of power: Ancient water systems and landscapes.* Santa Fe, NM: School for Advanced Research.

Scarborough, V. L., Fladd, S. G., Dunning, N. P., Plog, S., Owen, L. A., Carr, C., et al. (2018). Water uncertainty, ritual predictability and agricultural canals at Chaco Canyon, New Mexico. *Antiquity, 92*(364), 870–889.

Schiffer, M. B. (1986). Radiocarbon dating and the "old wood" problem: The case of the Hohokam chronology. *Journal of Archaeological Science, 13*(1), 13–30.

Sekaquaptewa, H. (1969). *Me and mine: The life story of Helen Sekaquaptewa.* Tucson, AZ: University of Arizona Press.

Snead, J. E. (2006). Mirror of the earth: Water, landscape, and meaning in the precolumbian southwest. In L. J. Lucero & B. W. Fash (Eds.), *Precolumbian water management: Ideology, ritual, and power* (pp. 205–222). Tucson, AZ: University of Arizona Press.

Touchan, R., Woodhouse, C. A., Meko, D. M., & Allen, C. D. (2011). Millennial precipitation reconstruction for the Jemez Mountains, New Mexico, reveals changing drought signal. *International Journal of Climatology, 31*(6), 896–906.

Whiteley, P. M. (1988). *Bacavi: Journey to Reed Springs.* Flagstaff, AZ: Northland Press Flagstaff.

Wilhite, D. A., & Buchanan-Smith, M. (2005). Drought as hazard: Understanding the natural and social context. In D. A. Wilhite (Ed.), *Drought and water crises: Science, technology, and management issues* (Vol. 847, p. 1). Boca Raton, FL: CRC Press.

Wills, W. H. (2017). Water management and the political economy of Chaco canyon during the Bonito phase (ca. AD 850–1200). *Kiva, 83*(4), 369–413.

Wilshusen, R. H., Churchill, M. J., & Potter, J. M. (1997). Prehistoric reservoirs and water basins in the Mesa Verde Region: intensification of water collection strategies during the great Pueblo period. American antiquity, 62(4), 664–681.

Index

A
Africa, 3, 5, 29, 36, 43, 45, 126–129, 132, 133, 166, 167, 173, 176–178, 219
Agriculture, 4, 33–37, 43, 59, 96, 131, 138, 140–142, 144, 145, 147, 150, 153, 157, 170, 218, 227, 247, 255, 285, 302
Akoneo, 43, 59, 60
American bison, 12, 28
Ancestral Puebloan, 7, 221, 282–286, 289, 295–301
Animal husbandry (pastoralism), 55, 78, 81, 96, 112, 115, 200, 221
Archaeology, 1, 6–8, 78, 89, 106, 190–192, 200–204, 213, 214, 216, 223, 229, 238, 239, 247, 256, 265, 266, 269, 282

C
California, 3, 6, 255–272, 282
Collective action, 2, 5, 23, 104, 119–121, 148, 153, 238, 248, 281–283, 285, 298, 301, 302
Cameroon, 3, 5, 167–169, 171, 174, 176
Chad Basin, 165–184
Chewa, 153
Common pool resources (CPRs), 1, 7, 8, 23, 37, 56, 122, 125–127, 132, 139, 144–146, 149–153, 156, 160, 281–302
Commons, 1–5, 7–20, 23–38, 41, 42, 45, 47, 53, 56, 58, 62, 65, 68, 96, 97, 104, 107–115, 121, 125–160, 165–167, 180, 181, 183, 184, 255–272, 281–302
Community, 1–5, 12, 13, 16, 19, 23–38, 41, 45, 46, 52, 62, 63, 66, 69, 78–97, 103, 105–107, 110, 111, 114, 116, 117, 119–122, 128, 130, 131, 138, 143–146, 152, 154, 170, 175, 179, 196, 197, 217, 222, 227, 240, 262, 264, 265, 283–286, 289, 297–299, 301, 302
Conflict, 1, 5, 14, 15, 17, 20, 26, 32, 96, 103–123, 129, 131, 140, 143, 145, 147, 151, 168, 173
Conservation, 3, 7, 9, 14, 18, 19, 24–29, 96, 150, 175, 176, 183, 190, 191, 195, 197, 199, 201–204, 240, 256, 263, 268, 269, 272, 289
Cooperation, 1–7, 17–19, 41–71, 93, 97, 103–123, 235, 236, 239
Cooperative aggregation, 214
Corporate social responsibility (CSR), 132, 134–136, 145, 152, 156–159

D
Discourses, 24, 26, 34–36, 126–130, 134–148, 151, 155, 157, 158

E
Ecology (human ecology, historical ecology, etc.), 1, 4, 8, 9, 26, 70, 80, 86, 128, 130, 131, 165, 204, 213–215, 219, 226, 229, 255, 265, 282
Ecosystems, 1, 5, 55, 84, 96, 129, 146, 165, 167, 199, 203, 214, 227, 281
Ethnographic and ethnoarchaeological data, 46, 55, 168, 191

European Union (EU), 8, 29, 116, 133, 136, 137, 140, 154, 157
Exclusion, 4, 12, 15, 16, 23–26, 28, 121, 154, 166, 183

F
Fiji, 4, 42, 43, 48–52, 56, 68
Folklore, 89, 91, 94, 95
Foraging (hunting and gathering), 7, 42, 48, 52, 54, 61, 69, 190–192, 194–197, 199, 200, 202, 203, 255, 258–262, 264, 298
France, 3, 4, 36, 105, 122
FulBe, 168, 170, 171, 174–179

G
Gabon, 3, 4, 23, 29–31, 37
Gender, 4, 24, 125–127, 130–132, 135, 136, 140, 153, 156
Geoarchaeology, 282, 289
Ghana, 3, 5, 126, 132, 140–145, 156–158
Governance, 1–3, 7, 8, 29, 30, 32, 35, 105, 120–122, 125, 128–130, 153, 154, 156, 182, 235–248

H
Hardin, G., 5, 9–11, 20, 184, 255, 264
Hadza, 41–43, 46, 52–54, 69
High-altitude pastures, 4, 104–107, 111, 112, 115, 116, 118, 120, 123
Historical ecology, 1, 4, 80, 204, 213
Hoodaande, 171, 172
Human Generosity Project, 5, 41–71

I
Iceland, 3, 4, 78–97, 121
Ideal free distribution, 177, 180, 183, 266
Identities, 24, 29, 105, 116, 118, 135, 228
Ik, 3, 42, 43, 46, 60–62, 66, 67, 103
Inclusion, 4, 28, 38, 183
India, 3, 4, 16, 23, 29, 31–33, 37, 127, 158
Institution shopping, 126, 139–141, 151, 154, 156–158

J
Jhors, 31–33, 37
Jemez Mountains, 7, 282–289, 295, 298, 302

K
Karamoja region, 59
Kenya, 3, 5, 42, 43, 46–48, 66, 126, 132, 145–148, 156–158, 167
Kerekere, 42, 49–51, 63
Keres, 285, 300, 301
Kijenge, 43, 46, 62–63, 69
Kiribati, 4, 6, 190, 191, 197, 199–201, 203
Kráka, 4, 78, 80–93, 95–97
Kushirikiana, 43, 62, 69

L
Land (land grabbing, land rights, open access, etc.), 1, 4–6, 9–17, 20, 24, 26–33, 36, 49–51, 55, 57, 58, 82, 84, 86, 89–91, 96, 103–106, 110, 115, 117–119, 121, 122, 125–160, 165–184, 191, 197, 199, 216, 223, 226, 227, 238, 247, 255–272, 282, 285
Land grabbing, 125, 128, 129, 132, 151
Landscape (cultural, natural, etc.), 4, 6, 7, 26, 80, 84, 85, 89, 90, 96, 97, 106, 123, 129, 146, 148, 158, 179, 213–229, 257, 263, 270–272
Landscape alteration, 223, 227
Large-scale land acquisition (LSLA), 5, 125–160
Local (indigenous) knowledge, vi, 79–81, 84, 91, 93, 189
Logone Floodplain, 5, 167, 168, 170, 171, 173–176, 179–181
Luo, 145–147, 158

M
Maasai, 41–43, 46–48, 57, 63, 67–70
Madagascar, 3, 4, 23–26, 28, 29, 37
Malawi, 3, 5, 126, 132, 153–157, 159, 160
Malpai Borderlands Group, 57
Mangrove, 24–26, 28, 193
Marine resources, 6, 16, 189, 190, 192, 197, 199, 200
Maya, 215, 218, 221–228, 240, 242, 246
Mesoamerica, 3, 217, 221, 235–248
Mollusc, 6, 189–204
Mollusc ecological and biological characteristics, 195, 199
Mongolia, 3, 42, 43, 55, 56, 70
Morocco, 3, 5, 126, 132–136, 156, 157
Mývatn, 4, 78–97

N
Native stewardship, 7, 269
Need-based transfers, 5, 41–71

New Institutionalism, 5, 126, 128, 130–132, 148, 156
New Mexico, 7, 43, 57, 265, 282–289
New World, 6, 217–219, 223, 228, 255
Ngikonei, 59, 60

O
Open access, 4–6, 11, 12, 15, 16, 20, 30, 103, 104, 106, 121, 129, 130, 132, 148, 165–184, 197, 199
Open property regimes, 182, 183
Optimal foraging, 7, 190, 191, 195, 200
Osotua, 42, 46–48, 63, 67, 69, 70
Outgrower scheme, 128, 143–145, 152–156, 159
Overkill hypothesis, 7, 265, 266

P
Pacific Islands, 4, 6, 189–204
Pajarito Plateau, 7, 283–285, 288, 295, 299–302
Panchayat, 32, 33
Pastoralism, 42, 116, 118, 142, 170, 179
Political economy, 240
Population, 7, 13, 16, 24, 29, 35, 36, 51, 52, 54, 55, 59, 82, 91, 117, 135, 148, 150, 153, 165, 168, 173, 174, 179, 180, 182, 190, 200, 215, 217, 218, 221–223, 225, 227, 228, 237, 240, 246, 256, 257, 261, 263, 265–272, 282, 284, 289, 295, 298–300
Property rights, 2, 10–12, 14–16, 59, 129, 138, 166
Pyrenees, 105–107, 115, 122

R
Rangelands, 16, 26, 57, 82, 86, 168, 176
Reforestation, 4, 24–26
Resilience, 36, 70, 115, 126–128, 132, 140, 147, 160, 189–204
Resource management, 1–4, 6, 7, 23–26, 28, 33, 34, 37, 38, 78–97, 103, 149, 150, 165–184, 189, 247, 248, 264, 282, 283, 285, 299, 301, 302
Risk management, 5, 41–45, 54, 55, 59, 66, 67, 69–71
Rural forest domain, 29–31

S
Salish, 26–28
Self-governance, 32, 121
Sierra Leone, 3, 5, 126, 132, 136–140, 156, 157, 160

Social sustainability, 104
Stability, 6, 84, 96, 204, 269
Sustainability, 1, 3, 6, 7, 80, 97, 104, 128, 181, 183, 189–204, 213, 235–248, 282, 283, 285, 289
Sustainable management, 96, 165
Swidden (horticulture), 4, 29, 34–37

T
Tanzania, 3, 5, 42, 43, 46, 47, 52, 62–63, 126, 132, 149–153, 156, 157, 159
Tewa, 285, 300, 301
Theory of common property, 9, 19
Tompon-tany, 24–26, 28
Tragedy of the commons, 5, 10, 23, 129, 132, 165–167, 179, 183, 184, 255, 256, 265, 267, 269, 272
Transhumance, 4, 116, 168, 170, 171, 173–176, 178–180
Tribelets, 256, 262–264, 266–267, 270–272
Trolls, 78–97

U
Uganda, 3, 42, 43, 59–61, 150
Urbanism, 235–237

V
Vahiny, 24–26
Viking Age, 81, 84, 89, 90
Vinyungus, 150–152

W
Wahehe, 149–151, 159
Water management, 7, 31, 37, 282, 283, 289, 298–302
Wbena, 149
Wetlands, 78, 82–84, 90–93, 95–97, 148, 216, 221–223, 227, 262, 300
Wildlife, 5, 9, 13, 26–29, 129, 146, 148, 176

Y
Yala Swamp, 139, 145–148, 158, 225, 227
Yasawa Island, 42, 43, 48–52, 67
Yucatán Peninsula, 223

Z
Zud, 55, 56

Printed by Printforce, the Netherlands